Genetic Programming Theory and Practice II

T0205370

GENETIC PROGRAMMING SERIES

Series Editor

John Koza
Stanford University

Also in the series:

The cover art was created by Leslie Sobel in Photoshop from an original photomicrograph of plant cells and genetic programming code. More of Sobel's artwork can be seen at www.lesliesobel.com.

Genetic Programming Theory and Practice II

Edited by

Una-May O'Reilly
Massachusetts Institute of Technology

Tina Yu
Chevron Texaco Information Technology Group

Rick Riolo
University of Michigan

Bill Worzel
Genetics Squared, Inc.

 Springer

Library of Congress Cataloging-in-Publication Data

A C.I.P. Catalogue record for this book is available
from the Library of Congress.

O'Reilly, U.
     Genetic Programming Theory and Practice II / edited by Una-May O'Reilly, Tina Yu, Rick Riolo,
Bill Worzel
        p.cm.

ISBN 978-1-4419-3589-2   Printed on acid-free paper.
e-ISBN 978-0-387-23254-6
© 2010 Springer Science+Business Media, Inc.

Printed in the United States of America.

9 8 7 6 5 4 3 2 1

springeronline.com

Contents

Contributing Authors

Sameer H. Al-Sakran is a Systems Research Programmer at Genetic Programming Inc. in Mountain View, California (al-sakran@sccm.Stanford.edu).

Wolfgang Banzhaf is Professor and Head of the Department of Computer Science at Memorial University of Newfoundland, St. John's, Canada (banzhaf@cs.mun.ca).

Ying Becker is a Principal, Advanced Research Center at State Street Global Advisors, State Street Corp (ying_becker@ssga.com).

Michael Caplan is a Principal, US Quantitative Active Equity at State Street Global Advisors, State Street Corp (michael_caplan@ssga.com).

Flor Castillo is a Research Specialist in the Statistics and Applied Math and Physics Groups within the Physical Sciences Research and Development of the Dow Chemical Company (Facastillo@dow.com).

Mike Cattolico is a consultant at Tiger Mountain Scientific, Inc. (mike@TigerScience.com).

Shu-Heng Chen is Director of AI-ECON Research Center and Professor of Economics at National Chengchi University in Taiwan (chchen@nccu.edu.tw).

Jason M. Daida is an Associate Research Scientist in the Space Physics Research Laboratory, Department of Atmospheric, Oceanic and Space Sciences and is affiliated with the Center for the Study of Complex Systems at The University of Michigan, Ann Arbor (daida@umich.edu).

Kurt DeMaagd is a STIET Fellow and Ph.D. student in the Business Information Systems department at the Michigan Business School in Ann Arbor, Michigan (demaagdk@umich.edu).

A. Beatriz Garmendia-Doval is a Software engineer at Quality Objects Ltd., Madrid, Spain (beatrizagd@yahoo.co.uk).

David E. Goldberg is the Jerry S. Dobrovolny Distinguished Professor in Entrepreneurial Engineering and Director of the Illinois Genetic Algorithms Laboratory at the University of Illinois at Urbana-Champaign (deg@uiuc.edu).

Erik D. Goodman is Professor of Electrical and Computer Engineering and of Mechanical Engineering at Michigan State University (goodman@egr.msu.edu).

John Hall is a computer scientist in the Digital Send Technology group at Hewlett-Packard Company (gpdesign@johnmhall.net).

Gregory S. Hornby is a computer scientist with QSS Group Inc., working as a member of the Evolvable Systems Group in the Computational Sciences Division at NASA Ames Research Center (hornby@email.arc.nasa.gov).

Daniel Howard is a QinetiQ Fellow and heads the Software Evolution Centre at QinetiQ in Malvern, UK (dhoward@qinetiq.com).

Jianjun Hu is a Ph.D. student in Computer Science and a member of Genetic Algorithm Research and Application Group (GARAGe) at Michigan State University (hujianju@msu.edu).

Cezary Z. Janikow is an Associate Professor of Computer Science at the University of Missouri, St. Louis (janikow@umsl.edu).

Lee W. Jones is a Systems Research Programmer at Genetic Programming Inc. in Mountain View, California (lj25@pacbell.net).

Martin A. Keane is a consultant to the gaming industry and works with Genetic Programming, Inc. (martinkeane@ameritech.net).

Maarten Keijzer is research scientist for KiQ Ltd, Amsterdam and researcher for the Strategic Research and Development Group at WL | Delft Hydraulics, Delft. He operates the research/consultancy company PrognoSys, Utrecht, The Netherlands (mkeijzer@xs4all.nl).

Arthur K. Kordon is a Research and Development Leader in the Applied Math and Physics Group within the Physical Sciences Research and Development of the Dow Chemical Company (akordon@dow.com).

Mark Kotanchek is the group leader for Applied Math and Physics within Physical Sciences Research and Development of the Dow Chemical Company, Midland, MI, USA (mkotanchek@dow.com).

John R. Koza is Consulting Professor at Stanford University in the Biomedical Informatics Program in the Department of Medicine and in the Department of Electrical Engineering (koza@stanford.edu).

Tzu-Wen Kuo is a Ph.D. student of Economics at National Chengchi University, Taiwan (kuo@aiecon.org).

Christian Lasarczyk is Research Assistant in the Department of Computer Science at the University of Dortmund, Germany (christian.lasarczyk@uni-dortmund.de).

Derek Linden is the Chief Technical Officer of Linden Innovation Research LLC, a company which specializes in the automated design and optimization of antennas and electromagnetic devices (dlinden@lindenir.com).

Jason D. Lohn leads the Evolvable Systems Group in the Computational Sciences Division at NASA Ames Research Center (jlohn@email.arc.nasa.gov).

Duncan MacLean is co-founder of Genetics Squared, Inc., a computational discovery company working in the pharmaceutical industry (dmaclean@acm.org).

Julian Francis Miller is a Lecturer in the Department of Electronics at the University of York, England (jfm@ohm.york.ac.uk).

Scott A. Moore is the Arthur F. Thurnau Professor and BBA Program Director at the Michigan Business School in Ann Arbor (samoore@umich.edu).

David Morley is the founder and Principal Consultant of Enspiral Discovery Ltd, and was previously the head of Computational Technology Development at Vernalis, Cambridge, UK (d.morley@enspiral-discovery.com).

Una-May O'Reilly is a research scientist in the Living Machines and Humanoid Robotics group in the Computer Science and Artificial Intelligence Laboratory at the Massachusetts Institute of Technology (unamay@csail.mit.edu).

Rick Riolo is Director of the Computer Lab and Associate Research Scientist in the Center for the Study of Complex Systems at the University of Michigan (rlriolo@umich.edu).

Simon C. Roberts is a senior engineer of the Software Evolution Centre at QinetiQ in Malvern, UK (scroberts@btinternet.com).

Conor Ryan is a senior lecturer and University Fellow at the University of Limerick, Ireland (conor.ryan@ul.ie).

Kumara Sastry is a member of Illinois Genetic Algorithms Laboratory and a graduate student of Material Science and Engineering at the University of Illinois at Urbana-Champaign (kumara@illigal.ge.uiuc.edu).

Guido Smits is a Research and Development Leader in the Applied Math and Physics group within Physical Sciences Research and Development of Dow Benelux, Terneuzen, Netherlands (GFSMITS@dow.com).

Terence Soule is a Professor at the University of Idaho, where is he a member of the Computer Science Department and of the Bioinformatics and Computational Biology Program (tsoule@cs.uidaho.edu).

Matthew W. Streeter is a Ph.D. student at Carnegie Mellon University and was formerly a Systems Research Programmer at Genetic Programming Inc. in Mountain View, California (matts@cs.cmu.edu).

Jeff Sweeney is a Senior Statistician within the Physical Sciences Research & Development Group of the Dow Chemical Company (Jsweeney@dow.com).

Eric A. Wollesen is a gradute of the University of Michigan. He is currently employed as a software developer by Genetics Squared, Inc., a computational discovery company working in the pharmaceutical industry (ericw@genetics2.com).

Bill Worzel is the Chief Technology Officer and co–founder of Genetics Squared, Inc., a computational discovery company working in the pharma- ceutical industry (billw@arroyosoft.com).

Tina Yu is a computer scientist in the Mathematical Modeling Team at Chevron- Texaco Information Technology Company (Tina.Yu@chevrontexaco.com).

Wayne Zirk is a Senior Statistician within the Physical Sciences Research & Development Group of the Dow Chemical Company (ZirkWE@dow.com).

Preface

The work described in this book was first presented at the Second Workshop on Genetic Programming, Theory and Practice, organized by the Center for the Study of Complex Systems at the University of Michigan, Ann Arbor, 13-15 May 2004. The goal of this workshop series is to promote the exchange of research results and ideas between those who focus on Genetic Programming (GP) theory and those who focus on the application of GP to various real-world problems. In order to facilitate these interactions, the number of talks and participants was small and the time for discussion was large. Further, participants were asked to review each other's chapters *before* the workshop. Those reviewer comments, as well as discussion at the workshop, are reflected in the chapters presented in this book. Additional information about the workshop, addendums to chapters, and a site for continuing discussions by participants and by others can be found at http://cscs.umich.edu:8000/GPTP-2004/.

We thank all the workshop participants for making the workshop an exciting and productive three days. In particular we thank all the authors, without whose hard work and creative talents, neither the workshop nor the book would be possible. We also thank our keynote speakers Lawrence ("Dave") Davis of NuTech Solutions, Inc., Jordan Pollack of Brandeis University, and Richard Lenski of Michigan State University, who delivered three thought-provoking speeches that inspired a great deal of discussion among the participants.

The workshop received support from these sources:

- The Center for the Study of Complex Systems (CSCS);

- Third Millennium Venture Capital Limited;

- State Street Global Advisors, Boston, MA;

- Biocomputing and Developmental Systems Group, Computer Science and Information Systems, University of Limerick;

- Christopher T. May, RedQueen Capital Management; and

- Dow Chemical, Core R&D/Physical Sciences.

We thank all of our sponsors for their kind and generous support for the workshop and GP research in general.

A number of people made key contributions to running the workshop and assisting the attendees while they were in Ann Arbor. Foremost among them was Howard Oishi. Howard was assisted by Mike Charters. We also thank Bill Tozier for helping with reading and copy-editing chapters. Melissa Fearon's editorial efforts were invaluable from the initial plans for the book through its final publication. Thanks also to Deborah Doherty of Kluwer for helping with various technical publishing issues. Finally, we thank Carl Simon, Director of CSCS, for his support for this endeavor from its very inception.

UNA-MAY O'REILLY, TINA YU, RICK RIOLO AND BILL WORZEL

Foreword

It was my good fortune to be invited to the 2004 Genetic Programming Workshop on Theory and Practice, held in May in Ann Arbor, Michigan. The goals of the workshop were unique, as was the blend of participants. To my knowledge, this workshop is alone in focusing on and promoting the interaction between theory and practice in the evolutionary computation world. There are many workshops and conference tracks that are oriented toward one or the other of these two, mostly disjoint, areas of evolutionary computation work. To participate in a workshop promoting interactions between the two subfields was a great joy.

The workshop organizers have summarized the various talks in the first chapter of this volume, and the reader can get a feel there for the talk I gave on the first day of the workshop. It is worth noting that a talk like mine – containing actual slides from training sessions for industrial practitioners of evolutionary computation, and containing a series of slides describing historically accurate but prickly interchanges between practitioners and theoreticians over the last twenty years – would most likely not have received a sympathetic hearing ten or twenty years ago. The attendees of this workshop, practitioners and theoreticians in roughly equal numbers, were able to laugh at some points, consider others, and during the course of the workshop, openly discuss issues related to the integration of theoretical and practical work in evolutionary computation. Our field is maturing in both areas, and so are our approaches to promoting interactions between our field's practical and theoretical subfields.

There is a good deal to be gained by all of this in these types of interactions, and by the change in focus that they create. The papers in this year's workshop are very stimulating, and I look forward as well to reading next year's workshop volume, containing even more work lying on the frontiers between theory and application of evolutionary computation.

Dr. Dave Davis, Vice President of Product Research
NuTech Solutions, Inc.,
Massachusetts, USA
June, 2004

Chapter 1

GENETIC PROGRAMMING: THEORY AND PRACTICE

An Introduction to Volume II

Una-May O'Reilly[1], Tina Yu[2], Rick Riolo[3] and Bill Worzel[4]

[1]CSAIL, Massachusetts Institute of Technology; [2]ChevronTexaco Information Technology Company; [3]Center for the Study of Complex Systems, University of Michigan; [4]Genetics Squared

Keywords: genetic programming, coevolution, theoretical biology, real-world applications

1. Theory and Practice: Mind the Gap

Genetic programming (GP) is a rapidly maturing technology that is making significant strides toward applications which demonstrate that it is a sustainable science. In this year's workshop, we are very pleased to receive more contributing papers describing the application of GP than last year. We therefore arranged to have Dave Davis , Vice President of Product Research at NuTech Solutions, Inc., kick off the workshop with a keynote entitled "Lessons Learned from Real-World Evolutionary Computation (EC) Projects."

Davis has over 15 years' experience in deploying EC in industry. He talked about EC project management by covering the project life cycle responsibilities of sales, proposal preparation, contract fulfillment and sustaining the client relationship. A successful sales presentation, advised Davis, is one that addresses the potential client's business problems rather than the EC technology being offered. When selling an EC solution, Davis warned, it is wrong to state the algorithm "is random, and can be run as long as you want to get better solutions." Instead, explain that the algorithm "is creative and can be used to improve on existing solutions." This approach of communicating the advantages of GP through the value of its solutions, rather than *how it works*, increases the likehood of EC being accepted by the clients. Both remarks resonated throughout subsequent workshop conversations.

In a provocative and admittedly somewhat exaggerated stance, Davis cited personal interchanges in the context of Genetic Algorithm theory and practice that might be interpreted as a warning call to the GP theory community and advice vis-a-vis theory to its practitioners. Davis stated that "the jury is out on the usefulness of theory to applications people." He advised that theory contributions should include their limitations. For example, it would be folly to advocate any one operator (or representation) as the best over all others when the operator has only been theoretically studied with simplifying assumptions or within the context of infinite measure that does not reflect the bias of reality. He felt that the knowledge of practitioners gained through experience, especially their discoveries concerning what things work well in different cases should be respected. Furthermore, he remonstrated that practitioners can not be expected to wait to use a technique until its theoretical underpinnings are well understood. Theoreticians should not hold experimenters back. As a constructive step, he suggested that successful demonstrations by practitioners should be used by theoreticians to choose what to examine and provide explanations for. He also pointed out that currently much theory focuses solely on EC. In the "real" world practitioners hybridize their EC with methods such as simulated annealing and tabu search, a practice which challenges the pertinence of the theory.

2.   The Accounts of Practitioners

Davis was followed by multiple contributions from application domains which substantiated his claim that real world problems demand more than the simplest form of GP that theory analyzes. In Chapter 2, Yu, Chen and Kuo report on their use of GP with lambda abstraction to discover financial technical trading rules that use historical prices to forecast price movement and recommend buy or sell actions. Lambda abstraction is a means of achieving modularity in GP. In contrast to Automatically Defined Functions where the position of a module in a program tree is determined by evolution, the position of a lambda abstraction is predefined to sit under a function node. This allows domain knowledge to be incorporated into design GP program structures. When properly used, the lambda abstraction module mechanism will lead to faster discovery of a solution. In this case study, the evolved GP trading rules yielded strong evidence that there are patterns (modules) in the S&P 500 time series. The authors made efforts to select data containing diverse financial market trends to prepare the training, validation and testing sets. They examined the evolved lambda abstraction GP rules, after simplification, and found there was discernible differentiation of technical indicators with appropriate buy or sell decisions for different factors in the data. This implies that a rule, regardless of market climate, is able to identify opportunities to make profitable trades and outperform a simple benchmark buy-and-hold strategy.

Researchers from the Dow Chemical Corporation have two contributions in the volume. In Chapter 3, Castillo, Kordon, Sweeney and Zirk outline how industrial statistical model building can be improved through hybridization with GP. When statistical analysis indicates that statistically derived models have inadequate fit, transformations of the input variables are the practical way to reduce the lack of fit . In this situation, the authors used GP symbolic regression models to suggest (a) non-linear input transformations that would reduce the lack of fit in designed data, and (b) linear input transformations that reduce input multicollinearity in undesigned data. The newly inferred statistical models demonstrated better fit and with better model structure than models derived by genetic programming alone.

In the undesigned data example of Chapter 3, the evolved solution that balanced accuracy with parsimony was derived using the Pareto front GP system of Smits and Kotanchek that is described in Chapter 17. This multi-objective approach to solving real-world symbolic regression problems allows one to select easily among multiple Pareto optimal solutions, trading between the performance and the complexity of the corresponding expression solution. Since an expression with the lowest residual error yet high complexity is likely to overfit the data, this argues for maintaining multiple solutions, and even components (subtrees) of those solutions. Without requiring additional preserving cost, these solutions are able to facilitate intelligent decision making. They may also suggest additional runs to be made with derived function sets.

On the first day, the audience heard a very experiential account of putting a GP-derived solution to the ultimate test. In Chapter 6 Caplan and Becker of State Street Global Advisors recount the journey that eventually led to the deployment of an evolved stock picking strategy in a quantitatively driven, risk-controlled, US equity portfolio. Rather than focus on the details of the specific market context, this story stressed how "success" depended not just on technical performance (that involved much adjustment and refinement of data for training and the fitness criteria) but also on winning the support of skeptical decision makers who were not entirely knowledgeable of the technology, but justifiably had to weigh the risk and uncertainty of the new approach. The sharp risk of the final step of using the result to automatically pick stocks was keenly conveyed, and made one deeply appreciative of the large amount of effort that must be expended to support the use of what seems to be a technically simple GP solution. This contribution is a perfect example of Dave Davis' earlier message: the non-technical aspects of GP must be considered in order to bring it to successful fruition in business.

Similar to the Caplan and Becker account, two stories of working with GP on problems that are not always well-behaved were presented on the final day of the workshop. In Chapter 16, Howard and Roberts of QinetiQ, Inc. have used GP for classification. Reminiscent of Yu, Chen and Kuo in Chapter 2, they communicate the large effort required to prepare the extensive data used in training, validation and testing to evolve detectors that classify alerts for night-time traffic incidents on the U.K. freeways. To cope with the many challenging aspects of the traffic data (e.g., missing, noisy), they used a two stage classification process. In stage one, high sensitivity was preferred over high specificity so there were a high number of false positive alerts. In stage two training was aimed to reduce false alarms while retaining at least a single alert per incident. Obvious in the account, and similar to Caplan and Becker, is how the problem-solving difficulty lay not in the GP technique itself, but in how much time and effort it took to prepare the data and to partition them so that a fairly straight-forward GP system could solve the problem. In both cases, their efforts have put GP solutions on the front line of real world usage.

MacLean, Wolleson and Worzel of Genetics Squared, Inc., like Howard and Roberts, have used GP for classification , though they work in the realm of biological and pharmaceutical data. In Chapter 15, they shared their experiences with a problem that exhibits good behavior and two problems that exhibit bad behavior when solved using GP. Their practical advice on both cases can be applied to problem domains where the number of explanatory (i.e., input) variables is large (e.g., thousands) and only relatively few examples are available, hence overfitting is highly likely to occur. They normally run GP multiple times and only consider a result reliable and the problem well behaved if the results show (a) good training-test set correspondence, (b) a distinct selection of variables unique to each class, (c) the same small number of features in classifiers from different runs and (d) no pattern to the samples that are misclassified across the different runs. In the instances of badly behaved problems, they counsel that GP should not be used "dogmatically" in the sense that when it does not work, the time spent understanding what GP may be revealing about the problem is as worthwhile as (or better than) simply trying to make a change to solve the problem. They demonstrated such practice by giving an example of how the difficulty in creating successful classifiers for one type of tumors led them to revisit the correspondence between molecular and physical level data. Analyzing this information suggested revising how the samples should be classified, and the new classifications led to more rational results.

3.　　GP Theory and Analysis

As GP systems in applications become more complex, the need for systematicity in the comprehension of their elements and behavior becomes more relevant. Last year, Sastry, O'Reilly and Goldberg insisted that ensuring adequate population size is crucial to systematic competent GP algorithm design. Now, in Chapter 4, they have taken a logical step forward from their population sizing model of a year ago. Whereas previously they considered sizing the population to ensure an adequate supply of raw building blocks in the initial population, now they derive a decision making model that determines population size based on ensuring a quantity sufficient to ensure, with some specifiable certainty, that the best building block is favored over its second best competitor. Such models do not directly transfer to practice because many of their factors are not measurable for a real GP problem. However, they provided insight by identifying critical factors that figure in population sizing, particularly ones unique to GP such as bloat and program size, and illuminating their relationships.

In Chapter 10, Hall and Soule showed experiments that examine whether GP uses a top-down design decomposition approach or not. Clearly, the tree representation of traditional GP can implicitly map top down design since a complete tree represents a solution to a full problem and solutions to subproblems exist at tree levels. However, the tree structure does not guarantee that the broader, more significant problem is decomposed first (at the root) and the successive subproblems are then either decomposed or solved. It appears that, while GP discovers a program from the root down, what is fixed at the root node does not reflect design decomposition but depends instead upon selection bias. When this selection bias leads to premature convergence, substantially increasing the population size might help because it will improve GP's sampling of root node choices. This heuristic concurs with the concept of sizing a GP population to ensure adequate optimal building block decision making as the contribution by Sastry, O'Reilly and Goldberg suggested but only to the extent that it ensures that the correct decision will be made among competing building blocks. Adequate population sizing will not enforce top-down design because in GP problems there is no structure dictating that the most salient building block is the first top-down design decision.

Chapter 5's contribution by Jason Daida is also systematic in its rigorous use of vast quantities of experimental data and its careful consideration of the role of structure in GP's ability to problem solve. Daida presented a tiered view of the roles of structure in GP: lattice, network and content. This view can be used to frame theory on how some problems are more difficult than others for GP to solve. Lattice, the lowest level, presumes structure independent of content and subsequent levels; network and context presume decreasing levels of content abstraction. Daida and his group have devised a tunably difficult test program to probe the behavior at each level. Their results indicate that GP may be hampered if overloaded with choice. Based on his systematic analysis, Daida offers speculative advice on using GP in real world problem solving: use large populations, use tournament selection, do not use an excessive primitive set, use structure-altering operations (e.g., automatically defined functions) to mitigate overloading and consider using meta-programs to pare down the size of primitive sets.

Last year, much discussion took place around a problematic issue with evolving modularity in GP: whenever both modules and the main solution must be evolved simultaneously, the latter frequently override the former due to the fitness criteria focusing on the performance of main solution. Consequently, evolutionary module identification and reuse occur on a slower timescale than the evolution of the main solution. The concept of Run Transferable Libraries (RTL) by Ryan, Keijzer and Cattolico in Chapter 7 seeks to address this issue. They show how libraries of functions can be evolved from one run and then be reused in a later run. In this way, the time gap between the evolution of main solution and its useful modules (library functions) may be reduced. The fitness of a library function is determined after each generation within a run, according to how much it is used in the population rather than the performance of the solutions that use it. In common with the standard programming libraries, the intent of RTL is to evolve general purpose sets of functions that can be used on different instances of a similar problem, hence enhance GP scalability to more difficult problems. Their simple initial results are encouraging and indicate that many of the choices opened up by this approach deserve further investigation.

Interestingly, the issues surrounding evolving modularity also present themselves in the problem of a GP system that learns its own rules of constraint and heuristically advantageous primitive combination. When should such heuristics and constraints be updated and how can they be learned when the system is focused on solving its problem?

inxACGP In Chapter 12, Janikow offers two means of doing this. First, weights assigned to existing heuristics can be strengthened when they produce an offspring fitter than its parents. Second, the distribution statistics of a pool of the best solutions in terms of fitness and secondarily size can be extracted and used to update the probabilities. This technique assumes that capturing distributional information in partial solutions will lead to better solutions and that first order statistics express essential structure of the genome. Janikow's method, like that of Ryan, Keizer and Cattolico, can be used within a run or for successive runs.

4.   Achieving Better GP Performance

The second day started with an invited talk entitled "Recent Results in Co-evolution" by Jordan Pollack . Pollack defines coevolution broadly: a coevolutionary algorithm differs from an evolutionary algorithm in that individuals are judged by relative fitness rather than absolute fitness. Not all coevolutionary dynamics facilitate the progress of a system and the evolution of complexity. Instead, some dynamics cause a system to stagnate. Pollack demonstrated such a coevolution model using a "Teacher's Dilemma" game in which the teacher chooses a problem, from easy to hard, and the student tries to solve it.

In this game, both student and teacher receive a "payoff" in terms of the utility (satisfaction and correctness) of the outcome from their perspective. Unfortunately, the strategy that dominates this game is one in which the teacher and student "secretly share" joint utility and collude in mediocrity. Besides collusive mediocrity, other non-progressive coevolutionary dynamics are "boom and bust", "winners take all", "disengagement" and "death spirals" . By presenting additional simple, formal models of coevolutionary dynamics, Pollack showed that competition alone does not drive progress. A system needs both competitiveness: fitness which is based on performance and *informativeness*: fitness which is based on the information that an individual provides to others. With this proper motivational structure, distributed self-interested adaptive agents can continuously create their own gradient for open-ended progress.

Pollack's talk encourages experimentation with coevolution because potentially informativeness will complement competition and prevent evolution from stymieing progress. Hu and Goodman in Chapter 9 note something similar in that GP is often in need of an explicit fair competition mechanism to sustain productive evolution. Last year, in this workshop they reported that too much competition in a GP system can prevent sufficient alternatives from being explored. They presented a sustainable evolutionary computation model called Hierarchical Fair Competition (HFC-GP). HFC-GP ensures that a sufficient variety of new candidates is continually introduced to the top level of the population. This year they examine robustness in the context of dynamic systems . Despite robustness being a key facet of dynamic systems, conventional dynamic system design decouples the functional or structural steps of designing a solution from the determination of robust operating procedures. They show how topologically open ended synthesis by GP offers an excellent alternative which allows robustness to be considered from the beginning of the solution design process. Their system exploits the representational advantages of bond graphs for both representing a dynamic system and for evolutionary search. To achieve their results they rely on a strongly typed GP tool enhanced with an improved version of HFC-GP.

In Chapter 13 Moore and DeMaagd report their progress on using GP to search for supply chain reordering policies. The system assigns fitness to agents that participate in a supply chain "game" based on how well the chain performs as a whole. This invites the question of how a coevolutionary view of the system might contribute to improving the dynamics as related to Pollack's definition of coevolutionary systems and his conclusions regarding competition and informativeness. Based on Pollack's model, a setup where the evolving agents need to cooperate with each other explicitly and to share information with each other may yield progressively better policies. In the investigation conducted, rather than evaluate GP's ability to find optimal restocking policies, the authors' primary goal was to understand how changes in a set of ten GP parameters (each with three settings) correlated with its ability to progressively and efficiently improve its policies for a given demand distribution and supply chain setup. They employed design of experiments to narrow the number of experiments down to 243 and evaluated five hypotheses concerning a parameter's influence ranging from the rate of improvement of the best solution to what generation gives the final best policy. Overall they have learned, under narrow conditions, a set of expectations for their system's behavior under the given parameter choices. This will prove useful as they use GP to search in the solution landscape.

In Chapter 14 Garmendia-Doval, Miller and Morley present a comprehensive contribution that deals with a real-world problem employing Cartesian GP , and analyze their system's performance with respect to bloat and neutral drift. The problem at hand is automating the removal of false positives from an initial stage classifier that estimates binding modes for input ligands. Using Cartesian GP, the evolved filter generalized well over the data by filtering out consistently bad compounds while retaining interesting hits. Cartesian GP encodes a graph as a string of integers that represents the functions and connections between graph nodes, and program inputs and outputs. The representation is very general for computational structures because it can encode a non-connected graph and supports a many-to-one genotype phenotype mapping. Additionally, despite having a fixed size, it can encode a variable-size graph. The evolutionary process effectively capitalized on neutral drift and experienced no program bloat, which seem to be inherent features of Cartesian GP's encoding.

Koza, Jones, Keane, Streeter and Al-Sakran combine a variety of means to upgrade previous approaches toward automated design of analog circuits with GP and present their results in Chapter 8. Whereas their previous goal was to show how GP can be used as an automated invention machine to synthesize designs for complex structures with a uniform set of techniques, now attention is turned to making the method " industrial-strength," to focus on analog circuit synthesis problems of challenging character. Making the technique industrial-strength involves using elementary general domain knowledge of analog circuits and exploiting problem specific knowledge about the required circuit. It also includes using automatically defined functions, faster simulators and an improved primitive set. The challenging factors are dealing with multi-objective fitness criteria and assessing circuits' performance at the corners of various performance envelope conditions. Using an ongoing project for illustration and assessment, the authors describe their improvements in detail.

In contrast to the amount of effort that has to be exerted to bring GP up to snuff for analog circuit synthesis, in Chapter 18, Lohn, Hornby and Linden present one of the most compelling examples of GP being used entirely in a standard manner to evolve something valuable: the design of an X-band antenna that may actually fly on a NASA spacecraft. The antenna design was greatly facilitated by a high fidelity simulator. Despite flight worthiness, remarkably a very simple GP primitive set that basically allowed branching and some standard construction primitives is sufficient for the task. The evolved antenna is compliant with its performance requirements and sports an unusual organic looking structure which seems unlikely to have been designed by hand. If successful at space qualification testing, it will become the first evolved hardware in space.

5.   How Biology and Computation Can Inform Each Other

Richard Lenski describes himself as a biologist who studies evolution empirically. One theme of his address was the study of contingency: the evolutionary pathway passes through thousands of improbable stages. The pathway contains events, that despite their apparent unimportance, if altered even so slightly, cause evolution to cascade into a radically different channel.

Lenski reported on his investigations with the bacterium, *E. coli*, and related how, in just one population, the ability to metabolize citrate (a carbon source) evolved. The experimental task of isolating the mutational changes upon which this adaptation is contingent will be arduous. Fortunately Avida, a fast and tractable artificial life system, is providing Lenski with additional insights into contingency. Lenski has established that only when he rewards simpler logic functions does the complex logic function EQU evolve in Avida. Relevant to GP (and all of evolutionary computation) he has shown that providing the rewards for building blocks is necessary for complex adaptation. He has observed considerable non-monotonicity in the mutational dynamics of populations that evolve EQU. Neutral and deleterious mutations occur. Sometimes a trade-off occurs – the final mutation leading to EQU will result in a simpler function being eliminated. Each population that evolved EQU did so by a different path and arrived at a different solution. In a case study of the lines of descent from one run where EQU evolved, at least one deleterious mutation was necessary for EQU because it interacted with the subsequent mutation to produce EQU.

Lenski's analysis produced much nodding of heads and emphatic acknowledgments from the audience. It indicates that we should not expect our evolutionary populations to monotonically improve. It confirmed intuition that we should choose representations and fitness functions to encourage and tolerate deleterious mutations on the adaptive trajectory. It resonates with experience using GP where GP runs for solving the same problem usually produce unique solutions evolved from contingent paths.

While Lenski has used computation to investigate biology, Banzhaf and Lasarczyk in Chapter 11 produced arguably the most provocative and speculative paper of the meeting by reversing this perspective and asking, instead, how biology might inform a new model of computation. The observation that concentration matters most in chemistry (e.g., consider the functioning of living cells) is mapped to programming terms by dissolving the sequential order associated with an algorithm's instructions. A program becomes an assemblage of a fixed quantity of instructions that are chosen randomly and executed in an arbitrary order. With that, what matters is the concentration of instructions and the concentration of multiple outcomes, rather than their order. This is admittedly inefficient on a small scale but if parallel and distributed computing were freed from the need to synchronize and to maintain order, and when thousands or millions of processors can be employed cheaply, the potential pay-off of this computational model is immense. The authors term this type of system an "algorithmic chemistry." The authors' perspective stimulates us to novelly regard GP as a program-based computation at the cellular chemical level not just the information processing level when this new notion of a program is considered.

6.   Wrap up: Narrowing the Gap

Few would deny that the simplest and most standard GP system is complex. The algorithmic definition of a population based search which uses an executable representation that can vary in structure and size, and which uses selection, recombination and perhaps mutation constitutes a rich, powerful complex system. Although such richness and power have made GP an attractive tool for solving real-world problems, they also make the establishment of GP's theoretical foundations very difficult. On top of that, many applied GP systems are coupled with extension or hybridization in order to provide solutions of a quality useful in the real world. Thus, it would seem that there is a widening gap between GP practitioners and theoreticians. However, the close encounters of the second time indicated otherwise. We heard laughter from theoreticians during Davis' provocative talk. We listened to practitioners defending theoretical work because they have benefited from their insights. At the end of the workshop, many participants expressed enthusiasm to continue this kind of close encounters to bridge GP theory and practice. Such open-minded attitudes make us believe that despite the current state of theory is imperfect to precisely describe the dynamics of GP and to strictly guide the use of GP (i.e., parameter and representation choices), there will always be links between theory and practice. Mapping the GP community to the coevolution model described by Pollack, we hope this workshop series will continue fostering healthy coevolutionary dynamics that allow each distributed self-interested adaptive researcher to create his/her own gradient for the GP open-ended progress.

Chapter 2

DISCOVERING FINANCIAL TECHNICAL TRADING RULES USING GENETIC PROGRAMMING WITH LAMBDA ABSTRACTION

Tina Yu[1], Shu-Heng Chen[2] and Tzu-Wen Kuo[2]

[1]*ChevronTexaco Information Technology Company;* [2]*National Chengchi University, Taiwan*

Abstract   We applied genetic programming with a lambda abstraction module mechanism to learn technical trading rules based on S&P 500 index from 1982 to 2002. The results show strong evidence of excess returns over buy-and-hold after transaction cost. The discovered trading rules can be interpreted easily; each rule uses a combination of one to four widely used technical indicators to make trading decisions. The consensus among these trading rules is high. For the majority of the testing period, 80% of the trading rules give the same decision. These rules also give high transaction frequency. Regardless of the stock market climate, they are able to identify opportunities to make profitable trades and out-perform buy-and-hold.

Keywords: modular genetic programming, lambda abstraction modules, higher-order functions, financial trading rules, buy-and-hold, S&P 500 index, automatically defined functions, PolyGP system, stock market, technical analysis, constrained syntactic structure, strongly typed genetic programming, financial time series, lambda abstraction GP.

1.   Introduction

In this chapter genetic programming (GP) (Koza, 1992) combined with a lambda abstraction module mechanism is used to find profitable trading rules in the stock market. Finding profitable trading rules is not equivalent to the problem of forecasting stock prices, although the two are clearly linked. A profitable trading rule may forecast rather poorly most of the time, but perform well overall because it is able to position the trader on the right side of the market during large price changes. One empirical approach to predict the price change is technical analysis. This approach uses historical stock prices and volume data to identify the price trend in the market. Originated from the work of Charles Dow in the late 1800s, technical analysis is now widely used by investment professionals to make trading decisions (Pring, 1991).

Various trading indicators have been developed based on technical analysis. Examples are *moving average, filter* and *trading-range break*. For the moving average class of indicators, the trading signals are decided by comparing a short-run with a long-run moving average in the same time series, producing a "buy" signal when the short-run moving average is greater than the long-run moving average. This indicator can be implemented in many different ways by specifying different short and long periods. For example, on the left side of Figure 2-1 is a moving average with a short of 10 days and a long of 50 days. For the filter indicators, the trading signals are decided by comparing the current price with its local low or with its local high over a past period of time. Similar to the moving average, it can be implemented with different time length. When multiple filter indicators are combined together similar to the one on the right side of Figure 2-1, it is called a *trading-range break indicator*.

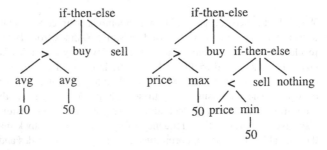

Figure 2-1.   A moving average (10,50) and a trading-range break indicator.

Previously, (Brock et al., 1992) reported that *moving average* and *trading-range break* give significant positive returns on Dow Jones index from 1897 to 1986. Similarly, (Cooper, 1999) showed that *filter* strategy can out-perform buy-and-hold under relatively low transaction cost on NYSE and AMEX stocks for the 1962-1993 period. These studies are encouraging evidence indicating that it is possible to devise profitable trading rules for stock markets.

However, one concern regarding these studies is that the investigated trading indicators are decided *ex post*. It is possible that the selected indicator is favored by the tested time period. If the investor had to make a choice about what indicator or combination of indicators to use at the *beginning* of the sample period, the reported returns may have not occurred. In order to obtain true out-of-sample performance, GP has been used to devise the trading rules for analysis. For the two attempts made, both of them reported that GP can not find trading rules that out-perform buy-and-hold on S&P 500 index (see Section

2 for details). One possible reason for this outcome is that the GP systems used are not adequate for this task. The work described in this chapter extends GP with a λ abstraction module mechanism and investigates its ability to find profitable technical trading rules based on S&P 500 index from 1982 to 2002.

This chapter is organized as follows. Section 2 reviews related work. Section 3 presents the λ abstraction module mechanism. In Section 4, the PolyGP system is described. In section 5, S&P 500 time series data are given. Section 6 explains the experimental setup while Section 7 presents the experimental results. We analyze the GP trading rules in Section 8 and 9. Finally, concluding remarks are given in Section 10.

2. Related Work

Targeted toward different financial markets, different researchers have applied GP to generate trading rules and analyzed their profitability. For example, (Allen and Karjalainen, 1999) studied S&P 500 index from 1928 to 1995. They reported that the evolved GP trading rules did not earn consistent excess returns over after transaction costs. In contrast, (Neely et al., 1997) reported that their GP trading rules for foreign exchange markets were able to gain excess returns for six exchange rates over the period 1981-1995. (Wang, 2000) suggested that this conflicting result might be due to the fact that foreign exchange markets have a lower transaction cost than the stock markets have. Another reason Wang suggested is that (Neely et al., 1997) did not use the rolling forward method (explained in Section 5) to test their results for different time periods while (Allen and Karjalainen, 1999) did. Finally, Wang pointed out that these two works used different benchmarks to assess their GP trading rules: (Allen and Karjalainen, 1999) used the return from buy-and-hold while (Neely et al., 1997) used zero return , because there is no well-defined buy-and-hold strategy in the foreign exchange markets.

Using a similar GP setup as that of (Allen and Karjalainen, 1999), Wang also investigated GP rules to trade in S&P 500 futures markets alone and to trade in both S&P 500 spot and futures markets simultaneously. He reported that GP trading rules were not able to beat buy-and-hold in both cases. Additionally, he also incorporated Automatically Defined Functions (ADFs) (Koza, 1994) in his GP experiments. He reported that ADFs made the representation of the trading rules simpler by avoiding duplication of the same branches. However, no comparison was made between the returns from GP rules and the returns from ADF-GP rules.

Another approach using GP to generate trading rules is by combining predefined trading indicators (Bhattacharyya et al., 2002, O'Neill et al., 2002). In these works, instead of providing functions such as *average* for GP to construct a moving average indicator and *minimum* to construct filter indicators, some of the trading indicators are selected and calculated. These indicators are then used to construct the leaves of GP trees. Since there are a wide range of trading indicators, this approach has an inevitable bias; only selected indicators can be used to construct trading rules. Modular GP relieves such bias by allowing any forms of indicators to be generated as modules, which are then combined to make trading decisions.

Our first attempt using modular GP to evolve financial trading rules was based on ADF-GP (Yu et al., 2004). There, the evolved rules trade in both stock markets and foreign exchange markets simultaneously. However, our study results showed that most ADF modules were evaluated into constant value of *True* or *False*. In other words, ADFs did not fulfill the role of identifying modules in the trading rules. Consequently, ADF-GP trading rules gave similar returns to those from vanilla GP trading rules; both of them were not as good as the returns from buy-and-hold. This suggests either that there is no pattern in financial market trading rules, or ADF is not able to find them. We find this outcome counter-intuitive, since it is not uncommon for traders to combine different technical indicators to make trading decisions. We therefore decide to investigate a different modular approach (λ abstraction) to better understand GP's ability in finding profitable trading rules.

3.   Modular GP through Lambda Abstraction

Lambda abstractions are expressions defined in λ calculus (Church, 1941) that represent function definition (see Section 4 for the syntax). Similar to a function definition in other programming languages such as C, a λ abstraction can take inputs and produce outputs. In a GP program tree, each λ abstraction is treated as an independent module, with a unique identity and purpose. It is protected as one unit throughout the program evolution process.

One way to incorporate λ abstraction modules in GP is using higher-order functions, i.e., functions which take other functions as inputs or return functions as outputs. When a higher-order function is used to construct GP program trees, its function arguments are created as λ abstractions modules. These modules evolve in ways that are similar to the rest of the GP trees. However, they can only interact with their own kind to preserve module identities.

For example, Figure 2-2 gives two program trees. Each contains two different kinds of λ abstraction modules: one is represented as a triangle and the other as a cycle. Cross-over operations are only permitted between modules of the same kind.

We use *type information* to distinguish different kind of λ abstraction modules. Two λ abstractions are of the same kind if they have the same number of inputs and outputs, with the same input and output types. For example, in this

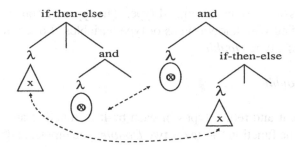

Figure 2-2. Cross-over between λ abstraction modules in two GP trees.

work we define a λ abstraction with type information $Time \to Boolean$: it takes one input with type *Time* and returns a *Boolean* output.

Unlike an ADF, whose position in a program tree is determined by evolution, a λ abstraction module is hard-wired to sit underneath a specified function node. Therefore, this module mechanism can be use to incorporate domain knowledge to design GP tree structure. In this work, we want GP to combine multiple technical indicators. To achieve that, we first add Boolean function combinators AND, OR, NAND, NOR to the function set. Additionally, we specify some of the combinators as higher-order functions. In this way, technical indicators can be evolved inside λ modules, which are then integrated together by the higher-order function combinators.

Incorporating domain knowledge to design can speed up the GP evolution process, and leads to faster discovery of meaningful solutions. In a previous work, a similar concept was used to design recursive program structure for the general even parity problem. With a very suitable design, the population program structures were quickly converged (in the first generation) and most GP evolution effort went to find the correct program contents (Yu, 2001).

4. The PolyGP System

PolyGP (Yu, 1999) is a GP system that evolves expression-based programs (λ calculus). The programs have the following syntax:

$$exp :: c \qquad \text{constant}$$
$$|\ x \qquad \text{identifier}$$
$$|\ f \qquad \text{built-in function}$$
$$|\ exp1\ exp2 \qquad \text{application of one expression to another}$$
$$|\ \lambda x.exp \qquad \text{lambda abstraction}$$

Constants and identifiers are given in the terminal set while built-in functions are provided in the function set. Application of expressions and λ abstractions are constructed by the system.

Each expression has an associated type. The types of constants and identifiers are specified with known types or type variables. For example, the stock price index has a type *Double*.

$$index :: Double$$

The argument and return types of each built-in function are also specified. For example, the function "+" takes two *Double* type inputs, and returns a *Double* type output.

$$+ :: Double \rightarrow Double \rightarrow Double$$

For higher-order functions, their function arguments are specified using brackets. For example, the first argument of function IF-THEN-ELSE can be specified as a function that takes two argument (one with type *Time* and the other with *Double* type) and returns a *Boolean* value.

$$IF - THEN - ELSE :: (Time \rightarrow Double \rightarrow Boolean) \rightarrow Boolean \rightarrow Boolean \rightarrow$$
Boolean

Using the provided type information, a type system selects type-matching functions and terminals to construct type-correct program trees. A program tree is grown from the top node downwards. There is a required type for the top node of the tree. The type system selects a function whose return type matches the required type. The selected function will require arguments to be created at the next (lower) level in the tree: there will be type requirements for each of those arguments. If the argument has a function type, a λ abstraction tree will be created. Otherwise, the type system will randomly select a function (or a terminal) whose return type matches the new required type to construct the argument node. This process is repeated many times until the permitted tree depth is reached.

λ abstraction trees are created using a similar procedure. The only difference is that their terminal set consists not only of the terminal set used to create the main program, but also the input variables to the λ abstraction. Input variable naming in λ abstractions follows a simple rule: each input variable is uniquely named with a hash symbol followed by an unique integer, *e.g.* #1, #2. This consistent naming style allows cross-over to be easily performed between λ abstraction trees with the same number and the same type of inputs and outputs.

5. S&P 500 Index Time Series Data

From *Datastream*, we acquired the S&P 500 index time series data between January 1, 1982 and December 31, 2002. Since the original time series is non-stationary, we transformed it by dividing the daily data by its 250-day moving average. This is the same method used by (Allen and Karjalainen, 1999) and (Neely et al., 1997). The adjusted data oscillate around 1 and make the modeling task easier.

A different approach to normalize financial time series is converting the price series into a return series . This is done by calculating the price difference between two consecutive days (first-order difference) in the original price series. Whether financial modeling should be based on price series or return series is still a subject under much debate (Kaboudan, 2002). We adopt the approach used by previous GP works on modeling technical trading rules so that we can make sensible performance comparisons.

Figure 2-3 gives the original and the transformed time series. There are three distinct phases in this time series. From 1982 to 1995, the market grew consistently; between 1996 and 1999, the market bulled; after 2000, the market declined. With such diversity, this data set is suitable for GP to model trading rules.

While the transformed series are used for modeling, the computation of the returns from GP trading rules are based on the original time series. One implication of this data transformation is that GP is searching for rules based on the *change of price trend* that give profitable trading rules.

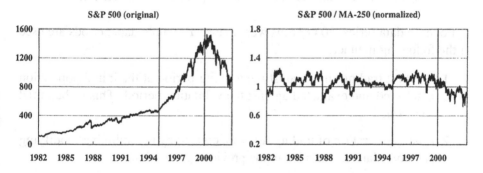

Figure 2-3. Time series data before and after normalization.

Over-fitting is an issue faced by all data modeling techniques; GP is no exception. When optimizing the trading rules, GP tends to make the rules producing maximum returns for the training period, which may contain noise that do not represent the overall series pattern. In order to construct trading rules that generalize beyond the training data, we split the series into training, validation and testing periods. We also adopted the rolling forward method, which was proposed by (Pesaran and Timmermann, 1995) and used by (Allen and Karjalainen, 1999) and (Wang, 2000).

To start, we reserved 1982 data to be referred to by time series functions such as *lag*. The remaining time series were then organized into 7 sequences, each of which was used to make an independent GP run. In each sequence, the training period is 4 years long, validation period is 2 years and testing period is 2 years. The data in one sequence may overlap the data in another sequence. As shown in Figure 2-4, the second half of the training period and the entire validation period of the first sequence are the training period of the second sequence. The testing period at the first sequence is the validation period at the second sequence. With this setup, each testing period is 2 years, and covers a different time period from 1989 to 2002.

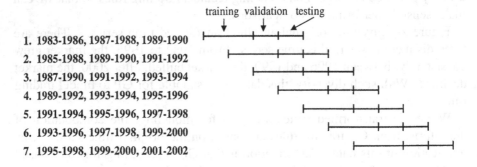

1. 1983-1986, 1987-1988, 1989-1990
2. 1985-1988, 1989-1990, 1991-1992
3. 1987-1990, 1991-1992, 1993-1994
4. 1989-1992, 1993-1994, 1995-1996
5. 1991-1994, 1995-1996, 1997-1998
6. 1993-1996, 1997-1998, 1999-2000
7. 1995-1998, 1999-2000, 2001-2002

Figure 2-4.   Training, validation and testing periods for 7 time sequences.

For each data series, 50 GP runs were made. The three data periods are used in the following manner:

1. The best trading rule against the training period at the initial population is selected and evaluated against the validation period. This is the initial "best rule".

2. A new generation of trading rules are created by recombining/modifying parts of relatively fit rules in the previous generation.

3. The best trading rule against the training period at the new population is selected and evaluated against the validation period;

4. If this rule has a better validation fitness than the previous "best rule", this is the new "best rule".

5. Goto step 2 until the maximum number of generation is reached or there is no fitter rule found after a certain number of generations (50 in this study).

6 The last "best rule" is evaluated against the testing period. This is what we use to evaluate the performance of the GP trading rule.

In summary, data from the training period are used to construct/optimize GP trading rules, while data from the validation period are used to select the GP trading rules, which are then applied to the testing period data to give the performance of the rule. The evaluation of performance of the GP trading rules is based on the results from testing periods.

6.   Experimental Setup

We made two sets of runs: one with λ abstraction modules and one without. The three higher-order functions defined for GP to evolve λ abstraction modules are:

$$AND :: (Time \rightarrow Boolean) \rightarrow Boolean \rightarrow Boolean$$

$$NOR :: (Time \rightarrow Boolean) \rightarrow Boolean \rightarrow Boolean$$

$$IF - THEN - ELSE :: (Time \rightarrow Double \rightarrow Boolean) \rightarrow Boolean$$
$$\rightarrow Boolean \rightarrow Boolean$$

The first argument of AND and NOR is a function with takes one input with type *Time* and returns a *Boolean* output. As described before, this function argument will be created as a λ abstraction in the GP trees. Since the two λ abstractions are of the same category, the left branch of an AND node in a GP tree is allowed to cross-over with the left branch of either an AND or a NOR node in another GP tree. The first argument of IF-THEN-ELSE, however, is a function with a different type. Its left branch is therefore only allowed to cross-over with the left branch of an IF-THEN-ELSE node in another GP tree. We constrain a GP tree to have a maximum of 4 higher-order functions to preserve computer memory usage.

Tables 2-1 and 2-2 give the functions and terminals that are used by both sets of GP runs. The function *avg* computes the moving average in a time window specified by the integer argument. For example, $avg(t,250)$ is the arithmetic mean of $index_{t-1}, index_{t-2}, \cdots, index_{t-250}$. The function *max* returns the largest index during a time window specified by the integer argument. For example, $max(t,3)$ is equivalent to $max(index_{t-1}, index_{t-2}, index_{t-3})$. Similarly, the function *min* returns the smallest index value during a time window specified by the integer argument. The function *lag* returns the index value lagged by a number of days specified by the integer argument. For example, $lag(t,3)$ is $index_{t-3}$. These functions are commonly used by financial traders to design trading indicators, hence are reasonable building blocks for GP to evolve trading rules. Also, the ranges for integer values are 0 and 250 while the ranges for double values are 0 and 1.

Table 2-1.   Functions and their types used for both sets of GP runs.

Name	Type
OR	$Boolean \rightarrow Boolean \rightarrow Boolean$
NAND	$Boolean \rightarrow Boolean \rightarrow Boolean$
>	$Double \rightarrow Double \rightarrow Boolean$
<	$Double \rightarrow Double \rightarrow Boolean$
+	$Double \rightarrow Double \rightarrow Double$
−	$Double \rightarrow Double \rightarrow Double$
*	$Double \rightarrow Double \rightarrow Double$
/	$Double \rightarrow Double \rightarrow Double$
AVG	$Time \rightarrow Integer \rightarrow Double$
MIN	$Time \rightarrow Integer \rightarrow Double$
MAX	$Time \rightarrow Integer \rightarrow Double$
LAG	$Time \rightarrow Integer \rightarrow Double$

Table 2-2.   Terminals and their types used for both sets of GP runs but rlr added some text to make this table caption go more than one line to see if that is also centered.

Name	Type	Name	Type
INDEX	*Double*	RANDOM-INT	*Integer*
TRUE	*Boolean*	RANDOM-DOUBLE	*Double*
FALSE	*Boolean*	T	*Time*

For GP runs without λ abstractions, we redefine the AND, NOR and IF-THEN-ELSE functions as follows:

$AND :: Boolean \rightarrow Boolean \rightarrow Boolean$

$NOR :: Boolean \rightarrow Boolean \rightarrow Boolean$

$IF - THEN - ELSE :: Boolean \rightarrow Boolean \rightarrow Boolean \rightarrow Boolean$

Both sets of GP runs used the same control parameters given in Table 2-3. The GP system is generation-based, *i.e.* parents do not compete with offspring for selection and reproduction. We used a tournament of size 2 to select winners. This means that two individuals were randomly selected and the one with a better fitness was the winner. The new population was generated with 50% of the individuals from cross-over, 40% from mutation (either point or sub-tree), and 10% from the copy operator. The best individual was always copied over to the new generation. A GP run stopped if no new best rule appeared for 50 generation on validation data, or the maximum number of generations (100) was reached.

Table 2-3.   GP control parameters.

Parameter	Value	Parameter	Value
Tree Depth	4	Cross-over Rate	50
Population Size	200	Mutation Rate	40
Number of Runs	50	Copy Rate	10
Maximum Generation	100	Maximum Non-Improvement	50

Fitness Function

The fitness of an evolved GP trading rule is the *return* (R) it generates over the tested period. Initially, we are out of the market, *i.e.* holding no stock. Based on the trading decisions, buy and sell activities interleave throughout the time period until the end of the term when the stock will be forcibly closed. When in the market, it earns the stock market return. While out of the market, it earns a risk free interest return. The continuous compounded return over the entire period is the *return* (R) which becomes the fitness of the GP trading rule.

There are three steps in computing the return of a GP trading rule. First, the GP rule is applied to the normalized time series to produce a sequence of trading decisions: *True* directs the trader to enter/stay in the market and *False* means to exit/stay out of the market. Second, this decision sequence is executed based on the original stock price series and the daily interest rate to calculate the compounded return. Last, each transaction (buy or sell) is charged with a 0.25% fee, which is deducted from the compounded return to give the final fitness.

Let P_t be the S&P 500 index price on day t, I_t be the interest rate on day t, and the return of day t is r_t:

$$r_t = \begin{cases} \log(P_t) - \log(P_{t-1}) & \text{, in the market} \\ I_t & \text{, out of the market} \end{cases}$$

Let n denote the total number of transactions, *i.e.* the number of times a *True* (in the market) is followed by a *False* (out of the market) plus the number of times a *False* (out of the market) is followed by a *True* (in the market). Also, let c be the one-way transaction cost. The return over the entire period of T days is:

$$R = \sum_{t=1}^{T} r_t + n * \log \frac{1-c}{1+c}$$

In this study, the transaction fee c is 0.25% of the stock price. Compared to the transaction cost used by (Allen and Karjalainen, 1999) (0.1%, 0.25% & 0.5%) and (Wang, 2000) (0.12%), we have a reasonable transaction cost.

7.   Results

Table 2-4 gives the returns from non-λ abstraction GP trading rules while Table 2-5 gives the returns from λ abstraction-GP trading rules. The last column in both tables gives the returns from trading decisions made by the majority vote over the 50 trading rules, generated from 50 different GP runs.

Table 2-4.   Returns from non-λ abstraction GP trading rules on testing data.

seq	year	mean	stdev	median	max	min	majority vote
1	1989-1990	0.4910	0.2667	0.4021	1.2768	0.1681	0.5639
2	1991-1992	0.5032	0.2614	0.3640	1.0306	0.2688	0.4997
3	1993-1994	0.1776	0.1540	0.1286	0.5660	0.0477	0.1996
4	1995-1996	0.6058	0.1901	0.4964	0.9212	0.3257	0.6808
5	1997-1998	0.8678	0.4177	0.7913	1.8019	0.2392	0.9145
6	1999-2000	0.4787	0.4354	0.3667	1.7774	0.0665	0.5058
7	2001-2002	0.2608	0.5796	0.0852	1.9405	-0.4109	0.7599

Table 2-5.   Returns from λ abstraction-GP trading rules on testing data.

seq	year	mean	stdev	median	max	min	majority vote
1	1989-1990	1.0353	0.2829	1.1287	1.2585	0.3081	1.1983
2	1991-1992	0.8377	0.2297	0.9507	0.9853	0.2120	0.9610
3	1993-1994	0.4479	0.1219	0.4905	0.5925	0.0477	0.5346
4	1995-1996	0.8007	0.1484	0.8537	0.9137	0.4548	0.9051
5	1997-1998	1.4917	0.4364	1.6450	1.8972	0.4976	1.8243
6	1999-2000	1.3321	0.5569	1.5488	1.9248	0.0665	1.6522
7	2001-2002	1.0167	0.7973	1.2671	1.9844	-0.1984	1.9651

Both sets of GP runs find trading rules that consistently out-perform buy-and-hold[1]. It is clear that their excess returns over buy-and-hold are statically significant. Also, λ abstraction-GP rules give higher returns than non-λ abstraction GP rules. Moreover, trading decisions based on the majority vote by 50 rules give the highest returns. These are encouraging results indicating that GP is capable of finding profitable trading rules that out-perform buy-and-hold.

---

[1] With buy-and-hold , stocks purchased at the beginning of the term are kept until the end of the term when they are closed; no trading activity takes place during the term. This is the most frequently used benchmark to evaluate the profitability of a financial trading rule. Buy-and-hold returns for the 7 testing periods are 0.1681, 0.2722, 0.0477, 0.4730, 0.5015, 0.0665, -0.4109 respectively

However, the GP rules returns may have two possible biases, from *trading costs* and *non-synchronous trading*.

Trading Cost Bias.   The actual cost associated with each trade is not easy to estimate. One obvious reason is that different markets have different fees and taxes. Additionally, there are hidden costs involved in the collection and analysis of information. To work with such difficulty, break-even transaction cost (BETC) has been proposed as an alternative approach to evaluate the profitability of a trading rule (Kaboudan, 2002).

BETC is the level of transaction cost which offsets trading rule revenue and lead to zero profits. Once we have calculated BETC for each trading rule, it can be roughly interpreted as follows:

- large and positive: good;

- small and positive: OK;

- small and negative: bad;

- large and negative: interesting.

We will incorporate BETC to measure the profitability of the evolved GP trading rules in our future work.

Non-Synchronous Trading Bias.   Non-synchronous trading is the tendency for prices recorded at the end of the day to represent the outcome of transactions that occur at different points in time for different stocks. The existence of thinly traded shares in the index can introduce non-synchronous trading bias. As a result, the observed returns might not be exploitable in practice. One way to test this is to execute the trading rules based on trades occurring with a delay of one day. This could remove any first order autocorrelation bias due to non-synchronous trading (Pereira, 2002). This is a research topic in our future work.

Another way to evaluate the GP trading rules is by applying them to a different financial index, such as NASDAQ 100. The returns may provide insights about the rules and/or the stock markets themselves.

8.   Analysis of GP Trading Rules

We examined all 50 rules generated from GP with λ abstraction modules on sequence 5 data and found most of them can be interpreted easily; each module is a trading indicator of some form. Depending on the number of λ abstraction modules it contains, a rule applies one to four indicators to make trading decisions (see Table 2-6). For example, $index > avg(28)$ is a *moving*

Table 2-6.   50 λ abstraction GP trading rules trained by sequence 5 data.

fitness	quantity	rules (after minor editing of non-executing code)
1.8972	2	$or(index > avg(2), index > lag(1))$
1.8937	1	$(index + index) > (avg(2) + avg(1))$
1.8535	1	$index > avg(1)$
1.8476	1	$if - then - else(max(1) < index, true, avg(3) < index)$
1.8059	7	$index > min(2)$
1.8034	1	$nand(if - then - else(index < avg(3), true, false),$ $if - then - else(index < min(2), true, false))$
1.7941	5	$index > avg(2)$
1.7941	1	$2 * index - avg(2) > min(21)$
1.7844	1	$and(or(avg(1) < index,$ $or(or(avg(6) < index, 1.30 < min(6)), avg(6) < index)), true)$
1.7002	1	$and(index > min(3), nand(index > avg(28), index < avg(3)))$
1.6936	1	$and(and(index < min(3), or(index > min(9),$ $index > min(11))), and(min(5) > index, true))$
1.6819	1	$or(index > 1.173, index > avg(2))$
1.6784	1	$nand(index < avg(5), index < min(3))$
1.6775	1	$nand(index < avg(4), nand(index < min(4),$ $nand(index < lag(4), nand(index < avg(13), true))))$
1.6126	1	$or(and(index > avg(5), true), and(index > min(5),$ $and(or(index > max(10), index < lag(5)), true)))$
1.5873	2	$index > min(4)$
1.5870	4	$index > avg(3)$
1.5539	1	$nand((0.00565 + index) < max(3), true)$
1.5149	1	$index > avg(4)$
1.5133	1	$and(min(5) < index,$ $nor((index + avg(175)) < (min(6) + avg(199)), false))$
1.5079	1	$and(index > min(13), and(index > min(5),$ $and(index > min(17), true)))$
1.4402	1	$and(index > min(8), or(nand(index > max(8),$ $nand(avg(165) < index, lag(45) > index)),$ $if - then - else(index > min(6), true, false)))$
1.4130	2	$index > avg(6)$
1.3283	1	$index < min(8)$
1.1427	1	$index > min(15)$
1.0650	1	$(0.01 + min(39)) < index$
0.7968	1	$2.44 * (index + index) > (avg(53) + (index * 3.86))$
0.7242	1	$index * index > avg(21)$
0.5996	1	$(index + 14.4) > (20.892/(0.28 + index))$
0.5611	1	$(index + 3.12) > (index/0.24)$
0.5611	1	$(min(84) + (8.8/index)) < ((index + 6.79) + lag(84))$
0.5015	2	$true(buy - and - hold)$
0.4976	1	$false$

average indicator which compares today's index (divided by its 250-days moving average) with the average index (divided by its 250-days moving average) over the previous 28 days. Another example is $index > max(8)$, which is a *filter* indicator that compares today's index (divided by its 250-days moving average) with the maximum index (divided by its 250-days moving average) of the previous 8 days.

Among the 50 λ abstraction GP trading rules, 23 use a combination of two to four indicators to make trading decisions. The most frequently used combinator is the AND function. This means many criteria have to be met before a stay-in-the-market decision (*True*) is issued. In other words, the GP rules use various indicators to evaluate the market trend and to make trading decisions. Such a sophisticated decision making process has led to more profitable trading.

In contrast, most (48) of the 50 rules generated from non-λ abstraction GP apply a single indicator to make trading decisions. Although some of the single trading indicators can also give high returns (see Table 2-6), they are not always easy to find. Without the structure protection, forming meaningful trading indicators during evolution is not always easy. We have found many rules having branches under a combinator (such as AND) that are evaluated into constant value of *True* or *False*, instead of a meaningful indicator. This is very different from the λ abstraction GP trading rules, where more meaningful indicators were evolved as λ abstraction modules under the branches of higher-order function combinators (AND & NOR & IF-THEN-ELSE).

Based on the analysis, we believe the λ abstraction module mechanism promotes the creation and combination of technical indicators. Such combined usage of different trading indicators gives a more, and leads to trades that generate higher returns.

We have also considered another possible benefit of the λ abstraction module mechanism: it provides good seeding , which helps GP to find fitter trading rules. However, after examining the initial populations of all the GP runs, we find no evidence to support such a hypothesis. Sometimes, λ abstraction-GP gives higher initial population fitness than the non-λ abstraction-GP does. Sometimes it is the other way around.

9.   Analysis of Transaction Frequency

As mentioned in Section 5, the S&P 500 index grew consistently between 1989 and 1995, bulled from 1996 to 1999 and declined after 2000. As expected, buy-and-hold gives the best return during the years 1996-1998 and the worst returns for the 2001-2002 period.

Regardless of the stock market's climate, GP trading rules were able to identify opportunities to make profitable trading. The average transaction frequency for non-λ abstraction GP rules is 22 for each testing period of 2 years: about one transaction every 33 days. The frequency for λ abstraction GP rules is 3 times higher, with an average of 76 transactions in each testing period. In both cases, the higher the transaction frequency, the higher the return. This is demonstrated at the bottom half of Figure 2-5 and 2-6 where 3 cross plots from the 3 distinct time periods are given.

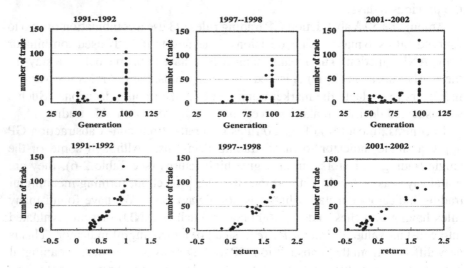

Figure 2-5. Transaction frequency *vs.* returns for non-λ abstraction GP rules.

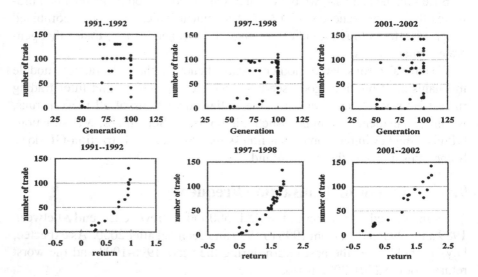

Figure 2-6. Transaction frequency *vs.* returns for λ abstraction GP rules.

We also compare the number of generations that each GP run lasted. As mentioned in Section 5, a GP run terminated when either no better rule on validation data was found for 50 generations or the maximum number of generation (100) has reached. This means that the number of possible generations of a GP run is between 50 and 100. We have found that on average λ abstraction GP runs lasted 6 generations longer than non-λ abstraction GP runs. This indicates that λ abstraction GP is better able to continue to find fitter trading rules.

Do longer runs always generate better trading rules? The top half of Figure 2-5 shows that non-λ abstraction GP rules which give higher than 20 were generated by runs terminated at generation 100 (there are a couple of exceptions). In other words, longer runs generated trading rules that gave higher trading frequency (> 20) and better returns. However, this pattern is not as evident in the λ abstraction GP runs (the top half of Figure 2-6). Some of the runs that terminated before generation 100 also generated trading rules that gave high trading frequency (> 20) and good returns. Nevertheless, all runs that terminated at generation 100 gave high trading frequency (> 20) which led to good returns.

Figure 2-7 and 2-8 present the proportion of the 50 trading rules signaling a *True* (in the market) over the entire testing period. They give a visual representation of the degree of consensus among 50 rules and of the extent to which their decisions are coordinated. The λ abstraction rules have high consensus; during most of the testing period, 80% of the rules give the same decisions. In contrast, non-λ abstraction rules have a slightly lower degree of consensus; about 70% of the rules give the same decisions over the majority of the testing period.

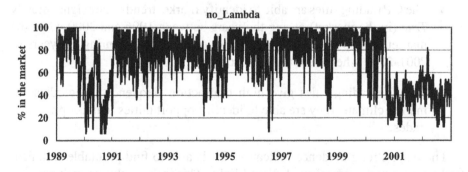

Figure 2-7.   Proportion of non-λ abstraction GP rules signals"in the market".

Both sets of GP rules were able to identify. They signaled mostly *True* (in the market) during the year between 1996 and 2000 when the market was up and mostly *False* (out of the market) during the year of 2001-2002 when the market was down.

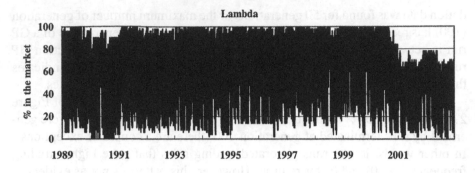

Figure 2-8. Proportion of λ abstraction GP rules signal "in the market".

10.   Concluding Remarks

The application of λ abstraction GP to find technical trading rules based on S&P 500 index has generated many encouraging results:

- The GP trading rules give returns in excess of buy-and-hold with statistical significance.

- The GP trading rules can be interpreted easily; they use one to four commonly used technical indicators to make trading decisions.

- The GP trading rules have high consensus; during the majority of the testing period, 80% of the rules give the same decision.

- The GP trading rules are able to identify market trends; they signal mostly *True* (in the market) during the years between 1996 and 2000 when the market was up and mostly *False* (out of the market) during the years of 2001-2002 when the market was down.

- The GP trading rules give high transaction frequency. Regardless of market climate, they are able to identify opportunities to make profitable trades.

These are strong evidence indicating GP is able to find profitable technical trading rules that out-perform buy-and-hold. This is the first time such positive results on GP trading rules are reported.

Various analysis indicates that the λ abstraction module mechanism promotes the creation and combination of technical indicators in the GP trading rules. Such combination of different trading indicators gives more sophisticated market evaluation and leads to trades that generate higher returns.

Lambda abstraction is a module mechanism that can incorporate domain knowledge to design program structures. When properly used, it leads to the discovery of good and meaningful solutions. This chapter gives one such example, in addition to the example of even parity problem reported in (Yu, 2001). We anticipate there are more such domain-knowledge-rich problems that the λ abstraction module mechanism can help GP to solve.

Future Work

The evolved GP trading rules give strong evidence that there are patterns in the S&P 500 time series. These patterns are identified by GP as various forms of technical indicators, each of which is captured in a λ abstraction module. This feature is exhibited in all the rules generated from 50 GP runs.

These patterns, however, do not seem to exist in the initial population. Instead, it is through the continuous merging (cross-over) and modification (mutation) of the same kind of modules for a long time (100 generations) when meaningful technical indicators were formed.

Based on these application results, we are planning on a theoretical work to formally define the convergence process of the λ abstraction GP:

- Define each indicator in the 50 GP rules as a building block;

- Formulate the steps to find one of the 50 rules.

We are not certain if such a theory is useful, since we might not be able to generalize it beyond this particular application or data set. Nevertheless, we believe it is a research worth pursuing.

Acknowledgments

We wish to thank John Koza and Mike Caplan for their comments and suggestions.

References

Allen, Franklin and Karjalainen, Risto (1999). Using genetic algorithms to find technical trading rules. *Journal of Financial Economics*, 51(2):245–271.

Bhattacharyya, Siddhartha, Pictet, Olivier V., and Zumbach, Gilles (2002). Knowledge-intensive genetic discovery in foreign exchange markets. *IEEE Transactions on Evolutionary Computation*, 6(2):169–181.

Brock, William, Lakonishok, Josef, and LeBaron, Blake (1992). Simple technical trading rules and the stochastic properties of stock returns. *Journal of Finance*, 47(5):1731–1764.

Church, Alonzo (1941). *The Calculi of Lambda Conversion*. Princeton University Press.

Cooper, Michael (1999). Filter rules based on price and volume in individual security overreaction. *The Review of Financial Studies*, 12(4):901–935.

Kaboudan, Mak (2002). Gp forecasts of stock prices for profitable trading. In *Evolutionary Computation in Economics and Finance*, pages 359–382. Physica-Verlag.

Koza, John R. (1992). *Genetic Programming: On the Programming of Computers by Means of Natural Selection*. MIT Press, Cambridge, MA, USA.

Koza, John R. (1994). *Genetic Programming II: Automatic Discovery of Reusable Programs.* MIT Press, Cambridge Massachusetts.

Neely, Christopher J., Weller, Paul A., and Dittmar, Rob (1997). Is technical analysis in the foreign exchange market profitable? A genetic programming approach. *The Journal of Financial and Quantitative Analysis*, 32(4):405–426.

O'Neill, Michael, Brabazon, Anthony, and Ryan, Conor (2002). Forecasting market indices using evolutionary automatic programming. In *Genetic Algoritms and Genetic Programming in Computational Finance*, pages 175–195. Kluwer Academic Publishers.

Pereira, Robert (2002). Forecasting ability but no profitability: An empirical evaluation of genetic algorithm-optimised technical trading rules. In *Evolutionary Computation in Economics and Finance*, pages 275–295. Physica-Verlag.

Pesaran, M. Hashem and Timmermann, Allan (1995). Predictability of stock returns: Robustness and economic significance. *Journal of Finance*, 50:1201–1228.

Pring, Martin J. (1991). *Technical Analysis Explained.* McGraw-Hill Trade.

Wang, Jun (2000). Trading and hedging in s&p 500 spot and futures markets using genetic programming. *The Journal of Futures Markets*, 20(10):911–942.

Yu, Gwoing Tina (1999). *An Analysis of the Impact of Functional Programming Techniques on Genetic Programming.* PhD thesis, University College, London, Gower Street, London, WC1E 6BT.

Yu, Tina (2001). Hierachical processing for evolving recursive and modular programs using higher order functions and lambda abstractions. *Genetic Programming and Evolvable Machines*, 2(4):345–380.

Yu, Tina, Chen, Shu-Heng, and Kuo, Tzu-Wen (2004). A genetic programming approach to model international short-term capital flow. *To appear in a special issue of Advances in Econometrics.*

Chapter 3

USING GENETIC PROGRAMMING IN INDUSTRIAL STATISTICAL MODEL BUILDING

Flor Castillo[1], Arthur Kordon[1], Jeff Sweeney[2], and Wayne Zirk[3]

[1]*TheDow Chemical Company*, Freeport, TX; [2]*TheDow Chemical Company*, Midland, MI [3]*TheDow Chemical Company*, South Charleston, WV.

Abstract   The chapter summarizes the practical experience of integrating genetic programming and statistical modeling at The Dow Chemical Company. A unique methodology for using Genetic Programming in statistical modeling of designed and undesigned data is described and illustrated with successful industrial applications. As a result of the synergistic efforts, the building technique has been improved and the model development cost and time can be significantly reduced. In case of designed data Genetic Programming reduced costs by suggesting transformations as an alternative to doing additional experimentation. In case of undesigned data Genetic Programming was instrumental in reducing the model building costs by providing alternative models for consideration.

Keywords: Genetic programming, statistical model building, symbolic regression, undesigned data

1. INTRODUCTION

Recently the role of statistical model building in industry has grown significantly. Many corporations have embraced the Six Sigma methodology (Harry and Schroeder, 2000) as the backbone of their manufacturing and new product development processes. One of the key objectives of Six Sigma is to improve the business decisions by making them entirely data-driven. An inevitable effect of this shift is that many people with wildly different backgrounds like process engineers, economists, and managers are building statistical models. Another industrial activity with growing demand for statistical model building is high-throughput discovery where the strategy for the designed experiments and the speed and quality of the analysis are critical (Cawse, 2003).

As a result of these large-scale efforts, the issue of reducing the cost of statistical model building in industrial settings becomes central. A significant component of the cost is due to the expense involved in running Design Of Experiments (DOE)[+]. This is evident in the chemical industry where running experiments can result in a temporary reduction in plant capacity or product quality. In the case of statistical model building using undesigned data (i.e. historical data), the cost is frequently based on non-linear models development and maintenance.

Recently, Genetic Programming (GP), with its capability to automatically generate models via symbolic regression, has captured the attention of industry (Koza, 1992, Banzhaf et al, 1998). It has been successfully implemented in several application areas like inferential sensors, emulators, accelerated new product development, etc. (Kotanchek et al, 2003). One of the areas where GP can significantly impact statistical modeling is the cost reduction associated with empirical modeling utilizing designed data and effective variable selection and alternative model building with undesigned data.

This chapter will present the results from the current efforts to use GP in industrial statistical model building at The Dow Chemical Company. The chapter is organized in the following manner. First, the potential benefits from the synergy between GP and statistical model building are defined, followed by description of a methodology for using GP in empirical model building from designed and undesigned data. The methodology is illustrated on real industrial applications. We describe a case involving designed data (data collected using designed experiments) where using GP reduced costs by suggesting transformations as an alternative to doing additional experimentation. Also we present a case involving undesigned data (observational data collected during production process) where GP was instrumental in reducing the model building costs by providing alternative models for consideration. Finally, topics for future research are proposed.

2.   SYNERGY BETWEEN GP AND STATISTICAL MODEL BUILDING

To our surprise, there are very few papers that address the synergy between statistical modeling and GP, especially in the statistical community (with exception of Westbury et al., 2003). Statistical modeling often refers to the local approximation of a functional relationship (affected by error) between the inputs and the outputs using a Taylor series expansion. In the

---

[+] A glossary of statistical terms is provided at the end of the chapter

GP community, the issues of statistical analysis in GP are discussed in (Banzhaf *et al*, 1998) and (Kaboudan, 1999). As a first step for analyzing the synergetic benefits of the both approaches, the unique features of each approach that are attractive to the other are discussed.

2.1 Unique Features of GP Attractive to Statistical Model Building

GP has the following features that might be beneficial for statistical modeling in industrial settings:
  (a) GP generates multiple diverse empirical models that could be used as an alternative to statistical models.
  (b) GP doesn't assume variable independence for model generation.
  (c) GP doesn't need the regular assumptions for least-squares estimators like multivariate normal distribution and independent errors with zero mean and constant variance.
  (d) GP can generate non-linear transforms that can linearize the problem and allow the use of linear regression with all the rigor and benefits of statistical analysis.
  (e) GP allows inputs sensitivity analysis and variable selection that reduces the dimensionality for statistical model building of undesigned data.
  (f) GP generates models from small data sets.

2.2 Unique Features of Statistical Model Building Attractive to GP

Statistical model building has the following important features that are beneficial for empirical model building using GP: [1]
  (a) Quantify the measure of performance of a model (ANOVA F test).
  (b) Ability to detect data outliers with respect to the data (Hat Matrix) and the model (residuals).
  (c) Provides multiple measures of model Lack Of Fit (R^2, LOF).
  (d) Calculates influence measures associated with data observations (Cook Distance).
  (e) Potential for making cause and effect conclusions (DOE).
  (f) Confidence intervals to assess model and model parameter uncertainty.

---

[1] A glossary of statistical terms is provided at the end of the chapter.

(g) Statistical hypothesis testing for assessing parameter statistical significance (t-test).
(h) Quantifiable ways to assess the stability of a model (multicollinearity and VIF).

2.3   Synergetic Benefits

It is obvious from the list of features attractive to both approaches that there is a big potential to improve model development and reduce its cost by their intelligent integration. First, the synergetic benefits in developing models based on GP and statistical models will be discussed, followed by the economic impact from the integration.

The key benefit from the synergy of GP and statistical model building in industrial model development is broadening the modeling capabilities of both approaches. On the one hand, GP allows model building in cases where it would be very costly or physically unrealistic to develop a linear model. On the other hand, statistical modeling with its well established metrics gives GP models all necessary measures of statistical performance. Some of these measures like the confidence limits of model parameters and responses are of critical importance for the model implementation in an industrial environment.

There are several economic benefits from the synergy between GP and statistical model building. The most obvious, as previously mentioned, is the elimination of additional experimental runs to address model Lack of Fit (LOF). Another case of economic benefit is the potential for the elimination of expensive screening DOE. Since the dimensionality of real industrial problems can be high (very often the numbers of inputs is 30-50), the screening process is often very time consuming and costly. Inputs screening can be addressed using the GP algorithm. An additional potential benefit from the synergy between GP and statistical model building is that the applied models may have higher reliability (due to the confidence limits and reduced instability) and require less maintenance in comparison to the non-linear models generated by GP alone.

3.   METHODOLOGY

We are suggesting a methodology that delivers the synergetic benefits described in Section 2 in the following two cases of high practical importance:
-   Designed data
-   Undesigned data

3.1   Methodology for Designed Data

The complexity of some industrial chemical processes requires that first-principle or mechanistic models be considered in conjunction with empirical models. At the basis of empirical models is the underlying assumption that for any system there is a fundamental relationship between the inputs and the outputs that can be locally approximated over a limited range of experimental conditions by a polynomial or a linear regression model. The term *linear model* refers to a model that is linear in *the parameters, β_k, not the input variables* (the x's)[2].   Suitable statistical techniques such as design of experiments (DOE) are available to assist in the experimentation process (Box *et al*, 1978).   The capability of the model to represent the data can often be assessed through a formal Lack Of   Fit (LOF) test when experimental replicates are available (Montgomery, 1999). Significant LOF in the model indicates a regression function that is not linear in the inputs; i.e., the polynomial initially considered is not adequate. A polynomial of higher order that fits the data better may be constructed by augmenting the original design with additional experimental runs. Specialized designs such as the Central Composite Design are available for this purpose (Box *et al.*, 1978).

However, in many situations a second-order polynomial has already been fit and LOF is still present. In other cases the fit of a higher order polynomial is impractical because runs are very expensive or technically infeasible because of extreme experimental conditions. Furthermore, the extra experimental runs introduce correlation among model parameters without guarantee that LOF is removed. This problem can be handled if appropriate input transformations are used, provided that the basic assumption of least-square estimation regarding the probability distributions of errors is not affected. These assumptions require that errors be uncorrelated and normally distributed with mean zero and constant variance.

Some useful transformations have been previously published (Box and Draper, 1987). Unfortunately, transformations that linearize the response without affecting the error structure are often unknown, at times based on experience and frequently becomes at best a guessing game. This process is time consuming and often non-efficient in solving LOF situations.

Genetic programming (GP) generated symbolic regression provides a unique opportunity to rapidly develop and test these transformations. Symbolic regression automatically generates non-linear input-output models. Several possible models of the response as a function of the input variables are obtained by combining basic functions, inputs, and numerical constants.

---

[2] A more detailed description of linear models is given in Appendix 2.

This multiplicity of models with different analytical expressions provides a rich set of possible transformations of the inputs, otherwise unknown, which have the potential to solve LOF.

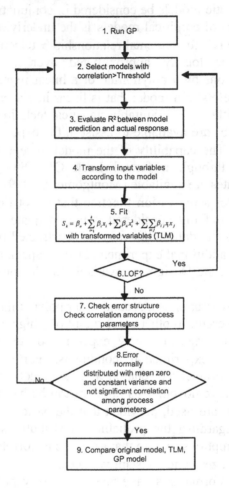

Figure 3-1. Methodology considered to find transforms that eliminate LOF.

Therefore, once LOF is confirmed with a statistical test and transformations of the inputs seems to be the most practical approach to address this situation, GP-generated symbolic regression can be used. The process is illustrated in Figure 3-1 and consists of selecting equations with correlation coefficients larger than a threshold level. These equations are analyzed in terms of the R^2. The original variables are then transformed according to the functional form of these equations. Then a linear regression model is fit to the data using the transformed variables. The adequacy of the transformed model is initially analyzed considering Lack Of Fit and R^2. Then the error structure of the models not showing significant LOF is considered and the correlation among model parameters is evaluated. This process ensures that the transformations given by GP not only remove LOF but also produce the adequate error structure needed for least square estimations with no significant correlations among the model parameters. This methodology is illustrated with the following specific example from a real industrial process.

3.1.1 Application- designed data

The data considered in this example is a Box-Behnken design of four input variables, x_1- x_4, with six center points (Castillo *et al*, 2004). A total of 30 experiments were performed. The output variable was the particle size distribution of a chemical compound. This output was fit to the following second-order linear regression equation considering only those terms that are significant at the 95% confidence level.

$$S_k = \beta_o + \sum_{i=1}^{k} \beta_i x_i + \sum_{i=1}^{k} \beta_{ii} x_i^2 + \sum \sum_{i<j} \beta_{ij} x_i x_j \tag{1}$$

The corresponding Analysis of Variance (obtained from the JMP[3] statistical software) showing evidence of Lack Of Fit (p = 0.0185) is presented in Table 3-1[4]. Typically p-values less than 0.05 are considered statistically significant.

Table 3-1. Analysis of variance (ANOVA table) and LOF for the linear model.

Source	DF	Sum of Squares	Mean Square	F Ratio
Model	14	4.7108333	0.336488	7.7751
Error	15	0.6491667	0.043278	p-value
C. Total	29	5.3600000		0.0002
				R^2=0.88
Lack Of Fit				
Source	DF	Sum of Squares	Mean Square	F Ratio
Lack Of Fit	10	0.6091667	0.060917	7.6146
Pure Error	5	0.0400000	0.008000	p-value
Total Error	15	0.6491666		**0.0185**

---

[3] JMP® is a registered trademark of SAS Institute Inc., Cary, NC, USA.
[4] Glossary of key statistical terms are given at the end of the chapter.

The ANOVA[5] p-value (p = 0.0002) given in Table 3-1 indicates that the model is statistically significant, however, the LOF p-value (p = 0.0185) suggests that there exists significant model lack-of-fit (LOF); i.e. p <0.05.

Variable x_1 was found to be insignificant and it along with terms involving x_1 was removed from the model fit. However, the resulting model with nine parameters still had significant LOF with a p-value of 0.046. Removal of LOF in this situation is particularly challenging because a second order polynomial has already been considered. Furthermore, the alternative of adding experiments to fit a third-order polynomial is not feasible because it is costly, introduces correlations among the model parameters, and can not guarantee that the resulting model will not have significant LOF. The methodology presented in Figure 3-1 was implemented and GP generated symbolic regression was employed. Function generation takes 20 runs with a population size of 100, run for 50 generations, 0.01 parsimony pressure, and correlation coefficient and sum of squares as fitness function. As a result, the analytical function given in equation 2 was obtained. This function is referred to as the GP model.

$$y = \frac{|x_2|^{0.54528}}{\sqrt{|\ln(x_3 x_2 + x_3)|} * x_2 x_4} \tag{2}$$

The transformations given in Table 3-2 were then applied to the data as indicated by the functional form of the derived GP function.

Table 3-2. Variable transformations suggested by GP model.

Original Variable	Transformed Variable
x_1	Z_1
x_2	$Z_2 = x_2^{0.5}$
x_3	$Z_3 = [\log(x_3)]^{0.5}$
x_4	$Z_4 = x_4^{-1}$

The transformed variables were used to fit a second order linear regression model shown in equation (1). The resulting model, referred to as the Transformed Linear Model (TLM), had an R^2 of 0.88, no evidence of significant Lack Of Fit (p=0.1131), no evidence of large correlation among the model parameters, and retained the appropriate error structure. A

---

[5] More details about Analysis of Variance (ANOVA), degrees of freedom (DF), Sum of Squares, Mean Square, and F Ratio can be found in any regression analysis book (see for example Draper & Smith, 1981).

summary of model numerical measures such as sum of square errors (SSE), R^2, and LOF significance is given for comparison purposes in Table 3-3.

Table 3-3. Model Comparison Summary.

	R^2	SSE	Number of Model Parameters	LOF Significance
Original Model	0.85	0.81	9	0.046
Transformed (TLM)	0.88	0.65	9	0.113
GP Model	0.77	1.19	na	na

It is evident that the sum of squares error for the Transformed Linear Model (TLM) is smaller than those of the original model and the GP model. Additionally, the TLM model shows no significant Lack Of Fit with a larger R^2.

It is also worth noting that the TLM and the original model considered the same number of parameters (9). This points out that the improvement of the TLM was not achieved by model overfitting. These results indicate that the input transformations suggested by GP successfully improved key model measures of performance while eliminating significant model Lack Of Fit without introducing additional experimental runs. The TLM with no significant LOF offers more reasonable predictions than the other models considered providing some assurance of the usefulness of the TLM model for prediction purposes. An additional application of this methodology to LOF situations in a 2^2 factorial design is available as well (Castillo *et al*, 2002).

3.2   Methodology for Undesigned Data

The main objective for collecting undesigned data is often process control (controlling the process variation not process improvement). In many industrial applications, lots of observational (undesigned) data is collected, stored, and later becomes the focus of a modeling exercise. Statistically modeling undesigned data provides many challenges, among them are data collinearity, the inability to draw cause-and-effect conclusions, and limitations on variable ranges, just to name a few.

One nice feature of designed data (data generated using DOE) is that the data structure relates to specific improvement objectives or scientific hypotheses to be examined. Therefore, there is typically a corresponding statistical model that can be fit to the designed data. Because undesigned data is not collected with any specific improvement objectives in mind, there may not be an obvious statistical model to fit. Thus, it is often entirely up to the modeler to decide what statistical model(s) to try. In situations where an obvious model to fit is not available, the GP algorithm can help to suggest several candidate models to consider. Using GP in this fashion can allow both a wider selection of models to be considered and reduce the amount of time required for empirical model identification.

Because undesigned data presents many challenges, there are many situations in which a Linear Regression Model (LRM) might be suspect (i.e. data collinearity). In those situations, the modeler may want to investigate using another model technique like PCR (Principal Component Regression), Neural Networks, or PLS (Partial Least Squares). One key advantage that GP has over these others is that the model terms are in the form of the original variables. Although the modeler should not consider this causal information, this may provide some additional understanding of the potential relationships between the variables studied and the response(s) of interest.

Sometimes the distinction between designed and undesigned data is not quite clear. Data collection may have been originally planned as DOE. However, the data may end up being undesigned because the defined levels of the input variables are not achieved in practice due to plant restrictions and operability conditions. Sometimes a set of data may even involve data collected using a DOE and other data outside the region of the DOE. In this case, the whole collection of data is often referred to as undesigned data.

3.2.1   Application- Undesigned data

The data to be illustrated in this example represents a typical situation involving undesigned data in an industrial application. Data collection was based on a three-month process history. Process conditions in four-hour intervals were used for the modeling effort. The output variable of interest (call it Y) is a measured concentration level of a process bi-product which is considered detrimental to the process. Thus, Y should be minimized for the process to operate successfully. One goal of this modeling effort was to predict the process conditions necessary to maintain the response variable (Y) at very low concentration levels. All other process conditions available in the extracted data were considered potential inputs (X's in a general Y = f(X) model form).

The first models investigated were linear polynomials. These models are often used because they tend to be very flexible and can approximate many different relationship patterns between the inputs and the output(s). However, because this was undesigned data, there was no obvious polynomial model form to fit. A first-order polynomial model (as shown in equation (3)) was fit to the data as a starting point.

$$Y = \beta_o + \sum_{i=1}^{k} \beta_i x_i \tag{3}$$

Characteristics of this model fit were assessed. The analysis of variance revealed a significant regression equation (F ratio <0.0001) with an R^2 of 0.96. A subsequent residual analysis did not show any indication of violations of the error structure required for least square estimation. This suggested that nothing else was missing from the model (i.e. no higher-order model terms required). With a high R^2 value (0.96) and no obvious patterns in the model residuals, very little improvement could be expected from investigating higher-order (more complex) polynomial models. The model parameter estimates are presented in Table 3-4.

Table 3-4. Parameter Estimates for Linear Regression Model.

Term	β Estimate	t Ratio	Prob>|t|	VIF
Intercept	230.70902	0.33	0.7432	
x1	0.9406677	19.31	<0.0001	3.84056
x2	-2.428614	-22.97	<0.0001	7.05279
x3	0.4005954	2.97	0.0041	9.42801
x4	-10.17105	-0.36	0.7217	861.2503
x5	2.956458	0.20	0.8385	343.7906
x6	10.223555	0.36	0.7164	918.9986
x7	-31.91927	-0.57	0.5686	3431.5002
x8	14.871442	0.35	0.7257	1976.0583
x9	-135.1481	-0.69	0.4919	1000231.8
X10	117.8077	0.68	0.4967	964097.17
X11	16.152238	0.40	0.6930	70850.669
X12	14.186557	0.89	0.3750	77.489476
X13	-19.53814	-0.67	0.5023	19404.123

Because this model was built using undesigned data, multicollinearity (correlation structure among the inputs) was examined. Variance Inflation Factors (VIF) [Montgomery and Peck, 1992] is a recommended method for assessing the severity of data multicollinearity. The presence of severe multicollinearty (strong relationships between the inputs) can seriously affect the precision of the estimated regression coefficients, making them very sensitive to the data in the particular sample collected and producing models with poor prediction. If multicollinearity is severe enough, it can cause real concerns with the stability, validity and usefulness of the resulting model.

The VIF for each model parameter (VIF_j) were calculated and are listed in Table 3-4. In general, high VIF's suggest that severe multicollinearity exists and the model is suspect; some authors suggest VIF's greater than 10 are too high (Myers & Montgomery, 1995). From the VIF's listed in Table 3-4, it was obvious that severe multicollinearity issues exist within the example data. This happens frequently with undesigned data from industrial situations. Many of the process variables will often vary together (being highly correlated) resulting in severely unbalanced data. One remedy often suggested is to remove any redundant inputs that may be included in the model together. If this is not possible or does not reduce the collinearity down to acceptable levels, then collecting more data (say from a suggested DOE) should be explored. However, in many situations, collecting more data to help with the modeling is not a viable economic solution. In our example, removing the redundant inputs did not reduce the multicollinearity to acceptable levels, and no additional data could be collected.

With a very unstable polynomial model, alternative candidate models, generated by GP were investigated. The parameters of the GP-generated models are as follows: functional set included addition, subtraction, multiplication, division, square, change sign, square root, natural logarithm, exponential, and power. The simulated evolution was done on 50 runs, each with 20 generations, a population size of 100; parsimony pressure 0.1, and the product between correlation coefficient and sum of squares as fitness function.

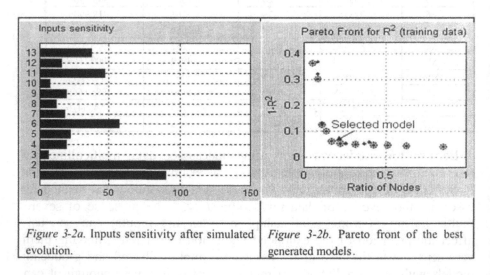

Figure 3-2a. Inputs sensitivity after simulated evolution.

Figure 3-2b. Pareto front of the best generated models.

The results from the sensitivity analysis are shown in Figure 3-2a, where the sensitivity of each of the 13 inputs is proportional to the frequency of selection in every functional tree or sub-tree during the whole simulated evolution (Kordon *et al.*, 2003). The inputs sensitivity analysis suggests five influential inputs (x_1, x_2, x_6, x_{11}, and x_{13}), thus reducing the dimensionality of the search space.

Multi-objective GP with $(1 - R^2)$ and relative number of nodes as fitness functions (Smits and Kotanchek, 2004) has been used for model selection. The models on the Pareto-front are shown in Figure 3-2b, where the final selected model with the "best" balance between performance and complexity is shown with an arrow. The model includes the suggested five influential inputs, has good performance, and acceptable error structure (see Figure 3-3)

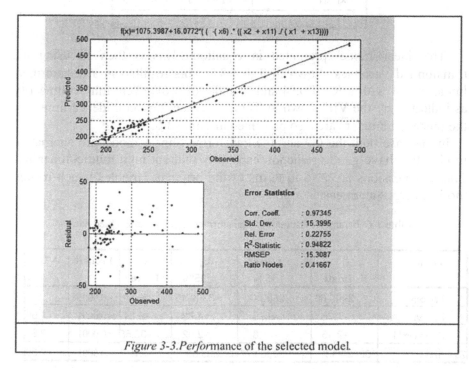

Figure 3-3. Performance of the selected model.

The following equation was selected:

$$Y = 10275 - 16078 * \frac{x_6(x_2 + x_{11})}{x_1 + x_{13}} \tag{4}$$

Note that the LRM shown in equation (3) and the GP model shown in equation (4) are both linear in the parameters. However, the GP model has a functional form that shows relationships between the different variables (x_1, x_2, x_6, x_{11}, x_{13}).

Equation (4) may be used to indicate that a transform can be applied to the linear model presented in equation (3). The transforms used are shown in Table 3-5.

Table 3-5. Original and transformed variables- Undesigned data.

Original Variable	Transformed Variable
x_2, x_{11}	$Z_1 = (x_2 + x_{11})$
x_1, x_{13}	$Z_2 = 1/(x_1 + x_{13})$
x_6	$Z_3 = x_6$

The linear model presented in equation (3) was then fit using the transformed variables shown in Table 3-5. This resulted in a transformed linear model with a R^2 of 0.94 and no indication of severe multicollinearity as indicated by the VIF shown in Table 3-6. The 95% confidence limits for the model parameters are also presented in Table 3-6.

In this case both the GP and the transformed linear model are alternative models that have good prediction capability without high multicollinearity. These expressions are also in terms of the original variables which makes model interpretation easier.

Table 3-6. Parameter Estimation Transformed model- Undesigned data.

Term	β Estimate	Lower 95%	Upper 95%	t Ratio	Prob>|t	VIF
Intercept	2955.60	2602.04	3309.15	16.62	<0.0001	
$Z_3 = x6$	-7.26	-9.75	-4.78	-5.81	<0.0001	1.50
$Z_1 = x2+x11$	-2.15	-2.28	-2.02	-32.65	<0.0001	2.50
$Z_2 = 1/x1+x13$	908023.43	993363.77	822683.09	-21.15	<0.0001	2.39

4.   FUTURE RESEARCH

The methodology discussed and illustrated with real industrial examples show the great potential of the synergy between statistical model building and genetic programming. Many research possibilities are foreseen both in applications of statistical model building to GP and in applications of GP to statistical model building. Among these are:

- The application of GP to pre-screening designs with available data. This is an attractive opportunity given the availability of online process data and the expense of industrial experimentation. In this situation GP offers a unique opportunity because sensitive inputs can be identified (Kordon, *et al*, 2003) and used as the starting point of discussion for further planned experimentation.

- Application of GP in regression models in principal component analysis (Hiden, *et al*, 1999). This may be an attractive alternative given that the interpretation of some principal components is not always obvious and can become quite difficult depending on the number of inputs included.
- Application of statistical model discrimination techniques. This would involve the evaluation of multiple models generated by GP in criteria other that the traditional fitness functions such as correlation or sum square errors. This represents a real opportunity given the number of models generated by GP and the difficulty in selecting the best model.
- Applications of designed of experiments prior to a GP run. In this work, the effects of GP running conditions (such as parsimony pressure, number of generations, and population size) on the quality of the models produced (Spoonger, 2000) would be better understood.

The possibilities are numerous and stem for the fact that both statistical model building and GP offer unique characteristics than can be combined to offer a better approach than each one individually.

5. APPENDIX 1: GLOSSARY OF STATISTICAL TERMS

- ANOVA F test: Overall statistical significance test (F-ratio) for a model.
- Center Points: A set of experiments usually at the middle levels of the input variable ranges which are often included as part of a designed experiment plan. In general, center points are typically included in a designed experiment for two reasons: 1. The experimental design plan specifically calls for inclusion of the center point run; or 2. Center points are added in order to test for model lack-of-fit (LOF) and provide an estimate of the reproducibility of the data under the same set of conditions.
- Cook Distance: Measures each observation's influence on the model fit by looking at the effect of the ith observation has on all n fitted values.
- Design of Experiments (DOE): A systematic approach to data collection in a research application such that the information

obtained from the data is maximized by determining the (cause-and-effect) relationships between factors (controllable inputs) affecting a process and one or more outputs measured from that process.

- Hat Matrix: diagonal values of the matrix $X(X'X)^{-1}X'$ where X is the input matrix of the original data.
- Input variable: Typically a controllable variable within the process to be modeled whose influence may or may not have an impact on the process output variables. In other sources, input variables may be referred to as predictors, factors, or X's.
- LOF: Lack Of Fit: measure that indicates that the models does not fit the data properly.
- Multicollinearity: Correlation structure among the inputs as measured by Pearson's correlation coefficient. Multicollinearity among the inputs leads to biased model parameter estimates.
- Output variable: Measure of process performance from changing input conditions. In other sources, output variables may be referred as responses, measures of performance, process quality characteristics, or Y's.
- p-value: the probability of incorrectly claiming a real effect.
- p-value in LOF test: the probability of concluding that significant LOF is present in the model when in fact it really is not. Typically p-values less than 0.05 are considered statistically significant.
- R^2: Proportion of total variability in the response that is explained by the model.
- Residual: differences between actual output and predicted output
- SSE: Sum of Squares Error: The sum of the square of the differences between actual output and predicted output.
- T test or Prob>|t|: the probability of incorrectly claiming a real effect. If the "Prob>>|t|:" values are smaller than 0.05, the factor is considered to be statistically significant.
- Undesigned Data: Data collected NOT in a systematic fashion through the use of internal DOW methodologies.
- VIF: Variance Inflation Factor; a measure of the collinearity between input variables.

6. APPENDIX 2: DEFINITION OF A LINEAR MODEL

A very important distinction that must be recognized is the difference between linear and non-linear models. This is one of the most widely misused and misunderstood terms. The term *linear model* refers to a model that is linear in *the parameters, β_k,* <u>not</u> *the input variables* (the x's). Indeed models in which the output is related to the inputs in a non-linear fashion can still be treated as linear provided that the parameters enter the model in a linear fashion (Montgomery and Peck.,1992; Seber and Wild, 1989). For example,

$$y = \beta_0 + \beta_1 e^{x_1}$$ is linear in the parameters, while

$$y = \beta_0 + e^{\beta_1 x_1}$$ is non-linear in the parameters (non-linear in β_1).

Another way to distinguish between linear and non-linear models is to differentiate the output with respect to the parameters. If the resulting derivatives are not a function of any of the parameters, the model is linear. Otherwise the model is non-linear.

References

Banzhaf, W., Nordin, P., Keller, R., and Francone, F. (1998). *Genetic Programming: An Introduction*, San Francisco, CA: Morgan Kaufmann.

Box, G., Hunter, W., and Hunter, J. (1978). *Statistics for Experiments: An Introduction to Design, Data Analysis, and Model Building.* New York, NY: Wiley.

Box, G. and Draper, N. (1987). *Empirical Model Building and Response Surfaces*. New York, NY: Wiley.

Castillo, F., Marshall, K, Greens, J. and Kordon, A. (2002). Symbolic Regression in Design of Experiments: A Case Study with Linearizing Transformations, In *Proceedings of the Genetic and Evolutionary Computing Conference (GECCO'2002)*, W. Langdon, *et al* (Eds), pp. 1043-1048. New York, NY: Morgan Kaufmann.

Castillo, F., Marshall, K, Greens, J. and Kordon, A. (2003). A Methodology for Combining Symbolic Regression and Design of Experiments to Improve Empirical Model Building In *Proceedings of the Genetic and Evolutionary Computing Conference (GECCO'2003)*, E. Cantu-Paz, *et al* (Eds), pp. 1975-1985. Chicago, IL:Springer.

Castillo, F., Sweeney, J., and Zirk, W. (2004). Using Evolutionary Algorithms to Suggest Variable Transformations in Linear Model Lack-of-Fit Situations, *accepted to CEC 2004.*

Cawse, J. (2003). *Experimental Design for Combinatorial and High Throughput Materials Development.* New York, NY: Wiley.

Cook, R. (1977). Detection of Influential Observations in Linear Regression, *Technometrics*, 19: 15-18.

Draper, N. R. and Smith, H. (1981). *Applied Regression Analysis (Second Edition)*. New York, NY: Wiley.

Harry, M. and Schroeder, R. (2000). *Six Sigma: The Breakthrough Management Strategy Revolutionizing the World's Top Corporations*. New York, NY: Doubleday.

Hiden, H. G., Willis, M. J., and Montague, G.A (1999). Non-linear Principal Component Analysis Using Genetic Programming, Computers and Chemical Engineering 23, pp 413-425.

Kaboudan M.(1999). Statistical Evaluation of Genetic Programming, *In Proceedings of the 5th International Conference on Computing in Economics and Finance (CEF'99)*, pp.24-26. Boston, MA.

Kordon, A., Smits, G., Kalos, A., and Jordaan, E. (2003). Robust Soft Sensor Development Using Genetic Programming, In *Nature-Inspired Methods in Chemometrics*, R. Leardi (Ed.), pp70-108. Amsterdam: Elsevier

Kotanchek, M, Smits, G. and Kordon, A. (2003). Industrial Strength Genetic Programming, In *Genetic Programming Theory and Practice, pp 239-258,* R. Riolo and B. Worzel (Eds). Boston, MA:Kluwer.

Koza, J. (1992). *Genetic Programming: On the Programming of Computers by Means of Natural Selection*. Cambridge, MA: MIT Press.

Montgomery, D and Peck, E. (1992). *Introduction to Linear Regression Analysis*. New York, NY: Wiley.

Montgomery, D. (1999) *Design and Analysis of Experiments*. New York, NY: Wiley.

Myers, R. H., and Montgomery, D. (1995). *Response Surface Methodology: Process and Product Optimization Using Designed Experiments*. New York, NY: Wiley.

Spoonger, S. (2000). Using Factorial Experiments to Evaluate the Effects of Genetic Programming parameters. In *Proceedings of EuroGP'2000*, pp. 2782-2788. Edinburgh, UK

Seber, G.A., and Wild, C. J. (1989). *Nonlinear Regression*, pp. 5-7. John Wiley and Sons, New York.

Smits, G. and Kotanchek, M. (2004). Pareto-Front Exploitation in Symbolic Regression, *Genetic Programming Theory and Practice, pp 283-300,* R. Riolo and B. Worzel (Eds). Boston, MA:Kluwer.

Westbury, C., Buchanan, P., Sanderson, M., Rhemtulla, M., and Phillips, L. (2003). Using Genetic Programming to Discover Nonlinear Variable Interactions, *Behavior Research Methods, Instruments, &Computers* 35(2): 2020-216.

Chapter 4

POPULATION SIZING FOR GENETIC PROGRAMMING BASED ON DECISION-MAKING

Kumara Sastry[1], Una-May O'Reilly[2] and David E. Goldberg[1]

[1]*Illinois Genetic Algorithms Laboratory, University of Illinois at Urbana-Champaign;*
[2]*Computer Science and Artificial Intelligence Lab, Massachusetts Institute of Technology*

Abstract   This chapter derives a population sizing relationship for genetic programming (GP). Following the population-sizing derivation for genetic algorithms in (Goldberg et al., 1992), it considers building block decision-making as a key facet. The analysis yields a GP-unique relationship because it has to account for bloat and for the fact that GP solutions often use subsolutions multiple times. The population-sizing relationship depends upon tree size, solution complexity, problem difficulty and building block expression probability. The relationship is used to analyze and empirically investigate population sizing for three model GP problems named ORDER, ON-OFF and LOUD. These problems exhibit bloat to differing extents and differ in whether their solutions require the use of a building block multiple times.

Keywords: genetic programming, population sizing, facetwise modeling, scalability

1.   Introduction

The growth in application of genetic programming (GP) to problems of practical and scientific importance is remarkable (Keijzer et al., 2004, Riolo and Worzel, 2003, Cantú-Paz et al., 2003). Yet, despite this increasing interest and empirical success, GP researchers and practitioners are often frustrated— sometimes stymied—by the lack of theory available to guide them in selecting key algorithm parameters or to help them explain empirical findings in a systematic manner. For example, GP population sizes run from ten to a million members or more, but at present there is no practical guide to knowing when to choose which size.

To continue addressing this issue, this chapter builds on a previous paper (Sastry et al., 2003) wherein we considered the building block supply problem for GP. In this earlier step, we asked what population size is required to ensure the presence of all raw building blocks for a given tree size (or size distribution) in the initial population. The building-block supply based population size is conservative because it does not guarantee the growth in the market share of good substructures. That is, while ensuring the building-block supply is important for a selecto-recombinative algorithm's success, ensuring a growth in the market share of good building blocks by correctly deciding between competing building blocks is also critical (Goldberg, 2002). Furthermore, the population sizing for GA success is usually bounded by the population size required for making good decisions between competing building blocks. Our results herein show this to be the case, at least for the ORDER problem.

This chapter derives a population-sizing model to ensure good decision-making between competing building blocks. Our analytical approach is similar to that used by (Goldberg et al., 1992) for developing a population-sizing model based on decision-making for genetic algorithms (GAs). In our population-sizing model, we incorporate factors that are common to both GP and GAs, as well as those that are unique to GP. We verify the population-sizing model on three different test problem that span the dimension of building block *expression*—thus, modeling the phenomena of bloat at various degrees. Using ORDER, with UNITATION as its fitness function, provides a model problem where, per tree, a building block can be expressed only once despite being present multiple times. At the opposite extreme, the LOUD problem models a building block being expressed each time it is present in the tree. To cover the range between the corners, the ON-OFF problem provides tunability of building block expression. A parameter controls the frequency with which a "function" can suppress the expression of the subtrees below it, thus affecting how frequently a tree expresses a building block. These experiments not only validate the population-sizing relationship, but also empirically illustrate the relationship between population size and problem difficulty, solution complexity, bloat and tree structure.

We proceed as follows: The next section gives a brief overview of past work in developing facetwise population-sizing models in both GAs and GP. In Section 3, we concisely review the derivation by (Goldberg et al., 1992) of a population sizing equation for GAs. Section 4 provides GP-equivalent definitions of building blocks, competitions (a.k.a partitions), trials, cardinality and building-block size. In Section 5 we follow the logical steps of (Goldberg et al., 1992) while factoring in GP perspectives to derive a general GP population sizing equation. In Section 6, we derive and empirically verify the population sizes for model problems that span the range of a BB being present and expressed. Finally, section 7 summarizes and provides key conclusions of the study.

2. Background

One of the key achievements of GA theory is the identification of the building-block decision-making to be a statistical one (Holland, 1973). Holland illustrated this using a 2^k-armed bandit model. Based on Holland's work, De Jong proposed equations for the 2-armed bandit problem without using Holland's assumption of foresight (De Jong, 1975). De Jong recognized the importance of noise in the decision-making process and also proposed a population-sizing model based on the signal and noise characteristics of a problem. De Jong's suggestion went unimplemented till the study by (Goldberg and Rudnick, 1991). Goldberg and Rudnick computed the fitness variance using Walsh analysis and proposed a population-sizing model based on the fitness variance.

A subsequent work (Goldberg et al., 1992) proposed an estimate of the population size that controlled decision-making errors. Their model was based on deciding correctly between the best and the next best BB in a partition in the presence of noise arising from adjoining BBs. This noise is termed as *collateral noise* (Goldberg and Rudnick, 1991). The model proposed by Goldberg et al., yielded practical population-sizing bounds for selectorecombinative GAs. The decision-making based population-sizing model (Goldberg et al., 1992) was refined by (Harik et al., 1999). Harik et al., proposed a tighter bound on the population size required for selectorecombinative GAs. They incorporated both the initial BB supply model and the decision-making model in the population-sizing relation. They also eliminated the requirement that only a successful decision-making in the first generation results in the convergence to the optimum. Specifically, Harik et al., modeled the decision-making in subsequent generations using the well known gambler's ruin model (Feller, 1970). The gambler's ruin population-sizing model was subsequently extended for noisy environments (Miller, 1997), and for parallel GAs (Cantú-Paz, 2000).

While, population-sizing in genetic algorithms has been successfully studied with the help of facetwise and dimensional models, similar efforts in genetic programming are still in the early stages. Recently, we developed a population sizing model to ensure the presence of all raw building blocks in the initial population size. We first derived the exact population size to ensure adequate supply for a model problem named ORDER. ORDER has an expression mechanism that models how a primitive in GP is expressed depending on its spatial context. We empirically validated our supply-driven population size result for ORDER under two different fitness functions: UNITATION where each primitive is a building block with uniform fitness contribution, and DECEPTION where each of m subgroups, each subgroup consisting of k primitives, has its fitness computed using a deceptive trap function.

After dealing specifically with ORDER in which, per tree, a building block can be expressed at most once, we considered the general case of ensuring an adequate building block supply where every building block in a tree is always expressed. This is analogous to the instance of a GP problem that exhibits no bloat. In this case, the supply equation does not have to account for subtrees that are present yet do not contribute to fitness. This supply-based population size equation is:

$$n = \frac{1}{\lambda}2^k \kappa \left(\log \kappa - \log \epsilon\right). \tag{4.1}$$

where κ enumerates the partition or building block competition, k is the building-block size, ϵ is supply error and λ is average tree size.

In the context of supply, to finally address the reality of bloat, we noted that the combined probability of a building block being present in the population and its probability of being expressed must be computed and amalgamated into the supply derivation. This would imply that Equation 4.1, though conservative under the assumed condition that every raw building block must be present in the initial population, is an underestimate in terms of accounting for bloat. Overall, the building block supply analysis yielded insight into how two salient properties of GP: building block expression and tree structure influence building block supply and thus influence population size. Building block expression manifests itself in "real life" as the phenomena of bloat in GP. Average tree size in GP typically increases as a result of the interaction of selection, crossover and program degeneracy.

As a next step, this study derives a decision-making based population-sizing model. We employ the methodology of (Goldberg et al., 1992) used for deriving a population sizing relationship for GA. In this method, the population size is chosen so that the population contains enough competing building blocks that decisions between two building blocks can be made with a pre-specified confidence. Compared to the GA derivation, there are two significant differences. First, the collateral noise in fitness, arises from a variable quantity of expressed BBs. Second, the number of trials of a BB, rather than one per individual in the GA case, depends on tree structure and whether a BB that is present in a tree is expressed. In the GP case, the variable, κ related to cardinality (e.g., the binary alphabet of a simple GA) and building block defining length, is considerably larger because GP problems typically use larger primitive sets. It is incorporated into the relationship by considering BB expression and presence.

We start with a brief outline of the population-sizing model of (Goldberg et al., 1992) in the following section.

3.   GA Population Sizing from the Perspective of Competing Building Blocks

The derivational foundation for our GP population sizing equation is the 1992 result for the selecto-recombinative GA by (Goldberg et al., 1992) entitled "Genetic Algorithms, Noise and the Sizing of Populations." That paper

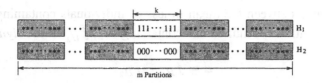

Figure 4-1. Two competing building blocks of size k, one is the best BB, H_1, and the other is the second best BB, H_2.

considers how the GA can derive accurate estimates of BB fitness in the presence of detrimental noise. It recognizes that, while selection is the principal decision maker, it distinguishes among individuals based on fitness and not by considering BBs. Therefore, there is a possibility that an inferior BB gets selected over a better BB in a competition due to noisy observed contributions from adjoining BBs that are also engaged in competitions.

To derive a relation for the probability of deciding correctly between competing BBs, the authors considered two individuals, one with the best BB and the other with the second best BB in the same competition. (Goldberg et al., 1992).

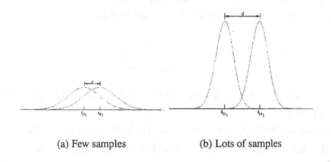

(a) Few samples   (b) Lots of samples

Figure 4-2. Fitness distribution of individuals in the population containing the two competing building blocks, the best BB H_1, and the second best BB H_2. When two mean fitness distributions overlap, low sampling increases the likelihood of estimation error. When sampling around each mean fitness is increased, fitness distributions are less likely to be inaccurately estimated.

Let i_1 and i_2 be these two individuals with m non-overlapping BBs of size k as shown in figure 4-1. Individual i_1 has the best BB, H_1 ($111 \cdots 111$ in figure 4-1) and individual i_2 has the second best BB, H_2 ($000 \cdots 000$ in figure 4-1). The fitness values of i_1 and i_2 are f_{H_1} and f_{H_2} respectively. To derive the probability of correct decision-making, we have to first recognize that the fitness distribution of the individuals containing H_1 and H_2 is Gaussian since we have assumed an additive fitness function and the central limit theorem applies. Two possible fitness distributions of individuals containing BBs H_1 and H_2 are illustrated in figure 4-2.

The distance between the mean fitness of individuals containing H_1, $\overline{f}_{H_1}$, and the mean fitness of individuals containing H_2, $\overline{f}_{H_2}$, is the *signal*, d. That is,

$$d = \overline{f}_{H_1} - \overline{f}_{H_2}. \tag{4.2}$$

Recognize that the probability of correctly deciding between H_1 and H_2 is equivalent to the probability that $f_{H_1} - f_{H_2} > 0$. Also, since f_{H_1} and f_{H_2} are normally distributed, $f_{H_1} - f_{H_2}$ is also normally distributed with mean d and variance $\sigma_{H_1}^2 + \sigma_{H_2}^2$, where $\sigma_{H_1}^2$ and $\sigma_{H_2}^2$ are the fitness variances of individuals containing H_1 and H_2 respectively. That is,

$$f_{H_1} - f_{H_2} \sim \mathcal{N}(d, \sigma_{H_1}^2 + \sigma_{H_2}^2). \tag{4.3}$$

The probability of correct decision-making, p_{dm}, is then given by the cumulative density function of a unit normal variate which is the signal-to-noise ratio :

$$p_{dm} = \Phi\left(\frac{d}{\sqrt{\sigma_{H_1}^2 + \sigma_{H_2}^2}}\right). \tag{4.4}$$

Alternatively, the probability of making an error on a single trial of each BB can estimated by finding the probability α such that

$$z^2(\alpha) = \frac{d^2}{\sigma_{H_1}^2 + \sigma_{H_2}^2} \tag{4.5}$$

where $z(\alpha)$ is the ordinate of a unit, one-sided normal deviate. Notationally $z(\alpha)$ is shortened to z.

Now, consider the BB variance, $\sigma_{H_1}^2$ (and $\sigma_{H_2}^2$): since it is assumed the fitness function is the sum of m independent subfunctions each of size k, $\sigma_{H_1}^2$ (and similarly $\sigma_{H_2}^2$) is the sum of the variance of the adjoining $m - 1$ subfunctions. Also, since it is assumed that the m partitions are uniformly scaled, the variance of each subfunction is equal to the average BB variance, σ_{bb}^2. Therefore,

$$\text{GA BB Variance:} \quad \sigma_{H_1}^2 = \sigma_{H_2}^2 = (m - 1)\sigma_{bb}^2. \tag{4.6}$$

A population-sizing equation was derived from this error probability by recognizing that as the number of trials, τ, increases, the variance of the fitness is decreased by a factor equal to the trial quantity:

$$z^2(\alpha) = \frac{d^2}{\frac{2(m-1)\sigma_{bb}}{\tau}} \tag{4.7}$$

To derive the quantity of trials, τ, assume a uniformly random population (of size n). Let χ represent the cardinality of the alphabet (2 for the GA) and k

the building-block size. For any individual, the probability of H_1 is $1/\kappa$ where $\kappa = \chi^k$. There is exactly one instance per individual of the competition, $\phi = 1$. Thus,

$$\tau = n \cdot p_{BB} \cdot \phi = n \cdot 1/\kappa \cdot 1 = n/\kappa \qquad (4.8)$$

By rearrangement and calling z^2 the coefficient c (still a function of α) a fairly general population-sizing relation was obtained:

$$n = 2c\chi^k(m-1)\frac{\sigma_{bb}^2}{d^2} \qquad (4.9)$$

To summarize, the decision-making based population sizing model in GAs consists of the following factors:

- **Competition complexity**, quantified by the total number of competing building blocks, χ^k.

- **Subcomponent complexity**, quantified by the number of building blocks, m.

- **Ease of decision-making**, quantified by the signal-to-noise ratio, d^2/σ_{bb}^2.

- **Probabilistic safety factor**, quantified by the coefficient c.

4.   GP Definitions for a Population Sizing Derivation

Most GP implementations reported in the literature use parse trees to represent candidate programs in the population (Langdon and Poli, 2002). We have assumed this representation in our analysis. To simplify the analysis further, we consider the following:

1 A primitive set of the GP tree is $\mathcal{F} \cup \mathcal{T}$ where $\mathcal{F}$ denotes the set of functions (interior nodes to a GP parse tree) and $\mathcal{T}$ denotes the set of terminals (leaf nodes in a GP parse tree).

2 The cardinality of $\mathcal{F} = \chi_f$ and the cardinality of $\mathcal{T} = \chi_t$.

3 The arity of all functions in the primitive set is two: All functions are binary and thus the GP parse trees generated from the primitive set are binary.

We believe that our analysis could be extended to primitive sets containing functions with arity greater than two (non-binary trees). We also note that our assumption closely matches a common GP benchmark, symbolic regression, which usually has arithmetic functions of arity two.

As in our BB supply work (Sastry et al., 2003), our analysis adopts a definition of a GP schema (or similarity template) called a "tree fragment". A tree fragment is a tree with at least one leaf that is a "don't care" symbol. This "don't care" symbol can be matched by any subtree (including degenerate leaf-only trees). As before, we are most interested in only the small set set of tree fragments that are defined by three or fewer nodes. See Figure 4-3 for this set.

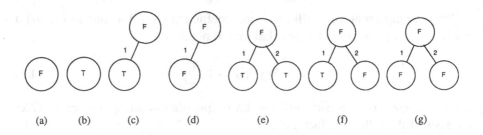

Figure 4-3. The smallest tree fragments in GP. Fragments (c) and (d) have mirrors where the child is 2nd parameter of the function. Likewise, fragment (f) has mirror where 1st and 2nd parameters of the function are reversed. Recall that a tree fragment is a similarity template: based on the similarity it defines, it also defines a competition. A tree fragment, in other words, is a competition. (At other times we have also used the term *partition* interchangeably with tree fragment or competition)

The defining length of a tree fragment is the sum of its quantities of function symbols, $\mathcal{F}$, and terminal symbols, $\mathcal{T}$:

$$k = N_f + N_t \tag{4.10}$$

Because a tree fragment is a similarity template, it also represents a competition. Since this chapter is concerned with decision-making, we will therefore use "competition" instead of a "tree fragment." The size of a competition (i.e., how many BBs compete) is

$$\kappa = \chi_f^{N_f} * \chi_t^{N_t} \tag{4.11}$$

As mentioned in (Sastry et al., 2003), because a tree fragment is defined without any positional anchoring, it can appear multiple times in a single tree. We denote the number of instances of a tree fragment that are present in a tree of size λ (i.e., the quantity of a tree fragment in a tree) as ϕ. This is equivalent to the instances of a competition as ϕ is used in the GA case (see Equation 4.8). For full binary trees:

$$\phi \approx 2^{-k}\lambda \tag{4.12}$$

Later, we will explain how ϕ describes the *potential* quantity, per tree, of a BB.

5.   GP Population Sizing Model

We now proceed to derive a GP population sizing relationship based on building block decision-making. Preliminarily, unless noted, we make the same assumptions as the GA derivation of Section 3.

The first way the GP population size derivation diverges from the GA case is how BB fitness variance (i.e., $\sigma_{H_1}^2$ and $\sigma_{H_2}^2$) is estimated (for reference, see Equation 4.6). Recall that for the GA the source of a BB's fitness variance was collateral noise from the $(m-1)$ competitions of its adjoining BBs. In GP, the source of collateral noise is the average number of adjoining BBs present and expressed in each tree, denoted as $\bar{q}$. Thus:

$$\text{GP BB Variance:} \qquad \sigma_{H_1}^2 = \sigma_{H_2}^2 = [\bar{q}_{BB}^{expr}(m,\lambda) - 1]\sigma_{bb}^2. \qquad (4.13)$$

Thus, the probability of making an error on a single trial of the BB can be estimated by finding the probability α such that

$$z^2(\alpha) = \frac{d^2}{2[\bar{q}_{BB}^{expr} - 1]\sigma_{bb}^2} \qquad (4.14)$$

The second way the GP population size derivation diverges from the GA case is in how the number of trials of a BB is estimated (for reference, see Equation 4.8). As with the GA, for GP we assume a uniformly distributed population of size n. In GP the probability of a trial of a particular BB must account for it being both present, $1/\kappa$, *and* expressed in an individual (or tree), which we denote as p_{BB}^{expr}. So, in GP:

$$\tau = \frac{1}{\kappa} \cdot p_{BB}^{expr} \cdot \phi \cdot n \qquad (4.15)$$

Thus, the population size relationship for GP is:

$$n = 2c\frac{\sigma_{bb}^2}{d^2}\kappa\,[\bar{q}_{BB}^{expr} - 1]\,\frac{1}{p_{BB}^{expr}\,\phi} \qquad (4.16)$$

where $c = z^2(\alpha)$ is the square of the ordinate of a one-sided standard Gaussian deviate at a specified error probability α. For low error values, c can be obtained by the usual approximation for the tail of a Gaussian distribution: $\alpha \approx \exp(-c/2)/(\sqrt{2c})$.

Obviously, it is not always possible to factor the real-world problems in the terms of this population sizing model. A practical approach would first approximate $\phi = 2^{-k}(\lambda)$ trials per tree (the full binary tree assumption). Then, estimate the size of the shortest program that will solve the problem, (one might regard this as the Kolomogorov complexity of the problem, λ_k), and choose a multiple of this for λ in the model. In this case, $\bar{q} = c_k m_k$. To ensure an initial supply of building blocks that is sufficient to solve the problem, the initial population should be initialized with trees of size λ. Therefore, the population-sizing in this case can be written as

$$n = c\frac{\sigma_{bb}^2}{d^2}\kappa\frac{(c_k m_k - 1)\,2^{k+1}}{p_{BB}^{expr}\,\lambda} \qquad (4.17)$$

Similar to the GA population sizing model, the decision-making based population sizing model in GP consists of the following factors:

- **Competition complexity**, quantified by the total number of competing building blocks, κ.

- **Ease of decision-making**, quantified by the signal-to-noise ratio, d^2/σ_{bb}^2.

- **Probabilistic safety factor**, quantified by the coefficient c.

- **Subcomponent complexity**, which unlike GA population-sizing, depends not only on the minimum number of building blocks required to solve the problem m_k, but also on tree size λ, the size of the problem primitive set and how bloat factors into trees (quantified by p_{BB}^{expr}).

6.   Sizing Model Problems

This section derives the components of the population-sizing model (Equation 4.16) for three test problems, ORDER, LOUD, and ON-OFF. We develop the population-sizing equation for each problem and verify it with empirical results. In all experiments we assume that $\alpha = 1/m$ and thus derive c. Table 4-1 shows some of these values. For all empirical experiments the the initial population is randomly generated with either full trees or by the ramped half-and-half method. The trees were allowed to grow up to a maximum size of 1024 nodes. We used a tournament selection with tournament size of 4 in obtaining the empirical results. We used subtree crossover with a crossover probability of 1.0 and retained 5% of the best individuals from the previous population. A GP run was terminated when either the best individual was obtained or when a predetermined number of generations were exceeded. The average number of BBs correctly converged in the best individuals were computed over 50 independent runs. The minimum population size required such that $m - 1$ BBs converge to the correct value is determined by a bisection method (Sastry, 2001). The results of population size and convergence time was averaged over 30 such bisection runs, while the results for the number of function evaluations was averaged over 1500 independent runs. We start with population sizing for ORDER, where a building block can be expressed at most once in a tree.

Table 4-1.   Values of $c = z^2(\alpha)$ used in population sizing equation.

m	8	16	32	64	128
c	.97	1.76	2.71	3.77	4.89

ORDER: At most one expression per BB

ORDER is a simple, yet intuitive expression mechanism which makes it amenable to analysis and modeling (Goldberg and O'Reilly, 1998, O'Reilly and Goldberg, 1998). For complete details refer elsewhere (Sastry et al., 2003).

The output for optimal solution of a $2m$-primitive ORDER problem is $\{X_1, X_2, \cdots, X_m\}$, and its fitness value is m. The building blocks in ORDER are the primitives, X_i, that are part of the subfunctions that reduce error (alternatively improve fitness). The shortest perfect program is $\lambda_k = 2m - 1$.

For the ORDER problem, we can easily see that $\sigma_{bb}^2 = 0.25$, $d = 1$, and $\phi = 1$. From (Sastry et al., 2003), we know that

$$p_{BB}^{expr} \approx \exp\left[-k \cdot e^{-\frac{\lambda}{2m}}\right]. \tag{4.18}$$

Additionally, for ORDER, $\bar{q}_{BB}^{expr}$ is given by

$$\bar{q}_{BB}^{expr} = 1 + \sum_{i=0}^{m-1} \binom{m-1}{i} i \sum_{j=0}^{i} \binom{i}{j} (-1)^j \left(\frac{i-j+1}{m}\right)^{n_l-1}, \tag{4.19}$$

where, n_l is the average number of leaf nodes per tree in the population. The derivation of the above equation was involved and detailed. It is provided elsewhere (Sastry et al., 2004).

Substituting the above relations (Equations 4.18 and 4.19) in the population-sizing model (Equation 4.16) we obtain the following population-sizing equation for ORDER:

$$n = 2^{k-1} z^2(\alpha) \left(\frac{\sigma_{bb}^2}{d^2}\right) [\bar{q}_{BB}^{expr} - 1] \exp\left[k \cdot e^{-\frac{\lambda}{2m}}\right]. \tag{4.20}$$

The above population-sizing equation is verified with empirical results in Figure 6.0. The initial population was randomly generated with either full trees or by the ramped half-and-half method with trees of heights, $h \in [h_k - 1, h_k + 1]$, where, h_k is the minimum tree height with an average of $2m$ leaf nodes. We observed that the population size scales quadratically with Kolmogorov complexity, $n = \mathcal{O}\left(2^k \lambda_k^2\right)$.

LOUD: Every BB in a tree is expressed

In ORDER, a building block could be expressed at most once in a tree. However, in many GP problems a building block can be expressed multiple times in an individual. Indeed, an extreme case is when every building block occurrence is expressed. One such problem is a modified version of a test problem proposed elsewhere (Soule and Heckendorn, 2002, Soule, 2003), which we call LOUD.

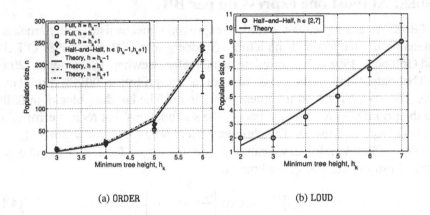

Figure 4-4.   Empirical validation of the population-sizing model (Equation 4.20) for ORDER and LOUD problems. Tree height h_k equals 2^m and $\lambda_k = 2m - 1$.

In LOUD, the primitive set consists of an "add" function of arity two, and three constant terminals: 0, 1 and 4. The objective is to find an optimal number of fours and ones. That is, for an individual with i 4s and j 1s, the fitness function is given by $F(\mathbf{x}) = |i - m_4| + |j - m_1|$. Therefore, even though a zero is expressed it does not contribute to fitness. Furthermore, a 4 or 1 is expressed each time it appears in an individual and each occurrence contributes to the fitness value of the individual. Moreover, the problem size, $m = m_4 + m_1$ and $\lambda_k = 2m - 1$.

For the LOUD problem the building blocks are "4" and "1". It is easy to see that for LOUD, $\sigma_{BB}^2 = 0.25$, $d = 1$, $\phi = \lambda/2$, and $p_{BB}^{expr} = 1/3$. Furthermore, the average number of building blocks expressed is given by $\bar{q}_{BB}^{expr} = 2n_l/3 \approx \lambda/3$. Substituting these values in the population-sizing model (Equation 4.16) we obtain

$$n = 2 \cdot 3^k z^2(\alpha) \left(\frac{\sigma_{bb}^2}{d^2} \right) \left[\frac{1}{3} \lambda - 1 \right] \cdot \left(\frac{2}{\lambda} \right). \qquad (4.21)$$

The above population-sizing equation is verified with empirical results in Figure 6.0. The initial population was randomly generated by the ramped half-and-half method with trees of heights $h \in [2, 7]$ yielding an average tree size of 4.1 (compared to the analytically derived value of 4.5). We observed that the population size scales as $n = \mathcal{O}\left(2^k \lambda_k^{0.5}\right)$.

ON-OFF: Tunable building block expression

In the previous sections we considered two extreme cases, one where a building block could be expressed at most once in an individual, and the other where every building block occurrence is expressed. However, usually in GP prob-

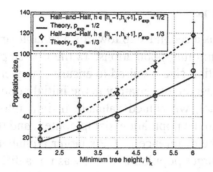

Figure 4-5. Empirical validation of the population-sizing model (Equation 4.22) required to obtain the global solution for ON-OFF problem. Note that $\lambda_k = 2m - 1$.

lems, some of the building blocks are expressed and others are not. Therefore, the third test function, which we call ON-OFF, is one in which the building-block expression probability is tunable (Sastry et al., 2004) and can approximate some bloat scenarios of standard GP problem (Luke, 2000a).

In ON-OFF, the primitive set consists of two functions EXP and $\overline{\text{EXP}}$ of arity two and terminal X_1, and X_2. The function EXP expresses its child nodes, while $\overline{\text{EXP}}$ suppresses its child nodes. Therefore a leaf node is expressed only when all its parental nodes have the primitive EXP. The probability of expressing a building block can be tuned by controlling the frequency of selecting EXP for an internal node in the initial tree. Similar to LOUD, the objective for ON-OFF is to find an optimal number of X_1 and X_2. The problem size, $m = m_{X_1} + m_{X_2}$ and $\lambda_k = 2m - 1$.

For the ON-OFF problem the building blocks are X_1 and X_2, $\sigma_{BB}^2 = 0.25$, $d = 1$, $\phi = \lambda/2$, and $p_{BB}^{expr} = p_{EXP}^h$. Here, p_{EXP} is the probability of a node being the primitive EXP. The average number of building blocks expressed is given by $\bar{q}_{BB}^{expr} = n_l \cdot p_{EXP}^h \approx \frac{s}{2} \cdot p_{EXP}^h$. Substituting these values in the population-sizing model (Equation 4.16) we obtain

$$n = 2^{k+1} z^2(\alpha) \left(\frac{\sigma_{bb}^2}{d^2} \right) \left[\frac{\lambda}{2} p_{EXP}^h - 1 \right] \cdot \left(\frac{2}{\lambda p_{EXP}^h} \right). \qquad (4.22)$$

The above population-sizing equation is verified with empirical results in Figure 4-5. The initial population was randomly generated by the ramped half-and-half method with trees of heights $h \in [h_k - 1, h_k + 1]$, where h_k is the minimum tree height with an average of m leaf nodes. We observed that the population size scales as $n = \mathcal{O}\left(2^k \lambda_k^{0.5} / p_{exp} \right)$.

7.   Conclusions

This contribution is a second step towards a reliable and accurate model for sizing genetic programming populations. In the first step the model estimated the minimum population size required to ensure that every building block was present with a given degree of certainty in the initial population. In the process of deriving this model, we gained valuable insight into (a) what makes GP different from a GA in the population-sizing context and (b) the implications of these differences. The difference of GP's larger alphabet, while influential in implying GP needs larger population sizes, was not a difficult factor to handle, while bloat and the variable length individuals in GP are more complicated.

Moving to the second step, by considering a decision-making model, we extended the GA decision-making model along these dimensions: First, our model retains a term describing collateral noise from competing BBs ($\bar{q}[m, \lambda]$) but it recognizes that the quantity of these competitors depends on tree size and the likelihood that the BB is present and expresses itself (rather than behaving as an intron). Second, our model, like its GA counterpart, assumes that trials decrease BB fitness variance; however, what was simple in a GA – there is one trial per population member – for the GP case is more involved. That is, the probability that a BB is present in a population member depends both on the likelihood that it is present in lieu of another BB *and* expresses itself, *plus* the number of potential trials any BB has in each population member.

The model shows that, to ensure correct decision-making within an error tolerance, population size must go up as the probability of error decreases, noise increases, alphabet cardinality increases, the signal-to-noise ratio decreases *and* tree size decreases and bloat frequency increases. This matches intuition. There is an interesting critical trade-off with tree size with respect to determining population size: pressure for larger trees comes from the need to express all correct BBs in the solution, while pressure for smaller trees comes from the need to reduce collateral noise from competing BBs.

The fact that the model is based on statistical decision-making means that crossover does not have to be incorporated. In GAs crossover solely acts as a mixer or combiner of BBs. Interestingly, in GP, crossover also interacts with selection with the potential result that programs' size grows and structure changes. When this happens, the frequency of bloat can also change (see (Luke, 2000a, Luke, 2000b) for examples of this with multiplexer and symbolic regression). These changes in size, structure and bloat frequency imply a much more complex model would be required if one were to attempt to account for decision-making throughout a run. They also suggest that when using the model as a rule of thumb to size an initial population, it may prove more accurate if the practitioner overestimates bloat in anticipation of subsequent tree growth causing more than the bloat seen in the initial population, given its average tree size.

It appears difficult to use this model with real problems where, among the GP-particular factors, the most compact solution and BB size is not known and the extent of bloat cannot be estimated. In the case of the GA model, the estimation of model factors has been addressed by (Reed et al., 2000). They estimated variance with the standard deviation of the fitness of a large random population. In the GP case, this sampling population should be controlled for average tree size. If a practitioner were willing to work with crude estimates of bloat, BB size and most compact solution size, a multiple of the size of the most compact solution could be substituted, and bloat could be used with that size to estimate the probability that a BB is expressed and present and the average number of BBs of the same size present and expressed, on average, in each tree. In the future, we intend to experiment with the model and well known toy GP problems (e.g., multiplexer, symbolic regression) where bloat frequency and most compact problem size are obtainable, and simple choices for BB size exist to verify if the population size scales with problem size within the order of complexity the model predicts.

Population sizing has been important to GAs and is now important to GP, because it is the principle factor in controlling ultimate solution quality. Once the quality-size relation is understood, populations can be sized to obtain a desired quality and only two things can happen in empirical trials. The quality goal can be equaled or exceeded in which case all is well with the design of the algorithm, or (as is more likely) the quality target can be missed, in which case there is some other obstacle to be overcome in the algorithm design. Moreover, once population size is understood, it can be combined with an understanding of run duration, thereby yielding first estimates of GP run complexity, a key milestone in making our understanding of these processes more rigorous.

Acknowledgments

We gratefully acknowledge the organizers and reviewers of the 2004 GP Theory and Practice Workshop.

This work was sponsored by the Air Force Office of Scientific Research, Air Force Material Command, USAF, under grant F49620-03-1-0129, the National Science Foundation under ITR grant DMR-99-76550 (at MCC), and ITR grant DMR-0121695 (at CPSD), and the Dept. of Energy under grant DEFG02-91ER45439 (at FS-MRL) , and by the TRECC at UIUC by NCSA and funded by the Office of Naval Research (grant N00014-01-1-0175). The U.S. Government is authorized to reproduce and distribute reprints for government purposes notwithstanding any copyright notation thereon. The views and conclusions contained herein are those of the authors and should not be interpreted as necessarily representing the official policies or endorsements, either expressed or implied, of the Air Force Office of Scientific Research, the National Science Foundation, or the U.S. Government.

References

Cantú-Paz, E. (2000). *Efficient and accurate parallel genetic algorithms*. Kluwer Academic Pub, Boston, MA.

Cantú-Paz, Erick, Foster, James A., Deb, Kalyanmoy, Davis, Lawrence, Roy, Rajkumar, O'Reilly, Una-May, Beyer, Hans-Georg, Standish, Russell K., Kendall, Graham, Wilson, Stewart W., Harman, Mark, Wegener, Joachim, Dasgupta, Dipankar, Potter, Mitchell A., Schultz, Alan C., Dowsland, Kathryn A., Jonoska, Natasa, and Miller, Julian F., editors (2003). *Genetic and Evolutionary Computation – GECCO 2003, Part II*, volume 2724 of *Lecture Notes in Computer Science*. Springer.

De Jong, K. A. (1975). *An analysis of the behavior of a class of genetic adaptive systems*. PhD thesis, University of Michigan, Ann-Arbor, MI. (University Microfilms No. 76-9381).

Feller, W. (1970). *An Introduction to Probability Theory and its Applications*. Wiley, New York, NY.

Goldberg, D. E. (2002). *The Design of Innovation: Lessons from and for Competent Genetic Algorithms*. Kluwer Academic Publishers, Boston, Mass.

Goldberg, D. E., Deb, K., and Clark, J. H. (1992). Genetic algorithms, noise, and the sizing of populations. *Complex Systems*, 6(4):333–362.

Goldberg, D. E. and Rudnick, M. (1991). Genetic algorithms and the variance of fitness. *Complex Systems*, 5(3):265–278.

Goldberg, David E. and O'Reilly, Una-May (1998). Where does the good stuff go, and why? how contextual semantics influence program structure in simple genetic programming. In Banzhaf, Wolfgang, Poli, Riccardo, Schoenauer, Marc, and Fogarty, Terence C., editors, *Proceedings of the First European Workshop on Genetic Programming*, volume 1391 of *LNCS*, pages 16–36, Paris. Springer-Verlag.

Harik, G., Cantú-Paz, E., Goldberg, D. E., and Miller, B. L. (1999). The gambler's ruin problem, genetic algorithms, and the sizing of populations. *Evolutionary Computation*, 7(3):231–253.

Holland, J. H. (1973). Genetic algorithms and the optimal allocation of trials. *SIAM Journal on Computing*, 2(2):88–105.

Keijzer, Maarten, O'Reilly, Una-May, Lucas, Simon M., Costa, Ernesto, and Soule, Terence, editors (2004). *Genetic Programming 7th European Conference, EuroGP 2004, Proceedings*, volume 3003 of *LNCS*, Coimbra, Portugal. Springer-Verlag.

Langdon, W. B. and Poli, Riccardo (2002). *Foundations of Genetic Programming*. Springer-Verlag.

Luke, Sean (2000a). Code growth is not caused by introns. In Whitley, Darrell, editor, *Late Breaking Papers at the 2000 Genetic and Evolutionary Computation Conference*, pages 228–235, Las Vegas, Nevada, USA.

Luke, Sean (2000b). *Issues in Scaling Genetic Programming: Breeding Strategies, Tree Generation, and Code Bloat*. PhD thesis, Department of Computer Science, University of Maryland, A. V. Williams Building, University of Maryland, College Park, MD 20742 USA.

Miller, B. L. (1997). *Noise, Sampling, and Efficient Genetic Algorithms*. PhD thesis, University of Illinois at Urbana-Champaign, General Engineering Department, Urbana, IL.

O'Reilly, Una-May and Goldberg, David E. (1998). How fitness structure affects subsolution acquisition in genetic programming. In Koza, John R., Banzhaf, Wolfgang, Chellapilla, Kumar, Deb, Kalyanmoy, Dorigo, Marco, Fogel, David B., Garzon, Max H., Goldberg, David E., Iba, Hitoshi, and Riolo, Rick, editors, *Genetic Programming 1998: Proceedings of the Third Annual Conference*, pages 269–277, University of Wisconsin, Madison, Wisconsin, USA. Morgan Kaufmann.

Reed, P., Minsker, B. S., and Goldberg, D. E. (2000). Designing a competent simple genetic algorithm for search and optimization. *Water Resources Research*, 36(12):3757–3761.

Riolo, Rick L. and Worzel, Bill (2003). *Genetic Programming Theory and Practice*. Genetic Programming Series. Kluwer, Boston, MA, USA. Series Editor - John Koza.

Sastry, K. (2001). Evaluation-relaxation schemes for genetic and evolutionary algorithms. Master's thesis, University of Illinois at Urbana-Champaign, General Engineering Department, Urbana, IL.

Sastry, K., O'Reilly, U.-M., and Goldberg, D. E. (2004). Population sizing for genetic programming based on decision making. IlliGAL Report No. 2004026, University of Illinois at Urbana Champaign, Urbana.

Sastry, Kumara, O'Reilly, Una-May, Goldberg, David E., and Hill, David (2003). Building block supply in genetic programming. In Riolo, Rick L. and Worzel, Bill, editors, *Genetic Programming Theory and Practice*, chapter 9, pages 137–154. Kluwer.

Soule, Terence (2003). Operator choice and the evolution of robust solutions. In Riolo, Rick L. and Worzel, Bill, editors, *Genetic Programming Theory and Practise*, chapter 16, pages 257–270. Kluwer.

Soule, Terence and Heckendorn, Robert B. (2002). An analysis of the causes of code growth in genetic programming. *Genetic Programming and Evolvable Machines*, 3(3):283–309.

Chapter 5

CONSIDERING THE ROLES OF STRUCTURE IN PROBLEM SOLVING BY COMPUTER
Cause and Emergence in Genetic Programming

Jason M. Daida
Center for the Study of Complex Systems and Space Physics Research Laboratory, The University of Michigan

Abstract: This chapter presents a tiered view of the roles of structure in genetic programming. This view can be used to frame theory on how some problems are more difficult than others for genetic programming to solve. This chapter subsequently summarizes my group's current theoretical work at the University of Michigan and extends the implications of that work to real-world problem solving.

Key words: GP theory, tree structures, problem difficulty, GP-hard, test problems, *Lid*, *Highlander, Binomial-3*

1.   INTRODUCTION

In genetic programming (GP), the general consensus is that structure has a role in GP dynamics. Beyond that general view, various researchers have presented conflicting views as to the nature of that role.

Most maintain that structure is of secondary importance to content, which involves the semantics and syntax of programs. After all, fitness is determined by the evaluation of programs; only in special cases is fitness determined by structure (e.g., Punch, Zongker et al., 1996; Clergue, Collard et al., 2002). Consequently, it is not structure, per se, that matters but schemata—building blocks of partial programs (e.g., Poli, 2000; Poli, 2001; Langdon and Poli, 2002).

Others would suggest that structure is an emergent property—an effect and not a cause—that arises as a result of fitness. Koza has actively promoted this by introducing mechanisms that allow GP to "choose" an architecture (i.e., the size and shape) that suits the functionality of its solutions (e.g., Koza, 1994; Koza, 1995; Koza, Bennett III et al., 1999). Other researchers have also designed such mechanisms (e.g., Rosca, 1995). Some have explored structure as an emergent property of fitness that occurs *without* any additional mechanisms (i.e., Goldberg and O'Reilly, 1998; O'Reilly and Goldberg, 1998). Emergent structure has not always been considered in a positive light, in particular, excess structure—bloat—is considered by some to be an emergent, albeit inefficient response to maintaining fitness (e.g., Angeline, 1994; Langdon and Poli, 1997; Banzhaf and Langdon, 2002; Soule and Heckendorn, 2002).

Still others consider structure as a causal influence that results in effects that either would occur in spite of content or would drive the determination of content. A number have studied the rapid convergence of a GP population to a common root structure, which tends to drive the solutions that are subsequently derived by GP (e.g., Rosca, 1997; Hall and Soule, 2004). Others have proposed a structure-as-cause alternative to hypotheses concerning evolution of size and shape and have proposed that the evolution of size and shape is the result of a random walk in GP on the probability distribution of possible sizes and shapes (e.g., Langdon and Poli, 2002). Still others (i.e., (Luke, 2003) have proposed an alternative hypothesis and a model of bloat that stems from a structural consequence of crossover.

My own group has also considered structure as a causal influence (Daida, 2003; Daida and Hilss, 2003; Daida, Hilss et al., 2003; Daida, Li et al., 2003). However, we have adopted a perspective that structure is not only a causal factor, but also a primary one, even when selection is specified solely on content. However, we would claim that this perspective is *not* at odds with any of the community's views on structure.

I would further argue that although it is possible for all of these views to be equally "correct," it is not the most beneficial way to consider the roles of structure. Structures that are causal are distinct from structures that are emergent, as are structures that correspond to primary factors are distinct from structures that correspond to secondary ones. What matters is the sense and scale that is being applied to the term *structure*, which in turn helps to determine which role to examine.

This chapter subsequently describes what these studies have to offer concerning the roles of structure in GP. In particular, Section 2 presents my group's hierarchical view of structure. Each of Sections 3, 4, and 5 discusses a level in this hierarchy. Section 6 concludes.

2.   A HIERARCHICAL VIEW OF STRUCTURE

In much of the field of GP, tree structures generally falls under the category of *problem representation* (e.g., Angeline, 1997; Banzhaf, Nordin et al., 1998). In spite of this, my group has considered tree structures as a matter distinct from problem representation.

When one does an analysis in problem representation, one implicitly assumes that what counts is information from a problem's domain, as opposed to the structure that carries that information. This view makes sense when considering many algorithms in genetic and evolutionary computation. In such cases, information structure—e.g., a matrix or a vector—does not change in size or length for the duration of that algorithm's processing. What changes is content. For all practical purposes, information structure can be (correctly) factored out of an analysis.

There are fields in computer science and in mathematics, however, where a static information structure is not a given. Of interest, instead, are the consequences of information structures that are variable and dynamic. Trees are one such structure. Consequently, when one does an analysis of trees as information structure, it is common to treat trees as mathematical entities *apart* from the information such trees would carry (e.g., Knuth, 1997). This treatment effectively renders information structure as a level of abstraction that is distinct from that of problem representation.

Nevertheless, a treatment of trees as pure mathematical entities *without* content can only go so far. GP ultimately produces programs, so at some point there needs to be a consideration of tree structures *with* content. For this and other reasons, my group has adopted a tiered view of structures. As shown in Figure 5-1, we consider three hierarchically arranged tiers: *lattice*, *network*, and *content*. Each level in this tiered view implies a certain level of abstraction concerning content. The lowest level—*lattice*—presumes structure *apart* from content, and subsequent levels—*network* and *content*—presume decreasing levels of content abstraction.

Furthermore, each level in this tiered view implies a certain set of behaviors and possibilities that apply to that level and that constrain possible behaviors and outcomes in the next level up.

Of interest to theoreticians is that just as it has been possible to design test problems that address theory in genetic algorithms, my group has designed test problems that address structural theory in GP. We have specifically devised test problems that address each tier to illuminate that level's behaviors and outcomes. Of

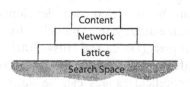

Figure 5-1. A tiered view for how GP works.

interest to practitioners is that findings associated with each tier also offer insights on how to leverage the technology for solving problems.

Sections 3, 4, and 5 highlight *lattice*, *network*, and *content*, respectively.

3.   LATTICE

The following summarizes the theoretical and practical implications concerning our work at the lowest tier—*lattice*.

3.1   Theory Concerning *Lattice*

The term *lattice* refers to the hierarchical information structures—trees— that GP uses without consideration of the content contained in the nodes of those trees. As it turns out, there are consequences of using a variable-length, hierarchical structure like a tree. Trees are not neutral to problem solving in GP. In our work (Daida, 2002; Daida, 2003; Daida and Hilss, 2003), we have described a "physics" that occurs when larger trees are assembled iteratively by using smaller trees. This "physics" is analogous to diffusion-limited aggregation (Witten and Sander, 1981; Witten and Sander, 1983)—a well-known process that describes diverse phenomena such as soot, electrolytic deposition, and porous bodies (Kaye, 1989).

Diffusion-limited aggregation results in fractal objects that have certain ranges for sizes and shapes. These sizes and shapes can be modeled so that theoretical ranges can be determined. In a similar fashion, processes in GP that iteratively assemble larger trees by using smaller ones result in fractal-like objects that have certain ranges for sizes and shapes. As in diffusion-limited aggregation, these sizes and shapes can be modeled; we developed our lattice-aggregate model for this purpose (Daida and Hilss, 2003). As in diffusion-limited aggregation, theoretical ranges can be determined.

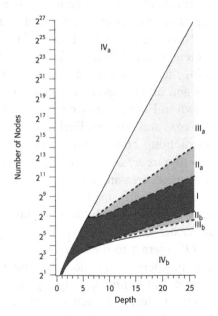

Figure 5-2. Predicted Regions. A map of likely tree structures can be derived based on a process that is analogous to diffusion-limited aggregation.

A map of these ranges is given in Figure 5-2.

There are four general regions in this map. Region I is where most GP binary trees occur. Region II is where increasingly fewer trees would be found. Region III is where even fewer trees would typically occur. In (Daida, 2002), we suggested that Region III might be impossible for all practical purposes. Since then, however, we have tentatively identified those conditions when the probability of trees occurring in this region approaches zero. Region IV represents impossible configurations of trees, which occurs in this case because the map presumes binary trees.

Region I occupies only a small fraction of the total allowable search space. Region I only seems large because the map is depicted on a logarithmic scale (which is a common convention). For the particular map shown in Figure 5-2, Region I represents less than 0.01% of the entire allowable search space in size and depth.

In (Daida, 2003; Daida and Hilss, 2003), we compared this map with empirical data from several different problems, including: *Quintic, Sextic, 6-Input Multiplexer, 11-Input Multiplexer*. We have also compared this map against the tunably difficult *Binomial-3* problem. In each case, nearly all of the solutions that were derived by GP fit inside the area delineated by Region I.

The model, however, presumes that the map applies to all GP problems, regardless of the substance of what these problems are. Consequently, to test for this, we de-vised a problem that is scored entirely on the structural metrics of a tree (as opposed to exe-cuting the pro-gram associated with a tree for evaluating and scoring that program). This test problem is called the *Lid*.

The premise behind the *Lid* problem is fairly straightforward. There have been efforts to limit bloat by including a structural metric, such as tree depth as in (Soule, Foster et

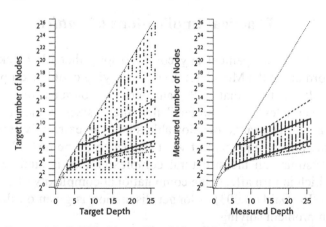

Figure 5-3. Lid Problem. The *Lid* problem demonstrates the effects of tree structure at the level of *lattice*. Dark bold lines indicate the boundaries for Region I; the dotted lines, the boundaries for Region II. (a) Input (i.e., target sizes that GP needs to reach). (b) Output (i.e., tree sizes that GP has derived in response to input).

al., 1996), as a part of the fitness measure. For the *Lid* problem, *all* of the selection pressure is directed towards identifying a tree of a given size and depth. A technical description of the *Lid* problem is given in (Daida, Li et al., 2003). The question is then, If one were to do this, would GP be able to cover the entire search space?

Our work has indicated "conditionally no" as an answer. Referring to Figure 5-3a, each dot shows the location of a target shape for a single trial; all GP would need to do is to assemble *any* tree with both a target number of nodes and a target depth to succeed. The targets were randomly distributed in the space of sizes and depths for depths 0–26. For this particular experiment, GP used a population size of 4,000 and fitness-proportionate selection. There were 1,000 trials in all.

Referring to Figure 5-3b, each dot shows the location of the best solution for a single trial. In spite of diverting all of computational effort in GP to simply coming up with a target tree shape, most solutions still exist within either Regions I or II. In particular, 66% of the solutions are contained within Region I; 94% of the solutions are contained within Regions I and II.

Our previous work on the *Lid* problem describes in detail empirical results from both horizontal and vertical cuts across this map (Daida, Li et al., 2003), instead of the Monte Carlo results shown here. In our current investigations, we are finding a significant difference when using tournament selection instead of fitness-proportionate selection. We suspect other structural mechanisms are involved, which are not currently included with the lattice-aggregate model.

3.2   Practical Implications of *Lattice*

"You can paint it any color, so long that it's black." (Attributed to H. Ford about the Model T.) A similar saying could be quipped about GP.

It is true that GP can derive programs of a great many sizes. Nevertheless, GP "prefers" that these sizes come in a specific range of shapes. The range of allowable shapes is extremely limited and amounts to fractions of a percent of what shapes could be possible. This limit implies a constraint on the structural complexity that is attainable for standard GP, which in turn affects the computational complexity of solution outcomes.

In (Daida, 2003), a longer discussion is given on the effects of structure on problem solving.

4.   NETWORK

Of course, GP does more than put together tree structures. At the core of it, GP builds up solutions from fragments of guesses. Somewhere scattered in these guesses—the initial population of solutions—are the elements from which GP must sift and reassemble. While many in the community would take this for granted, this ability to reconstitute working solutions from pieces does raise the following question: Just how small and just how scattered can those fragments be in an initial population for GP to work?

If one took the time to map out the topology of interconnections between various fragments in various individuals in an initial population, I would claim that this topology constitutes a network. What these networks look like in GP is currently an ongoing investigation. The following summarizes the theory and the practical implications concerning our work at the level of *network*.

4.1   Theory Concerning *Network*

We are not yet to the point of articulating a mathematical theory. We have, however, designed a test problem to probe for their existence and, if appropriate, their dynamics.

The chief difficulty in designing such a problem is a need to isolate the topology of interconnections away from its substance. In other words, if it is suitable to analyze networks in GP, there should be a set of behaviors and phenomena that occur at this level, regardless of whatever executable content is implicit in a GP population.

The closest parallel that the community of GP has in the discovery of a set of behaviors and phenomena at this level would be investigations on diversity (e.g., McPhee and Hopper, 1999; Burke, Gustafson et al., 2002a; Burke, Gustafson et al., 2002b; Burke, Gustafson et al., 2004). At one level, the goals between our study and these studies would be the same: an investigation of where and how scattered fragments are within the context of a population. At another level, the goals diverge. For example, what matters in the studies of diversity is the uniqueness of those fragments, which often presumes something about the content held within them. What also is presumed in the studies of diversity is a tacit acknowledgement that more diversity is better. Consequently, metrics that show a loss of diversity during problem solving might either call into question the definition of diversity that was used or whether the process of problem solving is somehow flawed (e.g., premature convergence).

While we acknowledge that there are parallels between biological diversity and the role of diversity in genetic and evolutionary computation, we have adopted a nuanced approach to this topic, similar to those taken in investigations of ecosystems and networks. In particular, one raw count of species in a given area is not by itself an indicator of ecosystem health. Likewise, introducing more diversity into an indigenous network does not necessarily result in a more diverse or robust ecosystem. For example, in cases where an exotic invasive species is introduced, it is entirely possible that a short-term increase in the number of different species for a given area is a prelude to a collapse of an indigenous ecosystem as described in (Sakai, Allendorf et al., 2001). Even in biology, *diversity* is a nuanced term.

The test problem that we have designed is called *Highlander* and was first described in (Daida, Samples et al., 2004). The premise behind this problem is simple and starts with a set of N uniquely labeled nodes, all of which are distributed among M individuals in an initial population. All GP has to do is to assemble an individual that contains a specified percentage of N uniquely labeled nodes.

Put another way, the *Highlander* problem is like a game that begins with a huge bag of marbles. Every marble corresponds to a node and there are as many marbles as there are nodes in an initial population. The number of marbles is known. Each marble has been labeled. Each label appears just once. The object of the game is to grab enough marbles from the bag so that one has a certain percentage of all of the unique labels in the bag.

Of course, the game would be easy if one had as many grabs as would be needed and no one does anything else to the bag (like adding marbles). Likewise, in GP, assembling an individual that consists of N uniquely labeled nodes would be trivial if GP were allowed as many recombinations as would be needed to create one individual while the population remained static over time. However, each "child" in GP is a result of just one recombination. Furthermore, the distribution of labels also changes over time, in part because GP selects some "parents" more frequently than others.

It is possible, then, for bloat to occur in the *Highlander* problem. A label counts just once, regardless of whether there is just one instance of that label or a hundred instances of them. Consequently, a tree could consist of thousands of nodes, but still have just three unique labels. Such a tree would score the same as a tree that had three nodes with three different labels.

By the same token, it is irrelevant to the test problem to categorize which fragments (i.e., subtrees) are introns and which are not, even if bloat were present. Introns presume executability (i.e., syntactically correct code) and functionality (i.e., upon execution, something happens). Neither applies to *Highlander* because code is not executed during the course of evaluating an individual. Consequently, it is entirely possible to point to a specific branch in a *Highlander* solution and not know whether it is an intron or whether it is *the* part of the tree that contributes to a fitness score. The specific programmatic content of nodes is rendered irrelevant in *Highlander*, which is desirable when probing for and isolating network behavior.

As a probe, *Highlander* was designed as a tunably difficult problem as a way to determine the conditions under which networking occurs in GP and as a way to determine the factors that influence the combination of material through networking. (For this reason, then, no mutation was used.) The tuning parameter β is the specified percentage of N uniquely labeled nodes that an individual tree must have. As a crude measure of problem difficulty, we used a successful-trials ratio: i.e., the number of trials that produced a correct solution, which is then normalized to the total number of GP trials. Figure 5-4 shows the results of problem difficulty as a function of tuning parameter β for two different population sizes for both tournament and fitness-proportionate selection. Each data point is the successful-trials ratio for 1,000 trials. A total of 82,000 trials is depicted.

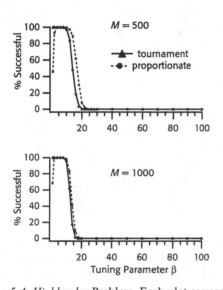

Figure 5-4. Highlander Problem. Each plot corresponds to a population size M and depicts the percentage of successful trials as a function of tuning parameter β. Parameter β values that correspond to easier settings have higher percentages of successful trials.

What is striking about the results shown is that GP is only able to assemble a fraction of the total number of possible fragments into a single individual. For population sizes that are commonly used in the GP community, that fraction amounts to something between 2 – 18%.

The other striking finding was what happened when a comparison was made between the map of Figure 5-2 and the shapes of the *Highlander* solutions. Figure 5-5 shows the size and depth results for population size 1,000 and tournament selection for various tuning parameter values. Each dot represents the size and depth for the best solution obtained for a trial. There are 1,000 dots per plot. What is noteworthy about these results is an *absence* of change in shape after the successful-trials metric goes to zero (i.e., no trial resulted in a successful solution for $\beta \geq 20\%$). An increase in β should result in an increase in the size of a tree, which is what happens when

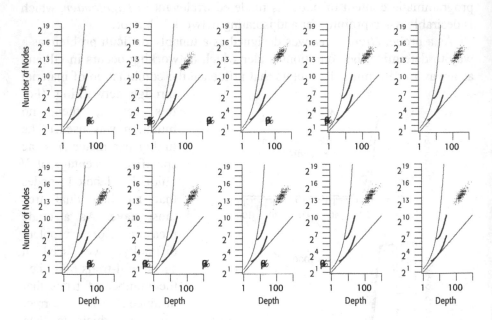

Figure 5-5. Size versus Depth Scatterplots for Tournament Selection, Population Size 1,000. The boundaries for Region I are shown in bold. Since Region I has only been computed up through depth 26, the Region I boundaries are truncated. An attractor is apparent when the tuning parameter $\beta \geq 20\%$.

GP is able to assemble a correct tree. The presence of an attractor at $\beta \geq$ 20%, in spite of what should be increasing selection pressure for trees to grow, is noteworthy. What makes this attractor particularly striking is that it exists even though there were no fitness criteria specified for either size or depth. Similar behavior occurs for the other configurations of population size and selection methods.

We speculate that the attractor represents an equilibrium point between the rate at which solutions can be assembled versus the rate of losing of individuals in a population due to selection.

GP can assemble a solution out of fragments that are distributed in a population only so quickly. Assembly is further constrained by lattice effects, which is evident in Figure 5-5. Although the boundaries for Regions I and II have not been computed at the depths for which the *Highlander* solutions lie, the shape and location of the attractor is consistent with a *lattice* constraint at those depths.

At the same time, GP can lose fragments because not all individuals in a population propagate. There has been work where it has been possible to compute the rate of diversity loss because of tournament selection (e.g., Blickle, 1997; Motoki, 2002). In actuality, the attrition rate would be even higher because GP has a tendency to select longer branches and not roots for subtree crossover (e.g., Luke, 2003), which subsequently means fragments proximal to roots are lost.

Our analysis as of this writing is only preliminary and we have not yet mapped out the topology of relationships between individuals. The *Highlander* results hint at a network topology that exists and that has an equilibrium point that is a consequence of how GP assembles all of its solutions.

4.2   Practical Implications of *Network*

There have been anecdotes where GP is said to work reasonably with a limited number of different kinds of functions and terminals. There have also been anecdotes where GP has been known to fail when too many different kinds of functions and terminals were needed to assemble a solution. Both sets of anecdotes may reflect the same phenomena that occur at the level of *network*.

GP has a sharply limited ability to assemble solutions from fragments that are scattered throughout a population. When it is possible to construct a solution from a limited number of different kinds of functions and terminals, there is likely to be a number of *redundant* fragments. Consequently, a loss of fragments would not likely be catastrophic.

However, if GP has to assemble a solution from many different kinds of functions and terminals, the chance for redundant fragments would decrease. The loss of fragments would be noticeable and consequential. The difficulty curves of Figure 5-4 definitely indicated that there is an upper limit to just how many different nodes can be used in the assembly of a solution. GP might not be able to solve a problem at all if this upper limit is reached before a solution is derived.

Furthermore, failure is likely to occur well before the upper limit is reached, since this upper limit presumes that it does not matter as to the way in which these nodes connect. If it does matter, which it does for most problems in GP, there would be further constraints. These additional constraints would occur at the next level of *content*.

5.   CONTENT

What matters most to many who use GP is the solutions that the technology generates. The solutions the technology is currently generating are compelling in their own right. In a series of books and papers, Koza and his colleagues have actively promoted GP as a discovery engine (Koza,

Bennett III et al., 1999; Koza, Keane et al., 2000; Koza, Keane et al., 2003). By 2003, 32 instances of solutions by GP met criteria that *humans* would also need to meet if *their* solutions are to be deemed innovative (e.g., by peer-review or by patent law). One of these 32 was sufficiently innovative to merit a patent application. Koza and his colleagues contend that someday GP will routinely make discoveries and inventions (Koza, Keane et al., 2003). I would agree that merits of GP as a technology ultimately reside in its substance, its solutions, and not whether it had the appropriate lattice structure or constructed an appropriate network.

Of course, the substance of a solution in GP depends on its programmatic content. The last and highest level—*content*—concerns how GP generates functional solutions, which happen to be subject to the constraints at the levels of *lattice* and *network*. The following summarizes the theory and the practical implications concerning our work at this tier.

5.1   Theory Concerning *Content*

I would say that much of the theoretical work in the GP community occurs at this level, where content is no longer abstracted away, where problem domains matter, and where fitness depends on executing code. Consequently, current theories on schema, bloat, and diversity (to name a few) have resided at this level. My own group's current work at this level is characterized by the following motivating question: "How do the consequences of *lattice* and *network* affect what happens at the level of *content*?"

We have just begun to explore what this question means, since much of my group's recent effort has involved *lattice* and *network*. Nevertheless, my group's oldest and first tunably difficult problem—*Binomial-3*—was designed for understanding content issues in problem difficulty (Daida, Bertram et al., 1999). Although it started off as a tool for exploring the role of building blocks in determining what makes a problem GP-hard, the *Binomial-3* has instead been instrumental in our current understanding of structure. Structure, as it seems to be turning out, plays various roles in problem solving by GP and is a major factor in determining problem difficulty (Daida, Polito 2 et al., 1999; Daida, Polito 2 et al., 2001; Daida, Li et al., 2003). The interplay between *lattice* and *content* was discussed at some length in (Daida, 2003) and so is not recapitulated here. Instead, what is discussed are some of the new developments in our group.

What is new to us since last year's workshop are the findings from the *Highlander* problem. If only a fraction of the material in the initial population can be assembled to form a solution, we wondered about how this fraction was distributed and what the dynamics were that governed content. To explore the consequences of the *Highlander* findings on content, we used the *Binomial-3* to focus on the interplay between *network* and *content*. See (Daida, Ward et al., 2004) for more details.

The *Binomial-3* is an instance taken from symbolic regression and involves solving for the function $f(x) = 1 + 3x + 3x^2 + x^3$. Fitness cases are 50 equidistant points generated from $f(x)$ over the interval [-1, 0). The function set is {+, −, ×, ÷}, which corresponds to arithmetic operators of addition, subtraction, multiplication, and protected division. Its terminal set is {x, **R**}, where x is the symbolic variable and **R** is the set of ephemeral random constants that are distributed uniformly over the interval [-α, α]. The tuning parameter is α, which is a real number. The *Binomial-3* can be tuned from a relatively easy problem (e.g., $\alpha = 1$) to a difficult one (e.g., $\alpha = 1,000$).

As in *Highlander*, my group modified the *Binomial-3* so that every node in the initial population was uniquely labeled. In this way, the use of nodes in any solution in any generation can be audited back to a particular individual in an initial population. For the purposes of illustration, we call an individual in an initial population an *ancestor*. Keeping track of ancestral lineages for a current population allows us a rough measure of how GP uses and assembles fragments from the initial population. For example, if GP uses fragments that are distributed broadly in an initial population, an audit would likely show a high number of ancestral lineages that belong to a current population. Likewise, if GP uses fragments that are distributed narrowly in an initial population, an audit would likely show a low number of ancestral lineages that belong to a current population.

We ran an experiment where we used representative settings for "easy" and "hard" problems (i.e., $\alpha = 1$ and $\alpha = 1,000$, respectively). We also used two different selection methods: fitness-proportionate selection (which is a selection method that is known to maintain diversity, e.g., Pincus, 1970; Galar, 1985) and tournament selection (which is a selection method that is known to lose diversity, e.g., Blickle and Thiele, 1995; Blickle, 1997)). This represents a total of four different experimental configurations. We ran 200 trials per configuration, with each trial consisting of a population size of 500 that ran for 200 generations. The results are shown in Figure 5-6.

Figure 5-6 is a complete summary of approximately 80 million trees that were audited into lineages of 400,000 ancestors. The summary is divided into four density plots, where each density plot corresponds to a different experimental configuration of selection method and tuning parameter α. Each plot shows the number of ancestral lineages present in a population as a function of time (in generations). The maximum number of ancestral lineages for each trial was 500, which happened to occur just at generation 0 (i.e., at population initialization). For visualization purposes, only the range [0, 150] is shown. Each density plot depicts 200 trials worth of data. Darker

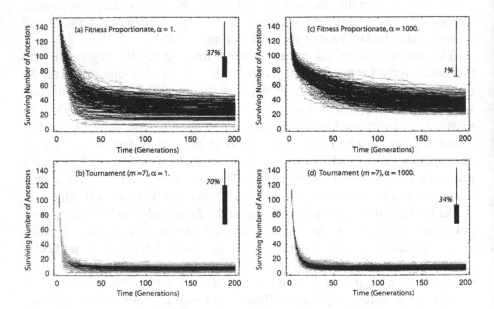

Figure 5-6. Surviving Number of Ancestor Lineages by Problem Difficulty and Selection Method. Each plot corresponds to a particular selection method and tuning parameter setting. The thermometer graph in each plot indicates problem difficulty: the lower the percentage, the harder it was for GP to solve.

tones in a plot correspond to more trials that have that number of lineages remaining at a given generation. The "thermometers" that are embedded in each plot correspond to the measured problem difficulty (i.e., a successful-trials ratio, where a higher percentage corresponds to an "easier" problem).

For our tiered view to be useful, the *Binomial-3* results should be constrained by the *Highlander* results. The results shown in Figure 5-6 do support the tiered view, since surviving lineages roughly correspond to the amount of material that is used. For each configuration, at most 12% of ancestral lineages remained intact through generation 200. The surprise in our findings was that fewer lineages are roughly correlated with easier problem solving. In other words, with less diversity, GP yielded a high success rate.

5.2   Practical Implications of *Content*

Barry Schwartz wrote in his recent book, *The Paradox of Choice: Why More is Less*, "…the fact that *some* choice is good doesn't necessarily mean that *more* choice is better…. there is a cost of having an overload of choice." (Schwartz, 2004), p. 3. Schwartz was talking about Americans, but he could have just as easily been talking about GP.

Having more choices from which to devise a solution would at first blush seem a reasonable strategy, particularly concerning genetic and evolutionary computation. Having more choices is like having more biological diversity. Nature has so many variations on a theme of life that even now there is not a complete species catalog (Wilson, 1992). If that wasn't enough, there have been compelling theoretical arguments for having diversity (e.g., Pincus, 1970; Galar, 1985).

Nonetheless, even in Nature, there are limits to diversity when one takes into account analogs for *lattice* and *network*. For example, if *lattice* corresponds to an island and *network* to that island's ecosystem, there have been seminal experimental and theoretical investigations (MacArthur and Wilson, 1967) that have shown that there are limits to the number of species that can coexist on that island. Although such works have been updated and are now regarded as somewhat simple, the original notion remains that the extent of a physical space is a constraining factor to the amount of biological diversity that this space can support.

The allowable "space" in GP, as constrained by *lattice* and *network*, is fairly small. For a set of commonly used conditions, the *lattice* constrains GP to about 0.01% of the entire search space. Within what amounts to a narrow strip of searchable space, something less than 20% of the material given in an initial population can be reintegrated into a single solution.

What Figure 5-6 indicates is that it may be possible to overload GP's "space" with too many choices. Fitness-proportionate selection allows for a significant fraction of what is theoretically allowable for recombination of initial population material. In the *Binomial-3*, much of this allowable material would be unique and in the form of ephemeral random constants. The configuration ($\alpha = 1,000$, fitness-proportionate selection) that retained the highest number of ancestral lineages and consequently the most number of unique nodes actually scored lowest in terms of GP's ability to provide correct solutions.

In GP, there is a basis for "hidden costs" for having too many choices. For example, all nodes may be statistically permissible for their use in assembling a solution, but not all nodes would be beneficial. The question then becomes, what does GP do with the material that is not beneficial, even detrimental, to problem solving? A number of different (emergent) methods that GP could use have been described in (Daida, Bertram et al., 1999). One could argue that each of these costs represents a penalty, since each consumes computational resources.

So what does one do? The following is a list of our speculations that could apply to real-world problem solving with GP:

- *Use large populations.* As Figure 5-6 indicates, GP recombines initial population material that is distributed among a *small* number of ancestors. Using large populations increases the probability of having suitable material concentrated in a handful of individuals in the initial population.

- *Use tournament selection.* For our work, we used a tournament selection size of 7. Although fitness-proportionate selection is beneficial in maintaining diversity, tournament selection removes "choices" as a natural consequence of the method. Fewer choices might result in fewer costs of overloading GP's "space."

- *Consider that having a large variety of different functions and terminals within GP solutions may actually initiate "overloading."* If this is the case, it could mean that the function or terminal set is too large and needs to be pared down.

- *Consider the use of structure-altering operations that delete material from a population.* Such structure-altering operations have been described in (Koza, Bennett III et al., 1999; Koza, Keane et al., 2003). It may help to mitigate against "overloading."

- *If a solution likely requires the use of a large number of different kinds of functions and terminals, consider the use of meta-programs.* In other words, GP wouldn't directly derive a solution, but instead derives a program that when executed, produces a solution. The meta-program could then use a more limited function and terminal set than what is required of a solution.

6.   CONCLUSIONS

The roles of structure in problem solving by GP are multifaceted and complex. This chapter has shown that it is possible for structure to be simultaneously a cause and an effect, simultaneously a primary factor and a secondary one. While these roles of structure may all be equally true, I shave uggested that they are all not equally scaled.

The tiered view featured three levels: *lattice*, *network*, and *content*. Each level corresponded to a particular structural scale. *Lattice* involved the largest scales in which structure was a causal factor and a primary influence. *Network* involved intermediate scales and allowed for emergent structures to occur. *Content* involved the fine scales and considered the specifics of what was in the network. It was at the level of *content* that structure was an effect and a secondary factor.

Each level can be examined for a different set of system behaviors, particularly with regards to how structure influences both problem solving and problem difficulty in GP. Although the theory is nascent, we have devised a tunably difficult test problem for each level to probe for behaviors. This chapter represents our first summary of how all three problems—*Lid*, *Highlander*, and *Binomial-3*—serve as part of an integrated investigation into the roles of structure in GP for problem solving.

The counterintuitive implication of our work was that because of structure, it is possible to overload GP with too many choices and with too much diversity implicit in those choices. The work indicated that there is a "season" when diversity is best leveraged by the technology and that this "season" occurs at population initialization (at least for standard GP). It is a reason why large populations are argued for in difficult real-world problems, rather than a strategy of maintaining diversity throughout the course of a run.

ACKNOWLEDGMENTS

Many colleagues and students were involved in the preparation of this work. I thank the following UMACERS teams: Borges (D. Ward, A. Hilss, S. Long, M. Hodges, J. Kriesel) for automated analysis tools and data mining support of the *Binomial-3*; Royal (H. Li, R. Tang) for their work on *Lid*; Niihau (M. Samples, B. Hart, J. Halim, A. Kumar, M. Byom) for their work on *Highlander*; Magic (M. Samples, P. Chuisano, R. O'Grady, C. Kurecka, M. Pizzimenti, F. Tsa) for their development of GP grid computer protocols and support infrastructure; Meta-Edge (R. Middleton, A. Mackenzie) for humanities research. Financial support of some of the students was given and administered through S. Gregerman. Supercomputer support was given and administered through both CAEN and the Center for Scientific Computation. The CSCS / Santa Fe Institute Fall Workshops have played significant roles in the formative development of the tiers. My interactions with J. Doyle, L. Sander, and J. Padgett have been brief, but thought provoking. Gratitude is extended to the workshop organizers T. Yu, U.-M. O'Reilly, R. Riolo, and W. Worzel, as well as to the reviewers of this chapter (i.e., T. Soule, C. Ryan, D. Howard, and S. Moore). Finally as ever, I extend my appreciation to S. Daida and I. Kristo.

REFERENCES

Angeline, P. (1994). Genetic Programming and Emergent Intelligence. In J. Kinnear, K.E. (Ed.), *Advances in Genetic Programming*, 75–97. Cambridge: The MIT Press.

Angeline, P. J. (1997). Parse Trees. In T. Bäck, D. B. Fogel and Z. Michalewicz (Eds.), *Handbook of Evolutionary Computation*, C1.6:1–C1.6:3. Bristol: Institute of Physics Publishing.

Banzhaf, W. and W. B. Langdon (2002). Some Considerations on the Reason for Bloat. *Genetic Programming and Evolvable Machines*, 3(1), 81 – 91.

Banzhaf, W., P. Nordin, et al. (1998). *Genetic Programming: An Introduction: On the Automatic Evolution of Computer Programs and Its Applications*. San Francisco: Morgan Kaufmann Publishers.

Blickle, T. (1997). Tournament Selection. In T. Bäck, D. B. Fogel and Z. Michalewicz (Eds.), *Handbook of Evolutionary Computation*, C2.3:1–C2.3:4. Bristol: Institute of Physics Publishing.

Blickle, T. and L. Thiele (1995). A Mathematical Analysis of Tournament Selection. In L. J. Eshelman (Ed.), *ICGA95: Proceedings of the Sixth International Conference on Genetic Algorithms*, 9–16. San Francisco: Morgan Kaufmann Publishers.

Burke, E., S. Gustafson, et al. (2002a). A Survey and Analysis of Diversity Measures in Genetic Programming. In W. B. Langdon, E. Cantú-Paz, K. Mathias, et al. (Eds.), *GECCO-2002: Proceedings of the Genetic and Evolutionary Computation Conference*, 716–723. San Francisco: Morgan Kaufmann Publishers.

Burke, E., S. Gustafson, et al. (2004). Diversity in Genetic Programming: An Analysis of Measure and Correlation with Fitness. *IEEE Transactions on Evolutionary Computation*, 8(1), 47–62.

Burke, E., S. Gustafson, et al. (2002b). Advanced Population Diversity Measures in Genetic Programming. In J. J. Merelo Guervós, P. Adamidis, H.-G. Beyer, J.-L. Fernández-Villacañas and H.-P. Schwefel (Eds.), *Parallel Problem Solving from Nature—PPSN VII: Proceedings*, 341–350. Berlin: Springer-Verlag.

Clergue, M., P. Collard, et al. (2002). Fitness Distance Correlation and Problem Difficulty for Genetic Programming. In W. B. Langdon, E. Cantú-Paz, K. Mathias, et al. (Eds.), *GECCO-2002: Proceedings of the Genetic and Evolutionary Computation Conference*, 724–732. San Francisco: Morgan Kaufmann Publishers.

Daida, J. M. (2002). Limits to Expression in Genetic Programming: Lattice-Aggregate Modeling. *The 2002 IEEE World Congress on Computational Intelligence: Proceedings of the 2002 Congress on Evolutionary Computation*, 273–278. Piscataway: IEEE.

Daida, J. M. (2003). What Makes a Problem GP-Hard? A Look at How Structure Affects Content. In R. L. Riolo and W. Worzel (Eds.), *Theory and Applications in Genetic Programming*, 99–118. Dordrecht: Kluwer Academic Publishers.

Daida, J. M., R. B. Bertram, et al. (1999). Analysis of Single-Node (Building) Blocks in Genetic Programming. In L. Spector, W. B. Langdon, U.-M. O'Reilly and P. J. Angeline (Eds.), *Advances in Genetic Programming 3*, 217–241. Cambridge: The MIT Press.

Daida, J. M. and A. M. Hilss (2003). Identifying Structural Mechanisms in Standard Genetic Programming. In E. Cantú-Paz, J. A. Foster, K. Deb, et al. (Eds.), *Genetic and Evolutionary Computation—GECCO 2003*, 1639–1651. Berlin: Springer-Verlag.

Daida, J. M., A. M. Hilss, et al. (2003). Visualizing Tree Structures in Genetic Programming. In E. Cantú-Paz, J. A. Foster, K. Deb, et al. (Eds.), *Genetic and Evolutionary Computation—GECCO 2003*, 1652–1664. Berlin: Springer-Verlag.

Daida, J. M., H. Li, et al. (2003). What Makes a Problem GP-Hard? Validating a Hypothesis of Structural Causes. In E. Cantú-Paz, J. A. Foster, K. Deb, et al. (Eds.), *Genetic and Evolutionary Computation—GECCO 2003*, 1665–1677. Berlin: Springer-Verlag.

Daida, J. M., J. A. Polito 2, et al. (1999). What Makes a Problem GP-Hard? Analysis of a Tunably Difficult Problem in Genetic Programming. In W. Banzhaf, J. M. Daida, A. E. Eiben, et al. (Eds.), *GECCO '99: Proceeding of the Genetic and Evolutionary Computation Conference*, 982–989. San Francisco: Morgan Kaufmann Publishers.

Daida, J. M., J. A. Polito 2, et al. (2001). What Makes a Problem GP-Hard? Analysis of a Tunably Difficult Problem in Genetic Programming. *Genetic Programming and Evolvable Machines*, 2(2), 165–191.

Daida, J. M., M. E. Samples, et al. (2004). Demonstrating Constraints to Diversity with a Tunably Difficult Problem for Genetic Programming. *Proceedings of CEC 2004*. Piscataway: IEEE Press.

Daida, J. M., D. J. Ward, et al. (2004). Visualizing the Loss of Diversity in Genetic Programming. *Proceedings of CEC 2004*. Piscataway: IEEE Press.

Galar, R. (1985). Handicapped Individua in Evolutionary Processes. *Biological Cybernetics*, *53*, 1–9.

Goldberg, D. E. and U.-M. O'Reilly (1998). Where Does the Good Stuff Go, and Why? In W. Banzhaf, R. Poli, M. Schoenauer and T. C. Fogarty (Eds.), *Proceedings of the First European Conference on Genetic Programming*, 16–36. Berlin: Springer-Verlag.

Hall, J. M. and T. Soule (2004). Does Genetic Programming Inherently Adopt Structured Design Techniques? In U.-M. O'Reilly, T. Yu, R. L. Riolo and W. Worzel (Eds.), *Genetic Programming Theory and Practice II*. Boston: Kluwer Academic Publishers.

Kaye, B. H. (1989). *A Random Walk Through Fractal Dimensions*. Weinheim: VCH Verlagsgesellschaft.

Knuth, D. E. (1997). *The Art of Computer Programming: Volume 1: Fundamental Algorithms*. Reading: Addison–Wesley.

Koza, J. R. (1994). *Genetic Programming II: Automatic Discovery of Reusable Programs*. Cambridge: The MIT Press.

Koza, J. R. (1995). Two Ways of Discovering the Size and Shape of a Computer Program to Solve a Problem. In L. J. Eshelman (Ed.), *ICGA95: Proceedings of the Sixth International Conference on Genetic Algorithms*, 287–294. San Francisco: Morgan Kaufmann Publishers.

Koza, J. R., F. H. Bennett III, et al. (1999). *Genetic Programming III: Darwinian Invention and Problem Solving*. San Francisco: Morgan Kaufmann Publishers.

Koza, J. R., M. A. Keane, et al. (2003). *Genetic Programming IV: Routine Human-Competitive Machine Intelligence*. Norwell: Kluwer Academic Publishers.

Koza, J. R., M. A. Keane, et al. (2000). Automatic Creation of Human-Competitive Programs and Controllers by Means of Genetic Programming. *Genetic Programming and Evolvable Machines*, *1*(1/2), 121–164.

Langdon, W. B. and R. Poli (1997). Fitness Causes Bloat. In P. K. Chawdhry, R. Roy and R. K. Pant (Eds.), *Soft Computing in Engineering Design and Manufacturing*, 23–27. London: Springer-Verlag.

Langdon, W. B. and R. Poli (2002). *Foundations of Genetic Programming*. Berlin: Springer-Verlag.

Luke, S. (2003). Modification Point Depth and Genome Growth in Genetic Programming. *Evolutionary Computation*, *11*(1), 67–106.

MacArthur, R. H. and E. O. Wilson (1967). *The Theory of Island Biogeography*. Princeton: Princeton University Press.

McPhee, N. F. and N. J. Hopper (1999). Analysis of Genetic Diversity through Population History. In W. Banzhaf, J. M. Daida, A. E. Eiben, et al. (Eds.), *GECCO '99: Proceeding of the Genetic and Evolutionary Computation Conference*, 1112 – 1120. San Francisco: Morgan Kaufmann Publishers.

Motoki, T. (2002). Calculating the Expected Loss of Diversity of Selection Schemes. *Evolutionary Computation*, *10*(4), 397–422.

O'Reilly, U.-M. and D. E. Goldberg (1998). How Fitness Structure Affects Subsolution Acquisition in Genetic Programming. In J. R. Koza, W. Banzhaf, K. Chellapilla, et al. (Eds.), *Genetic Programming 1998: Proceedings of the Third Annual Conference*, 269–277. San Francisco: Morgan Kaufmann Publishers.

Pincus, M. (1970). An Evolutionary Strategy. *Journal of Theoretical Biology*, *28*, 483–488.

Poli, R. (2000). Exact Schema Theorem and Effective Fitness for GP with One-Point Crossover. In L. D. Whitley, D. E. Goldberg, E. Cantú-Paz, et al. (Eds.), *GECCO 2000: Proceedings of the Genetic and Evolutionary Computation Conference*, 469–476. San Francisco: Morgan Kaufmann Publishers.

Poli, R. (2001). Exact Schema Theory for Genetic Programming and Variable-Length Genetic Algorithms with One-Point Crossover. *Genetic Programming and Evolvable Machines*, *2*(2), 123–163.

Punch, W., D. Zongker, et al. (1996). The Royal Tree Problem, A Benchmark for Single and Multiple Population Genetic Programming. In P. J. Angeline and J. K.E. Kinnear (Eds.), *Advances in Genetic Programming*, 299–316. Cambridge: The MIT Press.

Rosca, J. P. (1995). Genetic Programming Exploratory Power and the Discovery of Functions. In J. R. McDonnell, R. G. Reynolds and D. B. Fogel (Eds.), *Evolutionary Programming IV: Proceedings of the Fourth Annual Conference on Evolutionary Programming*, 719 – 736. Cambridge: The MIT Press.

Rosca, J. P. (1997). Analysis of Complexity Drift in Genetic Programming. In J. R. Koza, K. Deb, M. Dorigo, et al. (Eds.), *Genetic Programming 1997: Proceedings of the Second Annual Conference*, 286–94. San Francisco: Morgan Kaufmann Publishers.

Sakai, A. K., F. W. Allendorf, et al. (2001). The Population Biology of Invasive Species. *Annual Review of Ecology and Systematics*, *32*, 305–332.

Schwartz, B. (2004). *The Paradox of Choice: Why More is Less*. New York: HarperCollins Publishers, Inc.

Soule, T., J. A. Foster, et al. (1996). Code Growth in Genetic Programming. In J. R. Koza, D. E. Goldberg, D. B. Fogel and R. L. Riolo (Eds.), *Genetic Programming 1996: Proceedings of the First Annual Conference*, 215 – 223. Cambridge: The MIT Press.

Soule, T. and R. B. Heckendorn (2002). An Analysis of the Causes of Code Growth in Genetic Programming. *Genetic Programming and Evolvable Machines*, *3*(3), 283–309.

Wilson, E. O. (1992). *The Diversity of Life*. Cambridge: The Belknap Press.

Witten, T. A. and L. M. Sander (1981). Diffusion-Limited Aggregation: A Kinetic Critical Phenomenon. *Physics Review Letters*, *47*, 1400 – 1403.

Witten, T. A. and L. M. Sander (1983). Diffusion-Limited Aggregation. *Physics Review B*, *27*(9), 5686 – 5697.

Chapter 6

LESSONS LEARNED USING GENETIC PROGRAMMING IN A STOCK PICKING CONTEXT

A Story of Willful Optimism and Eventual Success

Michael Caplan[1] and Ying Becker[2]

[1]*Principal, Head of Quantitative US Active Equity, State Street Global Advisors, One Lincoln Place, Boston, MA 02111;*[2]*Principal, Advanced Research Center, State Street Global Advisors, One Lincoln Place, Boston, MA 02111;*

Abstract: This is a narrative describing the implementation of a genetic programming technique for stock picking in a quantitatively driven, risk-controlled, US equity portfolio. It describes, in general, the problems that the authors faced in their portfolio context when using genetic programming techniques and in gaining acceptance of the technique by a skeptical audience. We discuss in some detail the construction of the fitness function, the genetic programming system's parameterization (including data selection and internal function choice), and the interpretation and modification of the generated programs for eventual implementation.

Key words: genetic programming, stock selection, data mining, fitness functions, quantitative portfolio management.

1.   INTRODUCTION

This is the story of how the US Quantitative Equity Area and the Advanced Research Center of State Street Global Advisors (a unit of State Street Corporation) began using genetic programming techniques to discover new ways of stock investing in specific industries. The story begins with a poorly understood data mining technique, a discussion of previously developed underlying stock picking factors that we thought might make sense, and a lot of disagreement on how to (if not whether to) implement a final stock-picking model.   We describe our tribulations, technical and political, in defining the problem, codifying the solution, and finally convincing someone to invest using this model.   Importantly, we describe how the genetic programming process improved our knowledge of how the stock market worked in a small, but portfolio performance-significant, industry.

This paper has the following broad sections:

- The stock picking problems we faced,
- The financial elements that we had in place,
- Why a direct solution really wasn't possible and how we needed to construct (and adjust and adjust and adjust) our fitness function to proxy portfolio performance,
- How we avoided/sidestepped data mining/snooping concerns,
- How we interpreted and modified our raw genetic programs, and
- The political battle to use the new model.

We promise that there are no special financial insights contained within this paper and the details of the final model are absolutely proprietary and are left purposefully vague but we think the story may be interesting to those trying to find new applications for genetic programming techniques.

1.1   The Stock Picking Problems We Faced (a.k.a. Our Growth Market Problem)

As quantitative portfolio managers at one of the largest institutional money managers in the world, our task is to build risk-controlled, market-beating stock portfolios using a composite model made of individual stock-picking factors.   These stock-picking factors fall into the following general classes: valuation (price-based), market sentiment, and business quality.

An inherent part of our portfolio management task is to build portfolios that work in a variety of market conditions and minimize the investors' pain in periods where our stock picking isn't strong.   To this end, we do quite a bit of *ex post* analysis of our portfolio performance results and attempt to decompose our returns into elements of market risk and residual stock-picking performance as well as other more esoteric elements (volatility, market cap size, labor intensity, etc.).   The net result of this analysis is a series of statistics that are suggestive of areas in which we do well and poorly.   Often these statistics are quite time-period specific and require additional insight (or intuition) that is generally well beyond the degrees of freedom permitted by the data.

One area that needed improvement was our performance in the high technology manufacturing industry. We tend to have very good *average* stock-picking performance in this industry over time but had dismal performance in periods where the stock market was in a speculative growth market mode. Given that the speculative growth markets had been of relatively short duration during much of 1980s and early 1990s, our composite model's weakness in growth markets was masked by a preponderance of value markets in the prior 20 years. With a newly reinvigorated investor class gathering assets and market power (i.e., hedge funds and ultra-short term day-traders) as well as shorter-term client attitudes towards performance shortfalls, we needed to get our High Tech Manufacturing model into shape for both growth and value markets. For a relatively small industry of roughly 30 stocks and less than 4% of the market indices we typically benchmark our portfolios against, the performance impact of this industry (both positive and negative) was outsized and needed to be fixed.

Our traditional approach to solving this problem would be to go out and find a bunch of new (or old but unimplemented) factors that look like they might work in this area. This had already been attempted a few times and though we felt that we had sufficient elements to work with, we suspected that we hadn't combined them optimally. Given the number of possible factors, the various degrees to which they are correlated, and the sheer number of possible interactions that we would need to investigate, we turned to the genetic programming technique that had been used to create fairly straightforward portfolio trading rules in State Street Global Advisors' Currency Department.

2. PROJECT DESCRIPTION OVERVIEW

The flowchart shown in Figure 6-1 describes the development process for our project. Later sections of this paper describe in considerably more detail some of the decisions and compromises made in this project. We start with the upper left hand corner of the flowchart and begin with our set of presumptively useful factors (properly transformed for the project, we call these the alpha factors) pushed into the genetic programming system itself. Using the output of the genetic programming system, we then translate the models into mathematical formulae and calculate various translations to decipher seemingly impenetrable equations. We then hit a decision node, where we decide whether we have acceptable results for further testing or whether we need to make adjustments to our genetic programming process, in which case we loop again. Presuming we have acceptable equations to test, we would then compare these equations against our current factor combination.

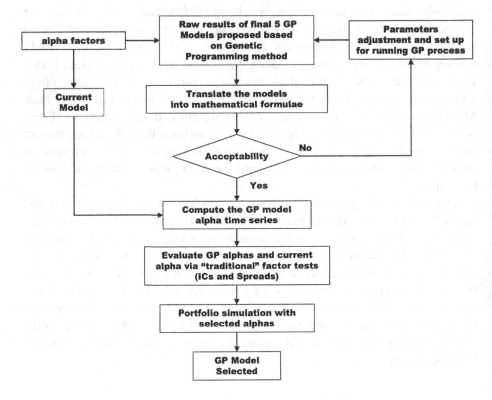

Figure 6-1. Genetic Program Project Flowchart

2.1   Acceptability Criterion – Does the resulting model agree with our intuition of how the markets work? Does it improve our knowledge?

The acceptability decision node requires a bit more explanation, as this is a central decision to the implementable goals of the project. As portfolio managers and observers of markets, it is a central requirement that any models used in our approach must be explainable and justified on economic or behavioral theory. Hard-won experience shows that trading data can mislead investors into drawing the wrong conclusions about history. Tying empirical research back into current theory provides us with comfort that we are at least looking at something potentially sustainable in the future.

One of the important questions that stirred this acceptability criterion was this one: If the genetic programming system came back with the square root of market capitalization, an equation that would have no theoretical basis, would we use it? The answer had to be a resounding NO. The net result of any implementable solution had to contain a link back into theoretical justification of how stock markets work.

From a research standpoint, we were stymied by more traditional approaches to the high technology manufacturing industry. By working from a largely assumption-free stance, i.e., mining reasonable data, we felt we would gain new intuition into how this challenging industry worked.

3. THE FINANCIAL ELEMENTS (THE DATA)

The data that we used in this project was initially drawn from a set of more than 60 factors that were used in prior component weighting exercises. These were financial factors of a variety of classes, such as technical models (e.g., moving averages and oscillators), fundamental ratios built from financial statements (such as a company's balance sheets and income statements), and a variety of other indicators from other data sources (such as earnings estimate data). Also included were the component factors that were already included in our existing composite model (also called Current Alpha Model).

The data was cleaned and transformed in a variety of meaningful ways (arctan, log, z-score, and percentiling transformations were used) to create an even bigger dataset for entry to our genetic programming system. An important side effect of this transformation work as well as the first genetic program runs was the discovery of a variety of data errors. As we put more pressure on our working dataset, we found a larger number of apparent anomalies that needed adjustment – nothing like a data-mining tool for discovering the errors in your data.

3.1 Factor Models Entering Problem

The final five alpha factors entering the last loop of our development process were:

- EP: 12 month forward Earnings-per-Share valuation Score
- CF: Free Cash Flow valuation Score

- ETD: Earnings Estimate Trend Score
- NOA: Net Operating Assets – Financial Quality Score
- WRSI: Price Trend Score

Monthly data were drawn from the time period: 1993-2003. Each of these factors was cross-sectionally (within time periods) transformed. On average, there were 30 stocks per month that entered our dataset. Earlier data was unsuitable for use in the project as the number of stocks in the high technology manufacturing industry quickly dropped below 15. 25 stocks per month was considered to be a reasonable cutoff, fewer data points would be too noisy, too sparse, and probably not representative of the future performance and population of this group.

4.   THE FITNESS FUNCTION

The fitness function, as we quickly found, was the linchpin to making the genetic program produce progressively better results. Due to the nature of the portfolio construction process, it is pretty hard to simulate the various portfolio tradeoffs necessary to emulate the performance of a particular model. In particular, there are a huge number of interactions of both risk and return that can create massive combinatorial problems even with a small number of candidate stocks.

As an illustration of this problem, imagine a portfolio holding exactly one stock. From a risk standpoint, that one stock could represent overall exposure to a variety of common market risks, such as volatility, industry exposure, market size, and trading liquidity. By adding additional stocks to the portfolio, covariance among stock returns has a non-linear impact on the overall risk of the portfolio. Any individual position change may cause other portfolio impacts seemingly unrelated to the choice of a particular stock. The upshot is that we needed to find a proxy for the performance of the tested model.

4.1   Fitness Elements as a Proxy for Portfolio Performance

Over time, we've developed a variety of tests that proxies a factor's (or combination of factors') performance within a portfolio context. These tests include, among others, information coefficients (rank correlation of *a priori* factor scores with *ex post* stock returns, also known as ICs) and top ranked quantiles versus bottom-ranked quantiles (also known collectively as spreads). Viewing spreads in relation to their temporal variance also provides an important metric called an information ratio, a measure of reward to risk. As both long-only (buy and sell stocks) and long-short (buy/sell as well as short/cover stocks) investment managers, we need to understand the whole distribution of returns.

In examining any factor, we look at a variety of these statistics and receive a tableau of results – never have we seen a completely positive report on any factor. There is always some tradeoff or compromise to be made. For example, a factor may have great ranking ability (via the IC statistics) but the overall spread may actually be very small or negative. When reviewing this statistical "tableau," experienced humans are quickly able to distinguish between good and poor models, though we might argue about finer gradations or a factor's appropriateness for various applications.

For a proper fitness function to operate in an automated fashion, it needs better specificity of what constitutes a good model and how various "warts" should be penalized.

4.2   Fitness Function Specification

After much trial and error, we decided on a weighted sum of two information ratios, penalized for non-monotonic results and program complexity. The first information ratio is based on the return spread between the highest ranked decile of stocks and the lowest ranked decile of stocks (i.e., for a 30 stock universe per month, which was typical during this period, a decile included 3 stocks). This provides a proxy into the returns resulting from a long/short portfolio management strategy. The second information ratio compared the top decile to the middle deciles, which provides a proxy for long-only management. Penalties were assessed at various weights for a lack of monotonic return spreads – high penalties if the top was below the bottom and somewhat lower penalties were assessed if the middle was out of order.

The genetic programming code that we used searched for the minimum fitness from the most perfect score possible, i.e., a perfect foresight score. This allowed for the possibility of a model of seemingly infinite "badness" without encountering numerical difficulties with scaling. You can well imagine that we created such models during our search! As an aside, the discussions that took place as we developed the fitness function were illuminating and incorporated a lot of really good suggestions – we'll see additional benefits from these discussions in future factor model research.

Equation (6-1) describes our fitness function. Recall that the genetic program was configured to minimize the fitness function value, i.e., the closer we got to "perfect" the more "fit" the formula.

$$\text{Fitness}_y = (\text{TB}_{\text{perfect}} + \text{TM}_{\text{perfect}}) - (\text{TB}_y + \text{TM}_y - \text{Penalties}_y) \qquad (6\text{-}1)$$

where

Fitness_y	=	the fitness score of formula y
$\text{TB}_{\text{perfect}}, \text{TB}_y$	=	top to bottom deciles spread Information Ratios for the perfect foresight and formula y cases
$\text{TM}_{\text{perfect}}, \text{TM}_y$	=	top to middle deciles spread Information Ratios for the perfect foresight and genetic program y cases
Penalties_y	=	non-linear penalties for non-monotonic formula y as well as a penalty on formula complexity based on the size of the tree developed

5.   GENETIC PROGRAMMING PARAMETERS

Next to the data and the fitness function definition, adjusting the genetic program parameters and program representation provided a great deal of fun in order to produce good results.

5.1   Program Representation

Our representation is a strongly typed (real numeric type) tree with at most two child nodes per parent node. Internal nodes represent mathematical or logical (converted to real) operations to be performed on its child nodes. Keeping the tree strongly typed permitted a wide variety of functions to be used without having to account for many incorrect function operations. We found that keeping the crossover/mutation operations simple was key to keeping the genetic program speedy.

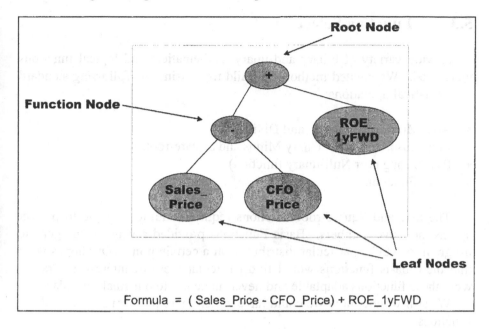

Figure 6-2. Sample Program Representation

5.2 Time-Series Selection: Avoiding Data Mining/Snooping Concerns

The data periods to be used were randomly selected upon program initialization from our dataset, without replacement, to one of three sets: Training, Selection, and Validation. The selection of dates was to be balanced across years and market conditions, if a random selection sufficiently violated our stratified sampling requirements, a new set of dates were selected. This helped us to avoid time-period specific problems (over fitting to a certain kind of market or calendar effect, for example). In addition, we kept back a sample of data that were NEVER used in any analysis until our final round of analysis was complete.

The training dataset, representing 50% of the in-sample data, was used to form the raw formula. Winners with the dataset went on to the selection dataset, a further 25% of the in-sample data. The winners from this round were then tested, after termination of the genetic programming process against our validation dataset, the last 25% of our in-sample data. By creating successively higher hurdles for the genetic program's formulae, we balanced getting good results against over fitting the available data.

5.3   Function Selection

A wide variety of binary and unary mathematical and logical functions were used. We created methods to build trees using the following standard mathematical operations:

- Add, Multiply, Subtract, and Divide,
- Log, Absolute Value, Unary Minus and Square-root,
- Pass-through (or Null-unary function)
- Basis Functions

The Log and Square-root functions required additional logic to protect against negative numbers. Basis Functions provided a way for the genetic program to "cut" a particular distribution at a certain point. Our hopes were that these basis functions would find particular areas of interest, but rarely were these functions adaptable and never made it into our final formulae.

We still wonder how we could have gotten more performance from these functions.

For the most part, the simpler mathematical functions enjoyed the most usage and were consistently used in the final acceptable formulae.

5.4   Other Genetic Program Parameters

We used many standard tree operators to grow, mutate, and express new formulae from good fitness candidates. We experimented with a wide variety of operators and found that the simplest crossover and mutation operators provided very good results.

Where we found somewhat more interesting results than the literature indicated was in the use of demes and limited migration.

5.4.1   Demes and Population Control

Given that we were using a SUN™ server with 16 CPUs, it made sense to try to use all of the CPUs. One element that we found early on in our research was that it was often quite possible for a single type of formula to do well in early generations and then fail to improve because they are locked into a local *extrema*. By using independent populations (loosely related to genetic demes or islands) that were permitted to grow "better adaptations" before subjecting them to greater competition (via migration to nearby populations), we were able to obtain a more robust set of formulae that were diverse enough to allow the formula to adapt beyond the sub-optimal models produced by single populations.

5.4.2   Other Controls and Genetic Program Tuning

A variety of other controls were important in guiding our search for a better genetic program, some with considerable effect, others with (surprisingly) little effect:

- Number and Type of Mutations
- Number and Type of Crossovers
- Termination Conditions, including the Number of Generations, Fitness Tolerance, and Fitness Invariance Over Time
- Population Size
- Number of Demes
- Migration Wait
- Depth of Allowable Tree

The genetic programming results seemed fairly insensitive to the number (probability) of mutations and crossovers, contrary to most literature that we've read. We did find that there were some reasonable levels that allowed convergence with fewer generations; it turns out they were awfully close to the genetic program library defaults. The population sizes and number of demes certainly had impact on the diversity of the initial formulae that were built – generally the higher the better if you have time. Migration wait is basically a parameter that controls how long the demes will act independently of other demes before "local best" formulae migrate to nearby populations. A moderate number (we used 100 generations) tended to work best. Depth of allowable tree prevented very large trees from being built. Note that this was also used as a penalty in our fitness function – less complex formulae are preferred.

The Termination Conditions were interesting controls to experiment with. We found that we got very good results under 500 generations, any more than 500 generations were essentially a waste of time as the complexity of the resulting genetic programs grew exponentially. We experimented with generations as much as 50,000 with no useful improvement in fitness. This "wait" for results also allowed us to experiment with other functions related to best fitness and the current number of generations. Knowing when to cut a run short seemed to be a useful way to getting more knowledge out of our process.

6.   GENETIC PROGRAMMING RESULTS

6.1   Simplification and Interpretation of Formulae

The genetic programming procedure, in its final run, provided five different formulae. Given the proprietary nature of these formulae, we are not able to display them in this paper.   Algebraic simplification and interpretation of these formulae helped inform our changing intuition about the high technology manufacturing industry and importantly, gain acceptance for eventual implementation.

Viewing the partial derivatives of the formula and simplifications (both numerical and analytical) of each formula provided additional insight into market behavior. In a gratifying moment of this project, we were able to provide significant improvement to our knowledge that was readily verifiable through additional, directed, independent tests.   We also performed various comparisons of the "new" genetic program formulae to our current model formulation to provide a reasonable benchmark of improvement.

Sample graphics of the partial programs in Figure 6-2 illustrate the extent to which we attempted to make the genetic program formulae accessible. Figure 6-3 illustrates how a particular formula was sensitive to a particular factor. We strongly recommend the use of a symbolic algebra program (such as MATHCAD™) to help with the analytical and numerical simplification, differentiation, and factoring of the formulae. Using these programs allowed non-mathematicians to readily grasp new insights by simply rearranging and grouping terms of the formula.

Fortunately, we found considerable similarity among the formulae: the same factors, at roughly equivalent ratios allowed us to consider them *en masse*. We then picked the simplest one (which strangely also had the best fitness function as well, *hmmm*) using the time-honored Occam's Razor.

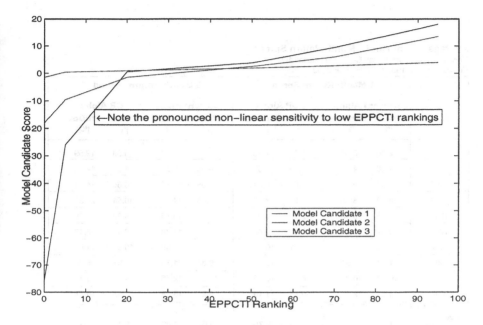

Figure 6-3. Partial Derivative Analysis

7. POST GENETIC PROGRAMMING PORTFOLIO SIMULATIONS

The penultimate step to final implementation of the new model was to backtest (or simulate) the newly found model in a full portfolio construction context. Recall that our genetic program's fitness function was only a proxy for this final, more involved step. Using our judgment, we produced results that were somewhat out of sample (though not completely out of sample due to data limitations). This process is similar to what we'd do in our more traditional factor testing approach.

Figures 6-4 and 6-5 demonstrate the effectiveness of the new model relative to our current model. Annual results, shown in Figure 6-4, as well as market style results found in Figure 6-5, showed a significant improvement over the current alpha model. The improvement of overall return and the effectiveness of the new model in both growth and value periods were noted as satisfying many of the investment goals for this project.

Average 1 Month and 3 Month Return Spreads
Universe: High Technology Cluster in Russell 1000
Period: January 1993 to December 2002

Year	1 Month Return Spread				3 Month Return Spread			
	Current Alpha		GP Alpha		Current Alpha		GP Alpha	
	Mean [%]	StdDev [%]	Mean [%]	StdDec [%]	Mean [%]	StdDev [%]	Mean [%]	StdDev [%]
1993	2.86	8.21	1.93	7.10	9.51	15.17	9.83	19.59
1994	1.48	4.69	-0.88	10.52	4.36	8.23	-1.74	14.88
1995	1.51	5.05	1.65	6.41	-2.98	11.49	6.66	14.01
1996	-0.80	8.45	1.54	7.85	1.65	14.52	10.54	20.35
1997	1.10	6.40	2.16	9.26	6.49	13.75	4.82	17.79
1998	2.32	10.71	3.88	12.45	-6.49	18.78	7.46	17.12
1999	-5.76	13.23	4.71	10.29	-9.85	17.62	16.36	14.48
2000	1.64	15.91	7.51	10.18	9.31	21.73	12.91	6.28
2001	6.16	10.08	6.63	10.35	17.93	12.75	14.03	19.35
2002	3.67	12.91	-0.26	11.49	6.23	18.28	0.67	10.77
Whole Period	1.42	10.24	2.89	9.75	3.61	17.03	8.15	16.35

Figure 6-4. New Formula Performance Measures

Average 1 Month and 3 Month Return Spreads
Universe: High Technology Cluster in Russell 1000
Period: January 1993 to December 2002

Market Regime	1 Month Return Spread				3 Month Return Spread			
	Current Alpha		GP Alpha		Current Alpha		GP Alpha	
	Mean [%]	StdDev [%]	Mean [%]	StdDec [%]	Mean [%]	StdDev [%]	Mean [%]	StdDev [%]
Growth Period (56 mo.)	-2.00	10.22	1.55	11.14	-2.10	16.86	4.20	16.56
Value Period (64 (mo.)	4.41	9.34	4.06	8.26	8.62	15.65	11.62	15.48
Overall Period (1/93 - 12/02)	1.42	10.24	2.89	9.75	3.61	17.03	8.15	16.35

Market Regime Indicator

•**Growth Period:** **R1K Growth - R1K Value > 0**

▪ Value Period: R1K Growth - R1K Value < 0

Figure 6-5. Growth and Value Market Measures

8.   FINAL STEP TO IMPLEMENTATION

The final step to the project was demonstrating this new model and investment capability to our Technical Committee (a sub-committee of our Investment Committee) that has to approve all substantive model and investment strategy changes. This is a bright and knowledgeable committee of portfolio managers, (i.e., practitioners, not technical statisticians.) Classical statistics (such as OLS regression) are well understood by this group; other statistical techniques much less so. In hindsight, we should have better prepared the committee members and given them more time to absorb the content. Let's just say our first presentation of this model to the committee was uncomfortable for all.

First, the committee was for the most part, ill-prepared to discuss or evaluate the genetic programming technique. We spent much of our time describing the genetic programming technique rather than discussing the results of the model. We highly recommend finding a really good metaphor for the genetic programming technique and sticking to it! Also concentrate on the results and touch on the technique only when necessary.

Second, there was just enough prior knowledge of the technique that members of the committee were able to brand the technique, *gasp*, "a data mining technique" – a highly pejorative label in our industry. By the time we'd finished describing how we avoided data snooping, we had tired out our audience.

Third, the new intuition developed from our process required bending the committee members' minds around the new concepts; concepts with which the project team members were working with for months. This was too much, too fast for the committee.

If we were to do this over again, we would have met with each committee member individually and discussed the project and its results prior to the acceptance meeting. This would have increased the time needed to gain approval but would have also decreased the initial unease that this project engendered in the committee.

9.   SUMMARY

At the end of this project we have a newly implemented stock-picking model (it is too early to tell how it is doing in "real life"). Along the way we learned quite a bit more about how markets operated; something that is informing our general opinion of market behavior and future research directions.

The use of the genetic programming techniques was important but not necessarily central to the success of the project. The use of additional analytics, algebraic simplification programs, and human judgment drove the project to a successful completion. Our original hopes that this would be essentially a drop-the-data-in-get-an-answer-out kind of analysis were quickly dashed but were replaced by a more considered view of the promise and limitations of the genetic programming technique.

REFERENCES

Koza, J. (1992). *Genetic Programming: On the Programming of Computers by Means of Natural Selection*, Cambridge, MA: MIT Press.

Thomas, J.D and K. Sycara (1999). The Importance of Simplicity and Validation in Genetic Programming for Data Mining in Financial Data. Freitas, (Ed.), *Data Mining with Evolutionary Algorithms: Research Directions*, AAAI Press.

Chapter 7

FAVOURABLE BIASING OF FUNCTION SETS USING RUN TRANSFERABLE LIBRARIES

Conor Ryan[1], Maarten Keijzer[2], and Mike Cattolico[3]

[1] *University of Limerick, Ireland,* [2] *Prognosys, Utrecht,* [3] *Tiger Mountain Scientific, Seattle, WA*

Abstract
This chapter describes the notion of Run Transferable Libraries(RTLs), libraries of functions which evolve from run to run. RTLs have much in common with standard programming libraries as they provide a suite of functions that can not only be used across several runs on a particular problem, but also to aid in the scaling of a system to more difficult instances of a problem. This is achieved by *training* a library on a relatively simple instance of a problem before applying it to the more difficult one.

The chapter examines the dynamics of the library internals, and how functions compete for dominance of the library. We demonstrate that the libraries tend to converge on a small number of functions, and identify methods to test how well a library is likely to be able to scale.

Keywords:
genetic programming, automatically defined functions, run transferable libraries.

1. Introduction

This chapter extends work initially (Keijzer et al., 2004) presented on the notion of Run Transferable Libraries(RTLs). Unlike traditional Evolutionary Algorithms, RTL enabled methods accumulate information from run to run, attempting to improve performance with each new iteration, but more importantly, trying to build a library that can be used to tackle new, related, problems.

RTLs are similar to programming libraries in that they attempt to provide a suite of functions that may be useful across a particular class of problems. For example, the initial presentation of this work showed how an RTL enabled system was able to outperform an ADF GP system after just a few iterations. Moreover, it was demonstrated that RTLs can be transferred across increasingly more difficult cases of a problem class, enabling the system to solve more difficult problems. For example, the system was able solve a number of parity problems (from 4-parity to 11-parity) with an increasing number of inputs faster than GP could solve each.

In the present chapter, the use of Run Transferable Libraries is investigated on a few selected logical problems. In contrast with earlier work, the investigation is not focused on performance *per se*, but on the contents of the libraries and how they evolve to meet the objectives in a set of problems. To study this, the parity problems are briefly revisited, but more effort is directed towards the Multiplexer problems. Particularly of interest are the balance between functions of different arity and the composition of the library, as these will give insights into not only how GP uses RTLs, but also into what are the most salient functions for the problems examined. Our hypothesis is that libraries that converge to a small number of functions will be the most useful. Given that we are examining Boolean problems, there is a finite number of possible functions that can appear, and it is possible to examine the functions to test if they are semantically identical. Furthermore, as the optimal functions are known for the Multiplexer and Parity problems, it is possible to examine if the libraries converge to these.

2.   Background

Modularity and re-usability are two features much desired in many high level programming languages. Modularity, in particular, can benefit most programming exercises in that it can help divide a problem into more manageable pieces. When this division is done on a logical basis, the overall effort required can also be reduced, as programmers dealing with a well defined logical block can concentrate their efforts on that, without concern for side effects such as the modification of other variables. Similarly, virtually all handwritten programs now depend to a large extent on prewritten libraries of functionality. Libraries provide sets of functionality, where functions of a similar type are grouped together, e.g. math functions, I/O functions etc.

There has been considerable work in GP on exploiting these features, mostly modularity. There are two reasons why the use of modules in GP can be beneficial. Firstly, taking a more *divide and conquer* approach to a problem can often significantly reduce the difficulty, and, secondly, once a useful module has been discovered, i.e. that at least partially solves part of the problem, it can be propagated through the population, quickly improving the performance.

Module Acquisition Strategies

A review (Keijzer et al., 2004) of module acquisition in GP examined a number of these schemes. Most can be described of their module acquisition strategy and their module exploitation strategy. Module acquisition strategies are usually either explicit, where the modules are in some way predefined before a run, or implicit, where modules are discovered during the run.

Examples of explicit strategies include standard Automatically Defined Functions (Koza, 1990, Koza and Rice, 1991, Koza, 1994) (ADFs) in which individuals evolve local functions which can be called by individuals. Typically, a user specifies the number and structure of ADFs that will be made available to the system. Koza demonstrated that, on problems in which solutions can exploit modularity, *any* form of ADF, even an inappropriate (e.g., having a badly chosen number of arguments) is better than having none.

Implicit module acquisition strategies are those that automatically discover modules during a run. Examples include ARL (Rosca and Ballard, 1994), Subtree Encapsulation (Roberts et al., 2001, Howard, 2003) and GLib (Angeline and Pollack, 1992). Each of these has some mechanism to harvest a population for useful modules that can be propagated through later populations. Most modularity techniques work within a particular run. For example, ADFs start with a similar random make up to the individuals that call them (the *Result Producing Branch*) and evolve in parallel. At the end of a particular run, any discovered ADFs are discarded and a new batch is generated for subsequent runs. When a run is capable of finding a good modularization of the problem, this is noticed as a success for the run, but no effort is undertaken to see if these particular ADFs can function outside of the limitations of this single problem.

An exception to this is Subtree Encapsulation, which only harvests the population for modules at the *end* of a run. This is done with a view to increasing the number of functions and terminals for subsequent runs, so modules discovered in one run are immediately available for the following one. However, the object of this encapsulation is to solve a single problem in later runs.

Run Transferable Libraries adopt this technique, thus discarding the notion of multiple independent runs for an evolutionary algorithm, as each run can modify the library of modules available, and creates a self-evolved API for a particular problem domain. The objective of a Run Transferable Library is thus to evolve a comprehensive set of functionality that can be used to tackle different problems in a problem domain. This is, effectively, an effort to automate what is currently limited to the "genetic programmer", the person who selects the function set for a problem.

3. Run Transferable Libraries

This section provides an abstract view of how RTL enabled systems can operate. It lists a few considerations and necessities to be able to develop a library based genetic programming system that can be used on different problems from a problem domain. In the present work, the domain is limited to logical problems, but it is thought that the considerations contained in this section have more wide applicability.

First and foremost: to be able to transfer knowledge from one run to the next, it is necessary to make a distinction between problem specific functionality and functionality that transcends specific problems and works in problem domains. For example, for logic problems, the distinction is clear-cut. Terminals are problem-dependent and cannot be expected to have the same meaning on a different problem, while functions are problem independent. Therefore, in this case, the library only contains logical functions, build up from some primitive, logically complete, basis set. It is up to the evolution of the library to find that set of functionality that helps in finding modular solutions. In particular this means that functions of arity 0 — subtrees — are not kept in the library. For other domains, where sensing the environment is a critical part of the functionality, such arity 0 *functions* could very well be part of the library.

Thus, an RTL-based system needs to operate using two subsystems: one that contains the problem-dependent information, the Result Producing Branches, and one that contains problem-independent, yet problem *domain* specific information, the library. The first subsystem needs a way to use the functionality in the library, a process we refer to as *linking*. Linking can take many forms: in a standard GP system with a pre-defined function set, it is simply the selection and insertion of functions in the trees (call by name); in our system, described below, it involves floating point *tags* that refer to localized functionality in the libraries (call by tag), as this provides a convenient way to resolve calls to non-existent tags, as discussed in section 4. Other approaches are imaginable. It seems a good choice to let the problem-dependent subsystem do multiple, relatively short runs, sampling from different sections of the library. The library is expected to evolve considerably slower, as information needs to be accumulated about the worth of its functionality in the face of changing requirements.

In contrast with the fixed-function set approach of standard GP, the elements in the library need to have some way of changing their functionality. In our approach this is done by using a similar syntax to ADFs for library functions, where each element in the library has a number of arguments, which can be used (and re-used) inside the function.

Finally, methods need to be devised to update the library in order to select that functionality that performs well, and to change functionality to try out new approaches. In this step the classical trade-off between exploration and exploitation is present, only in this case the trade-off does not only apply to a single run of the system, but to multiple runs, even runs done on new problems.

Currently, the concept of Run Transferable Libraries is mainly that, a concept. Below a concrete implementation is described that is used to tackle problems in logical problem domains.

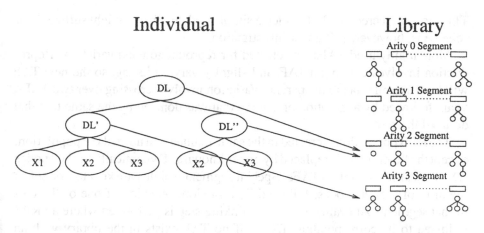

Figure 7-1. An overview of the Run Transferable Libraries system. Each DL-node consists of a floating point label which will be used to is used to look up the appropriate library segment, according to the arity of the function.

4.   Mnemosyne

An RTL-enabled system named *Mnemosyne*, a modified version of ECJ, has been written.

The library in Mnemosyne is divided into several segments, one for each legal arity. Each item in the library is referred to as a *Tag Addressable Function* (TAF) and is generated using a ramped half and half strategy, using the same type of syntax as ADFs, that is, the function set from the problem being tackled, and with parameters that will be bound at run time to **ARGS**. The actual problem inputs are not part of the terminal set for TAFs to promote re-usability not only in a particular run, but also across runs on a problem, and even across scaled up versions of the problem. Each TAF is tagged with a floating point number that is used by the main part of the trees, the *Result Producing Branch)*RPBs to reference it. If an RPB tries to reference a non-existent tag, then the TAF with the nearest tag in absolute terms is used.

The reference point in an RPB for a TAF is referred to as a *Dynamically Linked Node* (DL-node), and also contains a floating point number, known as its *label*. For example, in figure 7-1, each of DL and DL'' have their labels looked up in the arity 2 segment, while DL' is looked up in the arity 3 segment.

After each generation, and again after each run, the library can be updated, with TAFs being rewarded for their usage by the RPBs.

TAFs are assigned fitness based on their usage statistics, that is, the more a TAF is used by the RPB population, the fitter it will be. The reasoning behind this simple update strategy is that GP, operating on the RPBs, will assign more copies to better performing solutions. TAFs that are helpful in solving the problem will thus likely be sampled more often than those that are not helpful.

Thus, to assign credit to TAFs, such a simple update scheme might suffice. This scheme is, however, still under investigation.

More highly used TAFs are selected for reproduction and variation. Reproduction involves copying a TAF, and slightly varying its tag, so the new TAF will have a similar tag to the parent. Variation involves crossing over two TAFs, again followed by a mutation on the tag that was donated by the same tree that donated the root.

The RPB population is created in the same manner as a normal GP population, except the function set is replaced by nodes known as Dynamically Linked nodes (DL-nodes) which link to TAFs. Special segment weights are kept to first select the arity of the DL-nodes, followed by a random selection of one of the tags in that segment. At evaluation time, a linking step is performed where an RPB is linked to its corresponding TAFs. If no TAF exists in the library with an exact match, the closest one is chosen. As the initial population has exact tag matches, inexact matching can only happen after mutation of the tag values has occurred. This is an additional genetic operator. It permits the evolution of locality in the library, where it may be possible for TAFs with identical or similar tags to evolve in a locality. It is however still an open question what the worth of the tags and tag-mutation is in the system.

The rate at which a library is updated can have a direct effect on its usefulness. Libraries that aren't updated quickly enough may be slow to converge on a useful set of functions, while libraries that update too quickly may suffer from convergence on a less than optimal or even damaging set of functions. Currently, we use a simple moving average scheme on the usage statistics for driving the library updates, but future work will revisit this.. More details on the algorithm can be found in the appendix.

5.   Initial Results

Mnemosyne has been applied to several problems associated with ADFs, including the *Boolean even-n-parity* problems, the *Lawnmower* problem and the *Multiplexer* . In all cases, the average performance of the system increased as the number of library iterations increased. More importantly however, the performance on unseen, more difficult problems, increased as well, indicating that the library was able to find generalized functionality. As this chapter concentrates on the library activity for the even-n-parity and multiplexer problems we first present their performances.

In the Parity problems, initially examined in (Keijzer et al., 2004) the initial function set was {**AND, NAND, OR, NOR**} and the population size was 500, while in the Multiplexer problems, the function set was {**AND, OR, NOT**}, and the population size was also 500, except for the 11-multiplexer problems where it was 2500.

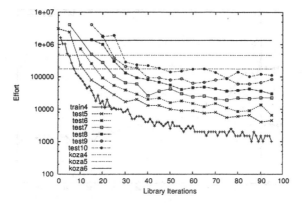

Figure 7-2. Number of individuals needed to be processed to obtain a solution with 99% probability on the parity problems using a library trained on parity 4, and applied to higher parity problems. As a benchmark, the results presented by Koza with ADFs are drawn as straight lines.

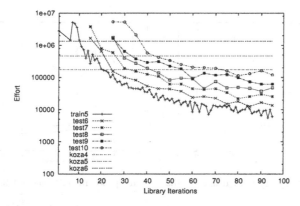

Figure 7-3. Number of individuals needed to be processed to obtain a solution with 99% probability on the parity problems using a library trained on parity 5.

Experiments

Figure 7-2 shows the results for training the library on the parity 4 and 5 problems and subsequently testing them on higher parities. Fifty independent libraries were trained on the lower parity problems for 95 iterations. The end-of-run libraries thus consisted of feedback obtained from 95 *dependent* runs, i.e., runs that use updated libraries. The system was also applied to the 6-multiplexer problem, and these results are shown in 7-4.

6. Bias in Function Sets

Function sets inherently contain bias. Although GP is capable of evolving required functions, as well as ignoring irrelevant functions, this information is

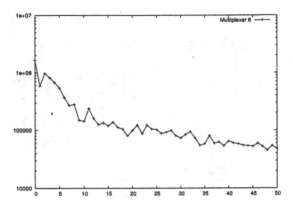

Figure 7-4. Number of individuals needed to be processed to obtain a solution with 99% probability on the 6-multiplexer problem using a population of 500. Koza reported 4,478,500 using a similar population.

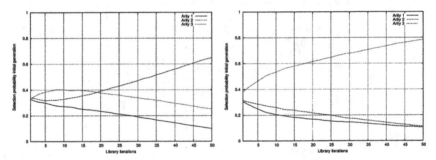

Figure 7-5. Library segment usage on the 4-parity problem, left, and on the 6-multiplexer problem, right.

typically lost for subsequent runs, each of which must make the same discoveries as all the others. The intention of RTLs is to evolve a standard library of functions that are useful for a particular problem domain, and thus bias function selection in favour of these. We tested to see if there were particular functions, or types of functions that were being favoured and, in each of the problems we examined, typically, one library segment dominated the population, typically being used around 60-80% of the time. Figure 7-5 shows how the segment usage varies over time. Note that on the parity 4 problem, initially the segment containing functions of arity 3 is sampled more often. Only when the optimal building blocks **XOR** or **EQ** of arity 2 are evolved does the arity 2 segment becomes more dominant. In both the multiplexer and the parity problem, the arity 1 segment shows a steady decline. Because this segment has only one non-trivial function to offer, **NOT**, this is not surprising.

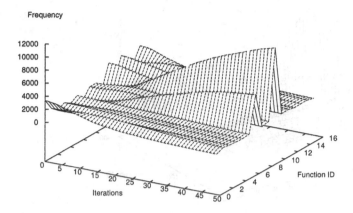

Figure 7-6. An overview of the evolution of the libraries for the Parity-4 problem.

Even Parity

The arity two segment was the most favoured in the parity problems. There are only 16 different functions of arity two, and by far the most common were **XOR** and **EQ**, two functions that are extremely helpful in solving the problem. Virtually all libraries that we trained converged to either one or both of these functions. Figure 7-6 shows the evolution of the TAFs over the lifetime of all the libraries used in these experiments. Each function in the possible set can be expressed as a decimal number from 0 to 15, where the decimal number is equivalent to the binary string output by that function given a standard enumeration of all possible inputs. For example, an **OR** outputs the string **1110**, where the 0 refers to the case of **0 OR 0** while an **AND** outputs the string **1000**. In Figure 7-6, the higher peak refers to the boolean function **EQ**, while the other refers to **XOR**. While both are increasing even at the end of the run, the curve for **EQ** is steeper. The difference is thought to be caused by the fact that the problem is *even* parity, where checking for equality instead of exclusive-or leads to shorter solutions. Once the library starts using **EQ** or the combination **XOR NOT** more often, the library starts to scale well, i.e., it has found the essential block of code that can solve this problem.

Multiplexer

Quite a different picture emerges for the Multiplexer problem, as illustrated in figure 7-7. In this case, the most favoured segment is the arity 3 segment. This segment can express 256 (2^8) different functions, although some of these

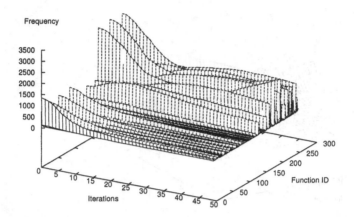

Figure 7-7. An overview of the evolution of the libraries for the 6-multiplexer problem. This indicates the *total* number of each function present across 50 different libraries.

are functionally identical. For example, the familiar **IF-THEN-ELSE** function can be expressed in six different ways, each of which is functionally identical. These other, less familiar forms, often use the second or third input as the test condition, and the order of the **THEN** and **ELSE** parts can also change. For example, functions such as **IF-ELSE-THEN** and **THEN-IF-ELSE** often appeared which, although unlikely to ever be used by a human programmer, offer the same functionality.

Figure 7-8 shows the distribution of the initial and final functions in the library. In this case, some functions are very common at the start, and not present in the final iteration, while two functions in particular are present in relatively high numbers at the end, both of which are forms of **IF-THEN-ELSE** . In all, ten functions made more than 1000 appearances in total in all the libraries. Somewhat surprisingly, only four of these were *bona fide* IFs, while the other six were all malformed **IF**s, similar in functionality to an IF, but with one set of inputs not giving the expected output. The other two genuine **IF**s, **THEN-IF-ELSE** and **ELSE-IF-THEN** made 970 and 643 appearances respectively. The total number of **IF-THEN-ELSE** variants that appeared was 7636, out of a total of 25000.

The three functions that are strongest in the first iteration of the library are 240, 204 and 170, which simply return **arg0**, **arg1** and **arg2** respectively. Their over-representation in the initial libraries is due to a combination of the initialisation strategy employed (ramped half-and-half) and the fact that so many boolean functions evaluate to the same thing. For example, **(arg0)** and **(arg0**

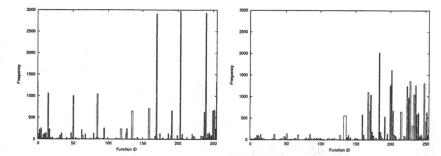

Figure 7-8. The initial (left) and final (right) distributions of functions in the arity 3 library for the Multiplexer problem.

AND arg0) are functionally equivalent. This is the language bias our system, in common with an ADF based system, has to overcome in order to solve the problem.

Although figures 7-7 and 7-8 shows that there is a lot less convergence in the libraries for the Multiplexer than with Parity, it should be stressed that this is an aggregate view across all libraries. Examining individual libraries, we observed that they tend to converge on one or two functions at the end of fifty iterations, usually with between another five and ten other functions represented in the library. Typically, one of the peaks was substantially higher than the other. Certain runs exhibited quite different behaviour from this, however. Figure 7-9 shows a case where a single function, represented by the decimal value 202, took over almost the entire library, occupying about 85% of the library. Function 202 corresponds to a standard IF-THEN-ELSE function. Another interesting run is shown in figure 7-10. In this case, the highest peak at the end of the iterations is actually substantially declining, indicating that, even at this late stage, the library is still evolving. A final example was the case in which two virtually identical (with a difference of one) peaks appeared, corresponding to functions 200 and 202 already encountered above. We don't show graph of these as the 3D nature of the graphs makes it impossible to see both curves at the same time. While the **(arg0 AND arg1) OR (arg1 AND arg2)** (200) maintains quite a healthy presence in the library from quite early on, the **IF-THEN-ELSE** (202) function only appears about halfway through the lifetime of the library, and rapidly begins to take over. The functional similarity between functions 200 and 202 can also be seen at the syntactic level, by noting that the standard **IF-THEN-ELSE** function can be written as (**(arg0 AND arg1) OR (NOT arg0 AND arg2)**).

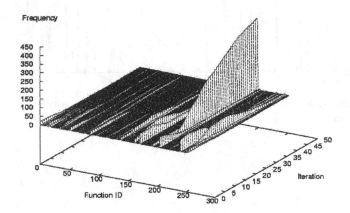

Figure 7-9.   A sample library run from the Multiplexer problem where one function dominates the library.

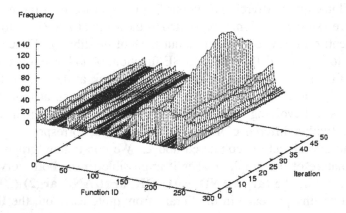

Figure 7-10.   A sample library run from the Multiplexer problem where the most common function is declines towards the end of the run

7. Subsequent Library Performance

Figures 7-2 and 7-3 show the performance of libraries trained on simpler versions of the parity problem and then applied to more difficult ones. Two sets of libraries, one trained on Parity 4 and the other on Parity 5, were applied to each parity problem up to Parity 10. These tests consisted of performing 50 independent runs of 100 iterations on each library and averaging the results. Both sets of Parity libraries performed extremely well, with even the library initially trained on Parity 4 being able to solve the Parity 10 problem with less computational effort than ADF based GP **on parity 4** after 50 iterations. Perhaps surprisingly, the library trained on Parity 5 took over 70 iterations on average to pass the same point. This level of performance wasn't entirely unexpected, however, when one considers the functions that appeared in the parity libraries, i.e. **EQ** and **XOR** as in figure 7-6. Both of these functions are known to be useful in all parity problems.

The libraries trained on 6-multiplexer were also successful when applied to the 11 multiplexer, but the performance of individual libraries varied considerably, as indicated in Figure 7-11. Here the mean performance (in hits) of the last 10 iterations for each library is plotted against the mean performance of 10 independent runs on the more difficult, 11-multiplexer problem.

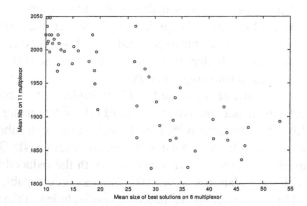

Figure 7-11. The performance of libraries trained on the 6-multiplexer problem, correlated with the average number size of the best performing expressions produced by the libraries on the 6-multiplexer problem. Performances are estimated using the last 10 iterations of the library on the training problem, and 10 independent runs for each library on the testing problem. Size is calculated only on the number of nodes in the RPB, thus ignoring size of the library elements.

Figure 7-11 shows how well these libraries did on the 11-multiplexer problem, and illustrates that the worst performer on 11-multiplexer also had the fewest mean hits on the 6-multiplexer, and, similarly, that the best had the highest mean hits. The correlation between performances is however weak with a value of $r = 0.43$. Also shown in figure 7-11 is how well libraries performed on 11-multiplexer given the average size of their best solutions on the 6-multiplexer. In this case there is a strong correlation ($r = -0.84$): the larger the expressions that are induced on the training problem, the lower their performance on the testing problem. The size of the expression on the training problem was however **not** indicative for their performance on the training problem, just the larger testing problem. The runs converging on the malformed **IF**s did almost equally well on the 6-multiplexer. This finding indicates that the size of proposed solutions during training might be a good indicator for the level of modularization that is achieved inside the library. This is to be expected as the optimality of the **IF-THEN-ELSE** function lies in its ability to be used in a minimal sized solution.

There are a number of reasons why the multiplexer libraries didn't enjoy the degree of convergence as the parity ones. Firstly, the important function for the multiplexer is an arity 3 function, and there are 256 possible functions in this set, compared to only 16 for arity 2 functions. Secondly, there is redundancy in this set, as there are six different ways to represent the crucial **IF** functionality. Thirdly, there is a substantial step up in difficulty when moving from a 6-multiplexer to an 11-multiplexer, and libraries with malformed **IF**s can still produce perfectly fit individuals for the simpler problem, but fail with the more difficult one.

As discussed in section 3, when updating the library, one is faced with a trade off between exploration and exploitation. However, these results suggest that libraries which will not be able to generalise well will produce, on average, larger and less fit individuals than those that will generalise well, and can thus be identified before compromising a library.

To compare the results obtained on the 11-multiplexer, two control experiments were performed: one involved a standard GP system using the function set {**AND,OR,NOT**} (the same as the initial function set for the library system), and one with a standard GP system using the function set {**AND,OR,NOT,IF**} , thus including the all-important **IF** function. With the reduced function set, over 50 runs with a population size of 2500, GP was only capable of finding a solution *once*. However, once the **IF** function was included in the function set, the success rate of GP rises to 76% (out of 100 runs), considerably higher than the 37% that was obtained using the library approach. Closer inspection of the library results reveals that 16 out of the 50 libraries did not produce a solution at all, while 12 libraries scored higher than 80% (over 10 independent runs). These libraries can all be identified by the size of the solutions they produced on the training set. It is, however, important to realize that the inclusion of the **IF** function in the function set trivializes the problem and presupposes that the user can select function sets for problems in an optimal or near optimal way. What is attempted to show here is that this process might be automatable, and indications are given to this effect. The fact that the system was able to

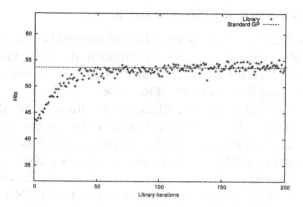

Figure 7-12. Iterations versus hits for the Mnemosyne system on random problems. As a comparison, standard GP performance is depicted as well.

bootstrap itself out of the difficult situation where GP was not able to perform well is indicative of this.

8. Debiasing Function Sets

As a final experiment, 40 libraries were trained for 200 iterations on random problems of 6 input variables, using an initial function set of {**AND,OR,NAND,NOR**}. For each iteration, for each library, a new random problem was constructed. As there is not much regularity to be found in such a problem, the best a library can hope to achieve is to induce some general set of functionality which works reasonably well across many problems. For comparison purposes 500 runs of a standard genetic programming system using the same initial function set were performed. Figure 7-12 shows the mean performance of the 40 libraries over the iterations.

Compared with a standard genetic programming system, the results on the first iterations are disappointing. It seems that again the initialization of the library is very biased toward very unhelpful functions. However, after a number of iterations, the RTL-based system is able to overcome this initial bias and induces a set of functionality that is comparable with the standard genetic programming setup. Although visually there seems to be a small slope upwards from iteration 50 to 200, giving a small indication that the library based method keeps on improving, this difference in comparison with the standard GP system is however not statistically significant.

Given our experience in in the multiplexer problem with badly initialized libraries, the 40 libraries that were induced on random problems for this section might very well be a better starting point than the ramped-half-and-half initialization procedure employed in the multiplexer and parity problems.

9.   Conclusions and future work

This chapter described the notion of Run Transferable Libraries, and showed how useful information can be passed from run to run in GP through an RTL. Furthermore, an RTL trained on a simpler version of a problem and can then be subsequently applied to a more difficult one.

Analysis of the contents and evolution of the libraries has shown that the libraries almost invariably converge to just one or two functions. In the case of the libraries trained on parity problems, all of them were dominated by **EQ** and **XOR**, two functions well known to be useful in parity problems.

The multiplexer library results were not so clear cut. The crucial function required for a multiplexer library to scale properly is **IF-THEN-ELSE** or one of its variants. The fact that there are six different forms of this function means that a dramatic convergence like that experienced with the parity libraries is unlikely to be repeated there. One surprising result, however, was the appearance and thriving of malformed **IF**s, functions which differ very slightly at a functional level. While these malformed functions weren't deleterious enough to cause a library to fail, they did make scaling the library to a more difficult problem a more demanding task, forcing the population to learn the idiosyncrasies of the malformed functions. Fortunately, there are indications that the size of the solutions induced on a library can be predictive for the scalability of the library.

The system we used for our experiments, *Mnemosyne*, is our first implementation of RTLs. As indicated in section 3, there is ample scope for research in this area, and many design decisions that were made for Mnemosyne were done so on the basis of simplicity to enable us to test the concept. Strategies such as how the library should be updated have not yet been examined.

As observed in section 7, it is possible for populations to thrive with suboptimal functions, only to fail when applied to more difficult problems. The results there suggest that the level of influence an individual run should have on a library should be related in some way to the quality of the final individuals produced. An estimate of the quality of an individual can be arrived at by examining the size of an individual relative to other, *best-of-run* individuals.

Appendix: The Mnemosyne Algorithm

Data : n segments, each with terminal set T and function set F;
n segment weights s;
m elements per segment;
functions $f_{n \times m}$, tag values $t_{n \times m}$ and usage weights $w_{n \times m}$;
moving average window $v \leftarrow 10$;

for *each segment i* **do**

  set segment weights: $s_i \leftarrow 1/\#\text{segments}$;

  for *each function j* **do**

    init function f_{ij} (ramped-half-and-half) using T_i and F_i;

    select tag value: $t_{ij} \leftarrow N(0,1)$;

    set usage weight: $w_{ij} \leftarrow 0$;

  end

end

for *each iteration* **do**

  set $u_{ij} \leftarrow 0$ for all functions i in all segments j;

  for *each individual in population* **do**

    Initialise using ramped-half-and-half

    use segment weights s to determine arity, uniform selection of functions;

  end

  for *each generation* **do**

    for *each individual* **do**

      relink individual to library;

      update for linked function f_{ij}:

      $u_{ij} \leftarrow u_{ij} + 1/\text{size(individual)}$;

      evaluate individual for fitness;

    end

    create new generation using reproduction, subtree crossover and tag mutation ;

  end

  $s_i \leftarrow (s_i * (v-1) + \sum_j u_{ij} / \sum_{kl} u_{kl})/v$;

  $w_{ij} \leftarrow (w_{ij} * (v-1) + u_{ij} / \sum_k u_{ik})/v$;

  for *each i, j for which $w_{ij} > 2\bar{w}_i$* **do**

    select replacement k for which w_{ik} is lowest;

    if *Reproduce (50%)* **then**

      $f_{ik} \leftarrow f_{ij}$;

    else

      select r uniformly from segment;

      $f_{ik} \leftarrow crossover(f_{ij}, f_{ir})$;

    end

    mutate tag value: $t_{ik} \leftarrow t_{ij} + N(0,1)$;

    $w_{ik} \leftarrow (w_{ij} + w_{ik})/2$;

    $w_{ij} \leftarrow w_{ik}$;

  end

end

References

Angeline, P. J. and Pollack, J. B. (1992). The evolutionary induction of subroutines. In *Proceedings of the Fourteenth Annual Conference of the Cognitive Science Society*, Bloomington, Indiana, USA. Lawrence Erlbaum.

Howard, Daniel (2003). Modularization by multi-run frequency driven subtree encapsulation. In Riolo, Rick L. and Worzel, Bill, editors, *Genetic Programming Theory and Practice*, chapter 10, pages 155–172. Kluwer.

Keijzer, Maarten, Ryan, Conor, and Cattolico, Mike (2004). Run transferable libraries — learning functional bias in problem domains. In Banzhaf, Wolfgang, Daida, Jason, Eiben, Agoston E., Garzon, Max H., Honavar, Vasant, Jakiela, Mark, and Smith, Robert E., editors, *Proceedings of the Genetic and Evolutionary Computation Conference*. Springer Verlag.

Koza, John R. (1990). Genetic programming: A paradigm for genetically breeding populations of computer programs to solve problems. Technical Report STAN-CS-90-1314, Computer Science Department, Stanford University.

Koza, John R. (1994). *Genetic Programming II: Automatic Discovery of Reusable Programs*. MIT Press, Cambridge Massachusetts.

Koza, John R. and Rice, James P. (1991). Genetic generation of both the weights and architecture for a neural network. In *Proceedings of nternational Joint Conference on Neural Networks*, pages 397–404. IEEE Press.

Roberts, Simon C., Howard, Daniel, and Koza, John R. (2001). Evolving modules in genetic programming by subtree encapsulation. In Miller, Julian F., Tomassini, Marco, Lanzi, Pier Luca, Ryan, Conor, Tettamanzi, Andrea G. B., and Langdon, William B., editors, *Genetic Programming, Proceedings of EuroGP'2001*, volume 2038 of *LNCS*, pages 160–175, Lake Como, Italy. Springer-Verlag.

Rosca, Justinian P. and Ballard, Dana H. (1994). Hierarchical self-organization in genetic programming. In *Proceedings of the Eleventh International Conference on Machine Learning*. Morgan Kaufmann.

Chapter 8

TOWARD AUTOMATED DESIGN OF INDUSTRIAL-STRENGTH ANALOG CIRCUITS BY MEANS OF GENETIC PROGRAMMING

John R. Koza[1], Lee W. Jones[2], Martin A. Keane[3,] Matthew J. Streeter[4] and Sameer H. Al-Sakran[2]

[1]Stanford University, Stanford, California; [2]Genetic Programming Inc., Mountain View, California; [3]Econometrics Inc., Chicago, Illinois; [4]Carnegie Mellon University, Pittsburgh, Pennsylvania.

Abstract: It has been previously established that genetic programming can be used as an automated invention machine to synthesize designs for complex structures. In particular, genetic programming has automatically synthesized structures that infringe, improve upon, or duplicate the functionality of 21 previously patented inventions (including six 21st-century patented analog electrical circuits) and has also generated two patentable new inventions (controllers). There are seven promising factors suggesting that these previous results can be extended to deliver industrial-strength automated design of analog circuits, but two countervailing factors. This chapter explores the question of whether the seven promising factors can overcome the two countervailing factors by reviewing progress on an ongoing project in which we are employing genetic programming to synthesize an amplifier circuit. The work involves a multiobjective fitness measure consisting of 16 different elements measured by five different test fixtures. The chapter describes five ways of using general domain knowledge applicable to all analog circuits, two ways for employing problem-specific knowledge, four ways of improving on previously published genetic programming techniques, and four ways of grappling with the multi-objective fitness measures associated with real-world design problems.

Key words: Automated design, automated circuit synthesis, analog circuits, amplifier, evolvable hardware, developmental process, genetic programming

1.   INTRODUCTION

Genetic programming is an automatic method for solving problems. It is an extension of the genetic algorithm (Holland 1975). Genetic programming starts from a high-level statement of the requirements of a problem and attempts to automatically create a computer program that solves the problem. Specifically, genetic programming starts with a primordial ooze of thousands of randomly created computer programs and uses the Darwinian principle of natural selection (fitness-based selection); analogs of recombination (crossover), mutation, gene duplication, gene deletion; and certain mechanisms of developmental biology to progressively breed an improved population over a series of generations (Koza 1992, Koza 1994; Koza, Bennett, Andre, and Keane 1999; Koza, Keane, Streeter, Mydlowec, Yu, and Lanza 2003; Banzhaf, Nordin, Keller, and Francone 1998; Langdon and Poli 2002).

Genetic programming can be used as an automated invention machine to synthesize designs for complex structures. In particular, genetic programming has automatically synthesized complex structures that infringe, improve upon or duplicate in a novel way the functionality of 21 previously patented inventions (e.g., analog electrical circuits, controllers, and mathematical algorithms), including six post-2000 patented inventions. These 21 patented inventions are listed in Table 8.14.1 of (Koza, Streeter, and Keane 2003). In addition, genetic programming has generated two patentable new inventions (both controllers) for which patent applications are currently pending (Keane, Koza, and Streeter 2002). Genetic programming has also generated numerous additional human-competitive results involving the automated design of quantum computing circuits (Spector 2004) and antennae (Lohn, Hornby, and Linden 2004). Genetic programming has generated results involving the automated design of networks of chemical reactions and metabolic networks (Koza, Mydlowec, Lanza, Yu, and Keane 2001) and genetic networks (Lanza, Mydlowec, and Koza 2000).

The six 21st-century patented inventions that were re-created by genetic programming were analog electrical circuits. Automatic synthesis of analog circuits from high-level specifications has long been recognized as a challenging problem. As Aaserud and Nielsen (1995) noted:

> "[M]ost ... analog circuits are still handcrafted by the experts or so-called 'zahs' of analog design. The design process is characterized by a combination of experience and intuition and requires a thorough knowledge of the process characteristics and the detailed specifications of the actual product.

> "Analog circuit design is known to be a knowledge-intensive, multiphase, iterative task, which usually stretches over a significant period of time and is performed by designers with a large portfolio of skills. It is therefore considered by many to be a form of art rather than a science."

And, as Balkir, Dundar, and Ogrenci (2003) stated:

> "The major reason underlying this lack of analog design automation tools has been the difficulty of the problem, in our opinion. Design in the analog domain requires creativity because of the large number of free parameters and the sometimes obscure interactions between them. ... Thus, analog design has remained more of an 'art' than a 'science.' "

There are seven promising factors suggesting that the previous results can be extended to deliver industrial-strength automated design of analog circuits and there are two countervailing factors that impede progress.

One promising factor is the unusually high success rate of previous work. Multiple runs of a probabilistic algorithm are typically necessary to solve a non-trivial problem. However, all 11 runs involving the six post-2000 patented circuits (ignoring partial runs used during debugging) yielded a satisfactory solution. This high rate suggests that we are currently nowhere near the limit of the capability of existing techniques.

A second promising factor (discussed in section 2) is that genetic programming has historically demonstrated the ability to yield progressively more substantial results in synchrony with the relentless increase in computer power tracked by Moore's law (thereby suggesting that evermore complex problems can be solved as increased computer power becomes available).

A third promising factor (discussed in section 3) is that our previous work (and most other previous work) involving the automated synthesis of circuits intentionally ignored many pieces of elementary general domain knowledge about analog circuits. For example, none of our previous runs culled egregiously flawed circuits, such as those drawing enormous amounts of current or those that lacked a connection to the circuit's incoming signal, output port, or power supplies. Instead, our previous work approached each problem with a relatively "clean hands" orientation—using as little human-supplied domain knowledge about electrical circuits as possible. Although this "clean hands" orientation highlighted the ability of genetic programming to produce human-competitive results in a "clean hands" setting, this orientation is entirely irrelevant to a practicing engineer interested in designing real-world circuits.

A fourth promising factor (discussed in section 4) is that our previous work (and most other previous work) intentionally ignored opportunities to employ problem-specific knowledge about the to-be-designed circuit. For example, the starting point for circuit development in our previous runs usually consisted merely of a single modifiable wire. Genetic programming was then expected to automatically create the entire circuit from scratch. However, a practicing engineer does not start each new assignment from first principles. Instead, the starting point for real-world design typically incorporates a core substructure that is known to provide a good head start.

A fifth promising factor (also discussed in section 4) is that the genetic programming techniques used in our previous work to produce the six post-2000 patented circuits were intentionally rigidly uniform. This uniformity had the advantage of emphasizing the ability of genetic programming to produce human-competitive results in a relatively "clean hands" setting. For example, we did not use automatically defined functions (subroutines) even on problems with manifest parallelism, regularity, symmetry, and modularity. However, a practicing engineer does not "reinvent the wheel" on each occasion requiring an already known solution to a sub-problem.

A sixth promising factor (discussed in section 5) is that current techniques used for circuit synthesis can be improved by applying various aspects of the theory of genetic algorithms and genetic programming. Many of the current techniques go back to early work on automated circuit synthesis and have not been critically reexamined since then.

A seventh promising factor is that considerable work has been done in recent years to accelerate the convergence characteristics and general efficiency of circuit simulators. For example, we used a version of the SPICE3 simulator (Quarles, Newton, Pederson, and Sangiovanni-Vincentelli 1994) that we modified in various ways (as described in Koza, Bennett, Andre, and Keane 1999). Today, there are numerous commercially available simulators that are considerably faster (e.g., up to 10 times faster).

There are, however, at least two countervailing factors that impede progress toward industrial-strength automated design of analog circuits.

The first countervailing factor (discussed in section 6) concerns the multi-objective fitness measures that are typically associated with industrial-strength problems. The fitness measures used in previously published examples of the synthesis of analog circuits by means of genetic programming (and genetic algorithms) typically consist of only a few different elements (rarely as many as four). In contrast, the data sheets used to specify commercial circuits typically contain a dozen or more different performance requirements. It is difficult to quantify the tradeoff between disparate elements of a fitness measure. Moreover, as the number of disparate elements in a fitness measure increases, the strategy for combining the various ("apples and oranges") elements of the fitness measure usually becomes vexatious. If, for example, gain, bias, and distortion (three characteristics that are relevant to amplifier design) are naively assigned equal weight in a fitness measure, an unadorned wire will immediately achieve a very good score (because a wire introduces no distortion and no bias to an incoming circuit). What's worse, almost any single modification applied to this wire will be highly deleterious—thereby creating a local optimum from which escape is difficult. The search for an amplifier may easily become trapped in an area of the search space containing distortion-free and bias-free circuits that deliver no amplification at all. Thus, the handling of the type of multi-objective fitness measures associated with industrial-strength design problems is a major issue.

The second countervailing factor arises from the need to evaluate candidate circuits at the "corners" of various performance envelopes. For example, circuit behavior depends on temperature. A real-world circuit might be required to operate correctly over a range between, say, –40° C and +105° C, not merely at room temperature (27° C). Separate simulations (or, if reconfigurable hardware is being used, separate test scenarios with different ambient temperatures) are required to measure the circuit's performance at each corner of the temperature envelope. Each additional simulation multiplies the required computer time by a factor of two (if only the two extreme values are considered), three (if the nominal value and two extremes are considered), or more (if more values are considered because of non-linear behavior). Similarly, a real-world circuit will be expected to operate correctly in the face of variation in the circuit's power supply (e.g., when the battery or other power supply is delivering, say, 90% or 110% of its nominal voltage). Again, separate simulations are required to measure the circuit's performance at each voltage corner. In addition, a real-world circuit will be expected to operate correctly in the face of deviations between the behavior of an actual manufactured component and the component's "model" performance. For example, separate measurements may be required for a entire circuit's "fast," "typical," and "slow" behavior or when a particular component is 75% or 125% of its nominal value. Circuits may also be expected to operate correctly in the face of variations in load, input, or other characteristics.

Thus, the answer to the question as to whether genetic programming can deliver industrial-strength automated design of analog electrical circuits depends on whether the seven promising factors overcome the two countervailing factors.

The remainder of this chapter reports on progress on an ongoing project in which we employed genetic programming to automatically synthesize both the topology and sizing of an amplifier circuit.

2.　ABILITY OF GENETIC PROGRAMMING TO PROFITABLY EXPLOIT INCREASED COMPUTER POWER

Genetic programming generally requires significant computational resources to solve non-trivial problems. Fortunately, the computer time necessary to achieve human-competitive results has become increasingly available in recent years because (1) the speed of commercially available single computers continues to double approximately every 18 months in accordance with Moore's law, (2) genetic programming is amenable to efficient parallelization, and (3) Beowulf-style parallel cluster computer systems can be assembled at relatively low cost.

As shown in Table 8-1, GP has historically demonstrated the ability to yield progressively more substantial results, given the increased computer power tracked by Moore's law. Column 1 lists the five computer systems used to produce our group's reported work on GP in the 15-year period between 1987 and 2002. Column 4 shows the speed-up of each system over the system shown in the previous row of the table. Column 7 shows the number of human-competitive results generated by each computer system.

Table 8-1. Human-competitive results produced by GP with five computer systems.

System	Period	Petacycles per day	Speed-up over first system	Used for work in book	Human-competitive results
Texas Instruments LISP machine	1987–1994	0.002	1 (base)	*Genetic Programming I* and *II*	0
64-node Transtech transputer machine	1994–1997	0.02	9	A few problems in *Genetic Programming III*	2
64-node Parsytec machine	1995–2000	0.44	204	Most problems in *Genetic Programming III*	12
70-node Alpha machine	1999–2001	3.2	1,481	8 of problems in *Genetic Programming IV*	2
1,000-node Pentium II machine	2000–2002	30.0	13,900	28 of the problems in *Genetic Programming IV*	12

The first entry in Table 8-1 is a serial computer and the next four entries are parallel computer systems. The presence of four increasingly powerful parallel computer systems reflects the fact that genetic programming has successfully taken advantage of the increased computational power available by means of parallel processing.

Table 8-1 shows the following:

- There is an order-of-magnitude speed-up (column 3) between each successive computer system in the table. Note that, according to Moore's law, exponential increases in computer power correspond approximately to constant periods of time.

- There is a 13,900-to-1 speed-up (column 4) between the fastest and most recent machine (the 1,000-node parallel computer system) and the slowest and earliest machine (the serial LISP machine).

- The slower early machines generated few or no human-competitive results, whereas the faster more recent machines have generated numerous human-competitive results.

Four successive order-of-magnitude increases in computer power are explicitly shown in Table 8-1. An additional order-of-magnitude increase was achieved by making extraordinarily long runs on the largest machine in the table (the 1,000-node Pentium® II parallel machine). The length of the run that produced the genetically evolved controller for which a patent application is currently pending (Keane, Koza, and Streeter 2002) was 28.8 days—almost an order-of-magnitude increase over the 3.4-day average for runs that our group has made in recent years. If this final 9.3-to-1 increase is counted as an additional speed-up, the overall speed-up is 130,660-to-1.

Table 8-2 is organized around the five just-explained order-of-magnitude increases in the expenditure of computing power. Column 4 of this table characterizes the qualitative nature of the results produced by genetic programming. This table shows the progression of qualitatively more substantial results produced by genetic programming in terms of five order-of-magnitude increases in the expenditure of computational resources.

The order-of-magnitude increases in computer power shown in Table 8-2 correspond closely (albeit not perfectly) with the following progression of qualitatively more substantial results produced by genetic programming:

- toy problems,

- human-competitive results not related to patented inventions,

- 20th-century patented inventions,

- 21st-century patented inventions, and

- patentable new inventions.

The progression in Table 8-2 demonstrates that genetic programming is able to take advantage of the exponentially increasing computational power tracked by iterations of Moore's law.

Table 8-2. Progression of qualitatively more substantial results produced by genetic programming in relation to five order-of-magnitude increases in computational power.

System	Period	Speed-up over previous	Qualitative nature of the results produced by genetic programming
Texas Instruments LISP machine	1987–1994	1 (base)	• Toy problems of the 1980s and early 1990s from the fields of artificial intelligence and machine learning
64-node Transtech transputer	1994–1997	9	•Two human-competitive results involving one-dimensional discrete data (not patent-related)
64-node Parsytec machine	1995–2000	22	• One human-competitive result involving two-dimensional discrete data • Numerous human-competitive results involving continuous signals analysed in the frequency domain • Numerous human-competitive results involving 20th-century patented inventions
70-node Alpha machine	1999–2001	7.3	• One human-competitive result involving continuous signals analysed in the time domain • Circuit synthesis extended from topology and sizing to include routing and placement (layout)
1,000-node Pentium II machine	2000–2002	9.4	• Numerous human-competitive results involving continuous signals analysed in the time domain • Numerous general solutions to problems in the form of parameterized topologies • Six human-competitive results duplicating the functionality of 21st-century patented inventions
4-week runs of 1,000-node Pentium II parallel machine	2002	9.3	• Generation of two patentable new inventions

3. EXPLOITING GENERAL KNOWLEDGE ABOUT CIRCUITS

The previously reported work involving the six 21st-century patented circuits intentionally did not take advantage of even the most elementary domain knowledge applicable to analog circuits. As part of our ongoing project of synthesizing commercially marketed amplifier circuits by means of genetic programming, we have incorporated general domain knowledge about circuits into our work in several ways.

First, in previously reported work, the initial population was created entirely at random and new individuals were created during the run using the usual problem-independent probabilistic genetic operations (e.g., crossover, mutation). Many individuals in these populations inevitably represent unrealistic or impractical electrical circuits. One particularly egregious characteristic of some circuits is that the circuit fails to make a connection to all input signals, all output signals, and all necessary sources of power (e.g., the positive power supply and the negative power supply). Circuits that do not satisfy these threshold requirements are now being culled from the population (by severe penalization). The removal of such egregiously flawed circuits not only conserves computational resources, but also increases the amount of useful genetic diversity of the population (thereby further accelerating the evolutionary process).

Second, another egregious characteristic of some circuits in unrestricted runs is that the circuit draws preposterously large amounts of current. In order to cull circuits of this type from the population, each circuit is examined for the current drawn by the circuit's positive power supply and negative power supply. Circuits that draw excessive current are now being culled from the population.

Third, the components that are inserted into a developing circuit need not be as primitive as a single transistor, resistor, or capacitor. Instead, component-creating functions can be defined to insert frequently occurring combinations of components that are known to be useful in practical circuitry. Examples include current mirrors, voltage gain stages, Darlington emitter-follower sections, and cascodes. Graeb, Zizala, Eckmueller, and Antreich (2001) identified (for a purpose entirely unrelated to evolutionary computation) a promising set of frequently occurring combinations of transistors that are known to be useful in a broad range of analog circuits. For the present work, we have implemented circuit-constructing functions that insert a current mirror, two types of voltage references, a loaded current mirror, and a level shifter from among these two-transistor groups. For certain problems, the set of primitives can be expanded to include higher-level entities, such as filters, amplifiers, and phase-locked loops.

Fourth, minimization of a circuit's total area is of great practical importance because the cost of manufacturing a chip depends directly on its size (because a given wafer contains more copies of a smaller chip and because a particular flaw on a wafer has a less deleterious effect on the wafer's yield percentage when the flawed chip is smaller). Resistors are often implemented on a silicon chip by laying down a serpentine chain of small patches of resistive material. Capacitors are often created by laying down two areas of conductive material. Thus, in many situations, a circuit's overall size is heavily influenced by the number of its resistors and capacitors. Our previous work on circuit synthesis typically permitted the creation of resistor and capacitor values over a very wide range (e.g., 10 orders of magnitude). Practical work requires choices of component values that lie in a particular range of only about three orders of magnitude.

Fifth, there are additional general principles of circuit design that might also be brought to bear on problems of circuit synthesis. For example, (Sripramong and Toumazou 2002) have combined current-flow analysis (and other improvements) into runs of genetic programming for the purpose of automatically synthesizing CMOS amplifiers.

4.   EXPLOITING PROBLEM-SPECIFIC KNOWLEDGE

The previously reported work involving the six 21st-century patented circuits intentionally did not take advantage of opportunities to use knowledge about the specific to-be-designed circuit. We have implemented such elementary knowledge in three areas as part of our ongoing project of synthesizing commercially marketed amplifier circuits by means of GP.

First, there are basic substructures that are known by practicing analog engineers to be useful for particular types of circuits. Just as an engineer would begin a design using these known substructures, every individual in a run can be hard-wired with a substructure of known utility, thereby relieving genetic programming of the need to "reinvent the wheel."

As an example, the LM124 amplifier is a well-known commercial amplifier that delivers 100 dB of gain. This circuit (described in detail by the National Semiconductor data sheet available on the web at http://www.national.com/pf/LM/LM124.html) has 13 transistors, two resistors, one capacitor, and four current sources. The LM124 has two inputs (an inverting input and non-inverting input) and one output. The circuit connects to a single +5 volt power source and ground. A differential pair that receives the inverting input and non-inverting input (shown in Figure 8-1) is a useful first stage in designing an amplifier with the characteristics of the LM124. In the figure, there are three construction-continuing subtrees (CCS1, CCS2, and CCS3) corresponding to the three output ports of the differential pair. After hard-wiring the differential pair, the evolutionary process is left with the task of automatically designing a satisfactory three-input sub-circuit that eventually connects to the overall circuit's single output port.

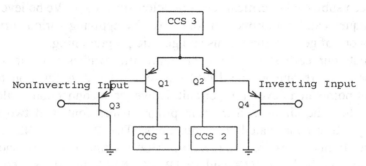

Figure 8-1. Substructure consisting of hard-wired differential pair.

The forced insertion of a substructure of known utility can be implemented in two different ways. In one approach, the desired substructure can be hard-wired into the embryo, thereby starting the developmental process off with the desired substructure (Koza, Bennett, Andre, and Keane 1999, section 52.2). In the second approach, when the initial population (generation 0) is created, an S-sub-expression that develops into the desired hard-wired structure can be hard-wired into the top of every program tree. In later generations, the functions and terminals in this fixed S-expression may either be immunized from modification by the genetic operations or, if desired, they may be permitted to change.

Second, previous work involving the six post-2000 patented circuits was intentionally uniform in terms of genetic programming technique in order to emphasize the ability of genetic programming to produce human-competitive results in a relatively "clean hands" setting. Thus, for example, even when a problem had manifest parallelism, regularity, symmetry, and modularity, we intentionally did not permit the use of automatically defined functions (subroutines). The benefits of using automatically defined functions in problems having parallelism, regularity, symmetry, and modularity are considerable (Koza 1990, Koza and Rice 1991, Koza 1992, Koza 1994). A practicing engineer would recognize that reuse is pervasive in at least two of the six post-2000 patented circuits (namely the mixed analog-digital integrated circuit for variable capacitance and the low-voltage high-current transistor circuit for testing a voltage source) and would instinctively take advantage of opportunities to reuse substructures.

5.   IMPROVING   TECHNIQUES   OF   GENETIC PROGRAMMING

Many of the current techniques for circuit synthesis by means of genetic programming originate with early work starting in 1995 (Koza, Bennett, Andre and Keane 1996). Many of these initially successful techniques have not been subjected to critical reexamination since then. We believe that these techniques can be improved in four ways by applying various principles of the theory of genetic algorithms and genetic programming.

First, our earliest work on the automatic synthesis of circuits (Koza, Bennett, Andre and Keane 1996) employed the VIA function to connect distant points in a developing circuit. However, a connection could be made only when the circuit-constructing program tree contained two (or more) appropriately coordinated VIA functions. The PAIR_CONNECT function (Koza, Bennett, Andre, and Keane 1999) eliminated this shortcoming. Nonetheless, both the VIA and PAIR_CONNECT functions were brittle in the sense that they were easily disrupted when crossover was performed on the circuit-constructing program trees. The premise behind the crossover operation in genetic programming (and the genetic algorithm) is that an individual with relatively high fitness is likely to contain some local substructures which, when recombined, will (at least some of the time) create offspring with even higher fitness. In genetic programming, the conventional crossover operation recombines a subtree from one parent's program tree with a subtree from the second parent. Over many generations, functions and terminals that are close together in a program tree tend to be preferentially preserved by crossover. In particular, smaller subtrees are preserved to a greater degree than larger ones. Moreover, when representing circuits by program trees containing the circuit-constructing (developmental) functions that we generally use, a subtree tends to represent a local area in the fully developed circuit. However, the VIA and PAIR_CONNECT functions are highly context-dependent. They have the disadvantage that when a subtree of one circuit-constructing program tree is swapped with a subtree of another circuit-constructing program tree, the connectivity of a point within both the crossover fragment and a point within the remainder is, almost always, dramatically altered in a highly disruptive way. That is, crossover usually significantly disrupts the nature of the preexisting connections formed by the VIA and PAIR_CONNECT functions within a local area of the developing circuit. However, it is precisely these local structures that may have contributed to the individual's comparatively high fitness and to the individual's being selected to participate in the genetic operation in the first place. To the extent that crossover almost always dramatically alters the characteristics of the swapped genetic material, it acquires the characteristics of the mutation operation. This, in turn, means that the problem-solving effectiveness of the crossover operation is reduced to the lesser level delivered by the mutation operation.

The issues caused by the excessive disruption of local substructures by the VIA and PAIR_CONNECT functions were addressed in later work (Koza, Keane, Streeter, Mydlowec, Yu, and Lanza 2003, section 10.1.1) by introducing a two-argument NODE function to connect two or more points in the developing circuit. However, recent experience with various problems has indicated that, in practice, the NODE function is overly restrictive in that it limits connections to a particular subtree. We have addressed this now-recognized deficiency in two ways. We have replaced the NODE function with a NODE_INCREASED_SCOPE function that permits connectivity within larger subtrees (one level higher in the program trees, in our current implementation). In addition, we have restored the original VIA function to the function set in order to again allow arbitrarily distant connections. We view these recent changes as an improvement, but not a complete solution.

Second, in our previous work on the automatic synthesis of circuits, a two-leaded component (e.g., resistor, capacitor) remained modifiable after insertion into the developing circuit whereas this was not the case for a component with three leads (e.g., a transistor) or one with more than three leads. We removed this asymmetric treatment of component-creating functions so that all inserted component are non-modifiable after insertion.

Third, to increase the variety of junctions, the three-argument Y division function was added to the repertoire of topology-modifying functions. This function had previously been used in some earlier work (Koza, Bennett, Andre, and Keane 1999, section 41.2.4).

Fourth, when the topology-modifying series division function is performed on a resistor, the resulting new resistor is assigned the same component value as the original resistor, thereby doubling the total resistance after the topology-modifying function is executed. When a parallel division function is performed on a resistor, the new resistor is also assigned the same component value as the original resistor, thereby halving the total resistance after the topology-modifying function is executed. The same thing happens for capacitors, except that a series division halves the total capacitance and a parallel division doubles the total capacitance. An argument can be made that the topology-modifying functions that are part of the overall circuit-constructing program tree (i.e., part of the developmental process) should concentrate exclusively on their overtly stated purpose of modifying topology so that the two components resulting from the series or parallel division are each assigned values so that the new topological composition has the same overall behavior as the original single component.

Thus, for example, the two resistors produced by a series division would each have half the resistance of the original single resistor.

6.   GRAPPLING   WITH   A   MULTI-OBJECTIVE FITNESS MEASURE

The fitness measures used in previously published examples of the automated synthesis of analog circuits by means of genetic programming and genetic algorithms have usually consisted of only a few elements (rarely as many as four). For example, only three elements (gain, bias, and distortion) were incorporated into the fitness measure employed to synthesize the amplifier in chapter 45 of Koza, Bennett, Andre, and Keane 1999 and only four elements (gain, bias, distortion, and the area of the bounding rectangle after placement and routing) were considered in chapter 5 of Koza, Keane, Streeter, Mydlowec, Yu, and Lanza 2003. In contrast, the data sheets for commercial circuits typically specify a circuit's performance for well over a dozen characteristics. As the number of disparate elements in a fitness measure increases, it becomes increasingly difficult to combine the elements in a way that enables the fitness measure to navigate a complex search space.

Moreover, circuit behavior is typically ascertained by mounting it into a test fixture. The test fixture feeds external input(s) into the circuit and has probe points for evaluating the circuit's output(s). The test fixture often has a small number of hard-wired non-modifiable components (e.g., a source resistor and a load resistor). In previous work involving genetic methods, a single test fixture was typically sufficient to measure all the characteristics under consideration. In contrast, the characteristics found in a typical commercial data sheet are so varied that multiple test fixtures (each consuming additional computational resources) are required.

In our ongoing project in which we are using genetic programming to try to synthesize commercially marketed amplifier circuits (such as the LM124 amplifier), we use a multiobjective fitness measure consisting of 16 elements measured by five different test fixtures. In this chapter reporting on our work in progress on this project, we focus on synthesizing a 40 dB amplifier.

The 16 elements of the fitness measure are (1) 10dB initial gain, (2) supply current, (3) offset voltage, (4) direction cosine, (5) gain ratio, (6) output swing, (7) output swing direction cosine, (8) variable load resistance signal output, (9) open loop gain for the non-inverting configuration, (10) 900 KHz unity gain bandwidth for the non-inverting configuration, (11) phase margin for the non-inverting configuration, (12) open loop gain for the inverting configuration, (13) 900 KHz unity gain bandwidth for the inverting configuration, (14) phase margin for the inverting configuration, (15) inversion enforcement across test fixtures for the inverting and non-inverting configurations, and (16) bias current.

When a human engineer designs an amplifier, all of the candidate circuits under consideration will usually perform amplification to some degree. However, when genetic and evolutionary methods are used to automatically synthesize complex structures, many of the candidate structures do not even remotely resemble the desired structure (i.e., do not perform amplification in any way). Thus, although most of the above elements of the fitness measure come from commercial data sheets for amplifiers, we included the direction cosine in the fitness measure in order to establish that the candidate circuit is doing something that resembles amplification of the difference between the circuit's two inputs. The direction cosine provides a measure of the alignment of two time-domain signals, independent of signal magnitude. We are interested in the difference, d, between the circuit's two inputs and the desired amplified output (called g). Specifically, the direction cosine is the inner product $\int d(t)^*g(t)\ dt$ divided by the product of the norms of d and g.

Figure 8-2 shows the first test fixture. This test fixture (with one probe point) is used to evaluate three elements of the fitness measure applicable to the non-inverting configuration, namely the open loop gain (in decibels), the 900 KHz unity gain bandwidth, and the phase margin. This figure (and Figure 8-3) contains the hard-wired differential pair of Figure 8-1; however, this space ordinarily contains the candidate circuit that is being evaluated.

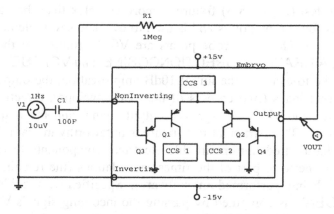

Figure 8-2. Test fixture for non-inverting configuration

A second test fixture (not shown) differs from Figure 8-2 only in that the inverting and non-inverting inputs are switched. This test fixture is used to evaluate, for the inverting configuration, the desired open loop gain, the 900 KHz unity gain bandwidth, and the phase margin. The first two test fixtures are used for inversion enforcement to ensure that specified values are achieved while the amplitude and phase of the output signals are inverted.

A third test fixture (not shown) measures the bias current. This test fixture differs from Figure 8-2 only in that there is no signal source, there is no capacitor, and there is a 1 mega-Ohm resistor between ground and the inverting input.

A fourth test fixture (not shown) measures the offset voltage (bias). This test fixture differs from Figure 8-2 only in that there is no signal source, there is no capacitor, and a wire replaces the 1 mega-Ohm feedback resistor.

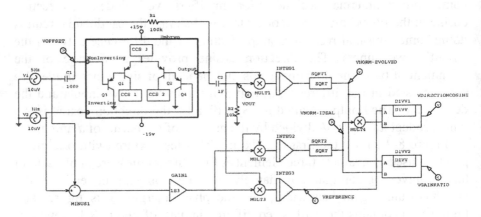

Figure 8-3. Test fixture with four probe points.

The fifth test (Figure 8-3) fixture is more complex than the others. The fifth test has four probe points and is used to evaluate seven elements of the fitness measure. The four probe points are VOUT (output of the evolved circuit), VGAINRATIO, VDIRECTIONCOSINE, and VOFFSET. This test fixture is used to evaluate the initial 10dB amplification, the output voltage under different loads (two corners of the load envelope), direction cosine, the gain ratio, the offset voltage, the output swing, and the output swing direction cosine. This particular test fixture is noteworthy in that it illustrates the use of hard-wired non-modifiable electrical components to enable the test fixture to perform part of the fitness calculations (the remainder of the calculations being performed in software). Specifically, the ideal norm, VNORM-IDEAL, is computed by passing the incoming signals V1 and V2 through subtractor block MINUS1 (to obtain the differential input of V1 and V2) and feeding the difference into gain block GAIN1 (which amplifies the signal according to the DC power value connected to it). Then, the signal GAIN1 is squared by feeding it to both inputs of multiplier block MULT2. The output of MULT2 is fed into integrator block INTEG2. The output of INTEG2 is then fed into square root block SQRT2 to produce VNORM-IDEAL. Similarly, the norm for the evolved circuit, VNORM-EVOLVED, is obtained using multiplier block MULT1, integrator block INTEG1, and square root block SQRT1. VREFERENCE is ascertained by multiplying GAIN1 by VOUT (at MULT3) and integrating at INTEG3. The direction cosine, VDIRECTIONCOSINE, is obtained by dividing VREFERENCE by the product of the two norms (VNORM-EVOLVED and VNORM-IDEAL). Finally, VGAINRATIO is obtained by dividing VNORM-EVOLVED by VNORM-IDEAL (at division block DIVV2).

Our focus here is on the engineering techniques for conducting an automated search in the absence of detailed information about the complex interrelationships among the various elements of the fitness measure.

First of all, even a little information can go a long way toward constructing a serviceable fitness measure that efficiently navigates a complex search space. For example, one thing that is almost always known is the identity of the preeminent element of the fitness measure (gain, in the case of an amplifier). The subspace of circuits that can actually amplify an incoming signal is an infinitesimal fraction of the space of possible circuits.

By heavily rewarding circuits that deliver even as little as 10 dB of gain (which can be obtained from even a single poorly deployed transistor), the search can be directed away from degenerate circuits (e.g., single wires) that deliver no gain at all, but which achieve alluringly good sub-optimal scores for secondary elements of the fitness measure (e.g., bias and distortion).

Second, after identifying the preeminent element of the fitness measure, we can weight the remaining elements equally in the sense that they will each make a certain common detrimental numerical contribution to fitness in a worst case that is likely to be occur. For this problem, an arbitrary common value of 30,000 was chosen.

Table 8-3. Elements of the fitness measure organized into four groups.

Preeminent element	Amplifier-like behavior	Single required value	Signal matching
• 10dB initial gain	• Phase margin (inverting) • Phase margin (non-inverting) • Unity gain bandwidth (inverting) • Unity gain bandwidth (non-inverting) • Phase and amplitude inversion	• Desired Decibel gain (inverting) • Desired decibel gain (non-inverting) • Output swing • Offset voltage • Bias current • Variable load performance • Supply current	• Direction cosine • Gain ratio • Output swing direction cosine

Third, the 16 elements of the fitness measure can be organized into four groups, as shown in Table 8-3. Column 1 of the table pertains to the just-discussed preeminent element of the fitness measure (gain). Column 2 contains elements of the fitness measure that ensure amplifier-like behavior. The unity gain bandwidth gives the upper limit to the useful passband of the amplifier. The phase margin is a mark of the amplifier's stability. Checking the phase and amplitude inversion ensures that we are dealing with a differential amplifier. When satisfied simultaneously, these elements of the fitness measure indicate the evolved circuit is a stable differential amplifier operating in a passband of interest. These characteristics would be a starting assumption of a practicing engineer when evaluating circuits for the remaining criteria. Usually, pace-setting best-of-generation individuals achieve satisfactory scores for these elements of the fitness measure during early generations of a run. Column 3 contains elements of the fitness measure that entail satisfactorily matching a single value. Column 4 contains elements of the fitness measure that entail satisfactorily matching a signal (curve) in the time-domain. The sum of the absolute errors is ideally 0; however, a satisfactory amplifier can have some residual error.

Fourth, because we do not have detailed information about the interrelationships among the various elements of the fitness measure, it is desirable to minimize the number of occasions where we need to quantify the tradeoff between disparate elements of the fitness measure. This can be accomplished by identifying all elements of the fitness measure for which there is no practical advantage to improvement once some minimal level of performance has been achieved. As soon as a satisfactory level is achieved for these elements, the detrimental contribution to fitness from that particular element is set to zero and no subsequent reward is given for additional improvement. In other words, these elements of the fitness measure are treated as constraints in that they make a non-zero detrimental numerical contribution to fitness only if the candidate circuit is considered to be in the infeasible region, but make no detrimental contribution once the constraint is satisfied. The elements in columns 2 and 3 of Table 8-3 can all be treated as constraints in this way, in the hope and expectation that their contribution to fitness will quickly become zero. If, and to the extent that, these contributions quickly become zero, we avoid having to quantify the tradeoff between these elements of the fitness measure.

There are four recognizable phases in typical runs of this problem: (1) initial topology search, (2) formation of a core topology, (3) component solution, and (4) refinement.

Phase 1 occurs in generations 0 and 1 and establishes initial topologies that deliver at least 10 dB of gain (column 1 of Table 8-3) and that exhibit amplifier-like behavior (the elements shown in column 2 of Table 8-3).

Figure 8-4 shows, for selected generations, the fitness of the best-of-generation individual for one run. The height of each bar represents the individual's fitness and the divisions within each bar show the contribution of eight selected elements of the fitness measure that illustrate the progress of the run. The eight selected elements are the differential gain direction cosine, gain ratio, offset voltage, supply current, output swing, output swing direction cosine, variable load resistance, and bias current. In Figure 8-5, the logarithm of these same eight fitness element are stacked on top of each other. The composition of each stack shows the progressive reduction (i.e., improvement) in the values of the eight elements.

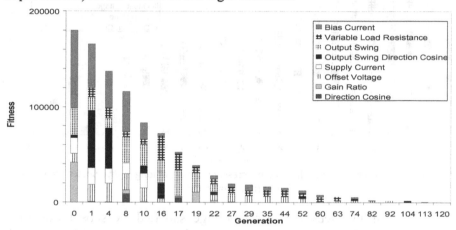

Figure 8-4. Progressive change among eight selected elements of the fitness measure.

Phase 2 of the run searches for a core topology. In generation 17, a core topology emerges that links the differential pair (Q1–Q4), a transistor (Q5), a resistor (R1), the positive power supply (V+), and the output. This topology persists for the remainder of the run. During this phase, the magnitude of each of the remaining elements of the fitness measure in Figure 8-5 is substantially reduced. Although none of the elements are driven to 0, this phase establishes a baseline value for the next phase.

In phase 3, the required values of the elements shown in the third column of Table 8-3 are driven to 0. As progress is made in reducing the various elements of the fitness measure, the core topology that first appeared in generation 17 is augmented by additional electrical components.

During phase 3, there are 3 sub-phases in which the run concentrates on one, two, or three elements of the six elements of the fitness measure shown in the second column of Table 8-3. For example, in the second sub-phase of phase 3 (between generations 18 and 29), a current mirror is added to the circuit to help drive the penalties associated with the gain ratio and output swing to 0. In the second sub-phase of phase 3 (between generation 30 and

73), the run concentrates on offset voltage, bias current, and variable load performance (i.e., the corners of the load envelope). The variable load performance becomes satisfied with the addition of current source I1.

In the third sub-phase of phase 3 (generations 74 to 113), the offset voltage and bias currents become satisfied. In generation 104 the bias current is pulled below the target value with the introduction of current source I4.

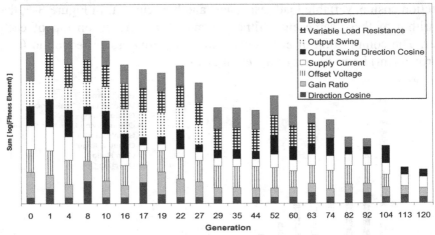

Figure 8-5. Logarithmic scale showing progressive change among eight selected elements of the fitness measure.

Generation 113 sees the offset voltage satisfied by substitution of a previously placed transistor with a current mirror consisting of **Q6** and **Q7**, completing what would be the core of the solution circuit.

In phase 4, the remaining residual error of the fitness measure elements in the third column of Table 8-3 are pushed toward their ideal values. The best-of-run individual from generation 120 (Figure 8-6) satisfies all constraints and all other minimum specifications, except that the supply current is 30 milliamperes. Although the supply current is not in compliance, its detrimental contribution to fitness is less than the sum of all of the errors.

A second run (using an arguably more realistic worst-case scaling for supply current), followed a similar four-phase chronology. The best-of-run individual satisfied all constraints and specifications except that the bias current was 112 nano-amperes (instead of less than 80 nano-amperes).

7.   CONCLUSIONS

The chapter discussed progress toward the synthesis of industrial-strength automated design of analog circuits by means of genetic programming by describing five ways for using general domain knowledge about circuits, three ways for employing problem-specific knowledge, four ways of improving on previously published genetic programming techniques, and four ways of grappling with the multi-objective fitness measure needed to synthesize an amplifier circuit.

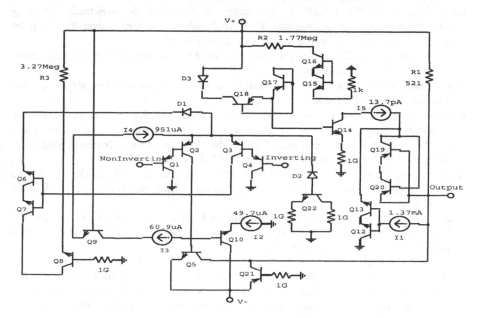

Figure 8-6. Best-of-run circuit from generation 120.

Acknowledgements

We are indebted to Trent McConaghy (formerly of Analog Design Automation Inc. of Ottawa, now a part of Synopsys) for suggesting this amplifier problem and useful discussions about it.

References

Aaserud, O. and Nielsen, I. Ring. (1995). Trends in current analog design: A panel debate. *Analog Integrated Circuits and Signal-Processing.* 7(1)5–9.

Balkir, Sina, Dundar, Gunhan, and Ogrenci, A. Selcuk. (2003). *Analog VLSI Design Automation.* Boca Raton, FL: CRC Press.

Banzhaf, Wolfgang, Nordin, Peter, Keller, Robert E., and Francone, Frank D. (1998). *Genetic Programming– An Introduction.* San Francisco, CA: Morgan Kaufmann.

Graeb, Helmut E., Zizala, S., Eckmueller, J., and Antreich, K. 2001. The sizing rules method for analog circuit design. Proceedings of the IEEE/ACM International Conference on Computer Aided Design. Piscataway, NJ: IEEE Press. Pages 343-349.

Holland, John H. (1975). *Adaptation in Natural and Artificial Systems: An Introductory Analysis with Applications to Biology, Control, and Artificial Intelligence*. Ann Arbor, MI: University of Michigan Press. Second edition. Cambridge, MA: The MIT Press 1992.

Keane, Martin A., Koza, John R., and Streeter, Matthew J. (2002). *Improved General-Purpose Controllers*. U.S. patent application filed July 12, 2002.

Koza, John R. (1990). *Genetic Programming: A Paradigm for Genetically Breeding Populations of Computer Programs to Solve Problems*. Stanford University Computer Science Dept. technical report STAN-CS-90-1314. June 1990.

Koza, John R. (1992). *Genetic Programming: On the Programming of Computers by Means of Natural Selection*. Cambridge, MA: MIT Press.

Koza, John R. (1994). *Genetic Programming II: Automatic Discovery of Reusable Programs*. Cambridge, MA: MIT Press.

Koza, John R., Bennett III, Forrest H, Andre, David, and Keane, Martin A. (1996). Automated design of both the topology and sizing of analog electrical circuits using genetic programming. In Gero, John S. and Sudweeks, Fay (editors). *Artificial Intelligence in Design '96*. Dordrecht: Kluwer Academic Publishers. Pages 151–170.

Koza, John R., Bennett III, Forrest H, Andre, David, and Keane, Martin A. (1999). *Genetic Programming III: Darwinian Invention and Problem Solving*. San Francisco, CA: Morgan Kaufmann.

Koza, John R., Keane, Martin A., Streeter, Matthew J., Mydlowec, William, Yu, Jessen, and Lanza, Guido.(2003). *Genetic Programming IV: Routine Human-Competitive Machine Intelligence*. Kluwer Academic Publishers.

Koza, John R., Mydlowec, William, Lanza, Guido, Yu, Jessen, and Keane, Martin A. (2001). Reverse engineering of metabolic pathways from observed data using genetic programming. In Altman, Russ B. Dunker, A. Keith, Hunter, Lawrence, Lauderdale, Kevin, and Klein, Teri (editors). *Pacific Symposium on Biocomputing 2001*. Singapore: World Scientific. Pages 434–445.

Koza, John R., and Rice, James P. (1991). Genetic generation of both the weights and architecture for a neural network. In *Proc. of International Joint Conference on Neural Networks, Seattle, July 1991*. Los Alamitos, CA: IEEE Press. Volume II. Pages 397–404.

Koza, John R., Streeter, Matthew J., and Keane, Martin A. (2003). Automated synthesis by means of genetic programming of complex structures incorporating reuse, parameterized reuse, hierarchies, and development. In *Genetic Programming: Theory and Practice* Riolo, R. and Worzel W. (eds.). Boston, MA: Kluwer Academic Publishers. Pp. 221–237.

Langdon, William B. and Poli, Riccardo. (2002). *Foundations of Genetic Programming*. Springer-Verlag.

Lanza, Guido, Mydlowec, William, and Koza, John R. (2000). Automatic creation of a genetic network for the lac operon from observed data by means of genetic programming. Poster paper accepted for First International Conference on Systems Biology in Tokyo on November 14–16, 2000.

Lohn, Jason, Hornby, Gregory, and Linden, Derek. (2003). Evolutionary antenna design for a NASA spacecraft. Chapter 18 of this volume.

Quarles, Thomas, Newton, A. R., Pederson, D. O., and Sangiovanni-Vincentelli, A. 1994. *SPICE 3 Version 3F5 User's Manual*. Department of Electrical Engineering and Computer Science, University of California. Berkeley, CA. March 1994.

Spector, Lee. 2004. *Automatic Quantum Computer Programming: A Genetic Programming Approach*. Boston: Kluwer Academic Publishers.

Sripramong, Thanwa and Toumazou, Christofer. (2002). The invention of CMOS amplifiers using genetic programming and current-flow analysis. *IEEE Trans. on Computer-Aided Design of Integrated Circuits and Systems*. 21(11). November 2002. Pages 1237–1252.

Chapter 9

TOPOLOGICAL SYNTHESIS OF ROBUST DYNAMIC SYSTEMS BY SUSTAINABLE GENETIC PROGRAMMING

Jianjun Hu and Erik Goodman

Genetic Algorithm Research & Application Group (GARAGe), Michigan State University

Abstract   Traditional robust design constitutes only one step in the detailed design stage, where parameters of a design solution are tuned to improve the robustness of the system. This chapter proposes that robust design should start from the conceptual design stage and genetic programming-based open-ended topology search can be used for automated synthesis of robust systems. Combined with a bond graph-based dynamic system synthesis methodology, an improved sustainable genetic programming technique - quick hierarchical fair competition (QHFC)- is used to evolve robust high-pass analog filters. It is shown that topological innovation by genetic programming can be used to improve the robustness of evolved design solutions with respect to both parameter perturbations and topology faults.

Keywords: sustainable genetic programming, automated synthesis,dynamic systems, robust design, bond graphs, analog filter

1.   Introduction

Topologically open-ended computational synthesis by genetic programming (GP) has been used as an effective approach for engineering design innovations, with many success stories in a variety of domains (Koza et al., 2003) including analog circuits , digital circuits, molecular design, and mechatronic systems (Seo et al., 2003a), etc. Much of the existing research focuses on employing genetic programming as a topologically open-ended search method to do functional design innovation – achieving a specified behavior without pre-specifying the design topology. In this chapter, we are interested in exploring more thoroughly how genetic-programming-based open-ended design synthesis can improve another dimension of engineering design: the robustness of the systems designed. Specifically, we examine whether topological innovation by genetic programming can facilitate design of robust dynamic systems with respect to environmental noise, variation in design parameters, and structural failures in the system.

Robustness, as the ability of a system to maintain function even with changes in internal structure or external environment (Carlson and Doyle, 2002, Jen, 2001), is critical to engineering design decisions. Engineering design systems, in reality, do not normally take into account all the types of uncertainties or variations to which the engineered artifacts are subjected, such as manufacturing variation, degradation or non-uniformity of material properties, environmental changes, and changing operating conditions. However, reliable systems, having the least sensitivity of performance to variations in the system components or environmental conditions, are highly desirable. Evolving robustness can also contribute to genetic-programming-based design synthesis by increasing the robustness of the evolved solutions, which make them easier to implement physically despite the discrepancy between the simulator and real-world model (Jakobi et al., 1995).

Our hypothesis here is that control factors (design variables) as used in the robust design framework in (Chen et al., 1996) should not be limited to changing the dimensions (or sizing) and other *numeric* parameters of the systems. As any given function of a dynamic system can be implemented in various ways, we believe that the *topological* or the *functional* design in the conceptual design phase may have a significant role in determining the robustness of the design solutions with respect to both topology variation as well as parameter perturbation in terms of traditional robust design. Actually, Ferrer i Cancho et al. (Ferrer i Cancho et al., 2001) gave an analysis of topological patterns in electric circuits and their relationship with the properties of the system behavior. There is already a body of research on how the structure of a system affects its functional robustness.For example, Balling and Sobieszczanski-Sobieski (Balling and Sobieszczanski-Sobieski, 1996) discussed how the coupling structure of the system may affect robust parameter design. But a systematic methodology and investigation of robust design of dynamic systems based on topologically open-ended search by genetic programming is still lacking.

2.   Related Work

Robust design, originally proposed by Taguchi (Tay and Taguchi, 1993), has been intensively investigated in the engineering design community since the 1980s and remains an important topic (Zhu, 2001). In robust design, a designer seeks to determine the control parameter settings that produce desirable values of the performance mean, while at the same time minimizing the variance of the performance (Tay and Taguchi, 1993).

Many aspects of traditional robust design such as performance sensitivity distribution have been investigated intensively (Zhu, 2001, Du and Chen, 2000). However, most of these robust design studies assume that there already exists a design solution for a system and the task of robust design is to determine its robust operating parameters with respect to various kinds of variations. The relation of how topological or functional structure of a system affects its robustness is often not treated. One reason why these issues are unresolved is that the prevailing approach for system design is a top-down procedure from functional design to detailed design, and robust design is applied only in the detailed design stage. Topologically open-ended synthesis by genetic programming provides a way to move robust design forward to the conceptual/functional design stage and thus consider design for robustness from the very beginning, which will augment the current practice of design for robustness in parametric design.

Application of evolutionary computation to robust design has been investigated since the early 1990s (Forouraghi, 2000) and can be classified into three categories. The first type of work applies evolutionary algorithms to parametric design for robustness, following the track of robust design in traditional engineering. Tsutsui et al. (Tsutsui and Ghosh, 1997) proposed to use noise on the design variables in the calculation of fitness values to evolve robust solutions. This approach was later applied to parametric robust design of MEMS by Ma and Antonsson (Ma and Antonsson, 2001). The second type of research on evolving robustness focuses on evolving robust solutions in a noisy environment (Hammel and Back, 1994). In these problems, the variation in the environment leads to uncertainty in the fitness function evaluation and the true fitness of a candidate solution needs to be evaluated based on sampling multiple environment configurations. In the evolutionary robotics area, for example, Lee et al. (Lee et al., 1997) evolved robust mobile robot controllers by training them in multiple trials of simulation, using genetic programming and a genetic algorithm, respectively. The active area of evolving robust systems is evolvable hardware (Thompson and Layzell, 2000). Most of these approaches employ genetic algorithms or evolution strategies as the search procedures. Very recent work is the evolution of robust digital circuits (Miller and Hartmann, 2001, Hartmann et al., 2002a). In this work, Miller, Hartmann, and their collaborators examine the feasibility of evolving robust digital circuits using a type of "messy gate." Hartmann et al.(Hartmann et al., 2002b) investigated how evolution may exploit non-perfect digital gates to achieve fault tolerance, including tolerance to output noise and gate failure. However, the noise introduced to improve robustness is not applied to parametric values of the components, but to the analog outputs of the messy gates, and an evolution strategy is used as the open-ended topology search tool. This method is thus not as instructive as might be desired in exploring effects of alternative topologies.

3.   Analog Filter Synthesis by Bond Graphs and Sustainable Genetic Programming

Dynamic systems in this chapter are represented as bond graphs (Karnopp et al., 2000). A strongly typed genetic programming tool, enhanced with the sustainable evolutionary computation model, the Hierarchical Fair Competition (HFC) model (Hu and Goodman, 2002), is used for topologically open-ended search. In this section, bond graphs, the bond graph synthesis approach by genetic programming and the HFC-GP algorithm (Hu and Goodman, 2002) are introduced briefly.

Bond Graphs

The bond graph is a multi-domain modeling tool for analysis and design of dynamic systems, especially hybrid multi-domain systems, including mechanical, electrical, pneumatic, hydraulic, etc., components (Karnopp et al., 2000). The multi-domain nature of bond graph modeling facilitates evolution of mechatronic system. Details of notation and methods of system analysis related to the bond graph representation can be found in (Karnopp et al., 2000). Figure 9-1 illustrates a bond graph that represents the accompanying electrical system. A typical bond graph model is composed of inductors (I), resistors (R), capacitors (C), transformers (TF), gyrators (GY), 0-Junctions (J0), 1-junctions (J1), and Sources of Effort (SE). In this chapter, we are only concerned with linear dynamic systems, or more specifically, analog filters as a case study represented as bond graphs, which are composed of I/R/C components, SE (as input signal),SF (as output signal access point).

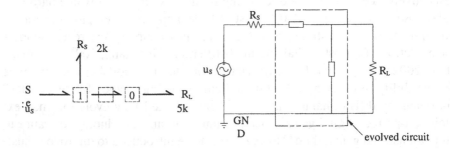

Figure 9-1. A bond graph and its equivalent circuit. The dotted boxes in the left bond graph indicate the modifiable sites (explained in next section)

Analog Filter Synthesis by Bond Graph and Genetic Programming

In previous work (Fan et al., 2001), we applied developmental genetic programming to automated synthesis of analog filters using a basic GP function set. In that approach, the GP functions for topological operation were:

F={Insert_J0/J1, Add_C/I/R, and Replace_C/I/R},

which allow evolution of a large variety of bond graph topologies. The shortcoming of this approach is that it tends to evolve redundant and sometimes causally ill-posed bond graphs (Seo et al., 2003b). In this chapter, we use a well-posed modular GP function set as shown below to evolve bond graphs, as in explained in (Hu et al., 2004):

F={ **Add_J_CI_R, Insert_J0CJ1I, EndNode, EndBond, ERC**}

where Add_J_CI_R adds a new alternative type of junction to an existing junction with a randomly specified attached elements like C/I/R; Insert_J0CJ1I inserts a pair of 0-junction and 1-junction into an existing bond, each junction with a randomly specified attached elements like C/I/R; EndNode and EndBond terminate the development (further topology manipulation) at junction and bond modifiable sites correspondingly; ERC represents a real number that can be changed by Gaussian mutation. As an example, the operation of Add_J_CI_R is illustrated in Figure 9-2.

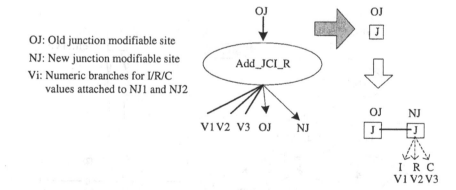

Figure 9-2. The Add_J_CI_R function, whose execution will attach a new junction with a certain number of attached components to an existing junction

In this modular set approach, the bond graphs are composed of only alternating 1-junctions and 0-junctions. Each junction is attached with three bits, each representing the presence or absence of corresponding C/I/R components. A flag mutation operator is used to evolve these flag bits. For the three C/I/R components attached to each junction, there are three parameters to represent the component values, which are evolved by a Gaussian mutation operator of the modified genetic programming system used here. This is different from our previous work in which the "classical" numeric subtree approach was used to evolve parameters of components. Figure 9-3 shows a GP tree that develops an embryo bond graph into a complete bond graph solution.

As a case study, we are interested in evolving analog filters (bond graphs) as defined in (Fan et al., 2001). The embryo bond graph and its equivalent circuit are illustrated in Figure 9-1. Note that the two junctions and one bond with dotted boxes are modifiable sites where further topological developments can proceed as instructed by a GP program tree.

The fitness of a candidate analog filter is defined as follows: within the frequency range of interest $[1, 10^5]$, uniformly sample 100 points. Compare the magnitudes of the frequency response at the sample points with target magnitudes, compute their differences, and get a sum of squared differences as raw fitness, defined as $Fitness_{raw}$. Then calculate normalized fitness according to:

$$Fitness_{norm} = \frac{100}{100 + Fitness_{raw}} \qquad (9.1)$$

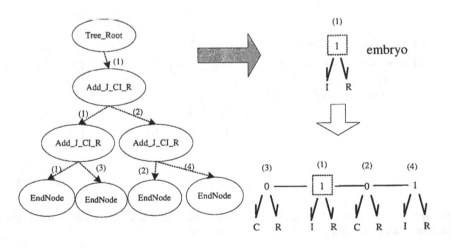

Figure 9-3. An example of a GP tree, composed of topology operators applied to an embryo, generating a bond graph after depth-first execution (numeric branches are omitted)

Sustainable Genetic Programming Based on the Hierarchical Fair Competition Model

Standard genetic programming has a strong tendency toward premature convergence of the GP tree structures, as illustrated by the visualization of GP tree populations by Daida et al. (Daida et al., 2003), which can be partially explained by the loss-of-exploration-capability hypothesis (Hu et al., 2003). In this work, we employ QHFC-GP, an improved version of the sustainable genetic programming method, HFC-GP, as introduced in (Hu and Goodman, 2002). The basic idea of the HFC artificial evolution model (HFC) for sustainable search is that evolutionary search needs to be sustained by continuously incorporating new genetic material into the evolving pool and by keeping lower- and intermediate-level evolutionary processes going on all the time, rather than relying only upon "survival of the fittest." The strategy of HFC is to stratify the population of standard genetic programming into cascading fitness levels and to put a random individual generator at the bottom fitness level. In this way, the convergent nature of conventional evolutionary algorithms is transformed into a non-convergent one, which can support sustainable evolutionary discovery of new solutions. Evolutionary algorithms based on the HFC sustainable evolution principle have proved to be able to improve robustness, efficiency, and scalability for both genetic algorithm and genetic programming problems (Hu et al., 2003, Hu et al., 2005).

The basic HFC algorithm (Hu et al., 2005) has been the subject of continuing experimentation and refinement. The continuous HFC model (CHFC) was introduced in (Hu et al., 2003), and a further refinement of HFC, Quick HFC (QHFC) is used in the work reported here in order to improve the efficiency and sustainability of the topological innovation. As the focus of this paper is on robust design by genetic programming rather than on the HFC model and algorithms, we refer our readers to (Hu et al., 2005) for a description of the QHFC algorithm and (Hu et al., 2003) for the ideas and advantages of HFC-based genetic programming compared to other techniques.

4. Evolving Robust Analog Filters by QHFC-GP

The typical approach for evolving robust designs is to use multiple Monte Carlo samplings with different environmental or system configurations to calculate an average fitness for a given candidate solution. One speciality of evolving robustness in genetic programming is that solutions evolved in GP are grown by a developmental process and the robustness of early intermediate individuals does not necessarily imply the robustness of the final solutions. But if the robustness is only evaluated after the fitness of the population reaches a high level, standard genetic programming has difficulty coming up with much variety in the space of solutions, because of convergence of the GP tree structure. The stratified sustainable search feature of QHFC tends to be able to solve this problem. In the following experiments, evaluation of the robustness of candidate solutions is only applied to individuals of the top level, as we only care about the final robustness rather than the robustness of intermediate solutions. This saves much computing effort. However, a sufficient variety of new topological candidates is continually introduced to the top level to allow for competition among various topologies according to their relative robustness.

The fitness evaluation for top-level individuals is as follows:

$$f_i = \sum_{k=1}^{SPI} f_i^k \tag{9.2}$$

where SPI is the number of Monte Carlo sampling evaluations for each individual, f_i^k is the fitness of the kth sampling evaluation with different Monte Carlo perturbation of the parameters or topology. In the case of topology perturbation, since some sampled systems after topology perturbation cannot be simulated because of ill-posed causality, SPI here would be replaced with a specific number of well-behaved perturbed systems (explained later).

5.   Experiments and Results

In this section, a series of experiments are conducted to verify the following hypotheses about robust design by genetic programming. The first hypothesis is that dynamic systems with equal performance in the deterministic formulation of the design problem have differential capacity for noise and fault tolerance. The second hypothesis is that topological innovation by genetic programming can improve the robustness to component sizing noise or component failures in dynamic systems.

As mentioned above, two types of robustness are examined. One is the robustness with respect to (w.r.t.) variation of parameter values of the components in the system; the other is the robustness with respect to failure of components, which in our case is simply modeled as removal of the components from the system. The perturbation of the component values during evolution is implemented by perturbing all component parameters with Gaussian noise $N(\mu, \sigma)$ with mean μ at 0 and standard deviation σ at 25% of parameter values. The failure of components during evolution is implemented by disconnecting a uniformly selected number (between 1 and 5) of components randomly from the systems. The number of Monte Carlo samplings for fitness evaluation of each individual with respect to parameter and topology perturbation is set as SPI =10. The robustness of an evolved solution w.r.t. parameter perturbation is evaluated against a series of perturbation magnitudes: Gaussian noise $N(\mu, \sigma)$ with mean μ at 0 and standard deviation σ at 5% to 50% of parameter values in steps of 5%, each tested with 5000 samplings with different configurations of the component parameter perturbations. The robustness of an evolved solution w.r.t. topology perturbation is evaluated against a series of topology perturbations: removing a certain number (1 to 10 in steps of 1) of components randomly from the systems, each tested with 100 samplings with different failure states of its components.

All the following experiments aim to evolve robust high-pass filters passing signals of frequency 100k Hz and higher. The running parameters for QHFC-GP used here are in Table 5:

Table 9-1. Shared running parameters of experiments

Total population size: 2000	Number of levels: 5
MaxDepth: 10	Crossover probability: 0.4
InitDepth: 3-5	Standard mutation probability: 0.05
Tournament size: 2	Parametric mutation probability: 0.3
Max evaluations: 20,000,000	Flag mutation probability: 0.3

Analog Filters with Different Topologies Have Different Noise Robustness and Fault Tolerance Capability

In this experiment, ten analog filters with approximately equal functional performance but with different topologies are evolved, each with 2,000,000 evaluations without incorporating a robustness criterion in the fitness function (9.1). We then choose two filters, one complex solution with 52 components and one compact solution with only 23 components, to test their capabilities for fault tolerance and noise tolerance over the degradation or variation of the component parameters with different perturbation magnitudes.

As described above, the evaluation of robustness w.r.t. parameter perturbation is conducted by running 5000 samplings of the configurations of the perturbations. The robustness w.r.t. component failures is evaluated with only 100 samplings as topological robustness is much more complex to evaluate. The reason is that topology modification usually leads to dramatic degradation of functional performance or leads to invalid physical system models, which can be checked out by the causality check procedure of a bond graph (Karnopp et al., 2000). Some systems with randomly perturbed topologies are causally valid but can not be simulated by our simulator. To deal with these difficulties, we first collect the fitness of all the topologically perturbed sampling systems that can be simulated. Then the average fitness of these performance values is calculated. To remove the dominance of a few dramatically degraded systems on the average fitness, we then remove all the fitness values that are worse than the average fitness and recalculate the average fitness to get the final fitness for the individual as f_i in (9.2). The performance degradation graphs of these two analog filters are shown in Figure 9-4.

From Figure 9-4 (a), we see that without incorporating a robustness requirement into fitness evaluation, the evolved filters are somewhat robust w.r.t. parameter perturbation compared to their performance degradation in face of topology perturbation in Figure 9-4 (b), which illustrates the principle that structure determines function. It can also be observed that the relatively simpler filter has higher robustness w.r.t. parameter perturbation than the more complex one. However, this advantage is offset by its very poor fault-tolerance capability: for the 100 sampling evaluations, removing only 2 components invariably leads to causally ill-posed systems or systems that cannot be simulated by our simulator. We also identify the fact that topology perturbation of a system with fewer components has much more dramatic effect on the function of the resulting system, usually leading to much higher percentage of causally ill-posed or non-simulatable systems among the 100 sampling topologically perturbed systems.

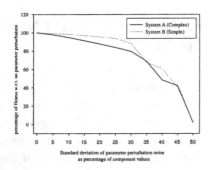 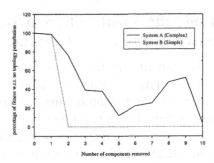

(a) Performance degradation w.r.t. component value perturbation magnitudes as percentages of original component values

(b) Performance degradation w.r.t. number of failed components. (Note: the superior performance of system A between 5-9 is because the perturbed system B had fewer valid systems for evaluating average performance withstanding topology perturbation)

Figure 9-4. Robustness of two evolved analog filters without incorporating a robustness criterion into fitness function.

Evolving Robustness to Component Sizing Perturbations

In the following experiments, we try to evolve a robust analog filter that has higher tolerance of the variation of component values and has graceful performance degradation. In mechanical systems, where bond graphs are widely used, component sizing is often constantly changing due to friction, wear, and damage. Figure 9-5 is the evolved bond graph (for simplicity, we omit the parameters here) and Figure 9-6 (a) is the performance degradation with respect to noise level.

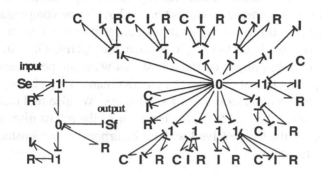

Figure 9-5. Evolved robust analog filter (represented in bond graph) w.r.t. parameter perturbation. Component sizing values are omitted for simplicity.

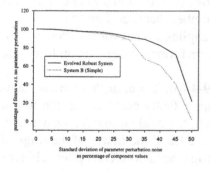 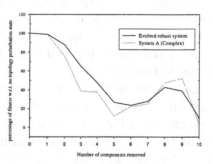

(a) Comparison of performance degradation w.r.t. component value perturbation magnitude as percentage of original component values between the robust system in Figure 9-5 and system B in Figure 9-4 (a)

(b) Comparison of performance degradation w.r.t. number of failed components between the evolved robust system in Figure 9-7 and system A in Figure 9-4 (b). (Note: the performance increase between 5-9 is because of fewer valid systems for evaluating average performance of topologically perturbed sampled systems)

Figure 9-6. Improved robustness of the evolved analog filters incorporating a robustness criterion in the fitness function.

The evolved robust filter in Figure 9-5 is very interesting. It has a central 0-junction with 11 1-junctions attached, which means that many serially connected C/I/R modules are connected in parallel. This topological structure reminds us of the scale-free topology (Ferrer i Cancho et al., 2001). One plausible explanation is that simultaneous parametric perturbations on the components of these symmetric modules tend to have some compensatory effects on each other, thus achieving higher robustness to parameter noise. Comparing Figure 9-6 (a) and Figure 9-4 (a), it is clear that QHFC-GP with robustness fitness evaluation has improved the robustness w.r.t. the perturbation over the component parameters of the filter. The performance degradation is smoother than that evolved without considering robustness. We also find that for a noise level below 20% or beyond 50%, the behavior of the robust filter is somewhat similar to that of the filter evolved without incorporating a robustness criterion in the fitness function.

Evolving Robustness to Component Failure

In the following experiments, we try to evolve a robust analog filter that can tolerate the failure of its components and has graceful performance degradation. The running parameters are the same as stated in the beginning of this section. Remember that because a significant portion of the topologically perturbed systems are causally ill-posed and can not be simulated with our simulator, the final fitness of the solutions (and the resulting conclusion) is much less reliable than that in the previous subsection. Topology perturbation during evolution is applied by removing a uniformly chosen number (between 1 and 5) of components from each candidate solution for 10 samplings. The evolved filter, in bond graph form, is shown in Figure 9-7 and the performance degradation levels are illustrated in Figure 9-6 (b).

Comparing Figure 9-6 (b) with Figure 9-4 (b), it is clear that a more fault-tolerant filter has been evolved. Removing 3 faulty components, the robust solution can still achieve 65% of the fitness of the original solution on average, while the non-robust filter can only achieve 39% of the fitness of the original solution. Another interesting observation is that the fault-tolerant filter in Figure 9-7 tends to be much more complex than the robust solution evolved in the previous subsection. This can be explained like this: more complex structures can have more redundancy, which serves as means for providing fault-tolerance. The lower degree of symmetry of this solution compared to that of Figure 9-5 seems to also contribute to its tolerance of component removal. It is clear that different perturbation patterns lead to different topological structures of the robust solutions.

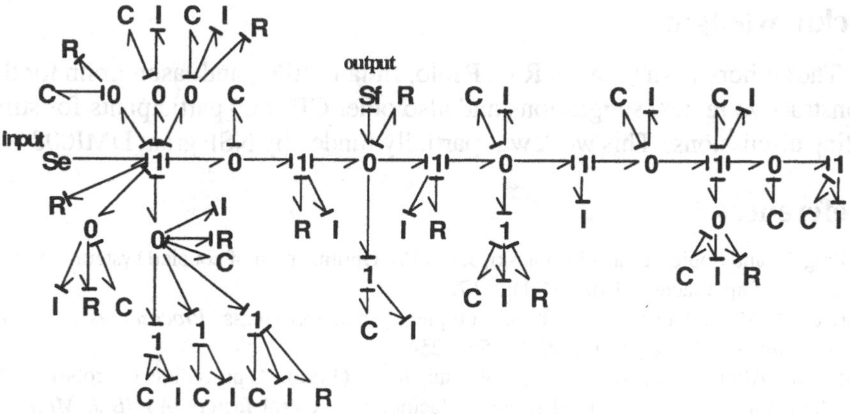

Figure 9-7. Evolved fault-tolerant filter represented as bond graph. Component sizing values are omitted for simplicity.

6. Conclusions and Future Work

This chapter proposes to exploit open-ended topology search capability of genetic programming for robust design of dynamic systems. We believe that topological or functional innovation in the conceptual design stage can improve the robustness of (the functionality of) the systems. Specifically, we apply an improved version of sustainable genetic programming-QHFC and a bond graph-based modular set approach to automated synthesis of robust dynamic systems. We find that our sustainable genetic programming enables us to find more robust analog filters with respect to the variations in their parameters and component faults.

Evolving robustness is a rich research theme and there are several interesting topics to be further investigated. First, we find that selection pressure for robustness w.r.t. parameter perturbation and component faults leads to different topological patterns. It would be interesting to investigate how simultaneous requirements for both types of robustness would affect topological structures. Another related study would be to examine how perturbation pattern would affect structures. For example, one could study how the evolutionary system responds differentially to component removal by an absolute number of or by a percentage of components. Next, our experiments suggest that symmetry or scale-free topology may have a role in system robustness. More experiments are needed to confirm this. Future work will also explore the tradeoffs between improving robustness by parameter search and by topological innovation will be studied and methods to control it will be developed.

Acknowledgments

The authors wish to thank Rick Riolo, Julian Miller, and Jason Lohn for their constructive review suggestions and also other GPTP04 participants for stimulating discussions. This work was partially funded by NSF grant DMI0084934.

References

Balling, R. and Sobieszczanski-Sobieski, J. (1996). Optimization of coupled systems: A critical review of approaches. *AIAA*, 34(1):6–17.

Carlson, J. M. and Doyle, J. (2002). Complexity and robustness. *Proceedings of National Academy of Science (PNAS)*, 99(1):2538–2545.

Chen, W., Allen, J. K., Mistree, F., and Tsui, K.-L. (1996). A procedure for robust design: Minimizing variations caused by noise factors and control factors. *ASME J. Mech. Des*, 118:478–485.

Daida, Jason M., Hilss, Adam M., Ward, David J., and Long, Stephen L. (2003). Visualizing tree structures in genetic programming. In Cantú-Paz, E., Foster, J. A., Deb, K., Davis, D., Roy, R., O'Reilly, U.-M., Beyer, H.-G., Standish, R., Kendall, G., Wilson, S., Harman, M., Wegener, J., Dasgupta, D., Potter, M. A., Schultz, A. C., Dowsland, K., Jonoska, N., and Miller, J., editors, *Genetic and Evolutionary Computation – GECCO-2003*, volume 2724 of *LNCS*, pages 1652–1664, Chicago. Springer-Verlag.

Du, X. and Chen, W. (2000). Towards a better understanding of modeling feasibility robustness in engineering design. *ASME J. Mech. Des*, 122(4):385–394.

Fan, Zhun, Hu, Jianjun, Seo, Kisung, Goodman, Erik D., Rosenberg, Ronald C., and Zhang, Baihai (2001). Bond graph representation and GP for automated analog filter design. In Goodman, Erik D., editor, *2001 Genetic and Evolutionary Computation Conference Late Breaking Papers*, pages 81–86, San Francisco, California, USA.

Forouraghi, B. (2000). A genetic algorithm for multiobjective robust design. *Applied Intelligence*, 12:151–161.

Hammel, U. and Back, T. (1994). Evolution strategies on noisy functions. how to improve convergence properties. *Parallel Problem Solving from Nature*, 3:159–168.

Hartmann, M., Haddow, P., and Eskelund, F. (2002a). Evolving robust digital designs. *Proc. 2002 NASA/DoD Conference on Evolvable Hardware (EH'02)*, pages 36–45.

Hartmann, Morten, Eskelund, Frode, Haddow, Pauline C., and Miller, Julian F. (2002b). Evolving fault tolerance on an unreliable technology platform. In Langdon, W. B., Cantú-Paz, E., Mathias, K., Roy, R., Davis, D., Poli, R., Balakrishnan, K., Honavar, V., Rudolph, G., Wegener, J., Bull, L., Potter, M. A., Schultz, A. C., Miller, J. F., Burke, E., and Jonoska, N., editors, *GECCO 2002: Proceedings of the Genetic and Evolutionary Computation Conference*, pages 171–177, New York. Morgan Kaufmann Publishers.

Hu, J., Goodman, E., and Rosenberg, R. (2004). Topological search in automated mechatronic system synthesis using bond graphs and genetic programming. *Proc. of American Control Conference ACC 2004*.

Hu, J., Goodman, E.D., Seo, K., Fan, Z., and Rosenberg, R. (2005). The hierarchical fair competition (hfc) framework for sustainable evolutionary algorithms. *Evolutionary Computation*, 13(1).

Hu, Jianjun and Goodman, Erik D. (2002). The hierarchical fair competition (HFC) model for parallel evolutionary algorithms. In Fogel, David B., El-Sharkawi, Mohamed A., Yao, Xin, Greenwood, Garry, Iba, Hitoshi, Marrow, Paul, and Shackleton, Mark, editors, *Proceedings of the 2002 Congress on Evolutionary Computation CEC2002*, pages 49–54. IEEE Press.

Hu, Jianjun, Goodman, Erik D., and Seo, Kisung (2003). Continuous hierarchical fair competition model for sustainable innovation in genetic programming. In Riolo, Rick L. and Worzel, Bill, editors, *Genetic Programming Theory and Practice*, chapter 6, pages 81–98. Kluwer.

Ferrer i Cancho, R., Janssen, C., and Sole, R. V. (2001). Topology of technology graphs: small world patterns in electronic circuits. *Physical Review E*, 64(046119).

Jakobi, N., P.Husbands, and Harvey, I. (1995). and the reality gap: The use of simulation in evolutionary robotics. *Proc. Third European Conference on Artificial Life*, pages 704–720.

Jen, E. (2001). Definitions of robustness. *Santa Fe Institute Robustness Site*,.

Karnopp, D.C., Margolis, D. L., and Rosenberg, R. C. (2000). *System Dynamics: Modeling and Simulation of Mechatronic Systems*. New York: John Wiley & Sons, Inc.

Koza, John R., Keane, Martin A., Streeter, Matthew J., Mydlowec, William, Yu, Jessen, and Lanza, Guido (2003). *Genetic Programming IV: Routine Human-Competitive Machine Intelligence*. Kluwer Academic Publishers.

Lee, Wei-Po, Hallam, John, and Lund, Henrik Hautop (1997). Applying genetic programming to evolve behavior primitives and arbitrators for mobile robots. In *Proceedings of IEEE 4th International Conference on Evolutionary Computation*, volume 1. IEEE Press. to appear.

Ma, L. and Antonsson, E.K. (2001). Robust mask-layout synthesis for mems. *Proceedings of the 2001 International Conference on Modeling and Simulation of Microsystems*.

Miller, Julian F. and Hartmann, Morten (2001). Evolving messy gates for fault tolerance: some preliminary findings. In Keymeulen, Didier, Stoica, Adrian, Lohn, Jason, and Zebulum, Ricardo S., editors, *The Third NASA/DoD workshop on Evolvable Hardware*, pages 116–123, Long Beach, California. IEEE Computer Society.

Seo, K., Fan, Z., Hu, J., Goodman, E. D., and Rosenberg, R. C. (2003a). Toward an automated design method for multi-domain dynamic systems using bond graphs and genetic programming. *Mechatronics*, 13(8-9):851–885.

Seo, Kisung, Fan, Zhun, Hu, Jianjun, Goodman, Erik D., and Rosenberg, Ronald C. (2003b). Dense and switched modular primitives for bond graph model design. In Cantú-Paz, E., Foster, J. A., Deb, K., Davis, D., Roy, R., O'Reilly, U.-M., Beyer, H.-G., Standish, R., Kendall, G., Wilson, S., Harman, M., Wegener, J., Dasgupta, D., Potter, M. A., Schultz, A. C., Dowsland, K., Jonoska, N., and Miller, J., editors, *Genetic and Evolutionary Computation – GECCO-2003*, volume 2724 of *LNCS*, pages 1764–1775, Chicago. Springer-Verlag.

Tay, E. and Taguchi, W. FG. (1993). *Taguchi on Robust Technology Development: Bringing Quality Engineering Upstream*. American Society of Mechanical Engineering Press, New York.

Thompson, A. and Layzell, P. (2000). Devolution of robustness in an electronics design. *Third Int. Conf., ICES 2000, volume 1801 of Lecture Notes in Computer Science. Evolvable Systems: From Biology to Hardware*, pages 218–228.

Tsutsui, S. and Ghosh, A. (1997). Genetic algorithms with a robust solution searching scheme. *IEEE Trans. Evolutionary Computation*, 1(3):201–208.

Zhu, J. (2001). Performance distribution analysis and robust design. *Journal of Mechanical Design*, 123(1):11–17.

Chapter 10

DOES GENETIC PROGRAMMING INHERENTLY ADOPT STRUCTURED DESIGN TECHNIQUES?

John M. Hall[1] and Terence Soule[2]

[1]*Hewlett-Packard Company;* [2]*University of Idaho*

Abstract   Basic genetic programming (GP) techniques allow individuals to take advantage of some basic top-down design principles. In order to evaluate the effectiveness of these techniques, we define a design as an evolutionary frozen root node. We show that GP design converges quickly based primarily on the best individual in the initial random population. This leads to speculation of several mechanisms that could be used to allow basic GP techniques to better incorporate top-down design principles.

Keywords: genetic programming, design, function choice, root node

1.   Introduction

Top-down design is one of the cornerstones of modern programming and program design techniques. The basic idea of top-down design is to make decisions that will divide each problem into smaller, more manageable subproblems (Lambert et al., 1997). The process is repeated on each of subproblem until the programmer is left with easily solved subproblems. This process is referred to as top-down because it focuses on the broader questions before addressing the more specific subproblems.

A simple example of this process is the problem of writing a program to calculate the area of a building. A typical top-down, approach might lead to the following design process. A) divide the problem into how to sum the areas of individual rooms and how to calculate the area of individual rooms. B) write a function to sum individual areas while assuming that the areas will be available. C) divide the problem of calculating the areas of individual rooms by the shape of the rooms: square, rectangular, circular, etc. D) write a function for each room shape. Note that the broader, more significant problems are addressed first; the design determines how to calculate the total area before addressing the problem of a specific room shape, that may only occur in a few buildings.

Top-down design can be implicitly mapped to a tree representation. (Indeed, top-down designs are often drawn as trees.) The complete tree represents the solution to the full problem. The root node divides the tree into two or more subtrees, which represent solutions to the first level of subproblems. The nodes at the next level further subdivides the subtrees into the subproblems, etc., until we reach problems that are simple enough to be solved via terminal instructions. Thus, the tree structure used in standard GP does inherently allow for a limited form of top-down design and problem decomposition (although this is no guarantee that GP uses a top-down approach). For example, if GP does inherently adopt a top-down design approach and if GP were used to address the problem of calculating the area of a building, we might expect to see numerous addition functions near the root nodes (to sum the area of the individual rooms) and multiplication functions near the leaves to calculate the areas of individual rooms.

The focus of this chapter is to determine whether or not GP does use a top-down approach. And, if so, to find out how quickly GP makes the decisions that have the largest impact on individual fitness. For this research, we limit ourselves to the first, and most significant, design decision–the root node choice. Our results suggest that GP does inherently perform limited top-down design for some problems, but is easily misled. Fixing the root node to the best design choice only marginally improves performance.

2.   Background

There is some evidence suggesting that GP does evolve trees following a generally top-down, structured order, fixing upper-level nodes early (top-down design) and fixing the overall tree structures (structured, decompositional design). However, it is unclear whether this order of evolution is followed because it is effective or because the natures of the GP operations favor fixing root nodes and structure early. McPhee and Hopper as well as Burke et. al. analyzed root node selection in simple, tree-based GP (McPhee and Hopper, 1999, Burke et al., 2002). They found that the upper levels of the individuals in a population become uniformly fixed in the early generations of a run and are very difficult to change in later generations. This suggests that GP adopts a structured design strategy; it works from the top-down, selecting higher level functions and decomposing the problem among the sub-trees.

Work by Daida et al. has shown that in the later generations of a GP run there is relatively little variation in the structure of the evolved trees (Daida et al., 2003) and is also discussed in chapter 5 of this volume. This suggests that GP selects a general structure and maintains it, adjusting the subtrees as necessary to improve fitness. However, it is unclear whether this structure is selected randomly or whether it represents a good design. It has also been shown that the typical GP tree structure falls within a region that can be defined by randomly generated trees (Langdon et al., 1999, Langdon, 2000). Similarly, Daida has shown that the typical GP tree structure can be defined using a stochastic diffusion-limited aggregation model (Daida, 2003). This model defines a relatively narrow region of the search space that most GP trees fall in. Thus, it is clear that the typical structure of GP trees is *bounded* by likely random structures. This suggests that the structure of GP trees is chosen randomly.

Within these bounded regions there are still a very large number of possible structures for evolution to choose from. It is possible that within these bounded regions GP is still actively selecting a beneficial structure. Further it is well known that the majority of code within a typical GP tree consists of non-coding regions. Non-coding regions are not subject to selective pressure based on content or structure. Thus, it is entirely possible that the structure of GP trees fall within the region bounded by random trees because the majority of the structure of a GP tree consists of non-coding regions that are effectively random. Whereas, the important coding regions, which are typically near the root (Soule and Foster, 1998), may in fact have structures that are selected by evolution.

It has also been shown that GP can be improved by explicitly incorporating structured design techniques into the evolutionary process. Several approaches have been proposed to incorporate these standard design techniques into GP. These examples are discussed here as examples of existing methods that allow GP to perform design better. Probably the best known approach is the use of automatically defined functions (ADFs) (Koza, 1994). In ADFs a normal GP tree is subdivided into a result producing branch and one or more function defining branches. Each of the function defining branches can be called from within the result producing branch (and possibly the other function defining branches). This makes typical top-down (or bottom-up) and decompositional design techniques possible; the problem can be decomposed into sub-problems solved by the function branches and the total program can be evolved either top-down (starting with the result producing branch) or bottom-up (starting with the function defining branches). ADFs have proven to be extremely successful at improving GP performance, which suggests that GP can take advantage of standard design techniques.

ADFs have been combined with architecture altering operators that allow the number and form of the function defining branches of a program with ADFs to be modified. Architecture altering operators further increase GP's ability to 'design' programs by making the number and form of the functions evolvable and the use of architecture altering operators have produced further performance gains.

Other, more limited, techniques for incorporating functions have also been proposed, including subtree encapsulation and module acquisition (Rosca and Ballard, 1996, Rosca, 1995, Angeline and Pollack, 1993). The techniques also improved GP performance, but to a much more limited extent.

The results described above are significant for two reasons. First, they show that GP algorithms that are capable of creating functions often perform better than those that aren't capable of creating functions. Second, they show that GPs with greater function creation capabilities perform better than GPs with poorer function creation capabilities. This suggests that GP uses, or at least imitates, top-down and decomposition design techniques when possible (i.e. when it can create separate reusable functions).

3.   Experimental Methods

Experiments

For these experiments we simplify the question of design by focusing only on the root node. The root node represents the first and most important design decision that can be made if a top-down methodology is used. Thus, if GP does follow a top-down, structured design process in evolving programs it should be most apparent in the selection of the root node.

Our first experiment forces a design on the evolutionary process by fixing the root node throughout the evolutionary process. In each of the experiments a different function is chosen to be the root node. It is fixed in the initial population and is not allowed to change either through mutation or crossover. In order to ensure significant results 500 trials are performed with each non-terminal function as the root. We then average the fitness of the best individual in each trial and define the function that generates the highest average fitness as the optimal root node and the best top-down design. The root node that produces the best performance in this experiment is assumed to represent the best initial design decision.

In the second experiment the population is initialized normally, that is with completely random trees. We then measure which function the population chose, via convergence, for the root node. Convergence is defined as at least 80% of the population having the same function at the root node, otherwise we assume the population is unconverged (in practice this very rarely occurred). In order to ensure significant results, 1000 trials are performed. This will determine whether the GP chooses the function for the root node as by experiment 1, and thus whether the GP is using 'good' design techniques.

The third experiment is designed to further understand the evolutionary forces that determine the root node choice. We identify the function at the root node of the best individual in each of the 1000 initial populations from the second experiment. This best, initial function is compared to the converged function from experiment 2 to determine how frequently GP simply converges on the best initial function.

The GP

Five test problems are used in this research: the Santa Fe Trail, intertwined spirals, symbolic regression, even parity, and battleship. The first four are chosen because they are commonly used benchmark problems. Additionally, they include representatives of classes of common application problems including classification, symbolic regression, and robot control. Thus, if inherent GP design is more or less likely in one type of problem, we should observe this in our results. Finally, these problems cover a wide range of non-terminal functions so if particular functions are more favorable to good design, we should also observe this in our results.

The general GP settings are fixed for all populations. All populations consist of 100 individuals. Populations are evaluated for 100 generations. It should be noted that these values are fixed despite the range of difficulties of test problems. Relatively small populations are used because we are not specifically interested in obtaining high fitness solutions, only in looking at the dynamics of root node selection. Previous research and our preliminary experiments demonstrated that in the majority of trials 100 generations is more than sufficient for the root nodes of a population to converge.

Individuals are created using ramped half and half (Koza, 1992). Grown trees have an 80% probability of each node being a non-terminal. In addition, all root nodes are non-terminals. As a slight simplification, all non-terminal nodes have the same number of branches. Operations which do not use all branches simply ignore the extra branches.

All individuals in the non-initial populations are created using the crossover and mutation genetic operators. Selection is rank based with a tournament of size 3. Crossover is performed 100% of the time. Crossover points are selected according to the 90/10 rule (Koza, 1992). Mutation is included in an effort to reduce any root node protectionism inherent to crossover. Mutation is applied with an average rate of 1 mutation per 100 nodes. Mutation never changes whether a node is a terminal or a non-terminal. New appropriate values are chosen uniformly. This gives a fair chance that a node is mutated back to its original value. A maximum depth limit of 20 is imposed. All individuals exceeding this depth are discarded. This limit is applied in an effort to limit code growth that may reduce the impact of crossover on the root of the tree.

In order to compare fitness values between test problems, the values are scaled to the range 0.0 to 1.0, where 1.0 is the optimal fitness. Parsimony pressure is applied as a tiebreaker in the event of an exact fitness match. This is more common with problems that have discrete fitness values.

Santa Fe Trail

The Santa Fe trail problem (Langdon and Poli, 1998), also known as the artificial ant problem requires a program to guide an ant along a path of food. The environment is modeled as a 32 by 32 discrete toroid. The ant starts in the Northwest corner facing east. The program is repeated until either all the food has been eaten or 500 actions have been performed. The fitness measure of a program is the percentage of food along this trail that is eaten.

Intertwined Spirals

The intertwined spirals problem (Koza, 1992a) is a classification problem. The goal is to evolve a program that correctly determines which of two spirals a given point is on. The points used include 96 points from each spiral. The fitness measure for a solution is what percentage of the 192 points are classified correctly. Because the classification requires a Boolean value, but the calculations use floating point numbers, the value produced by an individual is compared to 0. Values greater than or equal to zero are considered to be classified on the first spiral, and values less than zero are classified on the second spiral. The constants used for this problem are created uniformly on the interval -1.0 to 1.0. The division operator returns 1.0 when the divisor's magnitude is less than 0.000001.

Symbolic Regression

Symbolic regression attempts to evolve a function that approximates a group of sampled points. For this experiment, the sampled points are taken from the function $sin(x)$ at intervals of 0.5 starting at 0.

This simple regression function was chosen to simplify the problem which has many operators and tends to be 'difficult'. The error measurement used is simply the sum of the residuals between the actual points and the function evolved. In order to scale this error to the common 0.0 to 1.0 scale, the fitness function was 0.933^{error}. The constant 0.933 was chosen to give a fitness of 0.5 when the evaluation function had an average error of 1.0 per point. The constants used in this problem are generated uniformly on the interval -2.0 to 2.0. The division operator is protected in the same way as with the Santa Fe Trail problem.

Even Parity

The 6 bit even parity problem tries to evolve a Boolean function that returns the even parity of 6 input bits. The fitness of each individual is calculated by trying all 64 possible input configurations. The fitness is the percentage of these that give the correct output bit.

Battleship

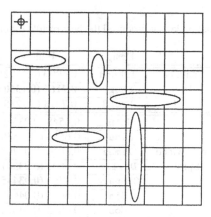

Figure 10-1. Battleship Problem

This chapter introduces the battleship problem. This problem is designed to be similar to the Santa Fe Trail problem, but it is hoped that the different states or behaviors allow more opportunity for design. The problem is based on the Battleship board game with only one player. The game is played on a 10 by 10 grid which contains one ship of length 5, one of length 4, two of length 3, and one of length 2. Figure 10-1 shows an example layout of ships. The goal is to hit the ships by moving a target over their location and firing. The target starts in the Northeast corner. The landscape does not wrap around from the left to right or top to bottom. A program is allowed up to 500 operations and up to 70 shots per game. In order to calculate the fitness of a solution, 25 games are played. The fitness is the total number of hits divided by the total number of possible hits. The 25 boards are created randomly and are not changed between generations.

The terminals for this problem are North, East, South, West, and No-Op. The first four move the target in the indicated direction one step. No-Op leaves the target unchanged. All 5 terminals count toward the 500 step limit.

The non-terminals for this problem are Fire, Prog2, and Loop. Fire conditionally executes either the left or the right branch based on whether there is a ship at the target location. This non-terminal counts toward the 70 shot limit and if there is a ship at the current target location, it is hit. Prog2 unconditionally executes its left and then its right branch. Loop is an unconditional loop that terminates only when the loop has no effect or the step limit is reached. For example if the only child of a Loop non-terminal is a West terminal, then the target would move all the way to the left of the board. Once there, the West terminal no longer has an effect and the loop terminates.

4. Results

Table 10-1. The fixed root node that produced the best results for each of the test problems.

	Design	Fitness
Santa Fe	IfFood	0.6900 (0.1192)
Trail	Prog2	**0.7162 (0.1360)**
	Prog3	0.7013 (0.1285)
	Plus	0.6548 (0.03569)
	Minus	0.6553 (0.03585)
Intertwined	Times	0.6616 (0.03708)
Spirals	Divide	0.6602 (0.03507)
	Compare	**0.6797 (0.03445)**
	Sin	0.6625 (0.04675)
	Cos	0.6542 (0.04012)
	Plus	0.9251 (0.02930)
Symbolic	Minus	0.9247 (0.03324)
Regression	Times	**0.9390 (0.02754)**
	Divide	0.9289 (0.04676)
	And	0.9661 (0.07339)
Even	Nand	0.9403 (0.08370)
Parity	Or	0.9618 (0.07272)
	Xor	**0.9907 (0.03135)**
	Fire	0.7259 (0.1174)
Battleship	Prog2	**0.7726 (0.06443)**
	Loop	0.7461 (0.09946)

Table 10-1 shows the average fitness for each of the functions for each problem. The fixed root design that averaged the best fitness for each of the test problems is shown in bold. For example, the best results for the Santa Fe Trail problem occur when the root is fixed as Prog2. In general, the differences in fitness are not statistically significant or, if significant, are fairly minor. This suggests that GP can easily adapt to whatever function is fixed at the root node.

Table 10-2 shows the results from the second experiment. This table shows the percentage of populations which converged to each function and the resulting average fitness and standard deviation (in parentheses). For reference, the values corresponding to the best design found in the *first* experiment are shown in bold. For example, with the Santa Fe Trail problem, in 42% of the 1000 trials the population converged on the IfFood function as a root node and in those trials the average best fitness was 0.6866.

These results show that the design/root node choice makes a small, but significant, difference in the final fitness. Comparison of the best and worst root

Table 10-2. Evolved Designs for Each Test Problem

	Converged Root	Evolved Fitness	% of Trials
Santa Fe Trail	IfFood	0.6866 (0.1159)	42%
	Prog2	**0.7163 (0.1300)**	**34%**
	Prog3	0.7115 (0.1259)	23%
	Unconverged	0.6899 (0.1366)	1.5%
Intertwined Spirals	Plus	0.6539 (0.03637)	17%
	Minus	0.6566 (0.02821)	15%
	Times	0.6638 (0.03450)	15%
	Divide	0.6726 (0.03641)	14%
	Compare	**0.6812 (0.03499)**	**18%**
	Sin	0.6729 (0.04009)	13%
	Cos	0.6485 (0.03580)	5%
	Unconverged	0.6539	3%
Symbolic Regression	Plus	0.9297 (0.02782)	12%
	Minus	0.9287 (0.02836)	11%
	Times	**0.9410 (0.02793)**	**30%**
	Divide	0.9364 (0.04157)	46%
	Unconverged	0.9251 (0.04460)	2%
Even Parity	And	0.9420 (0.08743)	10%
	Nand	0.9913 (0.03199)	7%
	Or	0.9815 (0.04180)	3%
	Xor	**0.9871 (0.03653)**	**73%**
	Unconverged	0.9954 (0.02280)	7%
Battleship	Fire	0.6591 (0.1074)	5%
	Prog2	**0.7685 (0.06788)**	**82%**
	Loop	0.7530 (0.08361)	6%
	Unconverged	0.7840 (0.05223)	7%

node choices shows a significant difference in all of the problems. In four of the five problems the best function selected via experiment one also produced the best fitness in experiment two. (The exception was the even parity problem where Xor is the best function with fixed root nodes, but Nand performed better as an evolved root node.) Thus, although the fitness differences seen in experiments 1 and 2 are small, the results are consistent between the fixed and evolved cases.

This supports the idea that for these problems there is a good design and a bad design as represented by the root node function. However, it is also clear that GP does not always select the optimal root node. In only two problems (parity and battleship) was the 'best' function, as determined in the first experiment, clearly favored by the GP and in only one case (battleship) did the favored function produce the best results. (Strictly speaking the favored function for intertwined spirals, Compare, also produced the best results, but it was favored by such a small margin that the results are not conclusive.)

With both even parity and battleship an argument that GP adopts a top-down design methodology could be made. In both cases the function that produced the best results when fixed is heavily favored and produces the best or nearly the best results when allowed to evolve. For these problems the evolutionary process appears to be recognizing and applying a beneficial design in the majority of trials. However, for the other problems this is not the case, instead the GP settles on a function that does not generate the best results when fixed or when evolved (e.g. for the Santa Fe Trail the GP settles on the IfFood root in the majority of trials even though Prog2 and Prog3 both produce better results on average, Table 10-2).

Table 10-3.   Initial Fitness for Each Operator for Each Problem

	Root Design	Best Initial	% of Trials
Santa Fe	IfFood	0.3089 (0.07572)	30%
Trail	Prog2	**0.3011 (0.07780)**	**35%**
	Prog3	0.2886 (0.06271)	35%
	Plus	0.5548 (0.01445)	16%
	Minus	0.5556 (0.01606)	15%
Intertwined	Times	0.5557 (0.01419)	16%
Spirals	Divide	0.5577 (0.01702)	16%
	Compare	**0.5557 (0.01460)**	**14%**
	Sin	0.5617 (0.01826)	18%
	Cos	0.5604 (0.01576)	5%
	Plus	0.7179 (0.05078)	10%
Symbolic	Minus	0.7100 (0.04861)	15%
Regression	Times	**0.6912 (0.03689)**	**32%**
	Divide	0.6883 (0.02609)	42%
	And	0.5754 (0.03314)	18%
Even	Nand	0.5776 (0.02904)	16%
Parity	Or	0.5728 (0.03246)	14%
	Xor	**0.5873 (0.03821)**	**53%**
	Fire	0.2197 (0.05904)	27%
Battleship	Prog2	**0.2452 (0.07965)**	**52%**
	Loop	0.2294 (0.05984)	21%

Our third experiment was designed to determine how GP selects the root function, given that it does not appear to select the function that results in the best solution. We hypothesize that GP either selects the function that produces the best overall fitness in the initial population or that GP selects the function that is most frequently the root node of the best individual in the initial population.

To test these hypotheses we examine the frequency with which a particular function produces the best of population member when that function is the root node and the average fitness of the best of population members with that function as the root node.

Table 10-3 shows how frequently each function is the root node of the best individual in the initial random populations and the average fitness of the best individuals with each function as the root node. E.g. for the Santa Fe Trail, in the initial population the best individual had the root node Prog2 in 35% of the trials and the average fitness of the best individuals from those 35% of the trials was 0.3011. The best design, as determined by the first experiment, is emphasized in bold.

The results suggest that both overall best fitness and frequency of best fitness are important. Table 10-3 shows that for both even parity and battleship (the two problems that seemed to adopt the best design) over half of the best individuals in the initial populations used the best top-level design, as determined by the first experiment, and that those individuals had the highest average fitness.

For the Santa Fe Trail, intertwined spirals, and symbolic regression problems the function producing the best fitness in the initial population is different from the function that most often produces the best fitness. For example, among the best programs for symbolic regression in the 1000 initial populations the programs with IfFood as the root node have the highest average fitness, but programs with Prog2 as the root are more likely to have the highest fitness. Also, for these three problems, the node leading to the greatest number of best of population programs is much less clearly defined.

Table 10-4. Design Evolution for Santa Fe Trail

Final Design

	IfFood	Prog2	Prog3
IfFood	70%	**15%**	14%
Prog2	28%	**55%**	16%
Prog3	31%	**31%**	36%

Tables 10-4-10-8 show a more detailed breakdown of the results of the third experiment. Each row in these tables shows the distribution of final designs given the initial design of the population. For example, in Table 10-4, the first row of data shows that with the Santa Fe Trail problem in the initial populations where IfFood is the design of the best individual, 70% of the populations converged to IfFood designs, 15% to Prog2 designs, and 14% to Prog3 designs. Thus, for the Santa Fe Trail, the root function of the best individual in the initial

Table 10-5.   Design Evolution for Intertwined Spirals

Final Design

	Plus	Minus	Mul	Div	Cmp	Sin	Cos
Plus	57%	8%	6%	7%	10%	4%	3%
Minus	10%	57%	6%	6%	10%	8%	1%
Mul	9%	8%	56%	7%	9%	4%	2%
Div	6%	9%	13%	52%	9%	5%	0%
Cmp	8%	9%	6%	4%	66%	4%	2%
Sin	15%	6%	4%	7%	11%	52	1%
Cos	12%	4%	2%	4%	10%	2%	66%

Table 10-6.   Design Evolution for Symbolic Regression

Final Design

	Plus	Minus	Times	Divide
Plus	33%	8%	22%	36%
Minus	9%	29%	25%	34%
Times	10%	10%	43%	35%
Divide	9%	7%	22%	60%

Table 10-7.   Design Evolution for Even Parity

Final Design

	And	Nand	Or	Xor
And	28%	6%	0%	54%
Nand	7%	19%	2%	65%
Or	4%	6%	10%	70%
Xor	6%	4%	2%	83%

population is significant in determining the converged root function after 100 generations.

In each table, the column which represents the best final design (from experiment 1) has been emphasized in bold. In most cases the function that the population converges on as the root node is the same function that generated the best of population individual in the initial, random population. One exception is Minus in the symbolic regression problem. In the trials where Minus was the root node of the best individual 34% of the populations converged on Divide

Table 10-8. Design Evolution for Battleship

Final Design

	Fire	Prog2	Loop
Fire	9%	79%	4%
Prog2	3%	87%	5%
Loop	5%	73%	12%

as the root node function and only 25% populations maintained Minus as the root node function.

These results suggest that in most cases the root node converges on a function before sampling sufficient individuals to identify the optimal design/function. This is mostly clearly shown for the Intertwined Spirals problem, Table 10-5. Along the diagonal where the initial best design matches the final design, all the values are over 50%. This implies that in over 50% of the trials, the final design is determined by the best individual in the initial random population. This could be viewed as premature convergence.

With Even parity, Xor seems sufficiently better than the other operators that it attracts from other designs. However, there is still a small 'trap' for the other operators. For example 28% of the time when And is the design of the best individual in the initial population, it is also the final design that is converged to. The percentages of Nand and Or are smaller. The same appears true for the battleship problem.

The 'designs' of the Santa Fe Trail, intertwined spirals, and symbolic regression problems are misleading. Table 10-3 shows that in all three problems the optimal root node function from the first experiment appears as the optimal root node function in less than half of the trials. In addition, in the cases of the intertwined spirals and symbolic regression problems, other designs appeared more frequently than the optimal designs. The data for Santa Fe Trail is less clear. It appears that there are several 'traps' with the initial design. If the initial best design is IfFood, 70% of the populations will evolve with the same design. With Prog2, the best design, only 55% of the populations will evolve to the same design. If the initial best design is Prog3, the final designs appear to be randomly distributed. For Symbolic Regression, Divide seems to trap and Plus and Minus seem to be redistributed. It is also interesting that different designs rarely result in a Plus or Minus in the final design. So, there is some 'design' away from specific functions.

5.   Discussion and Conclusions

Genetic programming appears to mimic top-down design methods in that it fixes programs from the root down. Thereby approaching the broadest problem first by subdividing it into two (or more) sub-problems. GP also settles on a general program structure early in the evolutionary process. However, the root function appears to be chosen largely based on the results of the first generation. This works well when the best initial root function is the overall best choice. However, many problems appear to be deceptive; the function that produces the best results in the initial population does not lead to the best results. For other problems there is no clear favorite in the initial population and the favored root node arises by chance.

In both of these cases the fixing of the root node can be viewed as an example of partial premature convergence; the population converges on a particular function for the root node without sufficient exploration to determine if that is the ideal root node. However, unlike a GA where prematurely fixing a bit can have significant affects on fitness, GP appears to be fairly adept at finding a near optimal solution even when a poor choice is made for the root node.

Given that genetic programming appears to be converging on the top-level nodes too quickly, at least for the more difficult and deceptive problems, there are several methods that may be useful to improve performance. Increasing the population size may allow the evolutionary process to sample enough individuals that the best design is more likely to be chosen. Sastry et al. have proposed specific rules for population sizes based on the need to sample available building blocks (Sastry et al., 2003) and see chapter 4 of this volume. It is unclear whether their sizing rules apply to our design question, as we are looking at functions at a specific location (the root) whereas their rules are based on position independent sampling.

An alternative, and more ad hoc approach, would be to begin with a very large population. This would improve the GP's sampling of the root node choices and may make it more likely that the population will converge on the optimal root function. After the population begins to converge, the population size would be reduced to more typical values. However, if design complexity were to increase linearly, it is expected that the population size would need to increase exponentially to be as effective. Another possibility would be to apply fitness sharing using the design of each individual. This would reduce the convergence problem, but would become more expensive and less reliable as the depth of the design considered increases. Manually forcing the root node to a predetermined best function would not improve performance very much (average fitness for experiments 1 and 2). In general, at least for these problems the difference in fitness between optimal and non-optimal root functions did not have a large effect on performance.

References

Angeline, P. J. and Pollack, J. B. (1993). Evolutionary module acquisition. In Fogel, D. and Atmar, W., editors, *Proceedings of the Second Annual Conference on Evolutionary Programming*, pages 154–163, La Jolla, CA, USA.

Burke, Edmund, Gustafson, Steven, and Kendall, Graham (2002). A survey and analysis of diversity measures in genetic programming. In Langdon, W. B., Cantú-Paz, E., Mathias, K., Roy, R., Davis, D., Poli, R., Balakrishnan, K., Honavar, V., Rudolph, G., Wegener, J., Bull, L., Potter, M. A., Schultz, A. C., Miller, J. F., Burke, E., and Jonoska, N., editors, *GECCO 2002: Proceedings of the Genetic and Evolutionary Computation Conference*, pages 716–723, New York. Morgan Kaufmann Publishers.

Daida, Jason M. (2003). What makes a problem GP-hard? In Riolo, Rick L. and Worzel, Bill, editors, *Genetic Programming Theory and Practice*, chapter 7, pages 99–118. Kluwer.

Daida, Jason M., Hilss, Adam M., Ward, David J., and Long, Stephen L. (2003). Visualizing tree structures in genetic programming. In Cantú-Paz, E., Foster, J. A., Deb, K., Davis, D., Roy, R., O'Reilly, U.-M., Beyer, H.-G., Standish, R., Kendall, G., Wilson, S., Harman, M., Wegener, J., Dasgupta, D., Potter, M. A., Schultz, A. C., Dowsland, K., Jonoska, N., and Miller, J., editors, *Genetic and Evolutionary Computation – GECCO-2003*, volume 2724 of *LNCS*, pages 1652–1664, Chicago. Springer-Verlag.

Koza, John R. (1992a). A genetic approach to the truck backer upper problem and the inter-twined spiral problem. In *Proceedings of IJCNN International Joint Conference on Neural Networks*, volume IV, pages 310–318. IEEE Press.

Koza, John R. (1992b). *Genetic Programming: On the Programming of Computers by Means of Natural Selection*. MIT Press, Cambridge, MA, USA.

Koza, John R. (1994). *Genetic Programming II: Automatic Discovery of Reusable Programs*. MIT Press, Cambridge Massachusetts.

Lambert, Kenneth A., Nance, Douglas W., and Naps, Thomas L. (1997). *Introduction to Computer Science with C++*. PWS Publishing Company, Boston, MA, USA.

Langdon, W. B. (2000). Quadratic bloat in genetic programming. In Whitley, Darrell, Goldberg, David, Cantu-Paz, Erick, Spector, Lee, Parmee, Ian, and Beyer, Hans-Georg, editors, *Proceedings of the Genetic and Evolutionary Computation Conference (GECCO-2000)*, pages 451–458, Las Vegas, Nevada, USA. Morgan Kaufmann.

Langdon, W. B. and Poli, R. (1998). Why ants are hard. In Koza, John R., Banzhaf, Wolfgang, Chellapilla, Kumar, Deb, Kalyanmoy, Dorigo, Marco, Fogel, David B., Garzon, Max H., Goldberg, David E., Iba, Hitoshi, and Riolo, Rick, editors, *Genetic Programming 1998: Proceedings of the Third Annual Conference*, pages 193–201, University of Wisconsin, Madison, Wisconsin, USA. Morgan Kaufmann.

Langdon, William B., Soule, Terry, Poli, Riccardo, and Foster, James A. (1999). The evolution of size and shape. In Spector, Lee, Langdon, William B., O'Reilly, Una-May, and Angeline, Peter J., editors, *Advances in Genetic Programming 3*, chapter 8, pages 163–190. MIT Press, Cambridge, MA, USA.

McPhee, Nicholas Freitag and Hopper, Nicholas J. (1999). Analysis of genetic diversity through population history. In Banzhaf, Wolfgang, Daida, Jason, Eiben, Agoston E., Garzon, Max H., Honavar, Vasant, Jakiela, Mark, and Smith, Robert E., editors, *Proceedings of the Genetic and Evolutionary Computation Conference*, volume 2, pages 1112–1120, Orlando, Florida, USA. Morgan Kaufmann.

Rosca, Justinian (1995). Towards automatic discovery of building blocks in genetic programming. In Siegel, E. V. and Koza, J. R., editors, *Working Notes for the AAAI Symposium on Genetic Programming*, pages 78–85, MIT, Cambridge, MA, USA. AAAI.

Rosca, Justinian P. and Ballard, Dana H. (1996). Discovery of subroutines in genetic programming. In Angeline, Peter J. and Kinnear, Jr., K. E., editors, *Advances in Genetic Programming 2*, chapter 9, pages 177–202. MIT Press, Cambridge, MA, USA.

Sastry, Kumara, O'Reilly, Una-May, Goldberg, David E., and Hill, David (2003). Building block supply in genetic programming. In Riolo, Rick L. and Worzel, Bill, editors, *Genetic Programming Theory and Practice*, chapter 9, pages 137–154. Kluwer.

Soule, Terence and Foster, James A. (1998). Removal bias: a new cause of code growth in tree based evolutionary programming. In *1998 IEEE International Conference on Evolutionary Computation*, pages 781–186, Anchorage, Alaska, USA. IEEE Press.

Chapter 11

GENETIC PROGRAMMING OF AN ALGORITHMIC CHEMISTRY

W. Banzhaf[1] and C. Lasarczyk[2]

[1]*Memorial University of Newfoundland;* [2]*University of Dortmund*

Abstract   We introduce a new method of execution for GP-evolved programs consisting of register machine instructions. It is shown that this method can be considered as an artificial chemistry. It lends itself well to distributed and parallel computing schemes in which synchronization and coordination are not an issue.

Informally, an *algorithm* is a well-defined computational procedure that takes some value, or set of values, as *input* and produces some value, or set of values, as *output*. An algorithm is thus a sequence of computational steps that transform the input into the output.

(Introduction to Algorithms, TH Cormen et al)

1.   Introduction

In this chapter we shall introduce a new way of looking at transformations from input to output that does not require the second part of the definition quoted above: a prescribed sequence of computational steps. Instead, the elements of the transformation, which in our case are single instructions from a multiset $I = \{I_1, I_2, I_3, I_2, I_3, I_1, ...\}$ are drawn in a random order to produce a transformation result. In this way we dissolve the sequential order usually associated with an algorithm for our programs. It will turn out, that such an arrangement is still able to produce wished-for results, though only under the reign of a programming method that banks on its stochastic character. This method will be Genetic Programming.

A program in this sense is thus not a sequence of instructions but rather an assemblage of instructions that can be executed in arbitrary order. By randomly choosing one instruction at a time, the program proceeds through its transformations until a predetermined number of instructions has been executed. In the present work we set the number of instructions to be executed at five times the size of the multiset, this way giving ample chance to each instruction to be executed at least once and to exert its proper influence on the result.

Different multi-sets can be considered different programs, whereas different passes through a multi–set can be considered different behavioral variants of a single program. Programs of this type can be seen as artificial chemistries, where instructions interact with each other (by taking the transformation results from one instruction and feeding it into another). As it will turn out, many interactions of this type are, what in an Artificial Chemistry is called "elastic", in that nothing happens as a result, for instance because the earlier instruction did not feed into the arguments of the later.[1]

Because instructions are drawn randomly in the execution of the program, it is really the concentration of instructions that matters most. It is thus expected that "programming" of such a system requires the proper choice of concentrations of instructions, similar to what is required from the functioning of living cells, where at each given time many reactions happen simultaneously but without a need to synchronicity.

Even if the reader at this point is skeptical about the feasibility of such a method, suppose for the moment, it would work. What would it mean for parallel and distributed computing? Perhaps it would mean that parallel and distributed computing could be freed from the need to constantly synchronize and keep proper orders. Perhaps it would be a method able to harvest a large amount of CPU power at the expense, admittedly, of some efficiency because the number of instructions to be executed will be higher than in deterministic sequential programs. In fact, due to the stochastic nature of results, it might be advisable to execute a program multiple times before a conclusion is drawn about its "real" output. In this way, it is again the concentration of output results that matters. Therefore, a number of n passes through the program should be taken before any reliable conclusion about its result can be drawn. Reliability in this sense would be in the eye of the beholder. Should results turn out to be not reliable enough, simply increasing n would help to narrow down the uncertainty. Thus the method is perfectly scalable, with more computational power thrown at the problem achieving more accurate results.

We believe that, despite this admitted inefficiency of the approach in the small, it might well beat sequential or synchronized computing at large, if we

---

[1] Elastic interactions have some bearings on neutral code, but they are not identical.

imagine tens of thousands or millions of processors at work. It really looks much more like a chemistry than like ordinary computing, the reason why we call it algorithmic chemistry.

2.   Background

Algorithmic Chemistries were considered earlier in the work of Fontana (Fontana, 1992). In that work, a system of λ-calculus expressions was examined in their interaction with each other. Due to the nature of the λ-calculus, each expression could serve both as a function and as an argument to a function. The resulting system produced, upon encounter of λ-expressions, new λ-expressions.

In our contribution we use the term as an umbrella term for those kinds of artificial chemistries (Dittrich et al., 2001) that aim at algorithms. As opposed to terms like randomized or probabilistic algorithms, in which a certain degree of stochasticity is introduced explicitly, our algorithms have an implicit type of stochasticity. Executing the sequence of instructions every time in a different order has the potential of producing highly unpredictable results.

It will turn out, however, that even though the resulting computation is unpredictable in principle, evolution will favor those multi-sets of instructions that turn out to produce approximately correct results after execution. This feature of approximating the wished-for results is a consequence of the evolutionary forces of mutation, recombination and selection, and will have nothing to do with the actual order in which instructions are being executed. Irrespective of how many processors would work on the multi-set, the results of the computation would tend to fall into the same band of approximation. We submit, therefore, that methods like this can be very useful in parallel and distributed environments.

Our previous work on Artificial Chemistries (see, for example (Banzhaf, 1993, di Fenizio et al., 2000, Dittrich and Banzhaf, 1998, Ziegler and Banzhaf, 2001)) didn't address the question of how to write algorithms "chemically" in enough detail. In (Banzhaf, 1995) we introduced a very general analogy between chemical reaction and algorithmic computation, arguing that concentrations of results would be important. The present contribution aims to fill that gap and to put forward a proposal as to how such an artificial chemistry could look like.

3.   The Method

Genetic Programming (GP) (Koza, 1992, Banzhaf et al., 1998) belongs to the family of Evolutionary Algorithms (EA). These heuristic algorithms try to improve originally random solutions to a problem via the mechanisms of recombination, mutation and selection. Many applications of GP can be described as evolution of models (Eiben and Smith, 2003). The elements of models are usually arithmetic expressions, logical expressions or executable programs.

Here, we shall use evolution of a sine function (an approximation problem) and of a thyroid pattern diagnosis problem (a classification problem). We represent a program as a set of instructions only stored as a linear sequence in memory due to technical limitations. These instructions are 2 and 3 address instructions which work on a set of registers.

It should be noted that — in contrast to tree-based GP — each change in an instruction of this representation will have global effects. If, as a result of a change in an instruction, a certain register holds a different value, this will affect all registers making use of this register as input argument.

Linear GP with Sequence Generators

Here we shall use 3-address machine instructions. The genotype of an individual is a list of those instructions. Each instruction consists of an operation, a destination register, and two source registers[2]. Initially, individuals are produced by randomly choosing instructions. As is usual, we employ a set of fitness cases in order to evaluate (and subsequently select) individuals.

Figure 11-1 shows the execution of an individual in linear GP. A sequence

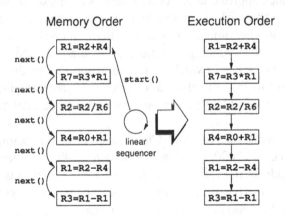

Figure 11-1.　Execution of an individual in linear GP. Memory order and execution order correspond to each other. Arrows indicate returned values of calls to the sequence generator.

generator is used to determine the sequence of instructions. Each instruction is executed, with resulting data stored in its destination register. Usually, the sequence generator moves through the program sequence instruction by instruc-

---

[2]Operations which require only one source register simply ignore the second register.

tion. Thus, the location in memory space determines the particular sequence of instructions. Classically, this is realized by the program counter.[3]

1–Point–*Crossover* can be described using two sequence generators. The first generator is acting on the first parent and returns instructions at its beginning. These instructions form the first part of the offspring. The second sequence generator operates on the other parent. We ignore the first instructions this generator returns[4]. The others form the tail of the offsprings instruction list.

Mutation changes single instructions by changing either operation, or destination register or the source registers according to a prescribed probability distribution.

A register machine as an Algorithmic Chemistry

There is a simple way to realize an chemistry by a register machine. By substituting the systematic incremental stepping of the sequence generator by a random sequence we arrive at our system. That is to say, the instructions are drawn randomly from the set of all instructions in the program[5]. Still, we have to provide the number of registers, starting conditions and determine a target register from which output is to be drawn.

As shown in Figure 11-2 the chemistry works by executing the instructions of an individual analogous to what would happen in a linear GP–System (cf. 11-1), except that the sequence order is different.

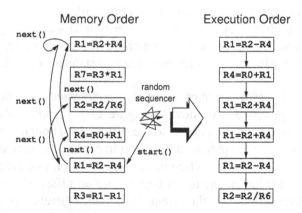

Figure 11-2. Execution in the AC system. The sequence generator returns a random order for execution.

---

[3](Conditional) jumps are a deviation from this behavior.
[4]Should crossover generate two offspring, the instructions not copied will be used for a second offspring.
[5]For technical reasons instructions are ordered in memory space, but access to an instruction (and subsequent execution) are done in random order.

It should be noted that there are registers with different features: Some registers are read-only. They can only be used as source registers. These registers contain constant values and are initialized for each fitness case at the start of program execution. All other registers can be read from and written into. These are the connection registers among which information flows in the course of the computation. Initially they are set to zero.

How a program behaves during execution will differ from instance to instance. There is no guarantee that an instruction is executed, nor is it guaranteed that this happens in a definite order or frequency. If, however, an instruction is more frequent in the multi-set, then its execution will be more probable. Similarly, if it should be advantageous to keep independence between data paths, the corresponding registers should be different in such a way that the instructions are not connecting to each other. Both features would be expected to be subject to evolutionary forces.

Evolution of an Algorithmic Chemistry

Genetic programming of this algorithmic chemistry (ACGP) is similar to other GP variants. The use of a sequence generator should help understand this similarity. We have seen already in Section 3.0 how an individual in ACGP is evaluated.

Initialization and mutation.   Initialization and mutation of an individual are the same for both the ACGP and usual linear GP.

Mutation will change operator and register numbers according to a probability distribution. In the present implementation register values are changed using a Gaussian with mean at present value and standard deviation 1.

Crossover.   Crossover makes use of the randomized sequences produced by the sequence generator. As shown in Figure 11-3 a random sequence of instructions is copied from the parents to the offspring. Though the instructions inherited from each of the parents are located in contiguous memory locations, the actual sequence of the execution is not dependent on that order. The probability that a particular instruction is copied into an offspring depends on the frequency of that instruction in the parent. Inheritance therefore is inheritance of frequencies of instructions, rather than of particular sequences of instructions.

Constant register values will be copied with equal probability from each parent, as is done for choice of the result register.

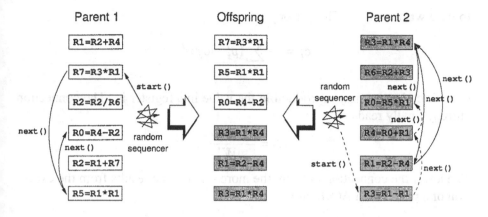

Figure 11-3. Crossover in an Artificial Chemistry.

Measures

Most measures, like the number of instructions of a program, can remain the same as in other GP systems, some are not observable at all, e.g. edit distance, or are completely new, as *connection entropy* described next.

If a register is written into from different instructions of a program which all might be equally frequent in the program, reproducibility of a result is strongly dependent on the sequence generator's seed. If, however, all registers are only written into from one instruction the result is more reproducible.

In order to increase reproducibility of results, the concentration of necessary instructions needs to be increased and that of other instructions needs to be decreased. One main influence on this is provided by crossover. At the same time, however, it is advantageous, to decouple flow of data interfering with the proper calculation. The connection entropy is designed to measure the progress along this line.

Let W be the set of connection registers participating in any data path. A connection register $i \in W$ might be written into by operations o_i^j of instructions j. Each of these instructions might be in multiple copies in the program, with $|o_i^j|$ the number of copies. We then have

$$O_i = \sum_{\forall j} |o_i^j|$$

the number of instructions that write into register i. Instruction o_i^j has probability

$$p_i^j = \frac{|o_i^j|}{O_i}$$

to have written into i. The entropy

$$e_i = -\sum_{\forall j}(p_i^j \cdot \log p_i^j)$$

of register i states how reproducible the value in a register is. The connection entropy finally reads

$$E = \frac{\sum_{i \in W} e_i}{|W|}.$$

The lower the connection entropy the more reliable the results from the execution of a program in ACGP are.

4.   Description of Experiments

We take two sample problems to demonstrate that the idea works in principle. The first one is approximation of the sine function, the second problem is classification of thyroid function on real world data. Table 11-1 lists parameters chosen identically for both problems. Table 11-2 shows settings that differ for

Table 11-1.   Common settings of both experiments.

Parameter	Value
Population	
Parents	100
Offsprings	500
Individual/Algorithmic Chemistry	
Connection registers	30
Evolved Constants	11
Operationset	add,sub,div,mult, pow,and,or,not
Init Length	100
Maximum Length	1000
Evaluation	
Nr. of randomly drawn instructions	5× length
Training set sampling	Stochastic subset sampling
Crossover rate	0.5
Mutation probability per entry	0.03
Evolution	
Generations	500

both problems. Additionally, both problems vary in their fitness function. In the following section we describe the applied fitness functions and give some more information about the two problems.

Table 11-2. Differences mainly concern the problem type and evaluation sets.

Parameter	Value	
	sine	**thyroid**
Problem type	regression	classification
Number of inputs	1 real value	21 values (6 real, 15 binary)
Training set size	1000	3772
subset (SSS)	100	400
Validation set size	400	1000
Testing set size	400	2428

Regression — Sine Function Approximation

Approximation of a sine function with non–trigonometric functions is a non–trivial but illustrative problem. The set of fitness cases $V = \{(x_1, y_1), (x_2, y_2), \ldots, (x_n, y_n)\}$ is created in the following way: In the interval $[-\pi, \pi]$ random values x_i are used to calculate values $y_i = sin(x_i)$, $i \in \{1, 2, \ldots, n\}$.

Given a subset V' of the training set V, the fitness function is the mean squared error of the individual I applied to all fitness cases of the subset:

$$f(I) = \left(\sum_{(x,y) \in V'} (I(x) - y)^2 \right) \bigg/ |V'| \ .$$

(x, y) denotes a fitness case in the subset V' of size $|V'|$, x the input and y the desired output.

Classification — Thyroid Problem

The thyroid–problem is a real world problem. The individual's task is to classify humans thyroid function. The dataset was obtained from the UCI–repository (Blake and Merz, 1998). It contains 3772 training and 3428 testing samples, each measured from one patient. A fitness case consists of a measurement vector containing 15 binary and 6 real valued entries of one human being and the appropriate thyroid function (class).

There are three different classes for the function of the thyroid gland, named *hyper function*, *hypo function* and *normal function*. As Gathercole (Gathercole, 1998) already showed, two out of these three classes, the hyper function and the hypo function, are linearly separable. Given the measurement vector as input, an individual of the ACGP system should decide whether the thyroid gland is normal functioning (class 1), or should be characterized as hyper or hypo function (class 2).

Because more than 92% of all patients contained in the dataset have a normal function, the classification error must be significantly lower than 8%. The classification error is the percentage of misclassified dataset. We use the classification error as our fitness function.

The selection algorithm picks its subsets out of the 3772 training examples. From the set of testing examples we remove the first 1000 examples to form a validation set. The remaining examples form the testing set.

We assign the following meaning to the output of the individuals. A negative output (< 0) denotes normal function, otherwise hyper or hypo function.

5.   Performance Observation

Figure 11-4 shows the characteristics of fitness, length and entropy for both experiments described in section 4. All results are averaged over 100 runs.

Fitness

Fitness characteristics are shown for population average as well as populations best individual, based on a subset of the training set. All individuals are tested on a validation set and the best individual is then applied to the testing set. The third characteristics shows fitness on this set in average.

In Figure 11.4(a) one can see their variation in time for the thyroid problem.

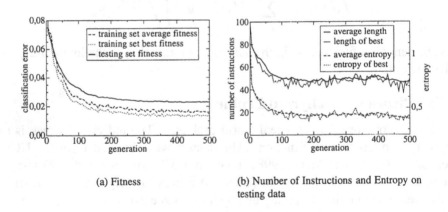

(a) Fitness

(b) Number of Instructions and Entropy on testing data

Figure 11-4.   Observations on classification of thyroid function.

In this example fitness is equal to classification error. The average classification error (on the test set) after 500 generations is 2.29%. The lowest classification error ever reached is 1.36%, observed after 220 generations. Using different settings, Gathercole (Gathercole, 1998) reports classification errors between 1.6% and 0.73% as best result using his tree–based GP system. He also cites a classification error of 1.52% for neural networks from Schiffmann et. al. (Schiffmann et al., 1992).

Figure 11.5(a) shows mean squared error (MSE) as fitness value for the sinus approximation problem. The lowest MSE observed ever is 0.026. One

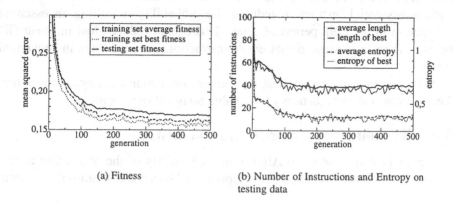

(a) Fitness

(b) Number of Instructions and Entropy on testing data

Figure 11-5. Observations on approximation of the sine function.

run achieved this value, but it got lost in subsequent generations. Runs better than average (0.17) show values next to 0.11. Certainly, there is room for improvement regarding these results.

The MSE might not be an adequate fitness function for Algorithmic Chemistries. No evaluation of a fitness case is like another, because a new random order of instructions is used for each fitness case. While an insufficient order leads to a low error on classification problems (one misclassification), it could lead to a large error on regression problems using MSE. Even if an Algorithmic Chemistry leads to good results on almost every fitness case, a single failure could have a large effect on the individual's fitness value. This complicates evolution. Limiting maximum error of a fitness case could be a possible way out.

Program Length and Connection Entropy

program length

Due to our definition of entropy, its variation in time is comparable to length of the individuals. For this reason they are shown in the same chart (Fig. 11.4(b) and 11.5(b)). We plotted the population means as well as the characteristics of population's best individual averaged over 100 runs. Values of the best individuals should give an impression on how selection pressure influences the mean value.

At the outset individuals loose between 20% and 40% of their initial length of 100 instructions immediately. Within the first 100 generations they reduce length even more and keep a nearly constant length afterwards. We cannot observe bloat by ineffective code as it is known in linear GP. For this behavior we take two reasons into account. First, bloat protects blocks of code belonging together in a specific order from being separated by the crossover operation. As there is no order in ACs, there is no need for such kind of protection. Second, each nonessential instruction reduces the probability of calling an essential instruction in the right period of time. This cannot reduce bloat in linear GP, because there it is assured that every instruction is called once in sequential order.

With decrease in average length, average connection entropy declines, too. This increases the uniqueness of the value assigned to a register.

Visualization of an Algorithmic Chemistry

Figure 11-6 represents an Algorithmic Chemistry of the population at two different time steps. Each register is represented by a node. Read-only registers

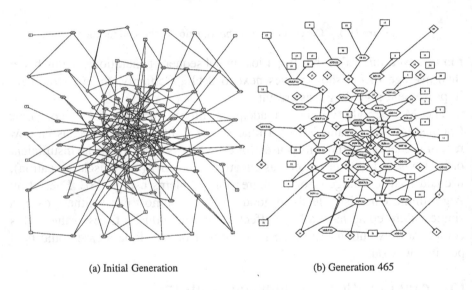

(a) Initial Generation   (b) Generation 465

Figure 11-6.   Graph of the best Algorithmic Chemistry for Thyroid problem at different generations.

are drawn as boxes. Other registers are symbolized by a diamond. Thus the output register is a diamond, and it is also drawn bold. Instructions are presented as hexagons. They are labeled by the name of the operation that belongs to the instruction they represent with number of identical instructions in parenthesis.

Every instruction–node is connected by an edge to the register it uses. The circle at the end of an edge symbolizes the kind of access. A filled circle shows a write access, an empty circle shows an read access. Flow of information between instructions happens when one instruction writes and the other reads a particular register.

Figure 11.6(a) shows a graph of an initial individual. It consists of 100 randomly assembled instructions. Nearly all instruction are single instances, and all registers are in use. Figure 11.6(b) shows a later time step in evolution. One can clearly see the reduced number of different instructions. Some instructions show a higher concentration than the others. Many registers that only allow read access, proved to be useless during evolution and are not accessed any more.

In Figure 11-7 one can see a part of the last graph with a different layout.

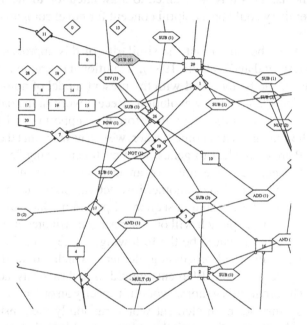

Figure 11-7. Most important part of the Chemistry shown in Figure 11.6(b). It shows all operations and registers responsible for the chemistries result. The number in parenthesis indicates how often this instruction is in the multiset. Brightness should indicate an instruction's frequency, with darker nodes having higher frequency.

The result register of this AC is register 11 shown at top left. Just one instruction is doing a write access on this register. It is a subtraction available six times in this AC. One of its source registers is register 29 of the register set that just allows read access. While the first 21 Registers in this set contain the inputs of the fitness case, the others contain evolved constants. The second input is a writable register (numbered 26). At this point of time in evolution there is also just one write access to this register. Here it is another subtraction available three times in this chemistry. It subtracts two values of the fitness case.

This illustrates how evolution achieves an evaluation with a high reproducibility within Artificial Chemistries. The two main mechanisms are reduction of competitive write-access to registers and an increase in the concentration of important instructions.

6.   Summary and Outlook

In this contribution it was not our intention to introduce simply a new representation for Genetic Programming. Instead, we wanted to show that goal-oriented behaviour is possible with a seemingly uncoordinated structure of program elements. This way we wanted to draw attention to the fact that an algorithmic chemistry could be a helpful concept for novel computer architecture considerations.

In fact a lot can be said about the similarity of this approach to data-flow architectures (Arwind and Kathail, 1981). Traditional restrictions of that architecture, however, can be loosened with the present model of non-deterministic computation, "programmed" by evolution. Recent work in the data-flow community (Swanson et al., 2003) might therefore find support in such an approach.

Spinning the analogy of a genome further, we can now see that the instructions used in ACGP are equivalent to genes, with each gene being "expressed" into a form that is executed. Execution of an instruction can, however, happen uncoordinated with execution of another instruction. So we are much nearer to a regulatory network here than to a sequential program (Banzhaf, 2003).

The strength of this approach will only appear if distributedness is taken into account. The reasoning would be the following: Systems of this kind should consist of a large number of processing elements which would share program storage and register content. Elements would asynchronously access storage and register. The program's genome wouldn't specify an order for the execution of instructions. Instead, each element would randomly pick instructions and execute them. Communication with the external world would be performed via a simple control unit.

It goes without saying that such a system would be well suited for parallel processing. Each additional processing element would accelerate the evaluation of programs. There would be no need for massive communication and for synchronization between processing elements. The system would be scalable at run-time: New elements could be added or removed without administrative overhead. The system as a whole would be fault-tolerant, failure of processing elements would appear merely as a slowed-down execution. Loss of information would not be a problem, and new processes need not be started instead of lost ones. Reducing the number of processors (and thus slowing down computation) could be allowed even for power management.

Explicit scheduling of tasks would not be necessary. Two algorithmic chemistries executing different tasks could be unified into one even, provided they used different connection registers. Would it be necessary that one task should be prioritized a higher concentration of instructions would be sufficient to achieve that.

Finally (though we haven't demonstrated that here) programs which are never sequentially executed don't need to reside in contiguous memory space. A good deal of memory management would therefore also become superfluous.

According to (Silberschatz and Galvin, 1994) "[a] computer system has many resources (hardware and software) that may be required to solve a problem: CPU time, memory space, file storage space, I/O devices, and so on. The operating system acts as a manager of these resources and allocates them to specific programs and users as necessary for their tasks". Architectural designs as the ones considered here would greatly simplify operating systems.

It is clear that non-deterministic programs resulting from runs of an ACGP system would not be suitable for all applications of computers. Already today, however, a number of complex systems (like the embedded systems in a car) have to process a large amount of noisy sensor data about the environment. It is frequently necessary to measure the same quantity repeatedly in order to arrive at safe observations. In such cases one would simply extend the repetition of tasks into computing. Adding processing would therefore simultaneously lead to more reliable conclusions from these observations.

Our real world is messy and non-deterministic. Would not a GP approach driving a messy and non-deterministic computational system be well suited for taking up these challenges?

Acknowledgements

The authors gratefully acknowledge support from a grant of the Deutsche Forschungsgemeinschaft DFG to W.B. under Ba 1042/7–3.

References

Arwind and Kathail, V. (1981). A multiple processor data flow machine that supports generalized procedures. In *International Conference on Computer Architecture (Minneapolis 1981)*, Los Alamitos, CA. IEEE Computer Society.

Banzhaf, W. (1993). Self-replicating sequences of binary numbers. *Comput. Math. Appl.*, 26:1–8.

Banzhaf, W., Nordin, P., Keller, R., and Francone, F. (1998). *Genetic Programming - An Introduction*. Morgan Kaufmann, San Francisco, CA.

Banzhaf, Wolfgang (1995). Self-organizing Algorithms Derived from RNA Interactions. In Banzhaf, W. and Eeckman, F.H., editors, *Evolution and Biocomputing*, volume 899 of *LNCS*, pages 69–103. Springer, Berlin.

Banzhaf, Wolfgang (2003). Artificial Regulatory Networks and Genetic Programming. In Riolo, R. and Worzel, B., editors, *Genetic Programming — Theory and Practice*, GP Series, pages 43–62. Kluwer, Norwell, MA.

Blake, C. L. and Merz, C. J. (1998). UCI repository of machine learning databases. http://www.ics.uci.edu/~ι

di Fenizio, P. Speroni, Dittrich, P., Banzhaf, W., and Ziegler, J. (2000). Towards a Theory of Organizations. In Hauhs, M. and Lange, H., editors, *Proceedings of the German 5th Workshop on Artificial Life*, Bayreuth, Germany. Bayreuth University Press.

Dittrich, P. and Banzhaf, W. (1998). Self-Evolution in a Constructive Binary String System. *Artificial Life*, 4(2):203–220.

Dittrich, P., Ziegler, J., and Banzhaf, W. (2001). Artificial Chemistries - A Review. *Artificial Life*, 7:225–275.

Eiben, G. and Smith, J. (2003). *Introduction to Evolutionary Computing*. Springer, Berlin, Germany.

Fontana, W. (1992). Algorithmic chemistry. In Langton, C. G., Taylor, C., Farmer, J. D., and Rasmussen, S., editors, *Artificial Life II*, pages 159–210, Redwood City, CA. Addison-Wesley.

Gathercole, Chris (1998). *An Investigation of Supervised Learning in Genetic Programming*. PhD thesis, University of Edinburgh.

Koza, John R. (1992). A genetic approach to the truck backer upper problem and the inter-twined spiral problem. In *Proceedings of IJCNN International Joint Conference on Neural Networks*, volume IV, pages 310–318. IEEE Press.

Schiffmann, W., M.Joost, and Werner, R. (1992). Optimization of the backpropagation algorithm for training multilayer perceptrons. Technical Report 15, University of Koblenz, Institute of Physics.

Silberschatz, A. and Galvin, P. B. (1994). *Operating System Concepts*. Addison-Wesley, Reading, MA, 4 edition.

Swanson, S., Michelson, K., and Oskin, M. (2003). Wavescalar. Technical Report UW-CSE-03-01-01, University of Washington, Dept. of Computer Science and Engineering.

Ziegler, J. and Banzhaf, W. (2001). Evolving Control Metabolisms for a Robot. *Artificial Life*, 7:171–190.

Chapter 12

ACGP: ADAPTABLE CONSTRAINED GENETIC PROGRAMMING

Cezary Z. Janikow

Department of Math and CS, University of Missouri - St. Louis

Abstract   Genetic Programming requires that all functions/terminals (tree labels) be given a priori. In the absence of specific information about the solution, the user is often forced to provide a large set, thus enlarging the search space — often resulting in reducing the search efficiency. Moreover, based on heuristics, syntactic constraints, or data typing, a given subtree may be undesired or invalid in a given context. Typed Genetic Programming methods give users the power to specify some rules for valid tree construction, and thus to prune the otherwise unconstrained representation in which Genetic Programming operates. However, in general, the user may not be aware of the best representation space to solve a particular problem. Moreover, some information may be in the form of weak heuristics. In this work, we present a methodology, which automatically adapts the representation for solving a particular problem, by extracting and utilizing such heuristics. Even though many specific techniques can be implemented in the methodology, in this paper we utilize information on local first–order (parent–child) distributions of the functions and terminals. The heuristics are extracted from the population by observing their distribution in "better" individuals. The methodology is illustrated and validated using a number of experiments with the 11-multiplexer. Moreover, some preliminary empirical results linking population size and the sampling rate are also given.

Keywords: genetic programming, representation, learning, adaptation, heuristics

1.   Introduction

Genetic Programming (GP), proposed by Koza (Koza, 1994), is an evolutionary algorithm, and thus it solves a problem by utilizing a population of solutions evolving under limited resources. The solutions, called chromosomes, are evaluated by a problem–specific, user–defined evaluation method. They compete for survival based on this fitness, and they undergo simulated evolution by means of crossover and mutation operators.

GP differs from other evolutionary methods by using different representation, usually trees, to represent potential problem solutions. Trees provide a rich representation that is sufficient to represent computer programs, analytical functions, and variable length structures, even computer hardware (Koza, 1994, Banzhaf et al., 1998). The user defines the representation space by defining the set of functions and terminals labelling the nodes of the trees. One of the foremost principles is that of *sufficiency* (Koza, 1994), which states that the function and terminal sets must be sufficient to solve the problem. The reasoning is obvious: every solution will be in the form of a tree, labelled only with the user–defined elements. Sufficiency will usually force the user to artificially enlarge the sets to ensure that no important elements are missing. This unfortunately dramatically increases the search space. Even if the user is aware of the functions and terminals needed in a solution, he/she may not be aware of the best subset to solve a subproblem (that is, used locally in the tree). Moreover, even if such subsets are identified, questions about the specific distribution of the elements of the subsets may arise — should all applicable functions and terminals have the same uniform probability in a given context? For example, a terminal t may be required, but never as an argument to function f_1, and maybe just rarely as an argument to function f_2. All of the above are obvious reasons for designing methodologies for:

- processing such *constraints* and *heuristics*,

- automatically extracting those constraints and heuristics.

Methodologies for processing user constraints (that is, strong heuristics) have been proposed over the last few years: structure–preserving crossover (Koza, 1994), type–based STGP (Montana, 1995), type, label, and heuristic–based CGP (Janikow, 1996), and syntax–based CFG–GP (Whigham, 1995).

This paper presents a methodology, called *Adaptable Constrained GP* (ACGP, for extracting such heuristics. It is based on CGP, which allows for processing syntax, semantic, and heuristic–based constraints in GP (Janikow, 1996)). In Section 2, we briefly describe CGP, paying special attention to its role in GP problem solving as a technology for processing constraints and heuristics. In Section 3, we introduce the ACGP methodology for extracting heuristics, and then present the specific technique, distribution statistics, that was implemented for the methodology. In Section 4, we define the 11-multiplexer problem that we use to validate the technique, illustrate the distribution of functions/terminals during evolution, and present some selected results in terms of fitness curves and extracted heuristics. Moreover, we also present some interesting empirical results linking population size, ACGP, and sampling rate for the distribution.

Finally, in concluding Section 5, we elaborate on current limitations and future work needed to extend the technique and the methodology.

2. CGP Technology

Even in early GP applications, it became apparent that functions and terminals should not be allowed to mix in an arbitrary way. For example, a 3–argument *if* function should use, on its condition argument, a subtree that computes a Boolean and not a temperature or angle. Because of the difficulties in enforcing these constraints, Koza has proposed the principle of *closure* (Koza, 1994), which allows any arity–consistent labelling, often accomplished through elaborate semantic interpretations. The working environment for such a GP system is illustrated in Figure 12-1 — initialization, and then mutation and crossover choose from the complete set of functions and terminals, with uniform distribution.

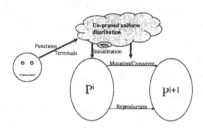

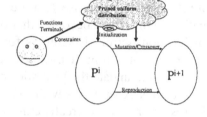

Figure 12-1. Working environment for a standard GP.

Figure 12-2. Working environment for a typed GP.

Structure–preserving crossover was introduced as the first attempt to handle some strong constraints (Koza, 1994) (the initial primary initial intention was to preserve structural constraints imposed by automatic modules — ADFs). In the nineties, three independent generic methodologies were developed to allow problem–independent strong constraints on tree construction. Montana proposed STGP (Montana, 1995), which uses types to control the way functions and terminals can label local tree structures. For example, if the function *if* requires a Boolean as its first argument, only Boolean–producing functions and terminals would be allowed to label the root of that subtree. Janikow proposed CGP, which originally required the user to explicitly specify allowed and/or disallowed labels in different contexts (Janikow, 1996). These local constraints could be based on types, but also on some problem specific semantics. In v2.1, CGP also added explicit type–based constraints, along with polymorphic functions. Finally, those interested more directly in program induction following specific syntax structure, have used similar ideas in CFG–based GP (Whigham, 1995).

CGP relies on closing the search space to the subspace satisfying the desired constraints. That is, only trees valid with respect to the constraints are ever processed. This is helped by the guarantee that all operators produce constraints–valid offspring from constraints–valid parents (Janikow, 1996). The allowed constraints, type–based, or explicitly provided, are only those that can be expressed in terms of *first–order constraints* (that is, constraints expressed locally between a parent and one of its children). These constraints are processed with only minimal overhead (constant for mutations, one additional traversal per crossover parent) (Janikow, 1996).

The working environment for a typed–based system such as the ones mentioned above is illustrated in Figure 12-2 — the representation space is locally pruned; however, the remaining elements are still subject to the same uniform application distribution.

CGP has one additional unique feature. It allows constraints to be weighted, in effect changing hard constraints into soft heuristics. For example, it allows the user to declare that some function f, even though it can use either f_1 or f_2 for its child, it should use f_1 more likely. Accordingly, the CGP working application environment becomes that of Figure 12-3 — with the final distribution of functions/terminals/subtrees for initialization, mutation, and crossover becoming non-uniform. This efficient technology is utilized in ACGP to express, process, and update the heuristics during evolution.

Previous experiments with CGP have demonstrated that proper constraints/ heuristics can indeed greatly enhance the evolution, and thus improve problem–solving capabilities. However, in many applications, the user may not be aware of those proper constraints or heuristics. For example, as illustrated with the 11-multiplexer problem, improper constraints can actually reduce GP's search capabilities, while proper constraints can increase them greatly (Janikow, 1996). ACGP is a new methodology allowing automatic updates of the weighted constraints, or heuristics, to enhance the search characteristics with respect to some user–defined objectives (currently tree quality and size).

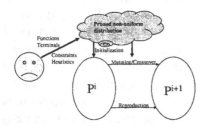

Figure 12-3. Working environment for CGP.

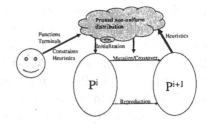

Figure 12-4. Working environment for ACGP.

3.   ACGP Methodology and the Local Distribution Technique

CGP preprocesses its input constraints into weighted mutation sets: the *mutation set* for a function f is the set of functions and terminals that can label the children of f (separately for all children). CGP v2.1 uses more elaborate mechanisms to process types and polymorphic functions. However, because the current ACGP methodology has not been extended to utilize those features, in what follows we will not be concerned with types and polymorphic functions (just plain constraints and heuristics).

ACGP v1 is a methodology to automatically modify the weights on typed mutation sets in CGP v1, thus to modify the heuristics during the evolution. Its working environment is presented in Figure 12-4 — the user may still provide initial constraints and heuristics, but these will be modified during the run. Of course, the obvious question is what technique to follow to do so. We have already investigated two ACGP techniques that allow such modifications. One technique is based on observing the fitness relationship between a parent and its offspring created by following specific heuristics. The heuristics are strengthened when the offspring improves upon the parent. A very simple implementation of this technique was shown to increase GP problem solving capabilities. However, mutation was much more problematic and not performing as well as crossover, due to the obvious bucket-brigade problem — in mutation, one offspring tree is produced by a number of mutations before being evaluated (Janikow and Deshpande, 2003).

The second technique explores the distribution statistics of the first–order contexts (that is, one parent — one child) in the population. Examples of such distributions are presented in Section 4. This idea is somehow similar to that used for CFG–based GP as recently reported (Shan et al., 2003), as well as to those applied in Bayesian Optimization Network (Pelikan and Goldberg, 1999), but used in the context of GP and functions/terminals and not binary alleles.

ACGP Flowchart and Algorithm

ACGP basic flowchart is illustrated in Figure 12-5. ACGP works in *iterations* — iteration is a number of generations ending with extracting the distribution and updating the heuristics. During a generation on which iteration does not terminate, ACGP runs just like GP (or CGP). However, when an iteration terminates, ACGP extracts the distribution information and updates the heuristics. Moreover, afterwards, the new population can be regrown from scratch (but utilizing the new heuristics) if the *regrow* option is set. The regrowing option seems beneficial with longer iterations, where likely some material gets lost before being accounted for in the distributions, and thus needs to be reintroduced by regrowing the population (as will be shown in Section 4).

The distribution information is collected from just the best samples. This information is subsequently used to modify the actual mutation set weights (the heuristics). The modification can be gradual (*slope* parameter on) or a complete replacement (*slope* off).

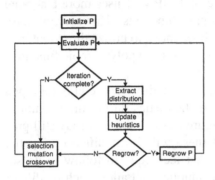

Figure 12-5. ACGP basic flowchart loop.   *Figure 12-6.* ACGP1.1 iterations.

To improve the statistics, ACGP can use simultaneous multiple independent populations. However, only one set of heuristics is currently maintained, as seen in Figure 12-6. ACGP can in fact correlate the populations by exchanging chromosomes. We have not experimented with this option, nor did we maintain separate heuristics — which is likely to result in solving the problem in different subspaces (via different constraints and heuristics) by different populations.

All trees are ordered with 2-key sorting, which compares sizes (ascending) if two fitness values are relatively similar, otherwise compares fitness (descending). The more relaxed the definition of relative similarity, the more importance is placed on sizes. The best trees (according to a percentage parameter) from individual populations are collected, resorted, and the final set is finally selected. This set is examined to extract the distribution and update the heuristics.

Distribution Statistics

The distribution is a 2-dimension matrix counting the frequency of parent-child appearances. For example, if the tree fragment of Figure 12-7 is in the selected pool, its partial distribution matrix would be as illustrated in Table 12-1. If these were the only extracted statistics, and the *slope* was off, at the end of an iteration heuristics would be updated so that if there is a node labelled f_1, and its right child needs a new subtree from mutation (initialization in *regrow*) or crossover, the tree brought by crossover (or the node generated by mutation) would be 1/3 likely to be labelled with f_1 and 2/3 with t_1.

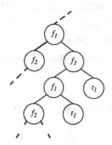

Figure 12-7. Sample partial GP tree.

Table 12-1. Examples of extracted distributions

	f_1	f_2	t_1	t_2
Function f_1 *arg1*	1	2	0	0
Function f_1 *arg2*	1	0	2	0

Off–line vs. On–line Environment

ACGP methodology can be used in two different settings. If our goal is to extract some knowledge about a particular problem or domain, to collect domain heuristics into a library , or to learn some heuristics for a simpler version of a problem in order to improve problem–solving capabilities when solving a more complex instance of the problem — we may run the system in *off–line* manner, meaning the heuristics are not extracted until the evolution converges. Iterations spanning over multiple generations are examples of these approaches.

On the other hand, if our goal is to solve a particular problem with the minimum effort and maximum speed, we would extract the heuristics as often as possible, possibly every generation — thus shortening iteration length to just one generation. This is the *on–line* environment.

Most of the experiments reported in Section 4 were conducted off–line, with just a few on–line results.

4. Illustrative Experiments

To illustrate the methodology and the distribution technique, we use the 11-multiplexer problem. Unless otherwise noted, all reported experiments used 1000 trees per population, the standard mutation, crossover, and reproduction operators at the rate of 0.10, 0.85, and 0.05, tournament (7) selection, and for the sake of sorting, trees with fitness values differing by no more than 2% of the fitness range in the population were considered the same on fitness (and thus ordered ascending by size). Moreover, unless otherwise noted, all results are averages of the best of five independent populations while executed with a single set of heuristics.

Illustrative Problem: 11–multiplexer

To illustrate the behavior of ACGP, we selected the well–known 11–multiplexer problem first introduced to GP in (Koza, 1994). This problem is not only well known and studied, but we also know from (Janikow, 1996) which specific constraints improve the search efficiency — thus allowing us to qualitatively and quantitatively evaluate the learned here heuristics.

The 11–multiplexer problem is to discover a function that passes the correct data bit (out of eight $d_0 - d_7$) when fed three addresses ($a_0 - a_2$). There are 2048 possible combinations. Koza (1994) has proposed a set of four atomic functions to solve the problem: 3-argument if, 2-argument and, or, and 1-argument not, in addition to the data and address bits. This set is not only sufficient but also redundant. In (Janikow, 1996) it was shown that operating under a sufficient set, such as not with and, degrades the performance, while operating with only if (sufficient by itself) and possibly not improves the performance. Moreover, it was shown that the performance is further enhanced when we restrict the if condition argument to choose only addresses, straight or negated (through not), while restricting the two action arguments to select only data or recursive if (Janikow, 1996). Again, this information is beneficial as we can compare ACGP discovered heuristics with these previously identified and tested.

First, we trace a specific off–line run, observing the population distribution dynamics, the change in fitness, and the evolved heuristics. Then, we empirically test the relationship between iteration length, regrowing option, and fitness. Finally, we empirically test the relationship between population size, sampling rate, and the resulting fitness, for an on–line case.

Off–line Experiment

In this section we experiment with $regrow$ on, iteration=25 generations, 10 sequential iterations, gradual update of heuristics ($slope$ on), and 4% effective rate for selecting sorted trees for distribution statistics.

Distribution.   We trace the distribution changes separately for the entire population (average of 5 populations is shown) and the selected best samples. Figure 12-8 illustrates the distribution change in a population when compared with the initial population. As seen, the distribution difference grows rapidly (each population diverges from the initial one), but eventually saturates.

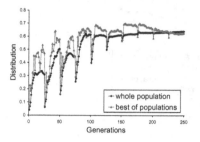

Figure 12-8. Distribution of the *if* function as a parent, with the initial population as the reference.

Figure 12-9. Distribution of the *if* function as a parent, with the previous generation as the reference.

Even though the distribution diverges from that of the initial population, does it converge to a single set of heuristics? The answer is provided in Figure 12-9 — it illustrates the same distribution difference when compared to the previous population. As seen, the changes diminish over subsequent iterations, except of narrow spikes when the populations are regrown. Therefore, the heuristics do converge.

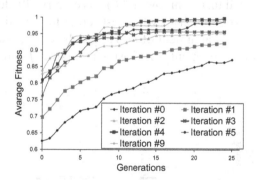

Figure 12-10. Fitness growth, shown separately for each iteration (*slope* on).

Fitness. The next two figures illustrate the resulting fitness (average of the best of each of the five populations) over sequential iterations: *slope* on (Figure 12-10), resulting in gradual changes in the heuristics, and *slope* off (Figure 12-11), resulting in a greedy instantaneous replacement of heuristics on every iteration. In both cases, subsequent iterations both start with better initially regrown populations (according to the newly acquired heuristics) and offer faster learning curves. However, the more greedy approach (Figure 12-

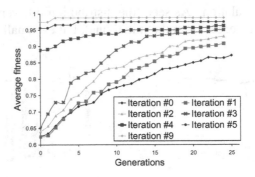

Figure 12-11. Fitness growth, shown separately for each iteration (*slope* off).

11) offers better initializations but also saturates below 100% - one of the five populations would consistently get stuck in a local minimum.

Altogether, we may see that off–line learning does improve subsequent runs. Thus, ACGP can learn meaningful heuristics (as also illustrated in the next section), and improve on subsequent runs. Later on we will see that ACGP can improve with on–line learning as well.

Heuristics.   Recall that (Janikow, 1996) has empirically determined that the best fitness curves were obtained when restricting the function set to use only *if* and *not*, with the test argument of *if* using only $a_0 - a_2$ straight or negated, and with the other two arguments of *if* using recursive *if* and the data bits only.

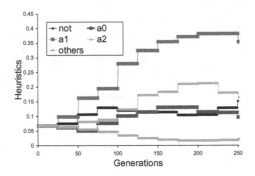

Figure 12-12. Direct heuristics on the test argument of *if*.

Figure 12-12 traces the evolving heuristics on the test argument over the course of the ten iterations. As illustrated, *if* has discovered to test addresses. However, only a_1 is highly represented, with a_2 and a_0 lower, respectively. This does not seem like the most effective heuristic. However, the puzzle is solved

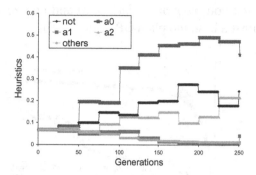

Figure 12-13. Indirect heuristics on the test argument of *if* (via *not*).

when we consider that *not* is also allowed as an argument. When considering indirect heuristics (the evolved heuristics for *not*, Figure 12-13), we can see that a_0 and a_2 are supported, with reversed proportions, and with a_1 virtually absent - since it was already highly supported directly.

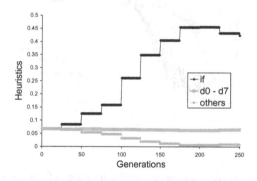

Figure 12-14. Combined heuristics on the two action arguments of *if*.

Figure 12-14 illustrates the evolved heuristics for the action arguments of *if*. As seen, recursion is highly evolved (to build deeper trees with multiple *if*s), and all data bits are supported with the other labels all virtually disappeared.

Varying Iteration Length and Regrow

All the results shown so far were obtained with *regrow* and off–line (iteration=25). The next question we set to assess is the impact of the iteration length and the *regrow* option on the problem solving capabilities.

We set four separate experiments, with iteration=1, 5, 10, and 25 generations, respectively. In all cases we used *slope* on and off without noticeable differences. We used both *regrow* ($what = 2$) and no *regrow* ($what = 1$), and compared against a baseline plain GP ($what = 0$).

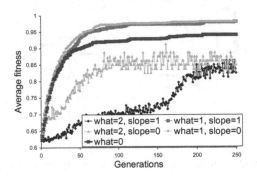

Figure 12-15.   Fitness growth for iteration = 1 generation.

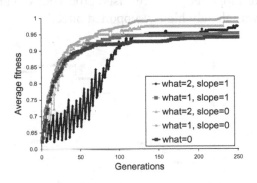

Figure 12-16.   Fitness growth for iteration = 5 generations.

The results are shown in Figure 12-15, 12-16, 12-17 and Figure 12-18. On–line runs, as seen in the top figures, suffer from the *regrow* option, but those without *regrow* beat the standard GP. In fact, the lengthened iteration to 5 generations does provide quality solutions even with *regrow*, but in one case it takes longer to obtain those solutions.

Off–line runs, as seen in the second figure, clearly benefit from *regrow*, especially for the longer iterations. Again, this may be justified by allowing sufficient time to converge to meaningful heuristics, but with this convergence it is advantageous to restart with a new population to avoid clear saturation.

As the iteration length decreases, regrowing causes more and more harm. This is apparent - there is no time for the GP to explore the space, and the run becomes a heuristics-guided random walk.

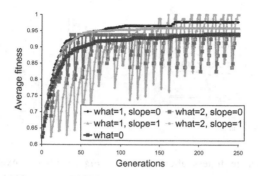

Figure 12-17. Fitness growth for iteration = 10 generations.

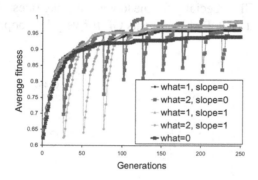

Figure 12-18. Fitness growth for iteration = 25 generations.

Varying Population and Sampling Sizes

All the previous runs were conducted with the assumed population size 1000 and effective sampling rate 4% for the trees contributing to the heuristics.

In this section, we empirically study the relationship between population size, sampling rate, and the resulting fitness. All results in this section were obtained with on–line runs (iteration=1 generation).

Figure 12-19 illustrates the average fitness of the best individuals from the 5 populations, after 50 generations, as a function of the population size. The top curve is that of a plain GP. As expected, the 50 generations lead to better fitness with increasing population size, due to more trees sampled. ACGP under–performs, but this was expected — Figure 12-15 already illustrated that *regrow* in combination with iteration=1 is destructive. One other observation is that decreasing effective sampling rate does improve the performance, which was observed especially for the larger populations.

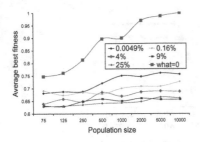

Figure 12-19. Average fitness after 50 generations with *regrow*.

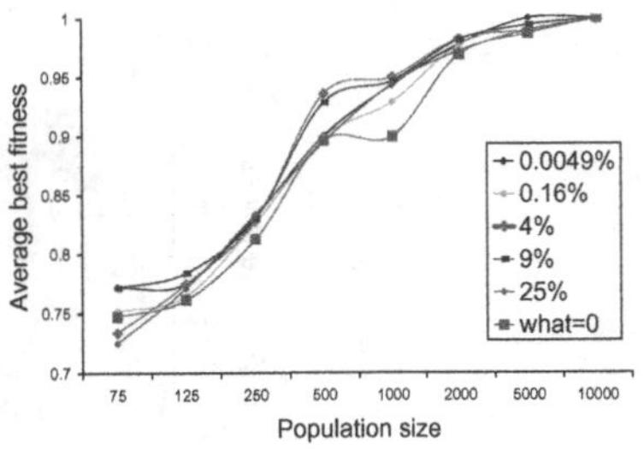

Figure 12-20. Average fitness after 50 generations no *regrow*.

Figure 12-20 presents the same fitness curves but for no *regrow*. As seen, ACGP does beat GP, especially for the lower sampling rates. Another important observation is that ACGP clearly beats GP for very low population sizes.

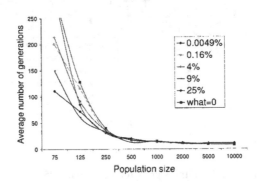

Figure 12-21. The number of generations needed to solve for 80% for varying population sizes.

The same can be seen in Figure 12-21, which presents the same fitness learning for no *regrow*, but presented differently. The figure illustrates the average number of generations needed to solve the problem with at least 80% fitness. As seen, the baseline GP fails to do so for the smallest population of 75, while ACGP accomplishes that, especially with the small–sampling runs. These results, along with the others, indicate that ACGP can outperform GP especially when working with smaller populations. One may speculate that ACGP is less dependent on population size — to be studied further in the future.

5.   Summary

We have presented the ACGP methodology for automatic extraction of heuristics in Genetic Programming. It is based on the CGP technology, which allows processing such constraints and heuristics with minimal overhead. The

ACGP algorithm implements a technique based on distribution of local first–order (parent–child) heuristics in the population.

As illustrated, ACGP is able to extract such heuristics to an advantage, and thus it performs domain learning while solving a problem at hand. Moreover, the extracted heuristics match those previously identified for this problem by empirical studies.

With the extracted heuristics, ACGP clearly outperforms a standard GP on subsequent runs (subsequent iterations) in the off–line settings, sometime solving the problem in the initial population. Moreover, with the proper setting, ACGP can also outperform GP even with the on–line settings, and it seems to be more robust with smaller population sizes.

ACGP v1 does rely exclusively on the first–order heuristics. By evaluating the resulting heuristics, one may say that the 11–multiplexer does possess such simple heuristics. For more complex problems, we may need to look at higher–order heuristics, such as those taking the siblings into account, or extending the dependency to lower levels. Such extensions can be accomplished by extending the distribution mechanism to compute deeper–level distributions, or by employing a Bayesian network or decision trees to the first-order heuristics.

Topics for further researched and explored include:

- Extending the technique to deeper-level heuristics.

- Using the same first–order heuristics, combined with the Bayesian network or a set of decision trees, to allow deeper-level reasoning.

- Linking population size with ACGP performance and problem complexity.

- Scalability of ACGP.

- Varying the effect of distribution and the heuristics at deeper tree levels, or taking only expressed genes into account while extracting the heuristics.

- The resulting trade–off between added capabilities and additional complexity when using deeper heuristics (CGP guarantees its low overhead only for the first–order constraints/heuristics).

- Other techniques for the heuristics, such as co–evolution between the heuristics and the solutions.

- Building and maintaining/combining libraries of heuristics with off–line processing, to be used in on–line problem solving.

References

Banzhaf, Wolfgang, Nordin, Peter, Keller, Robert E., and Francone, Frank D. (1998). *Genetic Programming – An Introduction; On the Automatic Evolution of Computer Programs and its Applications*. Morgan Kaufmann.

Janikow, Cezary Z. (1996). A methodology for processing problem constraints in genetic programming. *Computers and Mathematics with Applications*, 32(8):97–113.

Janikow, Cezary Z. and Deshpande, Rahul A (2003). Adaptation of representation in genetic programming. In Dagli, Cihan H., Buczak, Anna L., Ghosh, Joydeep, Embrechts, Mark J., and Ersoy, Okan, editors, *Smart Engineering System Design: Neural Networks, Fuzzy Logic, Evolutionary Programming, Complex Systems, and Artificial Life (ANNIE'2003)*, pages 45–50. ASME Press.

Koza, John R. (1994). *Genetic Programming II: Automatic Discovery of Reusable Programs*. MIT Press, Cambridge Massachusetts.

Montana, David J. (1995). Strongly typed genetic programming. *Evolutionary Computation*, 3(2):199–230.

Pelikan, Martin and Goldberg, David (1999). Boa: the bayesian optimization algorithm. In Banzhaf, Wolfgang, Daida, Jason, Eiben, Agoston E., Garzon, Max H., Honavar, Vasant, Jakiela, Mark, and Smith, Robert E., editors, *Proceedings of the Genetic and Evolutionary Computation Conference*, volume 1, pages 525–532, Orlando, Florida, USA. Morgan Kaufmann.

Shan, Y., McKay, R., Abbass, H., and Essam, D. (2003). Program evolution with explicit learning: a new framekwork for program automatic synthesis. Technical report, School of Computer Science, University of New Wales.

Whigham, P. A. (1995). Grammatically-based genetic programming. In Rosca, Justinian P., editor, *Proceedings of the Workshop on Genetic Programming: From Theory to Real-World Applications*, pages 33–41, Tahoe City, California, USA.

Chapter 13

USING GENETIC PROGRAMMING TO SEARCH FOR SUPPLY CHAIN REORDERING POLICIES

Scott A. Moore and Kurt DeMaagd
Michigan Business School

Abstract   The authors investigate using genetic programming as a tool for finding good heuristics for supply chain restocking strategies. In this paper they outline their method that integrates a supply chain simulation with genetic programming. The simulation is used to score the population members for the evolutionary algorithm which is, in turn, used to search for members that might perform better on the simulation. The fitness of a population member reflects its relative performance in the simulation. This paper investigates both the effectiveness of this method and the parameter settings that make it more or less effective.

Keywords: genetic programming, parameter tuning, supply chain, simulation, restocking policies, application

1.   Introduction

Analytically determining optimal restocking policies for members of a supply chain is difficult in many circumstances, impossible in many more. In such cases researchers and practitioners need tools for investigating the dynamics of the supply chain. Combining genetic programming (GP) (Koza, 1992) with a supply chain simulation as previously explored in (Parunak et al., 1998) allows a researcher to look for good heuristics, to investigate the impact of alternate supply chain configurations, and, generally, to research the supply restocking policy problem without worrying about whether or not he or she is able to find optimal restocking policies.

A problem with this approach is that it can be computationally burdensome. Thus, before investigating it, we aim to understand how changing GP's parameter values affects its ability to efficiently and effectively search the solution landscape for this supply chain problem. Some previous work has been done related to tuning GP's parameter values, but most researchers have simply used some sort of standard value for the settings and assumed that these would provide satisfactory results. Feldt and Nordin (Feldt and Nordin, 2000) investigated some of the settings in the context of different applications. Some of our results on a simple supply chain configuration confirmed expectations while others did not. More experiments are suggested before we can make firm conclusions.

In this paper we begin by describing the simulation and genetic programming in some depth. We also describe an addition to this process, necessitated by engineering concerns, that we call the championship rounds. In Section 3 we describe GP settings that we are investigating. In Section 4 we provide a short description of the experimental design we used to investigate the effects of different parameter settings. In Section 5 we present our hypotheses along with our results. We finish the paper in Section 6 with a short discussion.

2.   The computational process

As an alternative to the standard analytical techniques that look for provably optimal solutions, we have implemented (Moore and DeMaagd, 2004) a computer-based approach that has three parts. First, a program implements a simulation in which agents participate in a supply chain and use their re-stocking policies to help manage inventory. Second, we also implemented a GP-based approach in which the population members are valued by the quality of those policies. Third, the system has a process of keeping track of the one restocking policy (created during the algorithm's progress) that performs best on a wide variety of problems. We describe all of these in the sections that follow.

The simulation

The supply chain simulation has four members: retailer, wholesaler, distributor, and manufacturer (see Figure 13-1). A customer, exogenous to the

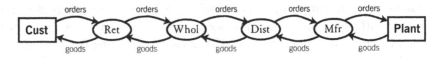

Figure 13-1.   Supply chain setup

system, demands goods from the retailer. The simulation allows demand to come from a variety of distributions but in the scenarios in this experiment it was selected from a uniform distribution from 50 to 150. (We refer to *scenarios* throughout this work; each is a particular, complete evolutionary process that was run with specific settings and under specific assumptions. For the work reported on herein we ran 243 scenarios.) We chose this distribution in this first

nal paths). Results highlight an alignment between the Bhandari's algorithm

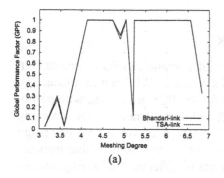
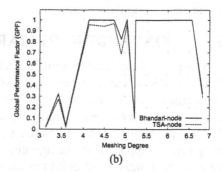

Figure 4. GPF in case of: (a) link-, and (b) node-disjointness computation.

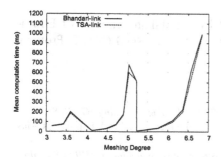
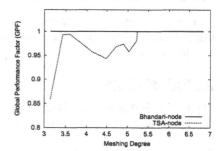

Figure 5. Mean Computation Time (ms) for an LSP request (link-disjointness case)

Figure 6. GPF for node-disj. and infinite resource availability

and the TSA when meshing degree increases. This is due to the higher resource availability in the network. However, this trend is strictly related to the variance of the TE-metric values for the TE-links: actually, other tests, not presented here, showed that the more TE-metrics were different between TE-links, the more the Bhandari's algorithm achieved the best performance w.r.t the TSA one. Moreover, these results confirmed that node disjointness proves to be a more exacting requirement than the link one, whatever algorithm is used (e.g., Bhandari's or TSA). In fact, link-disjoint algorithms provided generally a higher number of disjoined paths. The higher number of path computation failures at lower meshing degrees (e.g. interconnected rings and simple Manhattan) is strictly related to the resource availability on TE-links. In case of the TSA algorithm, this issue merges with the intrinsic sub-optimality of this algorithm. This assertion is supported by the results obtained for the 8-interconnected rings and the Manhattan topologies in case of theoretical infinite resource availability (ref. Figure 6). We observed that only the Bhandari's algorithm provided disjoint paths for every request, with an acceptable increase of the main computation time.

5. CONCLUDING REMARKS

This paper describes the implementation of a centralized Path Computation System (PCS) suited for transport networks with a GMPLS control plane. The requirements and the major design issues for the PCS are drawn, with particular emphasis on the centralized approach and on the strategies for achieving the connection survivability. Some results of an intensive testing campaign are given in support of the design choices w.r.t. survivability. Other tests are going to be completed to point out the effects of different Traffic Engineering functions on the load balancing into the GMPLS network.

ACKNOWLEDGMENTS

This work has been supported in part by the Italian Ministry of Education, University and Research through the project TANGO (MIUR Protocol No. RBNE01BNL5).

REFERENCES

[1] E. Mannie (Editor) et al., *Generalized Multi-Protocol Label Switching (GMPLS) Architecture*, draft-ietf-ccamp-gmpls-architecture-07.txt, Internet Draft, Work in progress, May 2003.

[2] L. Berger (Editor) et al., *Generalized Multi-Protocol Label Switching (GMPLS) Signaling Functional Description*, RFC 3471, Jan. 2003.

[3] R.K. Ahuja, T.L. Magnanti, and J.B. Orlin, *Network Flows - Theory, Algorithms and Applications*, Prentice Hall, 1993.

[4] J. Strand et al., *Issues for Routing in the Optical Layer*, IEEE Communications Magazine, pages 81-87, Feb. 2001.

[5] G. Carrozzo, *Algorithms and Engines for On line Routing in Generalized MPLS Networks*, PhD dissertation, Dept. Information Eng., University of Pisa, ITALY, 2004.

[6] G. Mohan-C and S. Ram Murthy, *Lightpath Restoration in WDM Optical Networks*, IEEE Network, pages 24-32, Nov./Dec. 2000.

[7] G. Carrozzo et al., *A Pre-planned Local Repair Restoration Strategy for Failure Handling in Optical Transport Networks*, Photonic Network Communication, vol. 4 (no. 3-4), pages 345-355, Jul./Dec. 2002.

[8] P. Lang (Editor) et al., *Generalized MPLS Recovery Functional Specification*, draft-ietf-ccamp-gmpls-recovery-functional-00.txt, Internet Draft, Work in progress, Jan. 2003.

[9] *Traffic models and Algorithms for Next Generation IP networks Optimization (TANGO) Project*, http://tango.isti.cnr.it/.

[10] R. Bhandari, *Survivable Networks - Algorithms for Diverse Routing*, Kluwer Academic Publisher, 1999

[11] J.W. Suurballe, *Disjoint Paths in a Network*, Networks, vol 4., pages 125-145, Jul. 1-3th 1974.

test of this approach simply to provide a baseline performance situation; we will use more structured and realistic distributions in later experiments. Orders for goods flow, one level at a time, toward the manufacturer (who makes the goods in the plant) while goods flow from the manufacturer toward the retailer. The orders take a constant 2 periods to go from one level to the next and the goods take the same amount of time to flow the other direction. Each member of the supply chain makes an independent decision about how much to order based on the information it has available — in this case, the player's current inventory, the amount of the most recent order received, the current week, and the total amount of backorders that it has to fulfill. The simulation consists of a set number of weeks (unknown to the player), and each week each player performs the same set of tasks (see Figure 13-2).

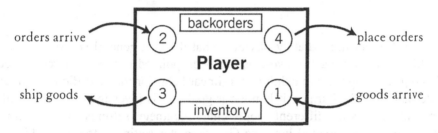

1 The player receives goods and adds them to the player's inventory.

2 The player receives orders and adds them to any currently unfilled orders (i.e., the set of *backorders*).

3 The player ships goods in order to fulfill any and all outstanding orders.

4 The player, in accordance with its restocking strategy, places an order for a certain amount of goods.

Figure 13-2. Player's tasks

Each period the players review inventory positions of the one type of product that they hold. The inventory does not deteriorate or in any way change while in storage. As discussed above, backordering is allowed; no sales are lost due to an out-of-stock position. Each player has an unlimited storage capacity and the plant has an unlimited manufacturing capability.

A player in the supply chain is assessed costs based on the inventory it carries (1 per unit per period), the amount of demand it is not able to meet that period (5 per unit per period), and the number of orders placed (10 per order). Other parameters are shown in Table 13-1. No players are given any revenue so the goal of the game is to minimize costs over the duration of the game.

Certainly the current simulation is fairly complex but it will be made more so in later investigations. We think the current simulation is complex enough

Table 13-1.   Settings for this experiment

Parameter	Setting
Demand distribution	U(50,150)
Inventory holding costs	1
Penalty costs	5
Setup costs per order placed	10
Travel time for orders	2
Travel time for goods	2
Beginning inventory	150
Goods in both shipments in transit	100
Goods received in last shipment	100

so that it is not immediately obvious what the best general solution is to the problem faced by each player; as has been pointed out in numerous places, this type of supply chain exhibits non-linear behavior that is difficult to predict (Sterman, 1989). Further, it is not our goal in this investigation to determine optimal policies for different supply chain parameter settings. We are simply attempting to understand how the GP parameter settings affects its ability to work well on this problem.

Evolutionary process

The simulation described above allows a researcher to see the effects of different settings for the game and for different restocking policies for each of the players. GP provides a tool for searching through a population (of restocking policies in this case) while the simulation provides the way of measuring the worth of the players (and, therefore, their restocking policies) in that population.

Figure 13-3 contains a representation of the general structure of the evolutionary scenario. The population (or, sometimes, populations — see discussion below) of agents is filled with agents whose restocking policies are randomly generated through various means ([1-2]). After this initialization, the agent population evolves through a series of generations in which the same process is repeated ([3-18]). For each new generation, the system generates a different instantiation of the demand distribution ([4]); for example, in generation 23 the demand might be [93, 78, 142,..., 103] while in generation 24 the demand might be [55, 134, 121,..., 76]. In each generation the demand does not change so all retailers in all games in a particular generation face the same demand.

After instantiating the demand pattern for that generation, the standard strategy's score is calculated ([5]). The standard strategy's score provides a useful

```
[ 1] Create each population of agents
[ 2] gen = 1
[ 3] repeat
[ 4]     Instantiate a particular demand pattern
[ 5]     Calculate the standard strategy's score
[ 6]     for each population
[ 7]         Choose agent j from the population at least M times
[ 8]             Fill all the roles in the game appropriately
[ 9]             Play the game for W weeks
[10]             Record the outcome for each agent
[11]         end-loop
[12]     end-for
[13]     Calculate and record fitness scores for all agents
[14]     Determine this generation's best agent
[15]     Determine the scenario's current champion so far
[16]     Breed the next generation of each population
[17]     gen = gen + 1
[18] until termination condition is met
```

Figure 13-3. Evolutionary scenario

yardstick against which to measure the success of the strategies created by GP because it plays the game under the same conditions and with the same demands. (See (Weiss, 1998, p. 125) for a discussion of the utility of yardsticks.) Generally, we set a scenario's standard strategy to be the analytical solution (if one is available), a well-known heuristic, or accepted standard practice. The choice of one standard strategy over another has absolutely no effect on the progress of evolution, it is simply reflected in the reports that the system generates.

The next two lines ([6-7]) define two loops that ensure that each agent from each population plays some minimum number of games in that generation. Then, after filling the other roles in the simulation with a random selection of agents ([8]; more on this below), the simulation runs for some W number of weeks ([9]). This value W is the same for each game in this generation but is randomly generated for each generation.

After each game played during a generation, the system records the scores for each agent who participated in that game ([10]). This is a rather complicated process but the score ends up reflecting how well the value chain performs as a whole. We could have made several different choices here but we wanted to choose those agents who help their value chains do better *as a whole* rather than doing well individually at the expense of the other agents. At the end of the games for each generation (that is, after line [13]), the system calculates both adjusted and normalized fitness values using as the basis of calculation the average of the agent's scores for each game it played during that generation (Koza, 1992, pp. 95–98). The system next records the agent that had the best

score for that generation ([14]), and then determines if this player is the scenario's current champion ([15]; more on this below). The system then breeds
the next generation of each population ([16]) using reproduction, crossover,
and mutation and starts over again if the termination condition has not been
met. (Other GP settings are discussed in Section 3.)

We are investigating three different ways in which to configure the number
of populations. The first one is as shown in Figure 13-4. In this situation four

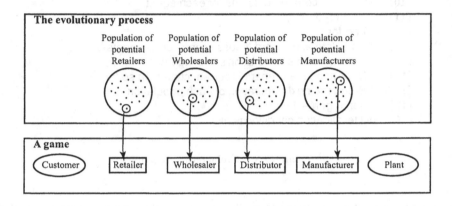

Figure 13-4. Selecting an agent from a population for the simulation

separate populations are maintained, and each population evolves in order to
play one specific role in the supply chain. The second setup is one in which one
population exists, one member is chosen from the population, and it plays all
four roles in the supply chain. The third setup is one in which one population
exists and four separate selections are made from the population, one for each
role. The assumption in the last two setups is that one type of restocking policy
is optimal at any level of the supply chain and, therefore, it is reasonable to
evolve agents for all four roles within just one population.

We have, so far, referred to the agents or players as having restocking policies,
and that these agents can go through the evolutionary process. Here we discuss
how this is possible. The restocking policies, while internally represented as a
Lisp *S-expression*, are commonly depicted as trees. Each leaf of the tree must
belong to the set of terminals (either an integer or a symbol; see Table 13-2
for related details) while each inner branch must belong to the set of functions
(again, see Table 13-2). At the beginning of the scenario, a set of random trees
between depths 2 and 6 are generated for the population using the ramped half-
and-half method (Koza, 1992, p. 93). Given the values that were in effect for
this experiment, there are approximately $10^{44\text{million}}$ different trees in the search
space for possible strategies. In future experiments we will look at investigating

Table 13-2. Settings for this experiment

Parameter	Setting
Integers in terminal set	0...4
Symbols in terminal set	InStk, OnOrd, Demnd, CurWk
Functions	+, −, round, remainder, ×, $\sqrt{x}$, max, min if-then, if-then-else
Player performance measurement	Value chain aggregate
Fitness measurement	Normalized fitness
Minimum depth for new individuals	2
Maximum depth for new individuals	6
Maximum depth for any individual	17
Championship comparison basis	Value chain aggregate
Demands in championship round	30
Standard strategy	Order amount demanded

the effects of such a large search space on GP and whether or not we should reduce the maximum depth of the trees.

Championship rounds

GP makes it possible that, at some time, the best performing agent from one generation will not make it into the next. Different GP settings provide different certainty levels for the high-performing strategies making it into the next generation — but, no matter what the settings, it is always going to be a random process. This is not a good state of affairs for the logistics researcher who wants to use GP to find the best performing strategy over the entire evolution, regardless of whether or not the strategy is present in the last generation. To correct for this, we have created a process external to the evolutionary process called the *championship rounds* (see Figure 13-5). The point of this process is to find the strategy that performs best against a wide variety of instantiations of the demand distribution used in this scenario.

The championship process is an engineering compromise. The full computational solution would require that in each generation each player plays not one game with a certain set of partners but all 30 games (with each one of the demand instantiations in the championship demand set) with those partners. This was not feasible given our resources. Further, "elitism" (guaranteeing that the top *N* members survive until the next generation), the usual approach to ensuring the best player survives, does not suffice for this problem since the top player against a particular demand distribution may not be a top player against the championship demand set — and it is performance against this set that we

1 Before evolution begins, generate a set of 30 different demand instantiations from the demand distribution used in the current experiment. Call this the *championship demand set*. If a player plays one game against each of the instantiations in the championship demand set, then it is said to have played the *championship games*.

2 Before evolution begins, have the standard strategy play the championship games. Call the average of these scores the *standard championship score*.

3 After the first generation, save the player with the lowest total costs as the *current champion*.

4 Have the current champion play the championship games. Average these scores. Call this the *current champion's score*. Divide the current champion's score by the standard championship score; call this the *current champion's ratio*.

5 Play the next generation.

6 After this generation, the player with the best score for that generation will be named as the *challenger* to the current champion.

7 The challenger will play the championship games. If the challenger's ratio for these games is lower than the current champion's ratio, then the challenger is declared the new champion.

8 Keep a record of the current champion's ratio.

9 Repeat starting at #5.

Figure 13-5. The championship process

are most interested in. One of the basic questions this experiment addresses is whether or not this compromise is effective.

3.   Genetic programming parameters

We need to run the evolutionary algorithm many times. Its settings can potentially affect the efficiency and effectiveness of this evolutionary search. These settings can also greatly affect the running time of the algorithm; for example, some of the scenarios took as little as 2 minutes while others took up to 107 hours (4.5 days). Table 13-3 shows the settings that we investigate in this experiment.

Number of generations After a number of preliminary tests, we decided to limit the upper end in this experiment to 150.

Selection method The three choices that we test are tournament, fitness proportionate, and rank. For the tournament method, two agents are selected for the tournament; the agent with the lower (better) score wins and is selected for the next generation. The more fit against the current demand instantiation is guaranteed to win but it is still the case that fitness against

Table 13-3. Factors

Factor		Values		
A	# of Generations	50	100	150
B	Selection Method	Tournament ($n = 2$)	Fitness Proportionate	Rank
C	% Internal Crossover Points	.7	.8	.95
D	Probability of Crossover	.6	.75	.9
E	Probability of Mutation	.01	.05	.09
F	# of Populations	4 Populations	1 Population, 1 Player	1 Population, 4 Players
G	Members per population	100	300	500
H	Games per member per population	1%	5%	10%
J	Weeks per game	35	65	100
K	Priming	none	quick-large	long-small

the current demand instantiation does not guarantee fitness against the championship demand set.

Probability of crossover When the system creates members for a new generation, it chooses between reproduction, mutation, and crossover. If a high crossover rate is chosen, then fewer members of the current generation will be directly transferred into the next generation.

Percent of internal crossover points The effects of crossover when done at an external point is more like point-mutation. We vary this parameter from 70% to 95% of all crossovers.

Probability of mutation We vary this parameter from 1% to 9%.

Priming The idea behind priming is that a set of agents, previously verified to be good performers, are put into the initial population. We have two different ways of priming a population of size P.

    quick large An evolution of 1 generation is run with a randomly-generated population of size $1.2 \times P$. At the end of the generation, the best P agents are chosen and put into the initial population. Evolution then runs as usual. The hypothesis is that it would be useful to get the worst of the worst performers out of the population because their bad performances also hurt the scores of other members of the population.

    long small An evolutionary process is run that is the same length as the standard evolution but with only $0.2 \times P$ members in the population.

At the end of this priming evolution, all members are put in the initial population while the remaining $0.8 \times P$ agents are randomly generated. The hypothesis is that the evolutionary process will start with at least some of the members being able to perform well while still having some variety in the initial population.

As a point of comparison with these two, we also ran scenarios without priming.

Number of populations As discussed above, we are investigating 3 different ways in which to configure the number of populations.

Members per population We looked at population sizes from 100 to 500 per population.

Games per member per population Each generation a population member (strategy) plays a certain number of games per generation. When the same member plays all four roles, this value is irrelevant — each member plays only one game per generation. In the other population setups, each role that the member plays in a game counts as a separate game. The value of this variable is stated in terms of a percent: a value of 1% means that each member has to play games with at least 1% of the members of the population.

Weeks per game Longer games minimize the effects of the initial position on the agent's performance. We look at games from 35 up to 100 periods in length in order to see how small this value can be while still effectively searching the space of restocking policies.

4.   Experimental design

The experiment examines ten factors and their influence on the effectiveness of GP with this application. Each of the ten factors is set to three different values. While similar experimental designs often test at only two levels, we tested at three levels to identify possible non-linear effects. To measure all combinations of the ten factors would require 3^{10} runs of the evolutionary algorithm, for a total of 59,049 runs. Assuming that each run requires $\frac{1}{2}$ hour on average, the simulation would require 3.37 years to complete. As a result, a more efficient measurement method must be employed. Factorial design is one such method and has been previously used to examine multiple genetic programming parameters (Feldt and Nordin, 2000).

To complete the computation in a reasonable time frame, a design that required less than 500 runs was desirable. A fractional factorial design with 3^{10-5} runs provided the greatest number of data points while still remaining computationally feasible. Given that only 243 runs were executed, not all combinations of the variables were looked at. Instead, an orthogonal array of the factors was created (Shell Internationale Research Maatschappij, 1998) to examine the different factors. The design generator for this orthogonal array is given in Table 13-4. Assume that each of the 10 factors to be considered is assigned a

Table 13-4. Design Generators

Factor	Generator
F	$ABCD$
G	AB^2CD
H	BC^2DE
J	AC^2D^2E
K	$AB^2C^2DE^2$

letter A-K. Factors A-E are assigned like a full factorial design; factors F-K are determined by a function of A-E.

This design is of resolution V which implies that main effects are confounded with four order interactions, two order interactions are confounded with third order interactions; therefore, assuming that higher order interactions are negligible, all of the main effects are strongly clear (Box et al., 1978). This design minimizes any confounding while examining the main factor and two factor interactions. For more details about developing fractional factorial designs, see (Box et al., 1978) and (Wu and Hamada, 2000).

5.   Hypotheses

For Hypotheses 5.3–5.5 we used ordinary least squares (OLS) to compute the estimators and p-values. We are testing at the 95% confidence interval for these hypotheses. For Hypotheses 5.1–5.2 we do not use OLS estimators. The champion and challenger slopes (related to the first two hypotheses) are mediating variables between the parameters and the final score, and the scores are serially correlated. We use a model that is a hybrid of (Gelfand et al., 1990) and (Waclawiw and Liang, 1993) to cope with these difficulties. The result is a two stage random effects hierarchical model for analyzing time series data. A Markov Chain Monte Carlo (MCMC) simulation using Gibbs sampling allows us to create highly accurate approximations of the estimator (Casella and George, 1992)). The MCMC was run for 50,000 iterations with 40,000 iterations of burn-in and thinning of 1/2.

As a result of the above, for these same two hypotheses we use Bayes factors instead of p-values to determine which variables increase the model's explanatory power. (For more information on using Bayes factors instead of p-values, see (Zellner, 1971).) Bayes factors of > 0.5 leads us to accept the null hypotheses. For each one of the experimental control parameters, we test the following hypotheses, iterating through all ten variables in the model to determine if each variable adds explanatory power. In theory, this method could be extended to computing all possible combinations of variables. This would require examining $2^{10} = 1024$ different models, which is not computationally feasible. Therefore we simplified the processes to only compare the full model versus the model of iteratively dropping each variable.

Table 13-5. Slope Hypotheses Results. The $p(w = 1)$ column indicates the probability that the variable should be included in the model.

Variable	Champ (5.1)		Challenger (5.2)	
	β	$p(w = 1)$	β	$p(w = 1)$
Internal Crossover Points	dropped	0.296	dropped	0.223
Probability of Crossover	dropped	0.194	dropped	0.428
Probability of Mutation	0.044620	0.853	-0.064150	0.720
Members per Population	-0.000037	1.000	0.000018	0.672
Games per Member per Pop	-0.013730	0.504	0.000299	0.689
Weeks per game	0.000012	0.900	0.000023	0.706
Priming		0.388		0.687
no prime	dropped		baseline	
quick-large	dropped		-0.003114	
long-small	dropped		0.001628	
Selection Method		0.502		0.698
tournament	baseline		baseline	
fitness proportionate	0.003589		0.009664	
rank	-0.000761		0.007962	
# of Populations		0.966		0.674
one pop per role	baseline		baseline	
one pop for all	-0.010390		0.005059	
one member for all roles	0.015830		0.005054	
Change per Generation	-0.016970		-0.024240	

In the following we highlight the most interesting results; the full set of results are presented in the tables.

Hypothesis 5.1 (Champion slope)   *The parameter influences the slope of the champion line.* This hypothesis tests whether or not the rate of change in the champions is affected by the parameter. This is a log-normal line so small values actually have a larger effect than the value might appear to indicate.

The results for the main factors are shown in the middle two columns of Table 13-5. Initial analysis indicated that the correct model should not include the variables representing internal crossover points, the probability of crossover, and priming. Of the remaining variables, increases in the probability of mutation lead to relatively large increases in the slope of the champion line. Surprisingly, increases in members per population had very little effect on the slope. Finally, changes in the population setup had relatively significant effects. One population for all gave the best results. This seems to indicate that some information in a population is transferable between roles.

Hypothesis 5.2 (Challenger slope) *The parameter influences the slope of the challenger line.* This hypothesis tests whether or not the rate of change in the challenger is affected by the parameter. Again, this is a log-normal line.

The results for the main factors are shown in the last two columns of Table 13-5. Initial analysis indicated that the correct model should drop the same variables as above except that priming should be included. A very interesting result is that almost every variable included in the model has a different sign than for the results from the first hypothesis. Related to this point, probability of mutation, which has the most positive effect on the champion slope, has the most negative effect on the challenger slope. Quick-large priming has the most negative effect on the challenger line while long-small priming was the most positive.

Hypothesis 5.3 (Ratio of last champion) *The parameter affects the ratio of the last champion.* With this first hypothesis we are testing if the setting changes the ability of GP to find a good champion. Smaller scores are better scores so negative beta values are better.

OLS estimators and p–values are shown in columns 2–3 of Table 13-6. In theory the result of Hypothesis 5.1 and this one should be highly correlated since the champion's last score is simply the last point on the downward trending champion line. However, some differences certainly can be found. It is still the case that internal crossover points, probability of crossover, and priming do not have a significant effect on the result. For the population setup it is again the case that one population for all is the best setup while one member for all roles dominates as the worst influence. On the other hand, probability of mutation dominates as the best (that is, the most negative) influence. This is exactly the opposite the result of the result for Hypothesis 5.1. Interestingly, the results related to members per population is insignificant — increasing the number of members in a population does not affect the performance of the algorithm in this dimension. Tournament selection is significantly better than either of the other two selection methods.

Hypothesis 5.4 (Generation of last champion) *The parameter influences in which generation the algorithm finds its last new champion.* This hypothesis tests if the setting helps GP continue to search effectively in later generations. Positive beta values mean that champions were found later than normal.

The results are shown in columns 4–5 of Table 13-6.

Table 13-6.   Champ Hypotheses

Variable	Ratio of Champ (5.3)		Generation of Champ (5.4)		New Champs (5.5)	
	β	p	β	p	β	p
Intercept	-1.205	0.376	45.385	0.000	14.805	0.000
Number of Generations	-0.013	0.000	0.583	0.000	0.028	0.000
Internal Crossover Points	0.376	0.758	-19.543	0.075	-2.638	0.072
Probability of Crossover	-1.420	0.165	-4.023	0.662	-0.550	0.654
Probability of Mutation	-13.279	0.001	70.815	0.040	1.826	0.692
Members per Population	0.001	0.438	-0.009	0.210	0.002	0.017
Games/Member/Pop	0.112	0.001	0.352	0.253	0.037	0.370
Weeks per game	0.073	0.000	0.088	0.026	0.016	0.002
Priming	F=0.519		F=0.190		F=0.001	
no prime	baseline		baseline		baseline	
quick-large	0.311	0.310	-2.051	0.457	0.998	0.007
long-small	0.294	0.339	-5.015	0.070	-0.337	0.361
Selection Method	F=0.000		F=0.000		F=0.000	
tournament	baseline		baseline		baseline	
fitness proportionate	3.758	0.000	-16.771	0.000	-3.449	0.000
rank	0.941	0.002	-0.546	0.844	0.220	0.552
# of Populations	F=0.000		F=0.000		F=0.000	
one pop per role	baseline		baseline		baseline	
one pop for all	-1.346	0.000	-14.021	0.000	-5.783	0.000
one member for all roles	11.168	0.000	-30.342	0.000	-9.783	0.000
$F(13, 715)$	107.89		44.58		57.14	
Prob > F	0.000		0.000		0.000	
Adj R^2	0.656		0.4377		0.5006	

Larger internal crossover rates are associated with a decreased incidence of finding new champions in later generations. On the other hand, increasing the probability of mutation significantly affects the algorithm's ability to find champions in later generations. As for the indicator variables, we can conclude the following: Tournament selection performs much better than fitness proportionate, allowing the algorithm to find more champions in later generations. Finally, one population for role allows champions to be found later than would be expected for either of the other approaches.

Hypothesis 5.5 (Number of new champions) *The parameter influences the number of new champions that the program finds.* This hypothesis tests if GP is able to make many improvements during its operations or if it makes just a few and then stops finding improvements. Positive beta values mean that an increase in the variable increases the expected number of champions found.

The results are shown in columns 6–7 of Table 13-6. Both the number of generations and the number of weeks only marginally increase the number of new champions found. For this hypothesis, the indicator variables have much more effect: quick large priming finds more champions than no priming; tournament selection finds more champions than fitness proportionate; and one population for role finds significantly more champions than either of the other approaches.

6. Discussion of results

The results here are limited in that the simulation was only played under one demand distribution and supply chain setup. It might be the case that different demand distributions or different supply chain configurations lead to different performance characteristics for genetic programming. Further, a wider range of parameter values should be investigated to determine if effects are seen outside the values looked at here. One of the more intriguing setups is related to populations: a member could be defined so that it defines possibly different strategies for all four roles. How would the benefits of evolving role players together measure up against the benefits of allowing role players to evolve separately? Other setups involving ways that better take advantage of co-evolution are also intriguing since the situation here is one in which different agents might evolve to play roles that need to cooperate with agents in other roles.

Also, many significant results based on the interaction of terms are possible; future analysis of existing data remains to be performed but preliminary work has indicated that they exist. Finally, it remains to be seen just how effective this method of searching for restocking policies actually is. We have, however, found some encouraging results even though we have only begun to understand genetic programming's performance on this problem. While the mean champion relative score was 3.9549, which means it found values about 300% higher than the standard heuristic, the best score was 0.2511 or about 75% less than the standard heuristic.

For now, let us see what we did find in this set of experiments. As expected, the maximum number of generations should be as big as possible given computing resources since it allows more champions to be found. The percent of internal crossover should be small since that is associated with both a small champion's relative score and finding champions in later generations. The experiments found no actually significant results pertaining to the probability of crossover or the number of games per member per population. More experiments, with a more difficult problem, might lead to different results — or, possibly, a different range of values should be investigated. Weak results were found for both size of population and number of weeks; further investigation is needed to say more about these.

Quick large priming led to both more champions being found and champions being found later in the evolutionary process. Quick large priming is also significantly less computationally expensive than long small priming while not being much more expensive than no priming at all. This is a fairly clear win for quick large priming (over quick large) which probably is not a surprise given that long small priming probably allowed too many very good members to take over the population too quickly. It is interesting that it is also a winner over no priming; this indicates that the negative effects of having very bad players in the population outweigh the positive effects of the diversity they bring to the population. The selection results also tell a relatively clear story. Selection, in general, had little effect on either of the slopes; however, tournament selection led to a significantly smaller final score, finding more champions in later generations, and finding more new champions.

As for the population setup indicator variables, all of the findings for the one member for all roles setting were negative. The negative finding was expected since this setup provides fewer degrees of freedom relative to the other settings. The comparison of the other two setups are more complex. One population for all led, in comparison with one population per role, to a lower final score but it took longer to find the last champion and found fewer champions in the process.

One of the underlying hypotheses being tested in the research reported in this paper is whether or not genetic programming combined with a simulation that measures fitness against one demand instantiation would be effective at generating strategies that would perform well against a large set of related demand instantiations. Early reports, as embodied in the research contained within, are positive. The evolutionary algorithm generated strategies that continued to improve the champion's score. Certainly, more results are needed before a final conclusion can be reached. Also, it is also nearly certain that improvements to this process could be made. For example, it might be the case that testing the top 5 strategies from the population at the end of each generation would lead to a significant reduction in the final champion score.

We have begun the process of investigating the effects of many parameters on GP and the championship process. Some effects have been found but many more experiments are necessary before we can make any firm conclusions. We are continuing with this process so that we can know more about this complex system.

References

Box, George E. P., Hunter, William G., and Hunter, J. Stuart (1978). *Statistics for Experimenters.* Wiley-Interscience.

Casella, George and George, Edward I. (1992). Explaining the Gibbs sampler. *American Statistician,* 46(3):167–174.

Feldt, Robert and Nordin, Peter (2000). Using factorial experiments to evaluate the effect of genetic programming parameters. In Poli, Riccardo, Banzhaf, Wolfgang, Langdon, William B., Miller, Julian F., Nordin, Peter, and Fogarty, Terence C., editors, *Genetic Programming, Proceedings of EuroGP'2000, LNCS* 1802, pages 271–282, Edinburgh. Springer-Verlang.

Gelfand, Alan E, Hills, Susan E., Racine-Poon, Amy, and Smith, Adrian F. M. (1990). Illustration of Bayesian inference in normal data models using Gibbs sampling. *Journal of the American Statistical Association,* 88(421):171–178.

Koza, John R. (1992). *Genetic Programming: On the Programming of Computers by Means of Natural Selection.* MIT Press, Cambridge, MA, USA.

Moore, Scott A. and DeMaagd, Kurt (2004). Beer game genetic program. http://sourceforge.net-/projects/beergame/.

Parunak, H. Van Dyke, Savit, Robert, and Riolo, Rick L. (1998). Agent-based modeling vs. equation-based modeling: A case study and users' guide. In *Proceedings of Multi-agent Systems and Agent-based Simulation (MABS '98), LNAI* 1534. Springer-verlag.

Shell Internationale Research Maatschappij (1998). Keyfinder.

Sterman, John D. (1989). Modeling managerial behavior: Misperceptions of feedback in a dynamic decision making experiment. *Management Science,* 35(3):321–339.

Waclawiw, Myron A. and Liang, Kung-Yee (1993). Prediction of random effects in the generalized linear model. *Journal of the American Statistical Association,* 88(421):171–178.

Weiss, Carol H. (1998). *Evaluation.* Prentice Hall, 2nd edition.

Wu, C. F. Jeff and Hamada, Michael (2000). *Experiments: Planning, Analysis, and Parameter Design Optimization.* Wiley-Interscience.

Zellner, Arnold (1971). *An Introduction to Bayesian Inference in Econometrics.* John Wiley & Sons, Inc.

Chapter 14

CARTESIAN GENETIC PROGRAMMING AND THE POST DOCKING FILTERING PROBLEM

A. Beatriz Garmendia-Doval[1], Julian F. Miller[2], and S. David Morley[3]

[1]*Galeon Software LTD, Spain;* [2]*University of York, UK;* [3]*Enspiral Discovery Ltd, UK*

Abstract   Structure-based virtual screening is a technology increasingly used in drug discovery. Although successful at estimating binding modes for input ligands, these technologies are less successful at ranking true hits correctly by binding free energy. This chapter presents the automated removal of false positives from virtual hit sets, by evolving a post docking filter using Cartesian Genetic Programming(CGP). We also investigate characteristics of CGP for this problem and confirm the absence of bloat and the usefulness of neutral drift.

Keywords: Cartesian genetic programming, molecular docking prediction, virtual screening, machine learning, genetic programming, evolutionary algorithms, neutral evolution

1.   Introduction

In this chapter we present the application of Cartesian Genetic Programming (CGP) to the real-world problem of predicting whether small molecules known as ligands will bind to defined target molecules. We have found CGP to be effective for this problem. The solution is currently in use in a commercial company. In addition to presenting a successful CGP application we have investigated empirically a number of methodological issues that affect the performance and characteristics of CGP. We have found, in accordance with previous studies of CGP on other problems, that neutral drift (see Section 2) in the genotype can be highly beneficial. In addition, unlike some other forms of GP we see very little bloat (even though we use many thousands of generations). The chapter consists of eight sections. In Section 2 we describe the CGP method and discuss some of its characteristics (some of which led us to adopt the technique). In Section 3 we describe the ligand docking problem and how we implemented a CGP system for it. In Section 4 we performed a large number of experiments to find optimum parameter settings and investigate how they influence the behaviour of CGP. In Section 5 we examine empirically the relative performance and behaviour of an algorithm which utilizes neutral drift with one that doesn't. In Section 6 we discuss the evolved post-docking filters and show how we selected the best candidates using seeded libraries. In Section 7 we examine the evolved filters on real data rather than idealised test sets. We end the chapter with our conclusions in section 8.

2.   Cartesian Genetic Programming

CGP (Miller and Thomson, 2000) is a graph based form of GP that was developed from a representation for evolving digital circuits (Miller et al., 1997, Miller, 1999). In essence, it is characterized by its encoding of a graph as a string of integers that represent the functions and connections between graph nodes, and program inputs and outputs. This gives it great generality so that it can represent neural networks, programs, circuits, and many other computational structures. Although, in general it is capable of representing directed multigraphs, it has so far only been used to represent directed acyclic graphs. It has a number of features that are distinctive compared with other forms of GP. Foremost among these is that the genotype can encode a non-connected graph (one in which it is not possible to walk between all pairs of nodes by following directed links). This means that it uses a many-to-one genotype phenotype mapping to produce the graph (or program) that is evaluated. The genetic material that is not utilised in the phenotype is analogous to junk DNA. As we will see, mutations will allow the activation of this redundant code or de-activation of it. Another feature is the ease with which it is able to handle problems involving multiple outputs. Graphs are attractive representations for programs as they are more compact than the more usual tree representation since subgraphs can be used more than once.

CGP has been applied to a growing number of domains and problems: digital circuit design (Miller et al., 2000a, Miller et al., 2000b), digital filter design (Miller, 1999), image processing (Sekanina, 2004), artificial life (Rothermich and Miller, 2002), bio-inspired developmental models (Miller and Thomson, 2003, Miller, 2003, Miller and Banzhaf, 2003), evolutionary art (Ashmore, 2000) and has been adopted within new evolutionary techniques cell-based Optimization (Rothermich et al., 2003) and Social Programming (Voss, 2003, Voss and James C. Howland, 2003).

In its original formulation, CGP was represented as a directed Cartesian grid of nodes in which nodes were arranged in layers (rows) and it was necessary to specify the number of nodes in each row and the number of columns. The nodes in each column were not allowed to be connected together (rather like a multi-layer perceptron neural network). In addition an additional parameter was

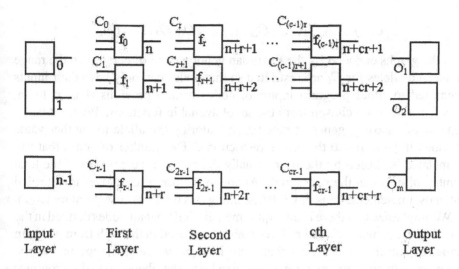

Figure 14-1. General form of Cartesian Program for an n input m-output function. There are three user-defined parameters: number of rows (r), number of columns (c) and levels-back (see text). Each node has a set of C_i connection genes (according to the arity of the function) and a function gene f_i which defines the node's function from a look-up table of available functions. On the far left are seen the program inputs or terminals and on the far right the program output connections O_i.

introduced called *levels-back* which defined how many columns back a node in a particular column could connect to. The program inputs were arranged in an "input layer" on the left of the array of nodes. This is shown in Figure 14-1

It is important to note that in many implementations of CGP (including this one) the number of rows (r) is set to one. In this case the number of columns (c) becomes the *maximum* allowed number of nodes (user defined). Also the parameter *levels-back* can be chosen to be any integer from one (in which case, nodes can only connect to the previous layer) to the maximum number of nodes (in which case a node can connect to *any* previous node). It should be noted that the output genes can be dispensed with by choosing the program outputs to be taken from the rightmost consecutive nodes (when only one row is used).

The Cartesian genotype (shown below) is a string of integers. C_i denotes in general a set of connection points that the inputs to the node are connected. Each node also has a function, f_i, chosen from a list of available functions (defined by the user). Sometimes it happens that the node functions in the function list have different arities (so the cardinality of C_i varies). Usually this is handled (as in this work) by setting the node arity to be the maximum arity that appears in the function list. Nodes with functions that require less inputs than the maximum ignore the extra inputs.

$$C_0, f_0, C_1, f_1, \ldots, C_{cr-1}, f_{cr-1}O_0, O_1, \ldots, O_m$$

If the graphs encoded by the Cartesian genotype are directed then the range of allowed alleles for C_i are restricted so that nodes can only have their inputs connected to either program inputs or nodes from a previous (left) column. Function values are chosen from the set of available functions. Point mutation consists of choosing genes at random and altering the allele to another value provided it conforms to the above restrictions. The number of genes that can be mutated is chosen by the user (usually defined as a percentage of the total number of genes in the genotype). Although the use of crossover is not ruled out, most implementations of CGP (including this one) only use point mutation.

We emphasize that there is no requirement in CGP that all nodes defined in the genotype are actually used (i.e. have their output used in the path from program output to input). This means that there is a many-one genotype phenotype mapping. Although the genotype is of fixed size the phenotype (the program) can have any size up to the maximum number of nodes that are representable in the genotype. It should also be observed that although a particular genotype may have a number of such redundant nodes they cannot be regarded as purely non-coding genes, since mutation may alter genes "downstream" of their position that causes them to be activated and code for something in the phenotype, similarly, formerly active genes can be deactivated by mutation.

When Cartesian genotypes are initialised one finds that many of the nodes are inactive. In many CGP implementations on various problems it is often found that this figure changes relatively little. Thus it is clear that during evolution many mutations have no effect on the phenotype (and hence do not change the fitness of the genotype). We refer genotypes with the same fitness as being neutral with respect to each other. A number of studies (mainly on Boolean problems) have shown that the constant genetic change that happens while the best population fitness remains fixed is very advantageous for search (Miller and Thomson, 2000, Vassilev and Miller, 2000, Yu and Miller, 2001, Yu and Miller, 2002). In the results section of this chapter we will show that such neutral search is also highly beneficial for the ligand docking problem.

To date no work on CGP has required any action to deal with bloat. Bloat is not observed even when enormous genotypes are allowed. Miller (Miller, 2001) investigated this phenomenon in CGP and found it to be intimately connected with the presence of genes that can be activated or deactivated. He argued that when the fitness of genotypes is high, it becomes more likely that *equally good* genotypes will be favourably selected. In tree-based GP models most equally good phenotypes differ from one another in useless (bloated) code sections, and they will be strongly selected for when fit. This, unfortunately, propagates the spread of such useless code but paradoxically compresses the useful code (Nordin and Banzhaf, 1995). On the other hand, in CGP, the increased proportion of *genetically different but phenotypically identical* code is able to exist without harm (i.e. it does not have to be processed as it is not in the phenotype). It is as if the bloat can exist in the form of genetically redundant code that resides in the genotype (but bounded by the fixed genotype size) but not in the phenotype. This has the side effect of *reducing* the size of the phenotype without requiring any parsimony pressure.

Evolutionary Algorithm

The evolutionary algorithm used for all experiments is that recommended in (Miller and Thomson, 2000). It is a simplified (1+4) Evolution Strategy for evolutionary search (Schwefel, 1965), i.e. one parent with 4 offspring (population size 5). The algorithm is described as follows:

1 Generate initial population of 5 individuals randomly;

2 Evaluate fitness for each individual in the population;

3 Select the best of the 5 in the population as the winner;

4 Carry out point-wise mutation on the winning parent to generate 4 offspring;

5 Construct a new generation with the winner and its 4 offspring;

6 Select a winner from the current population using the following rules:

    (a) If there are offspring that have a better fitness than the parent has, the best offspring becomes the winner.

    (b) *Otherwise, if there are offspring which have the same fitness as the parent then one is randomly selected and becomes the winner (NDEA)*

    (c) else the parent remains the winner.

7 Go to step 4 unless the maximum number of generations has reached.

The evolutionary strategy can be mistaken for a form of hillcimbing. However it should be remembered that the application of the mutation operator causes a sampling of a whole distribution of phenotypes. A single gene change *can* cause an enormous change in the phenotype, however when the genotype is quite fit, in most cases it will only cause little change (as large change is likely to be deleterious). Thus we can see that the genotype representation in CGP allows a very simple mutation operator to sample a large range of phenotypes. If the neutral drift is not allowed in selection of the genotype to be promoted to the next generation, the step emphasized (NDEA - neutral drift evolutionary algorithm) is removed. We refer to such an algorithm as simply an EA.

If this is done, the only way a genotype can supplant its parent is by having a superior fitness. Some have argued that allowing neutral drift is equivalent to using a higher mutation rate in an EA (Knowles and Watson, 2002). In results later we show empirically that this is not the case for the problem studied here, this accords with previous work reported on Boolean problems (Yu and Miller, 2001).

In this chapter, we show that fixing the output gene to be the rightmost node is sometimes advantageous. This accords with findings on other problems (Yu and Miller, 2001, Yu and Miller, 2002). It is important to note that CGP is continuing to develop and recently a form of automatically defined functions has been implemented that promises to make the technique more powerful (Walker and Miller, 2004).

3.　　Docking

Structure-based virtual screening (Lyne, 2002) is an increasingly important technology in the hit identification (identification of compounds that are potentially useful as drugs) and lead optimisation (process of refining the chemical structure of a hit to improve its drug characteristics) phases of drug discovery. The goal of structure-based virtual screening is to identify a set of small molecules (ligands) that are predicted to bind to a defined target macromolecule (protein or nucleic acid). Through the combination of fast molecular docking algorithms, empirical scoring functions and affordable computer farms, it is possible to virtually screen hundreds of thousands or even millions of ligands in a relatively short time (a few days). The output from the docking calculation is a prediction of the geometric binding conformation of each ligand along with a score that represents the quality of fit for the binding site. Only a small fraction of the top-scoring virtual hits (typically up to 1000) then are selected for experimental assay validation. If successful, this virtual hit set will be significantly enriched in bioactive molecules relative to a random selection and will yield a number of diverse starting points for a medicinal chemistry 'hit-to-lead' programme.

Although many factors contribute to the success of virtual screening, a critical component is the scoring function employed by the docking search algorithm. Whilst reasonably effective at reproducing the binding geometries of known ligands, empirical scores are less successful at ranking true hits correctly by binding free energy. This is a natural consequence of the many approximations made in the interests of high throughput and, as such, all virtual hit sets contain false positives to a greater or lesser extent. Many of these false positives can be removed manually by visual inspection of the predicted binding geometries by an expert computational chemist, but this is a time consuming process.

There have been previous studies that used Genetic Algorithms to improve the coefficients of the scoring function (Smith et al., 2003). Also Böhm (Stahl and Böhm, 1998) developed an empirical post-filter for the docking program FlexX using penalty functions. Here we present the results of our initial attempts to apply CGP techniques to automate the removal of false positives from virtual hit sets.

Virtual Screening

At Vernalis rDock (Morley et al., 2004) and its predecessor RiboDock (Afshar and Morley, 2004) were developed as docking platforms that can rapidly screen millions of compounds against protein and RNA targets.

During docking rDock tries to minimise the total score: $S_{total} = S_{inter} + S_{intra} + S_{restraint}$ where S_{inter} stands for the sum of all the intermolecular scoring functions, S_{intra} is the ligand intramolecular term and $S_{restraint}$ is a penalty term that considers the deviation from certain restraints, for instance when part of the ligand is outside the docking cavity.

Using this score rDock searches for the best conformation for a given ligand over a given docking site. At the end, rDock stores the ligands for which a conformation with a low enough score has been found. These are the ligands that will be considered virtual hits.

Filtering

Once all the hits are found, the value of the score is no longer meaningful. The score is good enough to compare two different conformations of a given ligand, but not good enough to accurately rank order different ligands.

rDock outputs the score and its constituents. rDock also outputs additional descriptors for both the ligand and the target docking site such as molecular weight, number of aromatic rings, charge, number of atoms, etc., that are not used directly during docking. This information is used in an ad hoc manner by the computational chemists to filter out manually the virtual hits, often on a per-target basis, for example to ensure a desired balance between polar and apolar interaction scores. We have explored the use of GP techniques to automatically evolve more complex, target-independent post-docking filters (Garmendia-Doval et al., 2004).

Implementation

In our experiments we used a single row of 200 nodes. We chose the levels-back parameter to be 100 and we counted the input variables as the first nodes. All nodes have three inputs and one output. So if their true arity is lower, the extra inputs are ignored. The operations implemented can be seen in Table 14-1.

The input to the program is the data returned by rDock. There are components to S_{inter}, S_{intra}, and $S_{restraint}$, ligand descriptors and docking site descriptors. Some of these descriptors are explained in detail in Table 14-2.

Apart from the input variables, there is also a pool of 15 constants introduced as program inputs. Each time the CGP is run, 13 of them will be created at random. The other 2 are the constants 0.0 and 1.0. A random constant is equal to $a * 10^b$ where a is a float (with just one decimal place) number between -10 and 10 and b is an integer between -5 and 5.

In total there were 66 input variables, although a given filter did not have to use all of them. On average 10 to 15 variables were used by individual filters.

Training Set

We assembled a set of 163 targets, such that for each of them there is a structure available of the target and of a native ligand, a compound which is experimentally known to dock into that target.

Each of the 163 ligands have been docked against each of the targets. If the scoring function used in docking were perfect, then the lowest (best) score for each target would be obtained for the native ligand bound.

As our current ability to calculate physical properties is quite limited, the native ligand only ranks first in a few cases. Therefore, this cross-docking set contains a large number of false positives. These can be used to drive a genetic program to evolve appropriate filters based on various calculated properties.

From the targets for which the corresponding native ligand ranks in the 9th position or higher, 30 were chosen at random. The training set is then these 30 targets, where the native ligands are considered hits and the ligands with a higher rank are considered misses.

Fitness Function

The CGP system implemented evolves numerical functions. For each input (i.e., docking score components of a given ligand over a given docking site, together with the ligand and docking site descriptors), a float number is returned. It was decided to interpret these numbers in the following manner:

$f < 0$ represents a hit
$f >= 0$ represents a miss

For each protein in the training set there is one hit (native ligand) and a list of size between 0 and 8 with misses (ligands that score better than the native ligand). The fitness function counts the number of proteins for which the hit was recognised as hit ($f < 0$) and at least $\frac{2}{3}$ of the misses were recognised as misses ($f >= 0$).

Table 14-1. Operators

Name	#Args	Description
+	2	Addition
−	2	Subtraction
*	2	Multiplication
/	2	$div(a,b) = \begin{cases} a & \text{if } \lvert b \rvert < 0.000001 \\ a/b & \text{otherwise} \end{cases}$
log	1	$log(a) = \begin{cases} 0 & \text{if } \lvert a \rvert < 0.000001 \\ log(\lvert a \rvert) & \text{otherwise} \end{cases}$
exp	1	$exp(a) = \begin{cases} 0 & \text{if } a < -200 \\ exp(200) & \text{if } a > 200 \\ exp(a) & \text{otherwise} \end{cases}$
if	3	$if(a,b,c) = \begin{cases} b & \text{if } a > 0 \\ c & \text{otherwise} \end{cases}$
Random constant	0	The first time this command is called for a given node, it will create a new random constant. That remains the value of the node for the rest of the program, unless a mutation operator changes the operation of the node.

4. Experiments Investigating CGP Behaviour with Parameter Variation

For all the following experiments, the results are the average of 100 runs. Every 500 generations the best individual and its program size was stored. The program size is understood as the phenotype size, i.e., the number of nodes, including the input variables, that are present in the function/program represented by the genotype. We are using the NDEA version of the evolutionary strategy discussed in Section 2.

Genome Sizes

Figure 14-2 is a comparison of results with different genome sizes. For all of them, the levels-back parameter was set equal to the genome size.

Examining the plot of average best of population fitness versus number of generations (Figure 14-3) we see that even after 10,000 generations the fitness is still improving. More interestingly we see that the maximum allowed number of nodes provides a good ordering of this behaviour: the larger the allowed number of nodes the higher the average best fitness. However, it looks like much larger genotypes would offer diminishing improvements over smaller, provided the allowed size is large enough. The growth in phenotype size is fairly rapid initially but settles down to a very small growth. It should be noted that even when 1000 active nodes are allowed the average best size eventually settles at about 43, leaving 957 inactive nodes. Despite this enormous level of redundancy in the genotype we find the evolutionary algorithm described is very effective.

Levels-Back

When the levels-back parameter is varied we see that with low values (25 out of a possible 200) the performance of the algorithm is much poorer and the program size is very much larger. Interestingly we find that intermediate values of local graph connectivity give the best results (levels-back 75 and 100).

Output Node

In the implementation used for the docking problem, the output of the filter was taken to be one of the CGP nodes taken at random. This output node could afterwards be mutated during the CGP run. Another option is to take always the last node as the output node without possibility of mutating it, i.e., it is taken out of the genome. A comparison of these two implementations was done using for both of them with 200 nodes, 0.08 mutation rate and NDEA

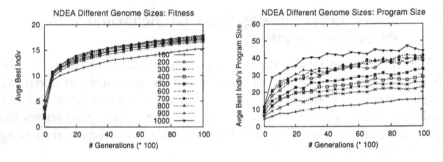

Figure 14-2. Comparison Genome Sizes

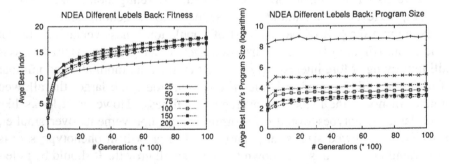

Figure 14-3. Comparison Levels-Back

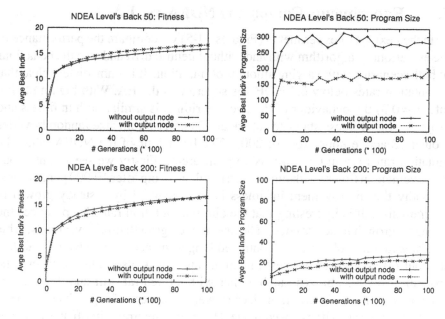

Figure 14-4. Comparison with/without output node: 50, 200

algorithm. A mutation rate of 0.08 means that for every mutation operation, each gene has a 0.08 probability of being mutated. With 200 nodes each one represented by 4 genes (3 inputs and the operator), it means on average 64 genes will be mutated. The parameter levels-back was modified to be 50, 75, 100, 150 and 200. The results for 50 and 200 can be seen in Figure 14-4. It is clear from the results that the performance of the evolutionary algorithm is not greatly affected by whether the program has a fixed output node or whether it is subject to evolution. However having no output gene appears to give better results when the levels-back parameter is large. Even though there is little difference in fitness improvement the average size of the best programs is very different especially with smaller values of levels-back. The weakness of the correlation between fitness improvement and the presence or absence of an output gene was unexpected as it has been found that in Boolean function search the performance is much more reliably good when the program output is taken from the rightmost node. This is because it can sometimes happen by chance that the best individual in the initial population has a small phenotype length. This means that nearly all mutations affect redundant code thus leading to trapping in a sub-optimum. The output gene is unlikely to hit by mutation and so sometimes one has to wait for many generations for a larger phenotype to be created. The continuous nature of the data may be the reason why the presence or absence of an output gene is of minor importance.

5.   Experiments Comparing NDEA vs. EA

In the next set of experiments (Figures 14-5) we compare the performance of the evolutionary algorithm with and without neutral drift and also the behaviour of both scenarios with varying amounts of mutation. It is immediately clear that at mutation rates below 0.3 NDEA is superior to the EA. With high mutation rates (>=0.3) the behaviour of the two algorithms is similar both in fitness and program size. Fitness stagnates at about 12 and program size randomly varies around 22 active nodes (out of 200). The behaviour of the NDEA when the mutation rates are much lower is very different. Firstly we see a continuous improvement in fitness with time which is still growing after 10,000 generations. Secondly the improvement in fitness is accompanied by a steady growth in program size. It is interesting that the optimal mutation rate also produces the strongest growth in active code. The rate of code growth drops eventually. This indicates that if evolution was continued longer the active code would stabilize at about 60 nodes (for the best mutation rate). It is also noteworthy that the program growth stabilizes much earlier without neutral drift and that there is much less variation in program sizes (lower variance). The graphs show very clearly that neutral drift is not equivalent to turning neutral drift off and allowing higher mutation rates.

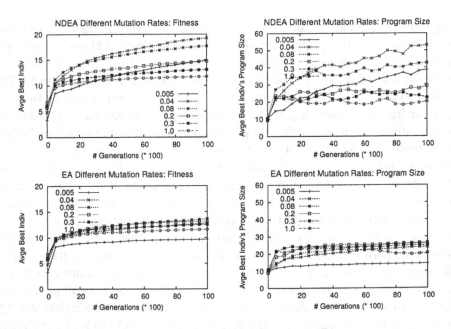

Figure 14-5.   Comparison of NDEA vs. EA

6. Application of NDEA over Docking

In the initial implementation of CGP for the docking problem, a series of experiments were conducted in which system parameters such as the structure of the matrix, mutation rate, etc. were varied, although not in such detail as the experiments shown in sections 4 and 5. At that time it was not possible to conduct very rigorous tests because of the severe time restrictions associated with the business environment, although another reason was caused by this being a classification problem. The fitness function in the CGP implementation is based on the result of applying the current filter on the training set. Since we are considering a classification problem, our aim is to maximize the classification accuracy over the test set. Our goal was not to find the global optimum for the training set as this would have almost surely been equivalent to overfitting and would have produced a filter that would have performed poorly over new data. Because of this, once a system capable of finding good local optima was identified, the system parameters were fixed to be the following: mutation rate 0.08, genome size 200 nodes and levels-back 100. From the results of the experiments described one can see that it was a good enough choice.

Test Set

The test set corresponded to the rest of the cross-docking matrix, i.e., the 133 proteins left after removing the 30 that were used for training. The reason for the test set being so much larger than the training set was due to the fact that only half of the matrix was available at the beginning of the project. Once the other half was made available, it was added directly to the test set.

CGP was run several hundred times and the filters that performed best over the test set were chosen. These were then further tested over our validation set.

Seeded Libraries

Seeded libraries are one of a number of methods that have been developed to assess the performance of virtual screening programs. A seeded library for a given target is a library of drug-like compounds that includes several native ligands known to bind to that target. All the compounds are docked into the given target using the docking platform. The output conformations are then sorted by the score. The ability of the virtual screening software to distinguish between the native ligands and the non native ones can then be measured, typically by calculating the percentage of native ligands found in the top $x\%$.

We tested the best filters over four seeded libraries, and the most promising was chosen. This filter can be seen in Figure 14-7. The variables used by this filter are described in Table 14-2 and the results obtained in the training set and the test set can be seen in Table 14-3.

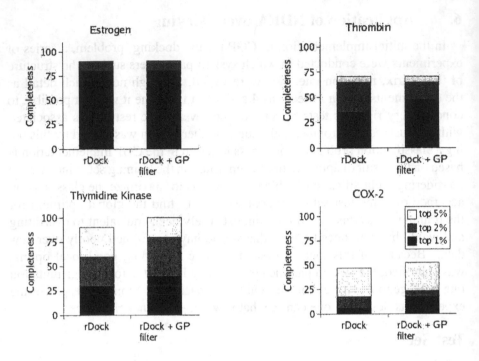

Figure 14-6. Seeded Libraries

Figure 14-6 shows the top 1% (black), top 2% (dark gray) and top 5% (light gray) completeness for these four seeded libraries, where completeness is defined as the percentage of true active retrieved in the slice. We had 10 native ligands for proteins Estrogen and Thymidine Kinase, and 17 for proteins Thrombin and COX-2. The first column shows the results of rDock. The second column shows the results of applying the Figure 14-7 filter.

For Estrogen, there is not a great improvement using the filter, as rDock already produces very good results and is therefore difficult to improve upon them.

Thrombin shows a nice improvement as some of the native ligands that were previously found on the top 2% are now found on the top 1%. Similarly for COX-2, all the native ligands found before in the top 2% are now found in the top 1%.

Finally Thymidine Kinase gives the best results as more native ligands are found in the top 1% (40% vs. 30%), more in the top 2% (80% vs. 60%) and again more in the top 5% (100% vs. 90%) where all the native ligands are found.

Best Filter

There were several filters that worked well for the cross-docking matrix but most of them did not generalise well for the seeded libraries. They either filtered out native ligands or, most commonly, they filter almost nothing out. However, we found the following filter to generalise quite well.

```
log(SCORE.INTRA.VDW.raw - 0.9913) *
    exp(SCORE.INTER.AROM.narom *
        exp(SCORE.INTER.POLAR.nhbd) * LIG_POS_CHG)
+ 684 *
    if  SCORE.INTER.REPUL.nhba > 0  then
        LIG_NEG_CHG
    else
        SCORE.INTER.VDW.nrep / SITE_PERC_AROMATOMS
    end

if (SCORE.INTER.POLAR.nhbd -
    SCORE.INTRA.REPUL.raw + LIG_TOT_CHG ) > 0  then
    SITE_NLIPOC
else
    exp(SITE_NEG_CHG) - log(LIG_NHBD)
end
```

Figure 14-7.   Best filter found to date

Table 14-2.   Descriptions of the Variables used by the best filter

variables	description
SCORE.INTRA.VDW.raw	sum of the intraligand van der Waals forces
SCORE.INTRA.REPUL.raw	sum of the intraligand repulsive polar contacts
SCORE.INTER.AROM.narom	number of aromatic rings involve in aromatic interactions
SCORE.INTER.POLAR.nhbd	number of ligand hydrogen bond donors involved in polar interactions
SCORE.INTER.REPUL.nhba	number of ligand hydrogen bond acceptors involved in repulsive polar interactions
SCORE.INTER.VDW.nrep	number of ligand atoms with overall repulsive van der Waals interactions (steric clash)
LIG_NEG_CHG	sum of formal negative charges of the ligand
LIG_NHBD	number of hydrogen bond donors in ligand
LIG_TOT_CHG	total formal charge of the ligand
SITE_PERC_AROMATOMS	percentage of atoms that are aromatic in the target site
SITE_NLIPOC	number of non-polar carbons in the site
SITE_NEG_CHG	sum of formal negative charges of the site

Table 14-3. Results of Best Filter for training set and test set

Training Set		Correctly Classified	Incorrectly Classified
	Native Ligands	28	2
	Non-Native Ligands	36	21
Test Set			
	Native Ligands	89	44
	Non-Native Ligands	1946	2417

It should be emphasised that the cross-docking matrix is a quite different experiment from the seeded libraries. The fact that this filter is able to filter out true misses while maintaining most of the true hits in both experiments is quite encouraging and is relatively safe to infer that somehow it has found some general trends in the data.

Although it is difficult to understand exactly what the filter is doing, the filter combines intermolecular score components (as used during docking) with both protein and ligand properties in a chemically meaningful way. For example, highly strained conformations (SCORE.INTRA.VDW.raw) and steric clashes between ligand and target (SCORE.INTER.VDW.nrep) are more likely to be rejected.

Finally it should also be noted that the only simplifications done over the original filter output by the CGP program and this filter were replacing the expression $\exp(-0.0087)$ for 0.9913 and the expression $-(900 * -0.76)$ for 684. Some parenthesis that were not necessary were also removed to make it more readable. As reported in (Miller, 2001), in all the programs found by CGP for this problem, there was "either very weak program bloat or *zero bloat*"

7. Results with Real Data

All the previous results shown were obtained over idealised test sets used routinely to measure docking performance. As a final validation we have applied the filter in Figure 14-7 to real virtual screening data from docking campaigns performed at Vernalis, specifically against an oncology target protein, HSP90.

From an initial docking library of around 700000 compounds, a total of around 40000 virtual hits were identified over several docking campaigns against HSP90. Around 1500 of the virtual hits were selected by a computational chemist for experimental assay using a variety of ad hoc post filters, and knowledge and experience of the target protein, in a process taking around a week. Thirty of the assayed compounds were confirmed as real hits, in that they showed significant activity against HSP90.

The filter shown in Figure 14-7 was applied to the virtual hits (see Table 14-4) and was able to remove 29% of the original unfiltered hits, whilst only removing 4% of the compounds manually selected for assay. Three of the true actives were also removed.

The GP-derived filter therefore shows very good agreement with the manual filtering process, in that the filter passes almost all of the original assayed compounds, but is able to reduce automatically the initial size of the data set by almost 30%. This provides further evidence that the filter is generalising across docking targets quite distinct from those in the training and test sets.

The filter is currently being used and tested with each new docking campaign, with very good results. It promises to be a useful additional tool in the computational chemist's armoury of post-docking filters.

Table 14-4.   HSP90

	Manual post-docking hits	+GP post-docking filter	Reduction
rDock virtual hits	39908	28374	−29%
Compounds assayed	1467	1409	−4%
True actives	30	27	−10%

8.   Conclusions

Removal of false positives after structure-based virtual screening is a recognised problem in the field. This chapter describes what we believe is the first attempt at using Genetic Programming to evolve a post-docking filter automatically. We found the simple 1+4 evolutionary strategy with neutral drift to be very effective and also confirmed that for this real world problem, program bloat was not a problem.

The cross docking matrix used for training and evolving post-docking filters is quite different from the seeded libraries and the HSP90 data. The post-docking filter chosen from the ones found by the GP platform is filtering out consistently bad compounds in all cases, while retaining interesting hits. We can say that it is generalising over the data. The HSP90 data is the first real data on which the filter has been tested and the results are very promising. This filter is now being used as standard in all the projects in the company. Early results confirm its usefulness.

The GP platform offers immediately a pragmatic, automated post-docking filter for cleaning up virtual hit sets. It can be easily applied again for different descriptors or scoring functions.

Longer-term the filters found may offer a way of "boot-strapping" docking scoring function improvements, by identifying non-obvious, yet systematic, defects in the scoring function.

This technique is also not specific to docking programs, and we plan to apply it in the near future for other problems where a list of variables and descriptors is available and there is a need for a generic filter.

References

Afshar, Mohammad and Morley, S. David (2004). Validation of an empirical rna-ligand scoring function for fast flexible docking using ribodock(r). J. Comput.-Aided Mol. Design, accepted.

Ashmore, Laurence (2000). An investigation into cartesian genetic programming within the field of evolutionary art. Technical report, Final year project, http://www.gaga.demon.co.uk/evoart.htm Department of Computer Science, University of Birmingham.

Garmendia-Doval, A. Beatriz, Morley, S. David, and Juhos, Szilvester (2004). Post docking filtering using cartesian genetic programming. In Liardet, P., Collet, P., Funlupt, C., Lutton, E., and Schoenauer, M., editors, *Artificial Evolution*, volume 2936 of *Lecture Notes in Computer Science*, pages 189–200. Springer.

Knowles, Joshua D. and Watson, Richard A. (2002). On the utility of redundant encodings in mutation-based evolutionary search. In J.-J. Merelo Guervós, P. Adamidis, H.-G. Beyer, J.-L. Fernández-Villacañas, H.-P. Schwefel, editor, *Parallel Problem Solving from Nature - PPSN VII, 7th International Conference, Granada, Spain, September 7-11, 2002. Proceedings*, number 2439 in Lecture Notes in Computer Science, LNCS, page 88 ff. Springer-Verlag.

Lyne, Paul D. (2002). Structure-based virtual screening: an overview. *Drug Discovery Today*, 7(20):1047–1055.

Miller, Julian (2001). What bloat? cartesian genetic programming on boolean problems. In Goodman, Erik D., editor, *2001 Genetic and Evolutionary Computation Conference Late Breaking Papers*, pages 295–302, San Francisco, California, USA.

Miller, Julian F. (1999). An empirical study of the efficiency of learning boolean functions using a cartesian genetic programming approach. In Banzhaf, Wolfgang, Daida, Jason, Eiben, Agoston E., Garzon, Max H., Honavar, Vasant, Jakiela, Mark, and Smith, Robert E., editors, *Proceedings of the Genetic and Evolutionary Computation Conference*, volume 2, pages 1135–1142, Orlando, Florida, USA. Morgan Kaufmann.

Miller, Julian F. (2003). Evolving developmental programs for adaptation, morphogenesis, and self-repair. In Banzhaf, Wolfgang, Christaller, Thomas, Dittrich, Peter, Kim, Jan T., and Ziegler, Jens, editors, *Advances in Artificial Life, ECAL 2003, Proceedings*, volume 2801 of *Lecture Notes in Artificial Intelligence*, pages 256–265. Springer.

Miller, Julian F. and Banzhaf, Wolfgang (2003). Evolving the program for a cell: from french flags to boolean circuits. In Kumar, Sanjeev and Bentley, Peter J., editors, *On Growth, Form and Computers*, pages 278–301. Academic Press.

Miller, Julian F., Job, Dominic, and Vassilev, Vesselin K. (2000a). Principles in the evolutionary design of digital circuits-part I. *Genetic Programming and Evolvable Machines*, 1(1/2):7–35.

Miller, Julian F., Job, Dominic, and Vassilev, Vesselin K. (2000b). Principles in the evolutionary design of digital circuits-part II. *Genetic Programming and Evolvable Machines*, 1(3):259–288.

Miller, Julian F. and Thomson, Peter (2000). Cartesian genetic programming. In Poli, Riccardo, Banzhaf, Wolfgang, Langdon, William B., Miller, Julian F., Nordin, Peter, and Fogarty, Terence C., editors, *Genetic Programming, Proceedings of EuroGP'2000*, volume 1802 of *LNCS*, pages 121–132, Edinburgh. Springer-Verlag.

Miller, Julian F. and Thomson, Peter (2003). A developmental method for growing graphs and circuits. In Tyrrell, Andy M., Haddow, Pauline C., and Torresen, Jim, editors, *Evolvable Systems: From Biology to Hardware, Fifth International Conference, ICES 2003*, volume 2606 of *LNCS*, pages 93–104, Trondheim, Norway. Springer-Verlag.

Miller, Julian F., Thomson, Peter, and Fogarty, Terence (1997). Designing electronic circuits using evolutionary algorithms arithmetic circuits: A case study. In Quagliarella, D., Périaux, J., Poloni, C., and Winter, G., editors, *Genetic Algorithms and Evolution Strategies in Engineering and Computer Science. Recent Advances and Industrial Applications*. John Wiley and Sons.

Morley, S. David, Juhos, Szilveszter, and Garmendia-Doval, A. Beatriz (2004). in preparation.

Nordin, Peter and Banzhaf, Wolfgang (1995). Complexity compression and evolution. In Eshelman, L., editor, *Genetic Algorithms: Proceedings of the Sixth International Conference (ICGA95)*, pages 310–317, Pittsburgh, PA, USA. Morgan Kaufmann.

Rothermich, Joseph A. and Miller, Julian F. (2002). Studying the emergence of multicellularity with cartesian genetic programming in artificial life. In Cantú-Paz, Erick, editor, *Late Breaking Papers at the Genetic and Evolutionary Computation Conference (GECCO-2002)*, pages 397–403, New York, NY. AAAI.

Rothermich, Joseph A., Wang, Fang, and Miller, Julian F. (2003). Adaptivity in cell based optimization for information ecosystems. In Press, IEEE, editor, *Proceedings of the 2003 Congress on Evolutionary Computation*, pages 490–497, Camberra.

Schwefel, H. P. (1965). Kybernetische evolution als strategie der experimentelen forschung in der stromungstechnik. Master's thesis, Technical University of Berlin.

Sekanina, Lukas (2004). *Evolvable Components: From Theory to Hardware Implementations*. Springer–Verlag.

Smith, Ryan, Hubbard, Roderick E., Gschwend, Daniel A., Leach, Andrew R., and Good, Andrew C. (2003). Analysis and optimization of structure-based virtual screening protocols (3). new methods and old problems in scoring function design. *J. Mol. Graphics Mod.*, 22:41–53.

Stahl, Martin and Böhm, Hans-Joachim (1998). Development of filter functions for protein-ligand docking. *J. Mol. Graphics Mod.*, 16:121–132.

Vassilev, Vesselin K. and Miller, Julian F. (2000). The advantages of landscape neutrality in digital circuit evolution. In *Proceedings of the Third International Conference on Evolvable Systems*, pages 252–263. Springer-Verlag.

Voss, Mark S. (2003). Social programming using functional swarm optimization. In *IEEE Swarm Intelligence Symposium (SIS03)*.

Voss, Mark S. and James C. Howland, III (2003). Financial modelling using social programming. In *FEA 2003: Financial Engineering and Applications*, Banff, Alberta.

Walker, James A. and Miller, Julian F. (2004). Evolution and acquisition of modules in cartesian genetic programming. In Keijzer, Maarten, O'Reilly, Una-May, Lucas, Simon M., Costa, Ernesto, and Soule, Terence, editors, *Proceedings of the Seventh European Conference on Genetic Programming*, volume 3003 of *LNCS*, pages 187–197. Springer-Verlag.

Yu, Tina and Miller, Julian (2001). Neutrality and the evolvability of boolean function landscape. In Miller, Julian F., Tomassini, Marco, Lanzi, Pier Luca, Ryan, Conor, Tettamanzi,

Andrea G. B., and Langdon, William B., editors, *Genetic Programming, Proceedings of EuroGP'2001*, volume 2038 of *LNCS*, pages 204–217, Lake Como, Italy. Springer-Verlag.

Yu, Tina and Miller, Julian F. (2002). Needles in haystacks are not hard to find with neutrality. In Foster, James A., Lutton, Evelyne, Miller, Julian, Ryan, Conor, and Tettamanzi, Andrea G. B., editors, *Genetic Programming, Proceedings of the 5th European Conference, EuroGP 2002*, volume 2278 of *LNCS*, pages 13–25, Kinsale, Ireland. Springer-Verlag.

Chapter 15

LISTENING TO DATA: TUNING A GENETIC PROGRAMMING SYSTEM

Duncan MacLean, Eric A. Wollesen and Bill Worzel
Genetics Squared Inc

Abstract: Genetic Programming (GP) may be used to model complex data but it must be "tuned" to get the best results. This process of tuning often gives insights into the data itself. This is discussed using examples from classification problems in molecular biology and the results and "rules of thumb" developed to tune the GP system are reviewed in light of current GP theory.

Key words: classifier, molecular biology, genetic programming, cancer, microarray, genetics

1. INTRODUCTION

Genetic Programming (GP) may be used to create a functional description of data by discovering classification functions or by modeling dynamic processes as described by (Banzhaf et al., 1996). The process of discovering such functions usually calls for successive iterations adjusting the parameters, fitness function, population size and other characteristics of the genetic programming system to arrive at a satisfactory result. Loosely speaking this may be viewed as "tuning" the GP system to the problem at hand. The process of tuning the system and the results arrived at may reveal something about the problem, the data and ultimately about genetic programming itself.

Several classifier problems will be described along with the tools and rules of thumb that were developed for tuning the GP system. A "well behaved" problem is described and two specific "ill behaved" problems are described. These studies are reviewed, information about the data and the problem that was discovered because of the behavior of the GP system is described, and the lessons learned discussed.

2.   BACKGROUND

Genetics Squared is a life science company focused on the analysis of biological and pharmaceutical data with the goal of developing better diagnostics and therapeutics. A common kind of problem we address is the development of diagnostic and prognostic rules that can inform treatment decisions by classifying disease characteristics into sub-types, often based on therapeutic results. Using genomic microarray data (Gerhold et al., 1999), it is often possible to gain insight into a disease state based on cellular behavior at the molecular level (Khan et al., 2001).

Because of the expense of developing microarray data, the number of tissue samples in a study are often limited, yet there may be up to 20,000 genes in a single microarray. This creates a challenge in that it is often easy to overfit the results to the training set and the difficulty of the problem varies tremendously from one to another. Typically studies that call for differentiating between healthy and diseased tissue are fairly easy to solve while problems involving prognostic outcomes or multiple sub-types (e.g., tumor stages) that are not necessarily tied to behaviors at the molecular level can be quite difficult. This provides a range of problems, some of which will demonstrate "good" behaviors (i.e., the behavior of a well-tuned GP system) and some of which are "bad" behaviors (i.e., the behavior of a badly-tuned GP system) in terms of the interaction of the GP system with the problem.

Given the small number of samples for the large number of variables, the standard procedure is to use an N-fold cross validation approach where the data is divided into N partitions and N-1 are used to produce classification functions and the Nth partition is used to test the best function discovered. Then the evolution of classifier programs starts over with a different partition used as the test set. This continues until all partitions have been used as the test set. The results from each separate fold are summed giving a cumulative result assessing the average ability of the GP system to find robust results.

We typically make a number of runs of N-folds to assess the tractability of a problem and GP parameters are changed to find the best combination for producing high-fitness, robust results. Typically the crossover and mutation rates are adjusted along with the population size, operator set and tournament size. If the average is good across several runs of multiple folds, then the entire set is taken as a whole and run as a single fold and the function with the best fitness on the entire set is selected as the diagnostic rule.

An example rule is shown in Figure 15-1 where the variables are represented by the name of genes whose expression levels were measured.

IF [KDR >= ((if (MAPK29 > sqr(FGFR4)) then GSTP1 else PDGFB) + MMP16)] THEN "Tumor Stage Ta"

Figure 15-1. Example Classification Rule

2.1 Post-Processing Analysis

Over the three years that Genetics Squared has worked on these classification problems, we have developed a set of post-processing tools that have proven useful for tracking the behavior of the GP system. While some of the tools are fairly usual, some were developed because of the unusual nature of the problems. These tools and the reasons for them are discussed below. By "post-processing," what is meant is the analysis of several GP runs to look for salient characteristics within the results.

2.1.1 Logfiles

During GP runs, logfiles are generated that record the current "front runner" or best function for classification across all demes. Typically multiple processors were used and the best individual may come from any processor. It is often the case that the successive front-runners will come from different processors.

2.1.2 Fitness Traces

A fitness trace is a plot of the fitness of the current frontrunner over time. An example of a fitness trace is shown in Figure 15-2. The fitness is the accuracy of the rule in predicting a sample's class membership with perfect being 1.0. The top line shows the fitness of the best individual from the training set. The bottom line is the fitness on the same individual when calculated on the test set.

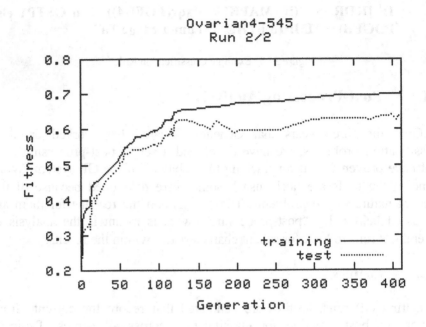

Figure 15-2. Example Fitness Trace

2.1.3   Gene Frequencies

Because many runs are typically made on the same data using the same parameters, we have developed a tool that tabulates the number of times a particular gene appears in each of the best-of-run functions. An example is shown in Figure 15-3.

30 rules found.
Gene{6720}: 24
Gene{410}: 23
Gene{5684}:20
Gene{3341}: 15
Gene{226}: 11
Gene{4862}: 10
Gene{2507}: 10
Gene{639}: 8
Gene{5061}: 6
Gene{2471}: 6

Figure 15-3. Example Gene Frequency List

In this example gene number 6720 appears in 24 best-of-run rules out of 30 rules altogether.

2.1.4 Misclassified Samples

Many of the studies are incorrectly classed or are based on gross physical characteristics that may not correspond to behaviors at the molecular level. For example, many cancers are diagnosed on the basis of cell staining and microscopic examination of the stained tumor cells. Occasionally mistakes are made and some of the samples that are used for training are incorrectly labeled. In this case the mislabeled samples will continually show up as being misclassified by the GP system, particularly when they appear in the test set. so we have developed a tool that counts the frequency of misclassification for each sample. Obviously a well characterized set will have few misclassifications and most will not be "repeat offenders."

2.1.5 Motifs

One of the things that we look for in classification studies are repeating "motifs" in the functions. These are combinations of genes and operators that appear repeatedly within a set of runs such as "GeneA * GeneB" or "(GeneC + GeneD) / GeneE". Because the rule expressions may be fairly complex, we have not yet developed a tool that can discover such motifs reliably since there may be many genes and other gene sub-calculations between two genes that appear in a motif. For example, consider the function fragment:

GeneA * (<long nested expression.> + GeneB)

The motif "GeneA*GeneB" is present but widely separated and could easily be missed without considering closely the algebra of the expression.

3. EXAMPLE STUDIES

What we have developed is an attitude that might best be summed up as "listening to the data." This is a case of working with a data set, changing GP parameters and then watching the response of the outcome to these changes. In tuning the GP parameters we have often found that the difficulties we encounter suggest something about the data being analyzed. It is easy to become dogmatic about how to use GP but in our experience, this will not get the best results nor will it achieve the ultimate goal of gaining insight into the problem being studied.

What follows are somewhat anecdotal examples of difficult problems and the "behavior" of the GP system as it struggled to find solutions. We start with a "well behaved" study (i.e., one where the GP system produced reliable results and showed a distinct behavior in how it reached the results) and then talk about two problems where the GP system struggled to find good answers but ultimately revealed more about the data than expected. All of these studies are cancer studies using gene expression profile data as inputs and some known physiological state as the class that is being predicted. Details of gene chip data and its application to diagnostics and therapeutics may be found in (Driscoll et al., 2003).

The characteristics of a run that we classify as well behaved are as follows:

- Good training-test set correspondence; few signs of overfitting
- Distinct selection of variables; each class uses different variables in the classification rules
- A small number of features that are selected in preference to any others across multiple runs
- Little or no pattern to the samples that are misclassified when viewed across multiple runs

Overfitting is the often a serious problem in GP, particularly when there are a limited number of samples from which to create a generally descriptive function. Contrary to what one might expect, it is not the difficulty of finding solutions that causes the most trouble, but the tendency of GP to find solutions that are too particularized to the training set. These solution tend to be "brittle" and don't generalize when applied to other data. A good correlation between accuracy (or other similar measures) on the training set and accuracy on the test set is the first and most important characteristic of a well-tuned classification system.

A distinct preference to select certain variables is a characteristic we have noticed in the high-dimensionality studies we have been involved in recently. (By "high-dimensionality" what is meant is that there are a very large number of inputs compared to the number of samples) Each class tends to have its "favorites" that the GP system "reaches for" in finding a solution. This may be because of the underlying biology where a few key marker genes often indicate the activation of specific pathways that distinguish the target classes but we have observed it in other studies of very different types of data, so it is not limited to biological problems.

There are a number of reasons why this may be a good sign: If the tree depth or number of terminals is too large in classification problems such as the ones described here, rather than introns becoming prevalent, overfitting occurs. One of the signs of this is that the choice of variables is very different in each run. While this may also occur if there are a large number of solutions to the problem, even in these cases some variables are better (or at least easier to find in useful combinations) than others so that we still find that the reinforcement of variables is consistent. We have seen all of these behaviors at one time or another and as a result this is one of the main features we look for.

Finally, because the data we are working with is often poor, not only because of noise in the data, but because of uncertainties in the sample labels used in training, looking at the frequency of misclassifications can provide insight into samples that may be skewing the results. If a sample is misclassified, GP will often "bend" the classification to try and include the wrongly labeled sample. Nonetheless this can either cause overfitting to include the sample or it may lead to consistent misclassification of samples that belong to the class that the mislabeled sample actually belongs to. For this reason we believe it is never enough to look only for overfitting in the training-test results: one should also look for patterns of misclassification that may indicate the problem is outside of the behavior of the GP system.

3.1 Well-behaved Runs

We recently completed a toxicity study of pre-clinical data for a major pharmaceutical company. Though the actual details of the results are confidential, the GP behavior is described here as it was a fairly interesting application of GP to a real problem having noisy data.

3.1.1 Toxicity Study

The data was composed of gene expression profiles for a number of samples taken from toxic doses of particular compounds. There were four separate types of toxicity in the study and the vehicle (carrier material for the compounds) as a control (i.e., it had nothing that would be expected to cause a toxic response). Of the five classes, two were relatively easy to match, one was moderately difficult and two were downright stubborn. As is often the case, there was more to be learned from the stubborn cases and in the end, reasonable classification rules were found for both of them.

The data was based on a common gene chip having 8,740 genes per sample as input and 194 samples for the entire data set. A summary of the data is provided in Table 15-1.

Table 15-1. Toxicity Data Set Characteristics

Number of Samples	Class A	Class B	Class C	Class D	Class V
194	19	16	55	12	92

In this study we typically used a 3-fold cross-validation scheme where the sample set was partitioned into 3 equal parts at random with roughly equal representation of each class in each partition. Each partition then took a turn as the test set and the other two folds were used as the training set. Each successive run started from scratch so that the results of the previous fold-trial did not influence the results in the next fold-trial. A number of runs were made using the same GP parameters and then, if overfitting was detected, the GP parameters were adjusted. While it may be argued that this amounted to "peeking" at the test set, since the results were run many times with the same settings and random recomposition of the folds for each run, there was no bias in the composition of partitions. However it has been argued that this biases the entire evolutionary process. Nevertheless, since it is impossible a priori to know when overfitting is going to occur on a particular data set with a particular set of GP parameters, this was the best compromise we could come up with while using the N-fold cross validation scheme.

We created classifiers that differentiated between a target class and "all the others" and then combined the best classifiers using the voting algorithm. The results were quite good with three of the five classes being perfectly classified and only two having any errors. Table 15-2 shows the results of combining the classifiers using the voting algorithm. This is a confusion matrix with the prediction read down each column and the truth for each sample read across a row. This shows that there was a Class A sample that was misclassified as an 'V' sample and 4 Class C samples identified as 'V' samples.

Table 15-2. Voting algorithm for combined classifiers

Class	A	B	C	D	V
A	18	0	0	0	1
B	0	16	0	0	0
C	0	0	51	0	4
D	0	0	0	12	0
V	0	0	0	0	92

The interesting thing about this is that the best single Class V rule had 12 errors and the best Class C rule had 5 errors but combined the rules covered the solution space very well. This result also showed some interesting points about this approach. The first is that the rules for classifying Vehicle samples frequently identified the Class C samples as belonging to the Vehicle class. However, by looking at the genes used, we can see that there are few genes that are used in both. This suggests that the characterization of Class C is weak in some samples and that the characterization of the vehicle is identifying these samples as belonging to the vehicle class because of the lack of the Class C response in these samples.

3.1.2 Gene Frequency Analysis

Table 15-3 shows the most commonly used genes from the logfile generated from a set of C class runs. This list shows the genes that were used most often in the best rules found (in all cases, "best" means "best on training") out of 30 folds. On average there were 7.1 genes in each rule. (Note: to protect the confidentiality of the data, the gene names or other identifiers are not used.)

Table 15-3. Gene Frequency from First Class C Runs

Gene{6720}: 24
Gene{410}: 23
Gene{5684}: 20
Gene{3341}: 15
Gene{226}: 11
Gene{4862}: 10
Gene{2507}: 10
Gene{639}: 8
Gene{5061}: 6
Gene{2471}: 6

Comparing this to the list in Table 15-4 from another set of 30 runs, one can see the difference: In the second set of runs, the most commonly used genes are much less strongly chosen. The first set shows the kind of profile that we have learned are often associated with robust rules: A few genes are used almost twice as frequently as any other gene and the selection frequency quickly falls off into long tails where genes appear only in one or two rules.

Table 15-4. Gene Selection from Second Set of Class C Runs

Gene{3228}: 8
Gene{2313}: 8
Gene{8}: 7
Gene{3341}: 7
Gene{2471}: 5
Gene{595}: 4
Gene{1156}: 4
Gene{7919}: 4
Gene{255}: 4
Gene{7447}: 4

3.1.3   Fitness Trace

Figure 15-4 shows a fitness trace of one of the runs from the logfile referred to in Table 15-3. Here the x-axis is time in generations and the y-axis is fitness scaled proportionally to the number of target class samples compared to the overall number of samples (i.e., if there are half as many target samples in the data set, then a false negative has twice the impact as a false positive). Figure 15-5 shows a typical fitness trace of one of the runs from the logfile associated with Table 15-4. Again, the traces show that the first set of runs were "well behaved," in this case they were not overfitting as often and the fitnesses were higher. The second set of runs tended to overfitting and lower fitness values. The fitness traces show this by the lack of correlation between the training and test fitnesses. Looking at the settings for the runs, they were identical except for an increased crossover rate of 0.9, mutation rate of 0.1 compared to a crossover rate of 0.5, mutation rate of 0.5 in the first set of runs. This result suggests that a higher crossover rate leads to faster convergence which may reduce the diversity in the population. This lack of diversity suggest that if the building blocks used are not desirable for generalization, overfitting may occur. This agrees with (Banzhaf et al., 1998), and (Banzhaf et al., 1996) where it is suggested that increasing the mutation rate on hard problems increases diversity and reducing the crossover rate allows this additional diversity to be preserved.

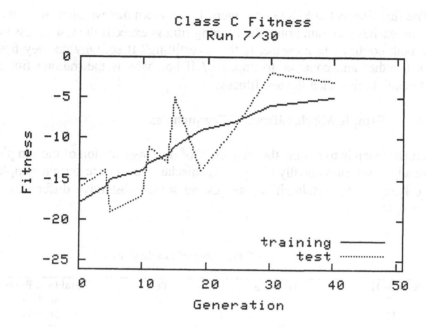

Figure 15-4. Fitness Trace From First Set of Class C Runs

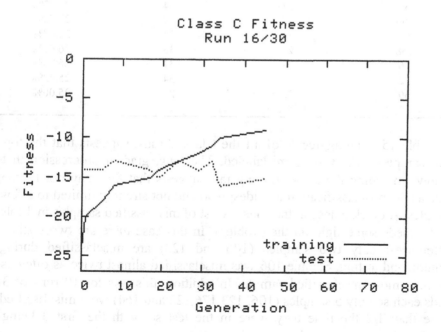

Figure 15-5. Fitness Trace From Second Set of Class C Runs

The first fitness trace shows an interesting pattern that we often see: Once the run reaches a certain point, the training fitness exceeds the test fitness but they both continue to increase. Is this overfitting? If so, why do they both track together and continue to improve? If not, why is the training fitness continually higher than the test fitness?

3.1.4   Sample Misclassification Frequencies

The last step is to review the frequency of misclassification of the samples – are all the samples equally likely to be misclassified, or are certain samples more likely to be misclassified, suggesting some substantive difference in the samples?

Table 15-5. Class C Frequency of Misclassification

Sample ID	Training	Test	Combined Percent
157	66	37	42.92%
117	53	39	38.33%
102	57	33	37.50%
156	51	26	32.08%
116	35	34	28.75%
61	33	34	27.92%
159	35	30	27.08%
67	31	33	26.67%
158	29	35	26.67%
66	32	31	26.25%
32	27	34	25.42%
69	33	27	25.00%
	<ETC.>		

Table 15-3, an aggregate of all the Class C runs, suggests that the top four samples may well be mislabeled. The long, gradual progression that follows including the heavy trailing tail suggests that this may not be the case as the misclassification is widespread and not strongly limited to a few samples. A quick glance at the Class A list of misclassified samples in Table 15-16 sheds some light on the problem. In this case there are two distinct differences: only two samples (106 and 123) are misclassified during training and testing. Sample 106 was misclassified almost twice as often as the next most misclassified sample. In addition, this was for 10 runs of 3 folds each so only 5 samples (106, 123,176,122 and 164) were misclassified more than 1/2 the time they were in the test set with the first 3 being misclassified every time they were in the test set.

Table 15-6. Class A Frequency of Misclassification

Sample ID	Training	Test	Combined Percent
106	9	10	31.67%
123	1	10	18.33%
176	0	10	16.67%
122	0	9	15.00%
164	0	7	11.67%
178	0	4	6.67%
129	0	3	5.00%
137	0	3	5.00%
78	0	3	5.00%
141	0	2	3.33%
58	0	2	3.33%
33	0	2	3.33%
119	0	2	3.33%
169	0	2	3.33%
120	0	2	3.33%
62	0	2	3.33%
128	0	1	1.67%
134	0	1	1.67%
193	0	1	1.67%
112	0	1	1.67%
75	0	1	1.67%

Compared to this, the Class C samples had many (most) samples misclassified when they were in both the training and test sets and there was not a dramatic drop in frequency between the first few samples and the later ones. This suggests a number of things:

1. The C class does not have a strong, independent signature. It resembles one or more of the other classes (primarily the V class)
2. The tendency toward overfitting in Class C is probably caused by this weak class signature
3. Sample 106 and possibly 123,176,122 and 164 in Class A may be mislabeled, causing difficulties in the classification of those samples.

This is a simple example of gaining insight into the data and the problem from the behavior of the GP system.

3.1.5 Summary

Even in a well behaved run there is something to be learned from looking at the "behavior" of the GP system. What follows are brief summaries of two particular studies that departed from the well behaved model and the possible causes of these departures. We will not present all of the analytic steps we took to reach our conclusions again but will summarize the results of our analysis.

3.2   Under-specified Behavior

(Shipp et al., 2002) studied Diffuse Large B-Cell Lymphoma (DLBCL) using gene expression profiles and postulated a different cause for this disease than (Alizadeh et al., 2000) had proposed. Using a number of different algorithms the authors were able to derive a correct prognosis for the disease in approximately 75% of the cases, depending on the algorithm used. This is about the best level of accuracy that can be reached in most prognostic studies as the outcome is a rather "soft" endpoint in the sense that while there are clearly bad outcomes (e.g., fast progressions of cancer development) and good outcomes (e.g., slow disease progression), there is inevitably a gray area where an outcome could be classed either way depending on how progression was defined. Nevertheless, a 75% accuracy level is still a useful result.

When we used GP to analyze the samples, approximately the same level of accuracy in classifying the patient's responsiveness to treatment was achieved. But what was most striking was that the behavior of the GP system when applied to this problem led to the conclusion that there were some difficulties with the data, since every effort to improve the accuracy of results actually *decreased* it. Specifically, the best results were achieved by making short, shallow runs (i.e., few generations and shallow GP trees). Longer runs or deeper trees produced severe signs of overfitting with much worse results on the blind test samples.

This behavior was much different from any other study we've done, including other prognostic studies. Furthermore, the samples that were misclassified using GP were almost identical to the samples misclassified by Shipp et al., which is significant given the very different approaches they used. Our first hypothesis was that the misclassified subset might be a third class that was perhaps "partially responsive". But attempts to classify by separately evolving classifiers for this set were complete failures. We concluded that that there is some other information needed to make a more accurate classification such as demographics or patient history.

Subsequent to this study Dr. Michael Krawetz of Wayne State University in a personal communication indicated that the problem with the study is that certain key genes were missing from the gene chip used. This suggests that the problem (and the associated behavior) is symptomatic of an underspecified problem, that is, one that has incomplete data, particularly key data.

It is also worth noting that this came to light not because of the accuracy of the GP prediction, but because of the behavior of the GP system. It was the uncharacteristic tendency to quickly overfit in the extreme not the results produced by the classification that led to this conclusion.

3.3 Unsupervised Results From Supervised Learning

The final study is a collaboration with Dr. Richard Cote's lab at the University of Southern California to correlate molecular data in the form of quantitative RT-PCR measurements with successive stages of bladder cancer. In this case the tumor stages refer to the degree of invasiveness and size of the tumor and range through five stages, Ta and T1-T4. Also included as a control were normal tissue samples taken from tissue near the tumor were included. In this case, while the primary goal was met, other unexpected results came from analysis of the behavior of the GP system.

3.3.1 Study Details

The study used a selection of 70 genes known to have an association with bladder cancer. They were profiled using a multiplexed RT-PCR system. The genes selected included anti-oxidant, angiogenesis, apoptosis, cell cycling, transcription factor, growth factor, invasion and signal transduction genes. There were 74 tissue samples in all, 36 of which were used to develop the rules and 38 were used as a blind test set. On the blind test set, 26 of 38 samples were correctly classified (68%) and 7 more predicted staging in advance of actual assigned stage (e.g., T2 for a T1 sample, T3 for a T2, etc.) which may indicate molecular changes in advance of physical evidence of the change. If these 7 samples are assumed to be correct then the rules were 86% accurate in predicting cancer stage.

3.3.2 System Behavior

As with the toxicity study, classifiers for each of the six classes were created and then combined in a voting algorithm. As mentioned in the previous paragraph, the results were quite good but some of the classes were simpler to classify than others. In particular, the T1 class was difficult to distinguish from the Ta and T2 classes and the normal samples were extraordinarily difficult to classify.

The system behavior with the normal samples was particularly odd in that they would be misclassified into quite different classes; sometimes they would be T3 or T4 misclassifications, sometimes T1 or T2. What we finally realized was that since most of the samples were taken during tumor resection from tissue from beyond the surgical margins, the "normal" tissue in these cases actually had the profile of the tumor type being removed – in other words the tumor was either invasive beyond the surgical margins or was causing a "sympathetic" behavior in nearby tissue. This is being investigated further but at a recent conference, other researchers reported the same results.

3.3.3   Reforming the Classes

The difficulty in creating successful classifiers for the T1 class led us to revisit the question of the correspondence between the molecular level and the physical level. While the Ta and T2 classifiers were reasonably solid, the T1 classifiers were much more problematic with many more misclassifications. It was not until we viewed the gene selection frequencies in the evolved classification rules that a pattern emerged.

Fundamentally the tumors broke down into two classes: early and late stage tumors. The genes used in the Ta, T1 and T2 classifiers were quite similar to one another with many of the same genes appearing in the "top 10" list of genes selected by the GP system. The T3 and T4 classifiers used an almost completely different set of genes with little overlap in the genes used in the earlier stage tumors.

The most interesting thing about the differences in the genes used between the early-stage and late-stage tumors is that they were biologically suggestive, providing an interesting validation of the GP result. In particular, early stage tumors had a consistent "motif" in the form of a Boolean expression comparing two particular genes, one an angiogenesis gene indicating blood vessel formation, the other was a growth factor associated with tumor growth. This indicated that as the tumor began to grow, certain growth factor genes were up-regulated while the blood vessels needed to supply the tumor with blood began to form in response.

In the late-stage tumors these genes did not appear, instead a set of cell signaling genes, a different set of growth factors genes and repressor genes were used. This suggests that the tumor had reached a stage that was the equivalent of cellular chaos with a blood supply to feed the tumor in place, normal communication between cells interrupted and, most interestingly, genes that would help stop growth had been down-regulated suggesting that the normal feedback mechanisms to stop cellular growth were shutting down.

Among other things these results, if valid, suggest that anti-angiogenesis therapies that stop the growth of blood vessels will only be effective in early stage tumors. This is significant because such re-purposed therapies are normally not given during early stage cancers because of the uncertainty of side effects. These results strengthen the likelihood that such drugs could be tested sooner in the disease cycle than would normally be the case for a new therapy.

Recently we have reclassified the samples into two classes: early-stage and late-stage tumors. The results bear out this supposition as the accuracy of this study was better than the earlier results.

This re-classing of tumor types was developed because of the behavior of the GP system and in particular, because of the variables selected by the system followed a different pattern than was suggested by the initialclasses. It might be considered an unsupervised result from a supervised learning approach.

4. CONCLUSIONS

The tools developed by Genetics Squared have proven helpful in solving classification problems such as those described here. In particular they help to identify unexpected features and combinations of genes that provide insight into the underlying nature of the problems considered.

The techniques described here illustrate some of the advantages of GP over other machine learning techniques. In particular the human readable nature of the solutions can be very important to understanding something about the data being studied. The variables selected, and how they are combined can be quite revealing and the stochastic nature of GP gives additional information about a problem by reinforcing the choice of features and confirming the robustness (or lack thereof) of a solution.

However the problem of overfitting is common to many machine learning techniques, including GP, particularly in problems such as those described here that have a large number of inputs and a comparatively small training set. What could be done to improve the robustness of the results? It is obvious that brining in additional information where possible can help. For example, (Keijzer and Babovic, 1999) describes the use of dimensional analysis for physical problems. Here they used a variety of techniques including brood selection ("culling") and multi-objective optimization to encourage consistency of units within functions.

In this domain, the literature of molecular biology is broadly focused on gene pathways (interacting sets of genes) and the impact of disease on normal cellular functioning. While much of the work we are doing is focused on understanding such disease functions, it may be possible to bring more of the domain knowledge into the GP world. The pathways that genes are associated with could be included into the GP process, either as part of the fitness function or as a multi-objective function where different niches are explicitly used that look for genes that belong to the same pathway. By creating separate niches for different solutions that are separated by pathway associations, it may be possible not only to reduce the amount of overfitting based on casual associations of genes found only in the training set, but it may make the results more accessible to domain experts. It may also suggest interacting networks of genes that were not previously known.

Finally adding these constraints to GP it may not only reduce the problem of overfitting, but may also introduce a more topic specific environment for evolution to take place in, increasing the utility of the results produced to the real world.

REFERENCES

Alizadeh, A.A., M.B. Eisen, R.E. Davis, C. Ma, I.S. Lossos, A. Rosenwald, J.C. Boldrick, H. Sabet, T. Tran, X. Yu, J.I. Powell, L. Yang, G.E. Marti, T. Moore, T. Hudson (2000). Distinct types of diffuse largeB-cell lymphoma identi®ed by gene expression profiling. Nature, Vol. 403, 503-511.Banzhaf, W., P. Nordin, R.E. Keller, F.D. Francone (1998). *Genetic Programming: An Introduction; On the Automatic Evolution of Computer Programs and its Applications."* Morgan-Kauffman

Banzhaf, W., F.D. Francone, P. Nordin (1996). "The Effect of Extensive Use of the Mutation Operator on Generalization in Genetic Programming Using Sparse Data Sets." In *Parallel Problem Solving from Nature IV, Proceedings of the International Conference on Evolutionary Computation,* H-M. Voigt, W. Ebeling, I. Rechenberg and H-P. Schwefel (eds.), Springer Verlag, Heidelberg, 300-309.

Driscoll, J.A., C.D. MacLean and W.P. Worze (2003). "Classification of Gene Expression Data with Genetic Programming." In Genetic Programming Theory and Practice, R. Riolo and B. Worzel (eds.), Kluwer, 25-42.

Gerhold, D., T. Rushmore, and Caskey, C.T. (1999). DNA chips: promising toys have become powerful tools. Trends in Biochemical Sciences; vol. 24, no. 5:168-173.

Keijzer, M. and V. Babovice (1999). "Dimensionally Aware Genetic Programming." In *Proceedings of the Genetic and Evolutionary Computation Conference,* W. Banzhaf, J. Daida, A. Eiben, M.H. Garzon, V. Honavar, M. Jakiela and R.E. Smith (eds.), Morgan Kaufmann, San Francisco, 1069-1076.

Khan, J., J.S. Wei, M. Ringner, L.H. Saal, M. Ladanyi, F. Westermann, F. Berthold, M. Schwab, C.R. Antonescu, C. Peterson, and P.S. Meltzer (2001). Classification and diagnostic prediction of cancers using gene expression profiling and artificial neural networks. Nature Medicine; vol. 7, no. 6:673-679.

Shipp, M., K.N. Ross, P. Tamay, A.P. Weng, J.L. Kutok, R.C.T. Aguiar, M. Gaaserbeek, M. Angelo, M. Reich, G.S. Pinkus, T.S. Ray, M.A. Koval, K.W. Last, A.L. Norton, J. Mesirov, D.S. Neuberg, E.S. Lander, J.C. Aster, and T.R. Golub (2002) Diffuse large B-cell lymphoma outcome prediction by gene-expression. profiling and supervised machine learning. Nature Medicine, Vol. 8, no. 1:68-74.

Chapter 16

INCIDENT DETECTION ON HIGHWAYS

Development of GP Alarms for Motorway Management

Daniel Howard and Simon C. Roberts

QinetiQ, Malvern, UK

Abstract   This chapter discusses the development of the Low-occupancy INcident Detection Algorithm (LINDA) that detects night-time motorway incidents. LINDA is undergoing testing on live data and deployment on the M5, M6 and other motorways in the United Kingdom. It was developed by the authors using Genetic Programming.

Keywords: automatic incident detection, freeway, motorway, highways, genetic programming, traffic management, control office, low flow, high speed, occupancy, reversing vehicles, roadworks, HIOCC, California Algorithm, MIDAS, LINDA.

1.   Introduction

A traffic incident on a freeway is something that would cause an inexperienced motorist to swerve or brake unnecessarily harshly. The development of automatic incident detectors on highways is motivated by the delays and dangers associated with incidents. In daytime, the cost of delays is very considerable indeed and the impact of an incident can be reduced by locating and removing it promptly. During the night, incidents are a great hazard because they occur in conditions of low traffic flow, high traffic speed and poor visibility. Danger is reduced if they are located quickly, reported to the traffic management center and remedial action is taken (e.g. send the police to the scene).

The UK Highways Agency protects the back of traffic queues, which have formed or are about to form on freeways, by automatically setting suitable signals to warn approaching traffic. The trigger is an algorithmic manipulation of the data that is generated by the MIDAS (Motorway Incident Detection and Automatic Signalling) system. MIDAS comprises double loop inductive sensors on each lane of a carriageway at 0.5 km intervals (see Figure 16-1). Each

Figure 16-1.   Photograph of the carriageway showing a single row of loops, with loops on the hard shoulder and in each of four lanes. Each loop occupies a square area with 2.0 meter long sides. More typically, double loops are arranged in two rows that are separated by 4.5 meters. The grey roadside chamber on the left is connected to a MIDAS outstation by loop feeder cables.

MIDAS double loop aggregates quantities such as 'occupancy' over 60 second intervals. Occupancy is the percentage of time a loop is occupied and is calculated every second. In the UK, the HIOCC algorithm (Collins, 1979) is used to trigger queue protection and signalling during periods of traffic criticality and congestion. A HIOCC alert is raised if a loop has 100% occupancy for 2 seconds. Loops are connected via the transmission network to an in-station which can either directly or indirectly operate motorway signalling systems (but queue protection signalling is always set indirectly). In some areas MIDAS data is used for congestion management (mandatory speed limits) and plays an important role in general traffic data collection.

This chapter discusses the development of the Low-occupancy INcident Detection Algorithm (LINDA) that locates night-time motorway incidents and their time of onset. LINDA uses the MIDAS loop sensor output during periods of low flow and high speed (usually between 10:30 pm and 5:30 am) to warn control offices of hazardous situations on the road. These include commencement of scheduled roadworks; breakdowns; debris; and reversing vehicles. The idea is to pick up any odd and often subtle anomaly in MIDAS patterns and to alert the operators immediately. Currently LINDA is undergoing trials on motorways that have large CCTV coverage. Its warnings will not only alert the control office staff but also point CCTV to the area of interest to reveal the nature of the "incident".

LINDA was developed by the authors with Genetic Programming (GP). GP was used in a two-stage strategy (Howard and Roberts, 1999) to evolve detectors by training and validating on archived traffic data. This exposure to extensive traffic data scales up our previous work (Howard and Roberts, 2002, Roberts and Howard, 2002) in order to evolve more robust detectors that can distinguish a greater variety of incidents from more diverse examples of normal traffic. Optimal detectors were selected during off-line validation. These detectors were then integrated into an on-line implementation.

2.   MIDAS Traffic Data

Incident detectors presented here were evolved and validated using archived MIDAS data for both carriageways of the M25 motorway which surrounds the city of London. This section explains how the traffic data was prepared for input to GP.

Traffic data types

The archived MIDAS traffic data comprised the following minute-averaged quantities, where the first four quantities were lane specific but the last quantity was carriageway specific.

- flow (vehicles per minute)
- occupancy (%)
- speed (km/h)
- headway (0.1s resolution)
- categorized flow using four vehicle length classes (vehicles per minute)

Manual incident identification

Automatic incident detectors were trained from examples of incident onsets and normal traffic. Hence, the precise locations of incident onsets needed to be manually identified and recorded. This was achieved by manually examining visualisations of archived MIDAS data for the specification given in Table 16-1.

Visualization software was developed to display traffic data in order to manually identify incidents to meet the following requirements:

- The station and minute axes must be displayed adequately to precisely locate a data point. It is essential to accurately identify an incident's onset time.
- Data for multiple lanes has to be displayed simultaneously, to facilitate the identification of questionable incidents.
- Data from multiple control offices associated with consecutive stations must be displayed simultaneously for continuity at the adjoining stations.

Table 16-1. MIDAS data specification for manual incident identification

Aspect	Specification
motorway	M25
carriageways	A and B
dates	March 1998 to August 2000
times	8 pm to 6 am the following morning
stations	4727 to 5010 (60 stations in total)
lanes	offside, offside-1 and offside-2

- A high display speed and and minimal user intervention (with simultaneous displays) makes the viewer practicable to examine many months worth of data from the two carriageways.

The visualization software was developed to display speed against station and time for a single night, carriageway and lane. Three images were simultaneously viewed for the three most offside lanes for each night and carriageway. Incidents were manually identified by examining these images to subjectively locate abnormal data on any of the lanes. Colour rectangles were drawn over the full extent of each incident, where the colour denoted the type of incident as shown in Table 16-2.

Major incidents spanned many stations and minutes, often affecting other lanes and upstream stations, and were typified by very slow speeds. Minor incidents were more localized, i.e. spanning few stations and minutes and perhaps only evident in a single lane, and they often involved only slight reductions in speed. Intermediate incidents were evident when the extent was between these extremes. Roadworks were evident by a very slow vehicle at the start and end of the incident (presumably laying-out and retrieving cones) and their onsets were staggered across adjacent lanes. An example of unusual traffic is a very slow vehicle that occupies multiple lanes (a police-escorted wide load).

The marked-up images were automatically processed to catalogue each incident's time limits and station limits on each specific lane. These lane-specific incidents were then automatically merged to give the final carriageway-specific incidents. The colour coding was automatically processed to specify incident class as given in Table 16-2.

Detectors were evolved to give alerts for incidents of class 1 to 3. Class 4 "incidents" were only used to discard spurious traffic data and the detectors were never exposed to this data. Preliminary detectors were evolved and common false alarms were manually analyzed to revise the incident set.

Table 16-2. Colour-coded incident types and classes.

Colour	Definition	Class
red	major incident	1
yellow	intermediate incident	2
green	minor incident	3
cyan	roadworks	2
magenta	other unusual traffic, spurious sensors	4

Correcting traffic data

The traffic data included the following anomalies: (a) missing data that resulted from single loop or double loop failure at a single station; (b) missing data due to lost connections between out-stations and control offices - this usually persisted for many hours at many adjacent stations; (c) "no-flow" data that was assigned when no vehicles occurred within the current minute - this was very common for night traffic especially on the outer lanes of the carriageway (speed and headway needed to be defined for the no-flow state to avoid discontinuities in the input data); (d) spurious data from faulty sensors; (e) Spurious data from incorrectly calibrated sensors. While the failure of a single loop results is no speed data the failure of the double loop results in no data at all.

Training on traffic data that included the anomalies was deemed to overcomplicate the problem by disguising the characteristic subtleties that distinguish incidents from normal traffic. Hence, a correction procedure was devised to improve the quality of the traffic data input to the detectors. The same procedure was used for each data type but headway correction had an additional algorithm dependent on the flow for the current and previous minutes.

Anomalous data was flagged by a value, val_{AD}, in order to invoke the correction procedure. The procedure attempted to correct the data by interpolating from the nearest current and previous valid raw data. The search for valid data was conducted first by station, then by lane and finally by time to analyze past data. Up to 4 adjacent stations were analyzed during the search to be equivalent to a maximum deviation of one minute, assuming a typical speed of 120 km/h (75 mph) and a station separation of 0.5 km. Weighted averaging was used to bias the interpolation towards nearer stations.

When corrective data was found on a different lane to the current lane, an offset was applied to represent the typical difference for the missing quantity for that particular lane combination. For example, a different offset applied when correcting the offside lane from offside-1 compared to correcting offside-1 from offside-2, as opposed to using the same offset to correct an adjacent outer lane of the carriageway.

The search process was terminated after no valid raw data was found during the previous 5 minutes worth of data. The current missing data thus remained at a value of val_{AD} and the correction procedure advanced to the next missing data. If a single application of the correction procedure could not correct all missing data from valid raw data, then the procedure was simply re-applied to correct from previously corrected data. Iterations were repeated until all missing data had been corrected. However, the iterative procedure could still fail for excessive missing data at the start of a night. In this case, the current night and carriageway was omitted from the data set unless it contained a worthwhile incident, in which case the night's start time was reset to an earlier time in order to allow the iterative procedure to succeed.

Empirical analysis of many months of known normal night-time traffic data allowed the setting of:

- headway based on flow in the current and previous minutes,

- lane offsets for each data type (except headway because there was a high variability in the difference between headway values on different lanes and so headway was not corrected from adjacent lanes),

- thresholds for each data type to retain data at faulty sensors when it was similar enough to the data at neighbouring valid stations,

- default values for each data type to be used when data could not be corrected in the on-line implementation.

Traffic data sets

The development of the incident detectors was data driven due to an evolutionary procedure that trained from traffic examples. Hence, it was important to define training, validation and test sets that represented similar distributions of incidents over a similar extent of valid raw traffic data.

The extent of missing data for each month was significant. A month was deemed to be "good" if it contained ample diverse incidents and had relatively little missing or spurious data. Consecutive months were partitioned to separate good months from bad months, and the resulting grouped months were then assigned to the following three traffic sets such that the numbers of each class of incident were fairly even: (a) 9 months for training: 06·1998-09·1998 and 01·2000-05·2000; (b) 9 months for validation: 07·1999-12·1999 and 06·2000-08·2000; and the remaining 12 months: 03·1998-05·1998, 10·1998-12·1998, 01·1999-03·1999 and 04·1999-06·1999 were left out of the exercise. The final specification for the training and validation sets is shown in Table 16-3. Note that the total number of nights is much larger than would correspond to 18 months (about 547 days). This is because data from the opposite carriageway

Table 16-3. Training and validation data specification.

Set	Number of incidents:				Number of nights:	Number of non -incident cases:
	Class 1	Class 2	Class 3	Total		
Training	10	147	102	259	504	8.4 million
Validation	7	120	99	226	450	7.0 million

is considered as data for 'another day'. Such data was included in training and validation sets when it was deemed to be "good" data.

Traffic data input to GP

Incident detectors were evolved and validated using the archived MIDAS data specification given in Table 16-1 but with time limits from 10:30 pm to 5:30 am the following morning. However, some nights used different time limits to capture slightly earlier or later incident onsets, or to avoid periods of spurious data or excessive missing data.

GP simultaneously processed local data on each lane (or vehicle class for categorized flow) via an input window as shown in Figure 16-2. A detector could process each of the five MIDAS quantities listed in Section 2.0 for the current minute and T previous minutes and for the current station and S downstream stations. The variables T and S were optimized during the evolution phase. The lane-specific quantities were input for each of the three most offside lanes.

3. First Detection Stage

This section discusses the evolution and validation of first-stage incident detectors.

Fitness Measure

GP evolves a population of GP trees. Each tree represents a detector and so the fitness measure should quantify the detection performance. A detector outputs a positive value when it judged the current traffic data to represent an incident onset. Each detector processed a set of training examples including incident cases and non-incident cases. Let TP denote the number of true positives (incidents detected) and FP denote the number of false positives (false alarms) that result after a detector had processed all the training cases. The detection performance was quantified by the following fitness measure where the variable fv controlled the balance between high sensitivity (high TP) and high specificity (low FP):

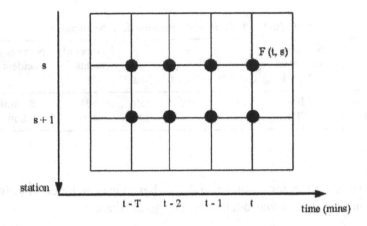

Figure 16-2. Input window showing quantity F at the current and previous minutes and at the current and downstream stations.

$$\text{fitness} = \frac{\text{TPS}}{\text{TPS}_{\text{max}} + fv\,\text{FP}} \tag{16.1}$$

TPS is an incident score and was calculated by weighting the incidents according to class, to give the detection of a class 1 incident the highest reward and the detection of a class 3 incident the lowest reward. This was because incidents of a lower-numbered class were rarer and furthermore such incidents were more major and thus should not be missed. TPS was the score obtained for the incidents detected and TPS_{max} was the score obtained when all incidents were detected (although a subjective 'incident class' was considered, evolved GP detectors detected 'incident' or 'no incident')

$$\text{TPS} = \sum_{i=0}^{i<\text{TP}} 4 - \text{class of incident}_i \tag{16.2}$$

Evolving first-stage detectors

Even though incidents occur at a single time and station, the incidents generally manifested themselves in the traffic data over many minutes (after the incident) and stations (more upstream than downstream). Furthermore, an incident could affect the traffic in a single lane or multiple lanes and, for the latter, the onset may be staggered in adjacent lanes (as was observed for roadworks). Therefore, even though the extent of an incident was manually marked-up for each lane, the precise position of traffic data that characterized an incident's onset could not be located manually. Hence, first-stage detectors were trained to automatically locate characteristic traffic data by sweeping from 5 minutes

Table 16-4. GP parameters.

Parameter	Setting
terminal nodes	traffic data via input window, integer and floating-point constants
function nodes	$+, -, *, /$, min(A,B), max(A,B), if (A<B) then C else D
maximum nodes in tree	1000
population size	1000
maximum generations	30

before to t_A minutes after the marked incident time, and by sweeping from upstream to downstream stations for each minute. The number of stations to sweep over was incident-specific and was obtained from the maximum extent of the marked-up incidents with an additional margin of a single station. The time limit t_A was dependent on total incident duration such that longer incidents had a longer post-onset sweep, as the onset was more likely to be staggered across adjacent lanes. The value of t_A was limited to between 5 and 20 minutes.

An incident's onset was said to be detected if a GP tree returned a positive output for any one of the times and stations in the onset sweep. During evolution, the sweep was terminated after the first positive output was obtained, because any further positive outputs for the current incident would not affect the detector's fitness. Non-incident training data was sampled at 10 minute steps using all possible stations at each minute. However, non-incident cases were sampled only from the nights on which the incidents occurred in order to minimize computation time.

Note that after the best first-stage detector was chosen, it was applied to process all times and stations in each incident onset sweep in order to locate all points to feed onto the second detection stage. Similarly, it processed all non-incident training data.

The general GP parameters are specified in Table 16-4. Some problem-specific parameters were varied to investigate their effect on detection performance (as explained below). At least 10 GP runs with different randomizer seeds were conducted for each parameter configuration.

The input window contained only a single downstream station (S=1) to encourage the evolution of a simple first-stage detector that was fast to apply in the final implementation. This was desirable because the first-stage detector processed all incoming data, whereas the second-stage detector processed only data at the first stage alerts and it could thus be more computationally expensive. The time width of the input window (T) was varied between 1 and 6 minutes. Setting T at 4 minutes tended to give better results than a smaller T setting, but no improvement was gained by using a larger setting. It was also desirable to

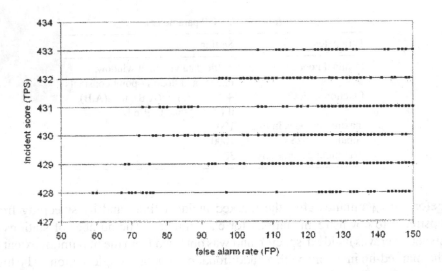

Figure 16-3. Incident score against false alarm rate for the first-stage detectors on training. More detectors were evolved but are not shown in the plot due to their worse performance.

use a smaller T setting to minimize the input window size to develop a simple first-stage detector.

First-stage detectors were trained to have high sensitivity in preference to high specificity in order to maximize the number of incident onset points to feed onto the second stage. The fitness variable fv was thus set to low values ranging from 10^{-4} to 1. Setting fv between 0.01 and 0.1 tended to give the best results, whereas higher settings caused incidents to be missed whilst lower settings tended to give an excessive false alarms.

Figure 16-3 plots the incident score against false alarm rate for the best first-stage detectors from all GP runs. A maximum score of 433 was obtained when all incidents were detected.

Validating first-stage detectors

First-stage detectors were only validated if they achieved a sufficient performance during training. The candidate detectors for validation were the best 10 from each generation of each GP run. A total of 8199 first-stage detectors were validated.

Figure 16-4 plots the incident score against false alarm rate for the validation results. Note that comparison of this plot against that for training (Figure 16-3) suggests that the false alarm rate greatly increased upon validation. This is misleading because the validation scheme used many more non-incident cases due to the following two issues. Firstly, non-incident validation data was sam-

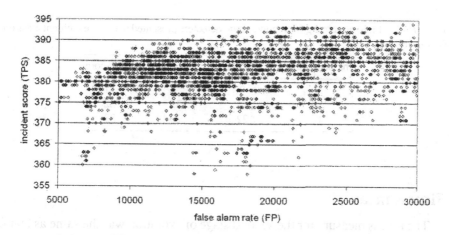

Figure 16-4. Incident score against false alarm rate for the first-stage detectors on validation. More detectors were validated but are not shown in the plot due to their worse performance.

pled at two minute steps using all possible stations at each minute, whereas the training scheme sampled at 10 minute steps. Secondly, non-incident validation cases were sampled from all nights whereas non-incident training cases were sampled only from the nights on which incidents occurred. The percentage false alarm rate was generally highly consistent on training and validation (as shown for the best first-stage detector in Table 16-6).

A maximum score of 396 was obtained when all 226 incidents were detected. In addition to having a near-maximal score, the best first-stage detectors were deemed to miss only minor incidents (class 3). Many detectors satisfied these requirements and thus the missed incidents were manually observed in order to select the best detector. It was discovered that some of the missed incidents were questionable, and thus the best detectors could have a score significantly lower than 396. Note that considering not only the performance on validation but on training also identified the best detectors.

All agreed that a low false alarm rate was desirable, even if this was at the expense of detection, in order to ensure the operators had faith in the system. Therefore, the final best detector was selected because of its relatively low false alarm rate as it gained a score of 380 and FP of 5156 (0.14%). Its performance is summarized in Table 16-6 after it processed all incident and non-incident validation data. Note that the best detector was trained using T=4 and fv=0.05.

4. Second Detection Stage

This section discusses the evolution and validation of second-stage incident detectors.

Table 16-5.   Incident scoring for second-stage detectors presented in reverse incident class order for clarity.

Incident class	Class score	Min score	Max score
3	0	1	11
2	11	12	22
1	22	23	33

Fitness measure

The fitness measure for the second stage of evolution was the same as that for the first stage (Section 3.0) but with the incident score (TPS) redefined to give a bias towards earlier onset alerts. This is explained by considering a single incident that obtained multiple first-stage hits distributed throughout its onset sweep. Each of these hits was assigned a score depending on its proximity to the onset time t that was manually defined during the incident mark-up phase. The hit score was initialized to 6. A hit before time t was rewarded with an extra point for each minute that it preceded t, and as the onset sweep started at t-5 the earliest possible hit was assigned a score of 11.

A similar scheme was devised for later hits but this was complicated by the fact that the onset sweep stopped at between t+5 and t+20 depending on the incident's total duration (Section 3.0). Hence, a time bin was set to equal a fifth of this post-onset sweep duration, so that a bin width was set between 1 and 4 minutes. A hit after time t was then punished by deducting a point for each time bin that it followed t, so the latest possible hit was assigned a score of 1. Note that a hit at time t retained the initial score of 6.

Therefore, when an incident was hit in the second stage it was assigned a score of between 1 and 11. However, an additional score was awarded based on the class of the incident, in a manner similar to that for the first-stage fitness measure. TPS was then simply set to equal the sum of the incident scores over all incidents.

Evolving second-stage detectors

When the best first-stage detector processed all incident and non-incident training data it produced 7756 alerts distributed across 259 incidents and it gave 12847 false alarms. Second stage detectors were trained to reduce these false alarms whilst retaining at least a single alert per incident. The first-stage incident alerts were processed in chronological order so that the processing of the current incident onset could be terminated after the second-stage detector produced its first positive output.

The use of extensive traffic data posed a challenging generalization task (compared to the proof of concept study (Howard and Roberts, 2002) (Roberts and Howard, 2002)). Hence, many GP runs were conducted to investigate the influence of many input parameters on detection performance. Some of these parameters were specific to GP (e.g. population size and tournament size) whereas others were problem specific. The population size was increased to range between 1000 and 32000, and in order to compensate for this with regards to computation time, the maximum number of generations was reduced to 20 (other GP parameters are given in Table 16-4). The most important problem-specific parameters were the fitness variable fv and the input window dimensions T and S (as explained below). At least 10 runs were conducted for each parameter configuration.

Second-stage detectors were trained to have high specificity in preference to high sensitivity in order to minimize the false alarm rate. The fitness variable fv was thus set between 0.1 to 10.0 to focus on two groups of detectors, those targeted at one false alarm per night and those targeted at one false alarm for every five nights.

The input window dimensions were varied to set T between 4 and 8 minutes and to set S between 1 and 7 stations. A larger input window allowed a detector to characterize incident onsets from more traffic data, but it resulted in a more complex search space due to an increase in the number of terminal nodes and thus a combinatorial increase in the number of possible GP tree structures. Furthermore, it was beneficial for the on-line implementation to use few downstream stations, i.e. low S, as explained in Section 5.0.

Figure 16-5 plots the incident score against false alarm rate for the best detectors from all GP runs. A maximum score of 3417 was obtained when all incidents were detected. Note that the plot was produced by re-evaluating detectors in order to gather detection properties that were not required on evolution, e.g. incident hit coverage. Furthermore, a detector had to have a sufficient performance to warrant re-evaluation and consequently the plot shows discontinuities in regions of relatively poor performance.

Validating Second-Stage Detectors

Second-stage detectors were only validated if they achieved a sufficient performance during training. The candidate detectors for validation were the best 10 from each generation of each GP run. When the best first-stage detector processed all incident and non-incident validation data it produced 8531 alerts distributed across all incidents and it gave 9753 false alarms.

Figure 16-6 displays the second-stage performance on validation. The plot shows two clusters of points due to the fact that the fitness variable fv was set to target for two different false alarm rates on evolution. The false alarm

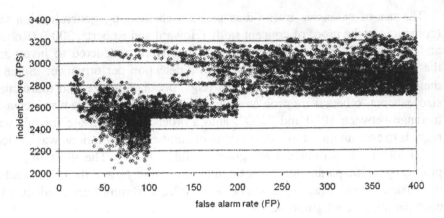

Figure 16-5. Incident score against false alarm rate for the second-stage detectors on training. More detectors were evolved but are not shown in the plot due to their worse performance (the two right angles pertain to stakeholder wishes).

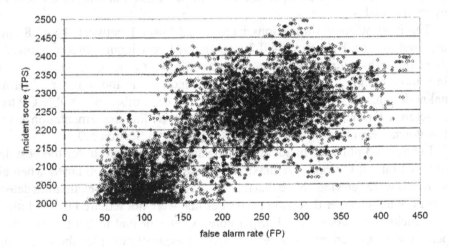

Figure 16-6. Incident score against false alarm rate for the second-stage detectors on validation. More detectors were validated but are not shown in the plot due to their worse performance (the two clusters correspond to stakeholder wishes).

rates achieved on validation were generally consistent with those obtained on training.

A maximum incident score (TPS$_{max}$) of 2827 was possible if a second-stage detector hit all incidents at the earliest opportunity. 25198 detectors achieved a score of at least 2000. Many detectors hit all major incidents and most intermediate incidents (approximately 95%) but a significant number of minor incidents could be missed (giving a hit rate of approximately 75%). However, this inability to detect the subtle differences that distinguish some minor incidents

Table 16-6. Performance metrics for the best first-stage and second-stage detectors on validation (unless training is stated). The following evolution metrics are also given: generation, fitness rank and size (metric definitions are given in the text).

Metric	First stage	Second stage
Generation	21	16
Fitness rank	2	8
Size (number of nodes)	107	987
Hit rate for major incidents (%)	100	100
Hit rate for intermediate incidents (%)	100	95
Hit rate for minor incidents (%)	99	76
First incident onset (minutes)	-0.10	-0.57
Average incident onset (minutes)	-2.32	-2.29
Hit coverage (%)	13	51
Hit score (validation)	380	2455
Hit score (% of max score on validation)	96	87
Hit score (training)	428	3203
Hit score (% of max score on training)	99	94
False alarm rate (validation)	9753	260
False alarm rate (% on validation)	0.14	0.0037
False alarm rate (% on training)	0.10	0.0041

from normal traffic may be deemed acceptable in order to achieve the target false-alarm rates. The overall incident detection rates prove that the detectors were not over-trained and could generalize across the validation data.

The best second-stage detectors were identified by considering not only the performance on validation but on training also. The best detectors were deemed to maximize the incident score by missing no major incidents and only very few intermediate incidents. Multiple detectors achieved this whilst satisfying the false alarm requirement of one false alarm per night.

The final best detector was selected because of its relatively low false alarm rate and its dependence on relatively few downstream stations. It gained an incident score of 2455 and a false alarm rate of 260, i.e. 2.7% of the false alarms output from the first stage and 0.0037% of the total number of non-incident validation cases. Note that the best detector was evolved using T=4, S=2 and fv=0.5 and that, on training, it achieved incident hit rates for major, intermediate and minor incidents of 100%, 99% and 93% respectively.

Performance metrics for the best first-stage and second-stage detectors are summarized in Table 16-6. The following evolution metrics are also given: the generation on which the detectors were evolved, their fitness rank (out of the 10 fittest detectors of their generation) and their GP tree size.

The onset metrics give the time between the detected hits and the incident onsets that were manually marked up. The first incident onset metric is the average earliest detected onset over all incidents, and the average incident onset metric is the average hit time over all hits (potentially many per incident). These times are negative showing that the incidents were generally hit after their marked-up onset, but most incidents were detected within two minutes.

The hit coverage metric is the average percentage hit coverage over all incidents. Its definition is slightly different for each detection stage because the maximum number of possible incident hits were derived from different sources. For the first stage, an incident's fractional coverage was calculated by dividing its number of hits by the total number of points in its onset sweep. For the second stage, an incident's fractional coverage was calculated by dividing its number of second-stage hits by its number of first-stage hits.

Comparison of the hit score (% of max score) and false alarm rate (%) metrics for training and validation shows that the detectors performed consistently on the two data sets, thus proving their generalization capability.

A false alarm rate of 0.004% translates to a single false alarm for every 25000 points processed. Recall that the traffic data corresponded to 60 stations and that two downstream stations were required in the second-stage detector's input window. Hence, 58 stations could be processed. Therefore, when the detector processed these stations it produced, on average, a single false alarm every 431 minutes (7 hours and 11 minutes). This approximates to a single false alarm per night for the time limits 10:30 pm to 5:30 am.

5.   Detection visualization

This section visualizes the performance of the best fused detector (the integration of the best first and second stage detectors) on archived MIDAS data from the validation set. Figure 16-7 show the output alerts superimposed on traffic data plotted in a manner similar to that used to manually mark-up the incidents. The horizontal axis presents advancing time in minutes (left to right) and the vertical axis presents stations from upstream (top) to downstream (bottom). Speed is plotted for each minute and station such that brighter cells represent lower speeds. All images correspond to lane offside-1 only. A coloured cross depicts each incident alert, where the colour corresponds to the value output by the second-stage detector. The detector was trained to output any positive value to indicate an alert, so the colours do not imply any detection property. Figure 16-7 shows examples of the hit coverage for major, intermediate and minor incidents. The images show multiple blocks of traffic data where each block corresponds to a single incident onset. The detectors were trained on incident onsets only and consequently incidents tended to be hit near the onset time and on the upstream approach.

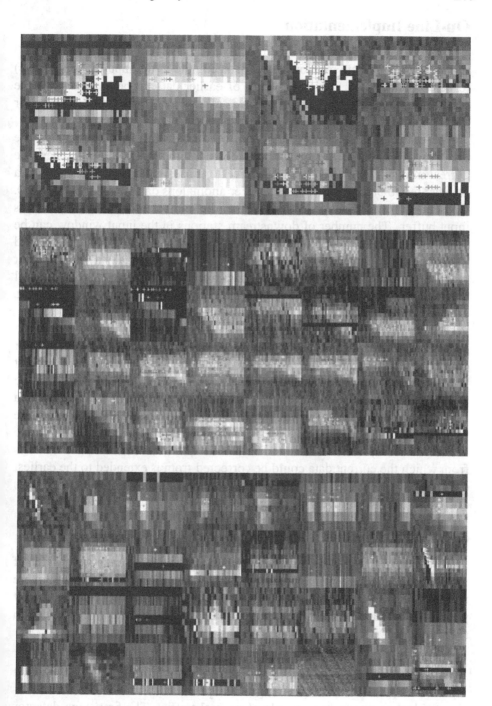

Figure 16-7. From top: hit coverage (crosses) for major, intermediate, and minor incidents.

On-Line Implementation

Differences arise due to on-line processing. LINDA's input buffer stores 10 minutes worth of data to allow the earliest minute in the input window (T=4) to be corrected from 5 minutes worth of earlier data, to be analogous to the off-line implementation. LINDA archives all raw and corrected traffic data for the three most offside lanes.

The online system gathers data from the out-stations in the order that the data arrives and thus data may not be received in time for LINDA to process the current minute. This gives another source for missing data and the absent data is defaulted to val_{AD}, similar to the other anomalous data listed in Section 2.0. Consequently, it is beneficial to minimize the number of stations in LINDA's input buffer. The number of downstream stations in the input window can be set to two during the off-line development, but this setting is made with regard to the current consideration. LINDA also requires additional stations adjacent to the input window to correct missing data from. However, only two additional upstream and downstream stations are used in the on-line implementation, as opposed to the four used in the off-line implementation, and thus the correction procedure is likely to fail more often (Section 2.0 describes the correction procedure). Therefore, LINDA's input buffer corresponds to 7 stations. For computational economy, the correction procedure does not iterate to correct from previously corrected data. Instead, data that remains missing after a single application of the procedure is simply corrected by averaging the corrected data for the previous minute. When no previous data is available, default values are used based on empirical analysis of archived MIDAS data. To minimize the use of previously corrected data or default data, the number of earlier minutes from which the current data could be corrected from is extended to the earliest data held in LINDA's input buffer , whereas the off-line implementation uses at most five earlier minutes on a single iteration.

6.   Conclusions

Motorway incident detectors were trained and validated on many months of archived MIDAS data from March 1998 to August 2000. The detectors were trained using GP to discriminate between incident onsets and normal traffic at periods of low occupancy (night traffic). The two-stage strategy introduced in (Howard and Roberts, 1999) was applied to evolve two detectors:

- A first-stage detector that automatically identified characteristic incident onset points by distinguishing traffic proximate to manually defined incident onsets from a sample of normal traffic. The first-stage detector was required to contain relatively few processor nodes in order to be computationally economical.

- A second-stage detector that filters the first-stage alerts to minimize the false alarm rate whilst maximizing the number of detected incidents. The second-stage detector was biased to detect incident onsets as early as possible to provide motorway controllers with a maximal response time.

Many detectors were evolved in each evolution stage but optimal detectors were chosen to achieve a desirable balance between sensitivity and specificity. Optimal detectors were deemed sensitive enough to miss only minor incidents whilst being specific enough to have relatively low false alarm rates. The best detectors were selected by considering detection performance on training and validation.

The incident hit rate and false alarm rate were consistent across training and validation, thus proving that the detectors had not memorized the training cases but instead could generalize across the validation data. The best first-stage and second-stage detectors were fused to give the following performance during off-line validation.

- Incident detection rates of 100% for major incidents, 95% for intermediate incidents and 76% for minor incidents were achieved.

- On average, incident onsets were detected within one minute after the manually marked-up incident onsets.

- Multiple alerts were raised for most incident onsets, although some minor incidents were hit only once due to their subtle difference from normal traffic.

- A false alarm rate of 0.004% was achieved which corresponds, on average, to a single false alarm every 7 hours and 11 minutes. This is equivalent to a single false alarm per night for the time limits 10:30 pm to 5:30 am.

GP evolved detectors in the form of explicit mathematical formulae, thus allowing the detection scheme to be interpreted and re-implemented (e.g. to minimize computation time).

On-line testing further verified the capability of generalized incident detection, but the fused detector tended to be over-sensitive to the subtle variations in the traffic data and thus produced false alarms. Fewer false alarms were output for the stations used in training, suggesting that different sections of carriageway have different traffic characteristics.

Currently, a different optimal second-stage detector is being experimented with to reduce the false alarm rate. For example, some second-stage detectors were evolved to produce on average a single false alarm for every five nights worth of archived MIDAS data. However, such detectors had a lower sensitivity and thus missed more minor incidents. As already stated, the end-user prefers to tolerate this to achieve fewer false alarms. Improvements will ensue with knowledge from the CCTV recording of incident alerts.

The processing of extensive traffic data poses a challenging generalization task because many diverse incident onsets need to be discriminated from many variations of normal traffic conditions. This chapter has shown that the two-stage detection strategy can scale-up to extensive training and validation data sets. Further algorithmic refinements and calibration has taken place in trials.

Acknowledgments

The authors acknowledge the UK Highways Agency for providing the data for this study. The opinions expressed in this paper are those of the authors and not necessarily those of the UK Highways Agency.

References

Collins, J. F. (1979). Automatic incident detection - TRL algorithms HIOCC and PATREG. TRL Report SR526, Transport Research Laboratory, UK.

Howard, Daniel and Roberts, Simon C. (1999). A staged genetic programming strategy for image analysis. In Banzhaf, Wolfgang, Daida, Jason, Eiben, Agoston E., Garzon, Max H., Honavar, Vasant, Jakiela, Mark, and Smith, Robert E., editors, *Proceedings of the Genetic and Evolutionary Computation Conference*, volume 2, pages 1047–1052, Orlando, Florida, USA. Morgan Kaufmann.

Howard, Daniel and Roberts, Simon C. (2002). Application of genetic programming to motorway traffic modelling. In Langdon, W. B., Cantú-Paz, E., Mathias, K., Roy, R., Davis, D., Poli, R., Balakrishnan, K., Honavar, V., Rudolph, G., Wegener, J., Bull, L., Potter, M. A., Schultz, A. C., Miller, J. F., Burke, E., and Jonoska, N., editors, *GECCO 2002: Proceedings of the Genetic and Evolutionary Computation Conference*, pages 1097–1104, New York. Morgan Kaufmann Publishers.

Roberts, Simon C. and Howard, Daniel (2002). Detection of incidents on motorways in low flow high speed conditions by genetic programming. In Cagnoni, Stefano, Gottlieb, Jens, Hart, Emma, Middendorf, Martin, and Raidl, G"unther, editors, *Applications of Evolutionary Computing, Proceedings of EvoWorkshops2002: EvoCOP, EvoIASP, EvoSTim/EvoPLAN*, volume 2279 of *LNCS*, pages 243–252, Kinsale, Ireland. Springer-Verlag.

Chapter 17

PARETO-FRONT EXPLOITATION IN SYMBOLIC REGRESSION

Guido F. Smits[1] and Mark Kotanchek[2]

[1]*Dow Benelux, Terneuzen, NV;* [2]*Dow Chemical, Midland, MI USA*

Abstract   Symbolic regression via genetic programming (hereafter, referred to simply as symbolic regression) has proven to be a very important tool for industrial empirical modeling (Kotanchek et al., 2003). Two of the primary problems with industrial use of symbolic regression are (1) the relatively large computational demands in comparison with other nonlinear empirical modeling techniques such as neural networks and (2) the difficulty in making the trade-off between expression accuracy and complexity. The latter issue is significant since, in general, we prefer parsimonious (simple) expressions with the expectation that they are more robust with respect to changes over time in the underlying system or extrapolation outside the range of the data used as the reference in evolving the symbolic regression.

In this chapter, we present a genetic programming variant, ParetoGP, which exploits the Pareto front to dramatically speed the symbolic regression solution evolution as well as explicitly exploit the complexity-performance trade-off. In addition to the improvement in evolution efficiency, the Pareto front perspective allows the user to choose appropriate models for further analysis or deployment. The Pareto front avoids the need to *a priori* specify a trade-off between competing objectives (e.g. complexity and performance) by identifying the *curve* (or surface or hyper-surface) which characterizes, for example, the best performance for a given expression complexity.

Keywords: genetic programming, Pareto front, multi-objective optimization, symbolic regression, ParetoGP

1.   Introduction

Unlike normal regression in which a model structure (e.g., second-order polynomials) is hypothesized and fit to available data, symbolic regression involves the discovery of the *structure* as well as the *coefficients* within that structure. One way to accomplish this is to use genetic programming (GP) techniques to evolve expressions which match the observed system behavior. In this section, we briefly review the practical motivations for symbolic regression as well as the classical problems characteristic to the GP approach. Finally, we outline a variant of GP which addresses some of the classical issues and has resulted in a significant improvement in the speed and robustness of symbolic regression. This variant focuses on the evolutionary effort on improving the Pareto front (which captures the trade-offs between competing objectives) rather than optimizing a single composite criteria. The rest of the paper is devoted to exploring the algorithm, its benefits and its performance.

In this chapter we assume that the reader has a working knowledge of GP concepts (Banzhaf et al., 1998, Jacob, 2001)) as well as its application to symbolic regression (Kotanchek et al., 2003).

Motivations for Symbolic Regression

In addition to the real-world benefits of empirical modeling for system modeling, emulation, monitoring and control, symbolic regression has several unique contributions. These contributions, which are especially important when faced with multivariate data from a nonlinear but unknown system, include:

- **Human insight** — examination of the evolved expressions can be indications of underlying physical mechanisms as well identification of *metavariables* (combinations or transforms of variables) which can simplify subsequent empirical modeling efforts. Additionally, examining the structure of an evolved model can be comforting in the sense that the model behavior, variables and metavariables agree with human expectation; this explainability helps to instill trust in the model(s).

- **Compact models** — generally solutions can be identified which perform well and are parsimonious with respect to structure complexity and/or number of input variables. Such models are attractive because they can be interpreted more easily and deployed easily in many environments. Such models may also be more robust and capture underlying fundamentals rather than system noise in the data.

- **Limited *a priori* assumptions** — unlike traditional regression which assumes a model structure for the data, symbolic regression allows the data to determine which structures of variables, functions and constants are appropriate to describe the observed behavior. Of course, appropriate functional building blocks as well as the pertinent data variables must be supplied for the evolution.

- **Natural variable selection** — the evolutionary processes of GP have a remarkable ability to focus on the driving variables necessary to capture the system behavior. Furthermore, post-processing can do sensitivity analysis on the evolved expressions to discard superfluous variables.

- **Diverse models (possibly)** — the evolutionary process will often develop models of similar performance using different variables (symbolic regression does not require that correlated variables be eliminated *a priori*) or different structures. Although it is difficult to characterize nonlinear model diversity, ensembles of diverse models can be useful to: (1) indicate operation outside the domain of the training data (due to divergence of model predictions) as well as (2) assemble robust online predictive models which are resistant to sensor failures and related pathologies.

- **Physical model integration** — integration with fundamental (first principles) models can control the extrapolation behavior of developed models and, thereby, result in more robust models which are aligned with the underlying physics. Of course, examining the structure of evolved models within the context of theoretical insight can help to identify the nature of the applicable fundamental behavior.

Problems with Symbolic Regression

Despite the plethora of advantages discussed above, there are at least three fundamental problems with symbolic regression via GP:

- **slow discovery** — classically, symbolic regression is very CPU intensive and slower than other nonlinear modeling techniques such as neural networks. That said, it is impressively efficient when the infinite size of the search space is considered.

- **difficulty in selection of good solutions** — during the course of an evolution, many candidate solutions will be evolved. Selecting the "best" solutions while balancing performance vs. model complexity trade-offs is a difficult exercise, as is the issue of detecting model pathologies in regions in which a model is not constrained by data.

- **good-but-not-great models** — other nonlinear techniques will typically outperform the symbolic regression models on training data. That said, symbolic regression can be a precursor to great models due to its capabilities for variable selection, metavariable identification, secondary rounds of symbolic regression evolutions and iterative prototyping including human input.

As will be demonstrated by the rest of this paper, the proposed symbolic regression variant which exploits the Pareto front can mitigate these problems.

New Variant: Exploit the Pareto Front

Unconstrained, GP has a terrible problem with *bloat* wherein the size of the evolved expressions grows to massive proportions due to the presence of *introns* (nonfunctional substructures) as well as the pursuit of mimicking each nuance of the data — i.e., modeling noise rather than fundamentals. Typically, the approach adopted to control this tendency has been to apply parsimony pressure so that the fitness metric considers both the performance of the evolved expression in terms of matching the data behavior *and* the complexity of the evolved expression. The problem with this single metric approach is that the complexity-performance trade-off cannot be made prior to model discovery despite the need to do so.

To resolve this quandary, we can leverage the notion of a Pareto front from the multi-objective optimization community. Given a population of solutions, the Pareto front considers all objectives to be equally important and identifies those solutions which are *nondominated*. This is illustrated in Figure 17-1 wherein the performance of a population is shown for two performance criteria with smaller values of each being preferable. The Pareto front consists of those members of the population for which there exists no solution which is better in *both criteria* than the Pareto set member. Thus, we can easily focus on the proper population members to explicitly make trade-offs of model complexity vs. performance.

Given that the Pareto front represents the best individuals in a population, it is reasonable to assume that we want to focus the evolutionary process on individuals on or near the Pareto front with a goal of pushing the Pareto down and to the left (in the case of the example shown in Figure 17-1) At the same time, given the limited size of the Pareto set relative to the overall population, we do not want to lose the diversity of building blocks present in that population nor the ability to discover new solutions and structures.

Once we realize the significance of the Pareto-based criteria, there are many ways to exploit the representation. As will be described below in more detail, an approach which has proven effective is to breed the Pareto set members with the best (in terms of model error) members of the population At the end of each generation, the Pareto set is updated to reflect any improvements in the Pareto set and the process is repeated. The Pareto archive is maintained across multiple GP *cascades* with each independent GP cascade contributing new genetic material in the exploration of the model structure space. Multiple independent *runs* (each containing their own set of cascades) are used to mitigate against evolutionary lock-in on a successful structure.

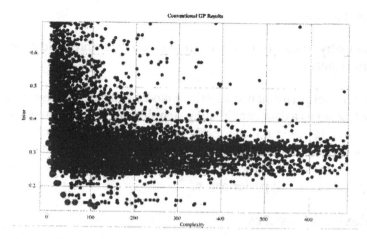

Figure 17-1. Here we illustrate the Pareto front (large red dots) in a population where the two axes represent competing objectives (with smaller values being better). This illustration uses the results from a conventional GP symbolic regression run; note that much of the computational effort was spent exploring entities of high complexity despite marginal (if any) incremental improvements over their less complex peers.

2. Pareto (Optimization) Axes

In this section, we discuss possible definitions of "good" — i.e., the various criteria which might be used to define the axes of the Pareto front. Symbolic regression will need to include model performance as well as model complexity; however, there are many possible definitions within these characteristics. Since the notion of a Pareto front is not constrained to two dimensions, we can also incorporate other performance metrics into the Pareto front. However, in general, the number of dimensions should be kept relatively low for computational performance reasons.

Model Performance

Model *performance* defines the absolute fitness (quality or accuracy) of an evolved structure and characterizes how well the model matches the observed data behavior. In our industrial applications, we have used:

- **1-norm** (sum of absolute values of error)

- **2-norm** (i.e., least squares criteria)

- *n*-**norm** (higher values of n weight large errors more; ∞-norm returns magnitude of largest error)

- **absolute correlation** (measures response surface matching independent of scaling and translation)

- **products** of the above

- **epsilon-insensitive zones** (only errors greater than some threshold count against performance)

Selection of the model performance criteria is model dependent. Also note the role of data balancing as a data conditioning step since the typical industrial symbolic regression data set is not the result of a designed experiment and, therefore, is likely to have some regions of parameter space over-represented relative to others — which can skew the performance metrics towards those regions at the expense of overall performance.

Model Complexity Measures

Characterizing the *complexity* of an expression should, in principle, consider two aspects: (1) the complexity of the expression structure and (2) the complexity of the derived response surface. Although the first aspect is difficult, it is much more tractable than the second aspect — especially for targeted systems having many input parameters. Hence, for computational simplicity reasons, we have chosen to define model complexity based upon the structure rather than the response. Even with this reduction in scope, there are many possible metrics for complexity; these include (assuming a tree-based GP implementation):

- **Tree depth** — the number of levels in the structure

- **Tree nodes** — the number of leaves and branch points in the structure

- **Component function nonlinearity** — e.g., "+" is less nonlinear than exponentiation, sines or if-than-else constructs

- **Number of variables** — either number of variables as leaves or the count of unique variables within the expression

- **Combinations of the above**

Although still an open area of research, we are currently using as a complexity metric the sum of the complexities of the tree structure and all subtrees — where the complexity is defined as the number of nodes (branch points plus leaves). This sort of metric has the advantage of favoring fewer layers as well as providing more resolution at the low end of the complexity axis of the Pareto front so that more simple solutions may be included in the Pareto front. Figure 17-2 illustrates the computation of this complexity measure whereas Figure 17-3 illustrates the complexity difference possible when two different genotype representations result in the same phenotype expression.

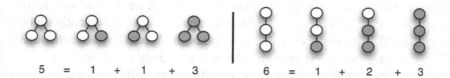

$$5 = 1 + 1 + 3 \qquad 6 = 1 + 2 + 3$$

Figure 17-2. Here we illustrate the computation of expression complexity with two simple three node structures. This complexity metric of the sum of the number of nodes of all subtrees will favor flatter and balanced structures for equivalent node counts.

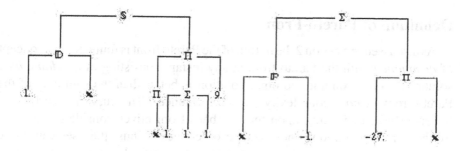

Figure 17-3. These two genome tree representations are equivalent to the expression $\frac{1}{x} - 27x$. Despite their equivalent raw performance, the left one has a complexity measure of 36 whereas the right one has a measure of 17; hence, the second structure would *dominate* the first from a Pareto perspective. (Here the genome representation is S $\rightarrow$ subtract, $\Sigma \rightarrow$ sum, D$\rightarrow$divide, P$\rightarrow$power, and $\Pi \rightarrow$product.)

Other Dimensions

There are other criteria which we may want to include in evaluating symbolic regression expressions. For example,

- performance on different data sets (e.g., training, test, and validation)

- uniqueness of included variables, number of variables, structures etc.

Although we could articulate these as additional dimensions in the multi-objective optimization space represented by the Pareto front, we generally want to keep the dimensionality as low as possible for practical reasons, since additional dimensions bring the "curse of dimensionality" to bear and greatly increases the difficulty of covering the Pareto front (hyper)surface.

3. Defining Pareto Optimality

Although defining the Pareto set is relatively straightforward since the definition if unambiguous, a definition of Pareto optimality is required if our interest extends to solutions not on the Pareto front or if we have an objective to fully populate the front (i.e., fill in gaps). This isn't as critical for the symbolic regression application as it is for more traditional multiobjective optimization where having a detailed understanding of the shape of the Pareto front is critical. For symbolic regression, "good enough" can be more easily achieved.

Although the subtleties of Pareto optimality are not critical for the currently proposed algorithm, an understanding of such issues may be important for successor algorithms. Hence, we include the discussion of this section. This section draws heavily from (Eckart Zitzler and Bleuler, 2004) and (Jensen, 2003).

Definition of Pareto-Front

As discussed in Section 2 the notion of the Pareto front is founded on a concept of *dominance* with the Pareto front at any instant consisting of *nondominated* solutions — for example, no other solution is better than the solutions of the Pareto front in *both* complexity and performance. The curve (or surface or hyper-surface, depending upon the number of objectives considered) defined by the Pareto points does not need to be convex. Thus, the user can judge whether an incremental gain in performance is worth the associated increase in expression complexity or if there is major improvement associated with an incremental increase in complexity.

Pareto Performance Metrics

There are a variety of ways to characterize the Pareto performance. We would, in general, prefer to fully explore and populate the Pareto front as well as refine and enhance the demonstrated success of the known members of the Pareto set. Thus, we are faced with the common problem of evolutionary algorithms of balancing exploration and exploitation.

A natural approach to ensuring the exploration of the Pareto front is to reward uniqueness. Unfortunately, explicitly rewarding this is difficult due to difficulty of choosing a proper scaling and distance metric for the diverse axes of the multiobjective optimization and, as a result, should typically be avoided. The alternative is to adopt a dominance-based criterion; there are three basic types of dominance-based building blocks:

- **Domination (or Dominance Rank)** — by how many entities is an entity dominated? A small number is good. This tends to reward exploration at the edges of the known Pareto front or in new regions.

- **Dominance (or Dominance Count)** — how many entities does an entity dominate? A large number is good. This tends to reward exploitation in the middle of the front.

- **Dominance Layer (or Dominance Depth)** — at which depth front is an entity located? This rewards being in layers (where a layer is defined as entities having a common dominance rank) close to the Pareto front.

From these fundamentals, many metrics have been derived, e.g., NGSA, NSGA-II, SPEA, SPEA2, MOGA, NPGA, DMOEA, VLSI-GA, PDE, PAES, PESA, etc. The summary is that it is possible — although not necessarily trivial — to shift the selection process away from the actual Pareto front to include those individuals near the front and reward uniqueness using the dominance based building blocks.

Computational Issues

As noted by Jensen (Jensen, 2003), brute force computation of the Pareto dominance of a population of N entities for M objectives will have a $O(MN^2)$ computational bound. For large population sizes, this can dominate algorithm performance. More clever algorithms can reduce that demand to $O(N \log^{M-1} N)$ or $O(N \log^{M-2} N)$ depending upon the Pareto performance metric flavor. However, as a general rule, the computational load effect of population size needs to be considered in the algorithm design.

4. Pareto Exploitation: User Selection

There are two potential users of the Pareto front: the human and the algorithm. Although the focus of this chapter is the algorithmic exploitation, we should note that the evolutionary process will identify a Pareto front of discovered solutions. The ability to characterize this front has two major benefits to the user:

- allows the user to focus on the top solutions for inspection and trade-offs of complexity vs. performance and

- provides insight into the problem difficulty by examining the shape of the Pareto front.

Of course, the user also benefits from the improved discovery speed and performance (both accuracy and robustness) which result from the algorithmic exploitation of the Pareto front. An example is shown in Figure 17-4 which displays the Pareto front for a biomass inferential sensor (Kordon et al., 2004). Every dot in this graph represents a GP-model with its associated fitness (in this case $1 - R^2$, i.e. lower values are better) and a normalized complexity measure indicated as the ratio of the number of nodes. Of the 88 models displayed, only 18 are lying on the Pareto front. The number of interesting models is actually even lower since it is clear that little can be gained by having models with a normalized complexity measure larger than 0.3.

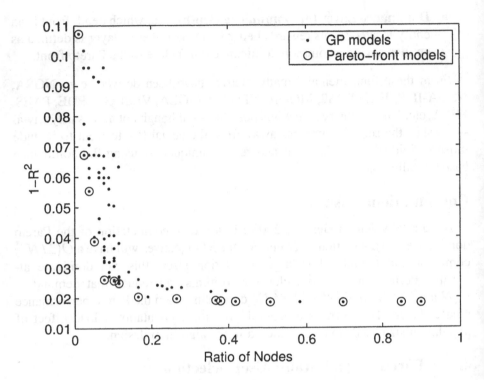

Figure 17-4.   Here we show the Pareto front of (normalized) complexity vs. performance for a biomass inferential sensor derived using GP. Lower complexity corresponds to lower ratio of the number of constituent nodes; hence, we see the diminishing returns from increases in expression complexity.

5.   Pareto Exploitation: GP Strategies

The Pareto front representation allows algorithms as well as humans to quickly scan for promising solutions from large populations of expressions and focus subsequent analysis effort on those solutions. In this section, we describe one algorithm to exploit that representation. Although exploiting the multi-objective representation is a relatively unexplored topic, there have been a number of other strategies proposed (e.g., (Bleuler et al., 2001, de Jong and Pollack, 2003, Saetrom and Hetland, 2003)); we will discuss these after presenting the ParetoGP algorithm.

Algorithm Objectives

The objectives of ParetoGP are threefold:

1 **Multi-Objective Characterization of Evolved Expressions** — Optimizing the Pareto front instead of a single fitness measure (even includ-

ing parsimony pressure) allows the automatic generation of a hierarchy of solutions of increasing complexity and fitness without having to specify a problem-dependent parsimony pressure *a priori.*

2 **Accelerated and Robust Evolution** — Significantly accelerate the search as well as improve the quality of the solutions. ParetoGP significantly alleviates the problem of bloat.

3 **Metavariable Identification** — Use the low-complexity equations as potential variable transforms that can lead to more physical insight.

The ParetoGP Algorithm

ParetoGP algorithm
In this section we'll discuss a number of aspects in which the proposed algorithm differs from a more conventional GP system. The main features are:

- Pareto front archive definition & persistence across generations and cascaded evolutions

- Generation-based update of the Pareto front archive

- Random crossover between Pareto archive members and generation population ranked by expression accuracy performance

- Random mutation of Pareto archive members

An archive of potential solutions is maintained between generations and between different cascades (except for the persistence of the archive, a cascade is an independent run with a freshly generated starting population). The end result of the computation is the archive which contains all the models on the Pareto front. As discussed before there are several benefits associated with this. One is that the shape of the Pareto front gives the user quite some insight into the intrinsic complexity of the problem. The shape of the Pareto front turns out to be very reproducible across independent runs. Also, the particular choice of the complexity measure (sum of the number of nodes of all subtrees) allows for additional resolution in the description of the Pareto front beyond that offered by a simple node count metric. An additional benefit is that the models at the low-complexity end of the Pareto front very often turn out to be "building blocks" or relatively simple variable transformations that can lead to more physical insight. These building blocks then sometimes can be used to develop linear models with new variables (Castillo et al., 2002). Of course the notion of extracting the Pareto front from a collection of models can also be used to analyze the population resulting from a conventional GP run. Here significant benefits can result from the fast analysis of large collections of models. There is, however, a significant difference between using a Pareto front as a post-run analysis tool vs. actively optimizing the Pareto front during a GP-run. In the latter case the Pareto front becomes the objective that is being optimized instead of the fitness (accuracy) of the "best" model.

At the end of every generation the archive is updated and contains the Pareto front of the combination of all models and (optionally) all the subtrees of the current population as well as the current archive. By including all the subtrees of all the models in the population (this involves no overhead in our MATLAB^{TM} implementation of the system) we are effectively using a population size equal to the sum of the number of nodes in all equations in the population. Depending on how much complexity we allow, this can lead to effective population sizes which are significantly larger than usual.

In generating the new population, crossover occurs between a random member of the archive and members of the current population. Selection of from the population is based on the conventional GP paradigm of accuracy. Random members of the archive are chosen to maintain diversity in the Pareto front. This is important since we want to develop the entire Pareto front and not bias the search into the low nor the high complexity region. It is important to note that in ParetoGP there is often still a lot of progress even while the model with the highest fitness does not change. This model is just one point at the high-complexity end of the Pareto front.

An archive of potential solutions is maintained not only between generations but also between different cascades. Whereas in a conventional GP system multiple runs are executed starting from scratch i.e. all runs are independent, the archive is maintained between runs in the current system. The result is that while the starting population is regenerated the subsequent generations quickly rediscover the results from the previous runs because of the cross-breeding with the archive. This changes the mode of execution to more runs with less generations compared to a conventional GP-system. The purpose of the independent runs is, therefore, to introduce new genetic material into the Pareto front development.

Practitioner Comments

Although ParetoGP has already proven itself to be a major addition to the Dow Chemical empirical modeling capability, we are still exploring the features and nuances of its behavior and performance. (Symbolic regression toolboxes have been developed internally in The Dow Chemical company both in Matlab and *Mathematica*.) Maintaining a minimum size archive (nominally 5-10% of the population size) helps the robustness of the symbolic regression in situations where a single variable explains a large portion of the targeted response behavior; if required, the additional models are assembled by adding Pareto layers until the threshold archive size is met. By construction, each layer has a different accuracy metric which, presumably, avoids inclusion of a more complex version of a model already contained within the archive.

Surprisingly, we often turn off parsimony pressure; however, we do maintain hard limits on expression complexity as a safety. Intuitively, assigning breeding rights to the population based upon accuracy would seem to make the evolution emphasis be model accuracy and, therefore, place the evolutionary effort on the complex side of the Pareto front — which, to some extent, is what we want for the symbolic regression. Using the Pareto archive as half of the breeding pool constrains the complexity of the overall population. Watching the shape of the evolving Pareto front is interesting in the sense that a "tail" of increasing complexity with incremental accuracy gains will be eliminated as a higher performing but much simpler expression is discovered. We also tend to see step changes (major jumps in accuracy) in the Pareto front backfilled in succeeding generations or cascades as the evolutionary process explores this new structure. Evaluating the constituent subtrees may help in this respect by maintaining a bias in the search process for simpler solutions.

The human aspect involved in assessing the evolved models is critical. Hence, we have developed tools for response surface visualization, statistical analysis, error analysis, etc. to facilitate understanding of the developed models.

Other Pareto Front Exploitation Algorithms

Other researchers have proposed algorithms to exploit the Pareto front. For example, (Bleuler et al., 2001) assign breeding rights based upon the SPEA2 metric of a population with members of the Pareto front persisting across generational boundaries. Their approach is not dependent upon the use of the SPEA2 metric — other than the requirement to have some scalar-valued criteria to award propagation rights. Philosophically, this is a conventional GP approach with the Pareto front used to transfer genetic material across generational boundaries and a selection metric which combines the competing objectives. (Saetrom and Hetland, 2003) have also essentially followed this approach. (de Jong and Pollack, 2003) propose a Pareto front-centric approach wherein they synthesize new entities each generation which are merged with a persistent Pareto front and used to define an updated Pareto front. The Pareto front has three criteria: performance, size and diversity. Genetic propagation is restricted to those entities on the Pareto front.

6. ParetoGP Algorithm Performance

In these following figures we compare the results of multiple runs for a polymer reactivity problem. Figure 17-5 shows the results from 300 runs of a conventional GP implementation for 128 generation; notice that conventional

GP was rarely able to generate any solutions with fitness greater than 0.9 for the 300 runs. In contrast, ParetoGP generated superior results with the maximum fitness exceeding 0.9 for almost every case of a similar set of 300 runs as shown in Figure 17-6. Similar results have been confirmed in a number of other projects (Kordon et al., 2004).

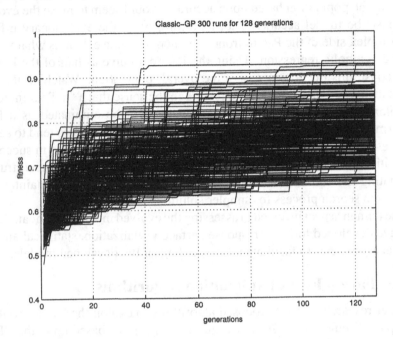

Figure 17-5. Example of ten runs of 150 generations with conventional GP for a polymer reactivity problem The highest performance (accuracy) is displayed.

7.   Conclusions

ParetoGP is a major advancement in Dow Chemical's empirical modeling tool portfolio due to greatly increasing the efficiency and robustness of symbolic regression. In this section we summarize the improvements as well as indicate future research directions.

Major Improvements Over Classical GP

The advantages of ParetoGP relative to classical GP implementations essentially reduces to (a) symbolic regression speed and robustness and (b) understanding of the complexity-accuracy trade-off of evolved models.

Changing the objective function from a single fitness criterion to the Pareto front of fitness versus a measure of complexity has proven to speed up symbolic regression significantly. Our current estimate is that the entire development

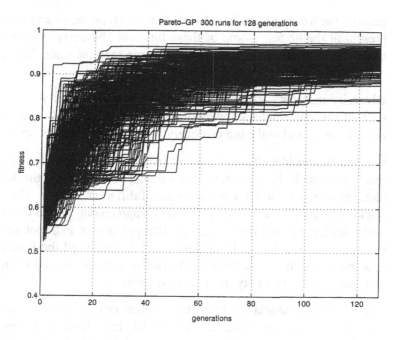

Figure 17-6. Example of five runs of thirty generations with Pareto GP for a polymer reactivity problem. The highest performance is displayed.

process speeds up at least tenfold — and even more if one includes the post-analysis phase. Because there are fewer problems with bloat and because of the improved discovery process, bigger problems can be tackled within the same CPU and memory constraints.

The fact that the user can pick one or more functions at the right level of complexity generates more buy-in from the end-user as well as more robust solutions. Also, the natural development of low-complexity transforms between variables at one end of the Pareto front helps to generate more physical insight and end-user buy-in.

Obvious Extensions

The current implementation of ParetoGP is still basic in many aspects and can be enhanced in various directions.

- **Metavariable identification** — One obvious direction is a more systematic consideration of the discovery of metavariables or building blocks that simplify the evolution process or to identify transforms that linearize the problem. This is currently being investigated.

- **Expression complexity metrics** — Another direction that is being explored is the generation of better complexity measures that not only depend on the tree structure but also take into account the functions that are present at the nodes. Some of these function obviously generate more nonlinearity than others. This is not a simple exercise since this needs to consider the particular scaling of the input variables.

- **Diversity metrics** — More work is probably also needed in developing explicit diversity metrics for the Pareto front. Perhaps this can also be used to direct and make the discovery process even more efficient.

- **Diverse model identification** — As in any empirical modelling effort, there is no such thing as the perfect model so very often the final implementation is built from an aggregate of different models. This model stacking helps us to calculate a "model disagreement" factor that is used to the decide whether the models are interpolating or extrapolating with respect to the original training data set. We have used the Pareto front as a source for these stacked models, but there is also a need for metrics that quantify the diversity in these model sets.

- **Convergence criteria** — Our convergence criteria are currently still based on the fitness of the best individual, but future measures could take the movement or lack of movement of the Pareto front into account to develop better measures.

One last point which is the subject of considerable research is more active control of the parsimony pressure as a function of the particular problem. Pare-toGP solves many of the practical problems related to bloat, but there still is a parsimony factor (which is far less critical compared to standard GP) that controls the maximum size of the equations that can be generated. In this sense it is used to control how far the Pareto front extends to the high complexity side.

References

Banzhaf, Wolfgang, Nordin, Peter, Keller, Robert E., and Francone, Frank D. (1998). *Genetic Programming – An Introduction; On the Automatic Evolution of Computer Programs and its Applications*. Morgan Kaufmann.

Bleuler, Stefan, Brack, Martin, Thiele, Lothar, and Zitzler, Eckart (2001). Multiobjective genetic programming: Reducing bloat using SPEA2. In *Proceedings of the 2001 Congress on Evolutionary Computation CEC2001*, pages 536–543, COEX, World Trade Center, 159 Samseong-dong, Gangnam-gu, Seoul, Korea. IEEE Press.

Castillo, Flor A., Marshall, Ken A., Green, James L., and Kordon, Arthur K. (2002). Symbolic regression in design of experiments: A case study with linearizing transformations. In Langdon, W. B., Cantú-Paz, E., Mathias, K., Roy, R., Davis, D., Poli, R., Balakrishnan, K., Honavar, V., Rudolph, G., Wegener, J., Bull, L., Potter, M. A., Schultz, A. C., Miller, J. F., Burke, E., and Jonoska, N., editors, *GECCO 2002: Proceedings of the Genetic and Evolutionary Computation Conference*, pages 1043–1047, New York. Morgan Kaufmann Publishers.

de Jong, Edwin D. and Pollack, Jordan B. (2003). Multi-objective methods for tree size control. *Genetic Programming and Evolvable Machines*, 4(3):211–233.

Eckart Zitzler, Marco Laumanns and Bleuler, Stefan (2004). A tutorial on evolutionary multi-objective optimization. In Xavier Gandibleux, Marc Sevaux, Kenneth Sšrensen and T'kindt, Vincent, editors, *Metaheuristics for Multiobjective Optimisation*, chapter 1, pages 1–32? Springer Verlag.

Jacob, Christian (2001). *Illustrating Evolutionary Computation with Mathematica*. Morgan Kaufmann.

Jensen, Mikkel T. (2003). Reducing the run-time complexity of multiobjective eas: The nsga-ii and other algorithms. *IEEE Transactions on Evolutionary Computation*, 7(5):503–515.

Kordon, Arthur, Jordaan, Elsa, Chew, Lawrence, Smits, Guido, Bruck, Torben, Haney, Keith, and Jenings, Annika (2004). Biomass inferential sensor based on ensemble of models generated by genetic programming. In in process, editor, *GECCO-2004*, page tbd, New York, New York.

Kotanchek, Mark, Smits, Guido, and Kordon, Arthur (2003). Industrial strength genetic programming. In Riolo, Rick L. and Worzel, Bill, editors, *Genetic Programming Theory and Practise*, chapter 15, pages 239–256. Kluwer.

Saetrom, Pal and Hetland, Magnus Lie (2003). Multiobjective evolution of temporal rules. In B. Tessem, P. Ala-Siuru, P. Doherty and Mayoh, B., editors, *Proceedings of the 8th Scandinavian Conference on Artificial Intelligence*. IOS Press.

Chapter 18

AN EVOLVED ANTENNA FOR DEPLOYMENT ON NASA'S SPACE TECHNOLOGY 5 MISSION

Jason D. Lohn[1], Gregory S. Hornby[1,2], and Derek S. Linden[3]

[1]*NASA Ames Research Center;* [2]*QSS Group, Inc.;* [3]*Linden Innovation Research, LLC.*

Abstract   We present an evolved X-band antenna design and flight prototype currently on schedule to be deployed on NASA's Space Technology 5 (ST5) spacecraft. Current methods of designing and optimizing antennas by hand are time and labor intensive, limit complexity, and require significant expertise and experience. Evolutionary design techniques can overcome these limitations by searching the design space and automatically finding effective solutions that would ordinarily not be found. The ST5 antenna was evolved to meet a challenging set of mission requirements, most notably the combination of wide beamwidth for a circularly-polarized wave and wide bandwidth. Two evolutionary algorithms were used: one used a genetic algorithm style representation that did not allow branching in the antenna arms; the second used a genetic programming style tree-structured representation that allowed branching in the antenna arms. The highest performance antennas from both algorithms were fabricated and tested, and both yielded very similar performance. Both antennas were comparable in performance to a hand-designed antenna produced by the antenna contractor for the mission, and so we consider them examples of human-competitive performance by evolutionary algorithms. As of this writing, one of our evolved antenna prototypes is undergoing flight qualification testing. If successful, the resulting antenna would represent the first evolved hardware in space, and the first deployed evolved antenna..

Keywords: design, computational design, antenna, wire antenna, spacecraft, genetic programming, evolutionary computation.

1.   Introduction

Researchers have been investigating evolutionary antenna design and optimization since the early 1990s (e.g., (Michielssen et al., 1993, Haupt, 1995, Altshuler and Linden, 1997a, Rahmat-Samii and Michielssen, 1999)), and the field has grown in recent years as computer speed has increased and electromagnetics simulators have improved. Many antenna types have been investigated, including wire antennas (Linden and Altshuler, 1996), antenna arrays (Haupt, 1996), and quadrifilar helical antennas (Lohn et al., 2002). In addition, the ability to evolve antennas *in-situ* (Linden, 2000), that is, taking into account the effects of surrounding structures, opens new design possibilities. Such an approach is very difficult for antenna designers due to the complexity of electromagnetic interactions, yet easy to integrate into evolutionary techniques.

Below we describe two evolutionary algorithm (EA) approaches to a challenging antenna design problem on NASA's Space Technology 5 (ST5) mission (ST5). ST5's objective is to demonstrate and flight qualify innovative technologies and concepts for application to future space missions. Images showing the ST5 spacecraft are seen in Figure 18-1. The mission duration is planned for three months.

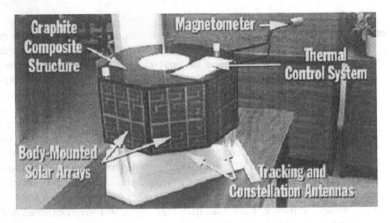

Figure 18-1. ST5 satellite mock-up. The satellite will have two antennas, centered on the top and bottom of each spacecraft.

2.   ST5 Mission Antenna Requirements

The three ST5 spacecraft will orbit at close separations in a highly elliptical geosynchronous transfer orbit approximately 35,000 km above Earth and will communicate with a 34 meter ground-based dish antenna. The combination of wide beamwidth for a circularly-polarized wave and wide bandwidth make for a challenging design problem. In terms of simulation challenges, because the diameter of the spacecraft is 54.2 cm, the spacecraft is 13-15 wavelengths across which makes antenna simulation computationally intensive. For that reason, an infinite ground plane approximation or smaller finite ground plane is typically used in modeling and design.

The antenna requirements are as follows. The gain pattern must be greater than or equal to 0 dBic (decibels as referenced to an isotropic radiator that is circularly polarized) at $40° \leq \theta \leq 80°$ and $0° \leq \phi \leq 360°$ for right-hand circular polarization. The antenna must have a voltage standing wave ratio (VSWR) of under 1.2 at the transmit frequency (8470 MHz) and under 1.5 at the receive frequency (7209.125 MHz) – VSWR is a way to quantify reflected-wave interference, and thus the amount of impedance mismatch at the junction. in the At both frequencies the input impedance should be 50 Ω. The antenna is restricted in shape to a mass of under 165 g, and must fit in a cylinder of height and diameter of 15.24 cm.

In addition to these requirements, an additional "desired" specification was issued for the field pattern. Because of the spacecraft's relative orientation to the Earth, high gain in the field pattern was desired at low elevation angles. Specifically, across $0° \leq \phi \leq 360°$, gain was desired to meet: 2 dBic for $\theta = 80°$, and 4 dBic for $\theta = 90°$.

ST5 mission managers were willing to accept antenna performance that aligned closer to the "desired" field pattern specifications noted above, and the contractor, using conventional design practices, produced a quadrifilar helical (QFH) (see Figure 18-2) antenna to meet these specifications.

3.   Evolved Antenna Design

From past experience in designing wire antennas (Linden, 1997), we decided to constrain our evolutionary design to a monopole wire antenna with four identical arms, each arm rotated 90° from its neighbors. The EA thus evolves genotypes that specify the design for one arm, and builds the complete antenna using four copies of the evolved arm.

In the remainder of this section we describe the two evolutionary algorithms used. The first algorithm was used in our previous work in evolutionary antenna design (Linden and Altshuler, 1996) and it is a standard genetic algorithm (GA) that evolves non-branching wire forms. The second algorithm is based on our previous work evolving rod-structured, robot morphologies (Hornby and Pollack, 2002). This EA has a genetic programming (GP) style tree-structured representation that allows branching in the wire forms. In addition, the two EAs use different fitness functions.

Non-branching EA

In this EA, the design was constrained to non-branching arms and the encoding used real numbers. The feed wire for the antenna is not optimized, but is specified by the user. The size constraints used, an example of an evolved arm, and the resulting antenna are shown in Figure 18-3.

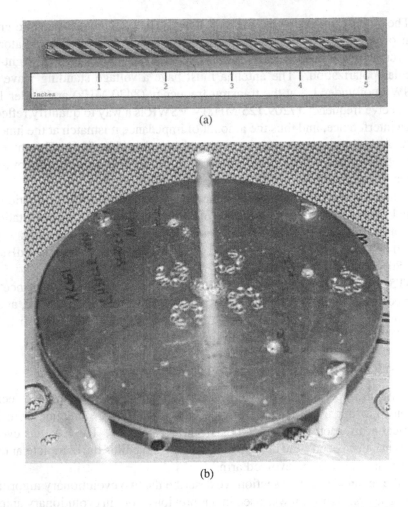

(a)

(b)

Figure 18-2. Conventionally-designed quadrifilar helical (QHF) antenna: (a) Radiator; (b) Radiator mounted on ground plane.

Representation

The design is specified by a set of real-valued scalars, one for each coordinate of each point. Thus, for a four-segment design (shown in Figure 18-3), 12 parameters are required.

Adewuya's method of mating (Adewuya, 1996) and Gaussian mutation are used to evolve effective designs from initial random populations. This EA has been shown to work extremely well on many different antenna problems (Altshuler and Linden, 1997b, Altshuler, 0002, Linden and MacMillan, 2000).

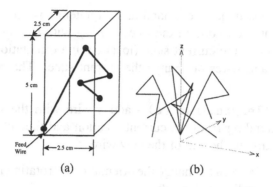

Figure 18-3. (a) size constraints and evolved arm; (b) resulting 4-wire antenna after rotations.

Fitness Function

This EA used pattern quality scores at 7.2 GHz and 8.47 GHz in the fitness function. Unlike the second EA, VSWR was not used in this fitness calculation. To quantify the pattern quality at a single frequency, PQ_f, the following was used:

$$PQ_f = \sum_{\substack{0° < \phi < 360° \\ 40° < \theta < 80°}} (\text{gain}_{\phi,\theta} - T)^2 \quad \text{if gain}_{\phi,\theta} < T$$

where $\text{gain}_{\phi,\theta}$ is the gain of the antenna in dBic (right-hand polarization) at a particular angle, T is the target gain (3 dBic was used in this case), ϕ is the azimuth, and θ is the elevation.

To compute the overall fitness of an antenna design, the pattern quality measures at the transmit and receive frequencies were summed, lower values corresponding to better antennas:

$$F = PQ_{7.2} + PQ_{8.47}$$

Branching EA

The EA in this section allows for branching in the antenna arms. Rather than using linear sequences of bits or real-values as is traditionally done, here we use a tree-structured representation which naturally represents branching in the antenna arms.

Representation

The representation for encoding branching antennas is an extension of our previous work in using a linear-representation for encoding rod-based robots (Hornby and Pollack, 2002). Each node in the tree-structured representation is an antenna-construction command and an antenna is created by executing the commands at each node in the tree, starting with the root node. In constructing an antenna the current state (location and orientation) is maintained and commands add wires or change the current state. The commands are as follows:

- `forward(length, radius)` - add a wire with the given length and radius extending from the current location and then change the current state location to the end of the new wire.

- `rotate-x(angle)` - change the orientation by rotating it by the specified amount (in radians) about the x-axis.

- `rotate-y(angle)` - change the orientation by rotating it by the specified amount (in radians) about the y-axis.

- `rotate-z(angle)` - change the orientation by rotating it by the specified amount (in radians) about the z-axis.

An antenna design is created by starting with an initial feedwire and adding wires. For the ST5 mission the initial feed wire starts at the origin and has a length of 0.4 cm along the Z-axis. That is, the design starts with the single feedwire from (0.0, 0.0, 0.0) to (0.0, 0.0, 0.4) and the current construction state (location and orientation) for the next wire will be started from location (0.0, 0.0, 0.4) with the orientation along the positive Z-axis.

To produce antennas that are four-way symmetric about the z-axis, the construction process is restricted to producing antenna wires that are fully contained in the positive XY quadrant and then after construction is complete, this arm is copied three times and these copies are placed in each of the other quadrants through rotations of 90°/180°/270°. For example, in executing the program `rotate-z(0.523598776) forward(1.0,0.032)`, the `rotate-z()` command causes the the current orientation to rotate 0.523598776 radians (30°) about the Z axis. The `forward()` command adds a wire of length 1.0 cm and radius 0.032 cm in the current forward direction. This wire is then copied into each of the other three XY quadrants. The resulting antenna is shown in Figure 18-4(a).

Branches in the representation cause a branch in the flow of execution and create different branches in the constructed antenna. The following is an encoding of an antenna with branching in the arms, here brackets are used to separate the subtrees:

```
rotate-z(0.5235) [ forward(1.0,0.032) [ rotate-z(0.5235)
[ forward(1.0,0.032) ] rotate-x(0.5235) [ forward(1.0,0.032)
] ] ]
```

This antenna is shown in Figure 18-4(b).

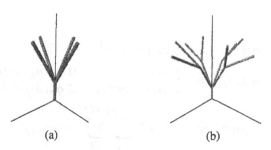

Figure 18-4. Example antennas: (a) non-branching arms; (b) branching arms.

To take into account imprecision in manufacturing an antenna, antenna designs are evaluated multiple times, each time with a small random perturbation applied to joint angles and wire radii. The overall fitness of an antenna is the worst score of these evaluations. In this way, the fitness score assigned to an antenna design is a conservative estimate of how well it will perform if it were to be constructed. An additional side-effect of this is that antennas evolved with this manufacturing noise tend to perform well across a broader range of frequencies than do antennas evolved without this noise.

Fitness Function

The fitness function used to evaluate antennas is a function of the VSWR and gain values on the transmit and receive frequencies. The VSWR component of the fitness function is constructed to put strong pressure to evolving antennas with receive and transmit VSWR values below the required amounts of 1.2 and 1.5, reduced pressure at a value below these requirements (1.15 and 1.25) and then no pressure to go below 1.1:

$$
v_r = \text{VSWR at receive frequency}
$$
$$
v_r' = \begin{cases} v_r + 2.0(v_r - 1.25) & \text{if } v_r > 1.25 \\ v_r & \text{if } 1.25 > v_r > 1.1 \\ 1.1 & \text{if } v_r < 1.1 \end{cases}
$$
$$
v_t = \text{VSWR at transmit frequency}
$$
$$
v_t' = \begin{cases} v_t + 2.0(v_t - 1.15) & \text{if } v_t > 1.15 \\ v_t & \text{if } 1.15 > v_t > 1.1 \\ 1.1 & \text{if } v_t < 1.1 \end{cases}
$$
$$
vswr = v_r' v_t'
$$

The gain component of the fitness function uses the gain (in decibels) in $5°$ increments about the angles of interest: from $40° \leq \theta \leq 90°$ and $0° \leq \phi \leq$

$360°$:

$$gain_{ij} = \text{gain at } \theta = 5°i, \; \phi = 5°j$$

$$gain(i,j) = \begin{cases} 0 & \text{if } gain_{ij} > 0.5 \\ 0.5 - gain_{ij} & \text{if } gain_{ij} < 0.5 \end{cases}$$

$$gain = 1 + 0.1 \sum_{i=8}^{i<19} \sum_{j=0}^{j=72} gain(i,j)$$

While the actual minimum required gain value is 0 dBic for $40° \leq \theta \leq 80°$, and desired gain values are 2 dBic for $\theta \geq 80°$ and 4dBic for $\theta = 90°$ only a single target gain of 0.5 dBic is used here. This provides some headroom to account for errors in simulation over the minimum of 0 dBic and does not attempt to meet desired gain values. Since achieving gain values greater than 0 dBic is the main part of the required specifications, the third component of the fitness function rewards antenna designs for having sample points with gains greater than zero:

$$outlier(i,j) = \begin{cases} 0.1 & \text{if } gain_{ij} < 0.01 \\ 0 & \text{otherwise} \end{cases}$$

$$outlier = 1 + \sum_{i=8}^{i<19} \sum_{j=0}^{j=72} outlier(i,j)$$

These three components are multiplied together to produce the overall fitness score of an antenna design:

$$F = vswr \times gain \times outlier$$

The objective of the EA is to produce antenna designs that minimize F.

4.   EA Run Setup

As mentioned earlier, the ST5 spacecraft is 13-15 wavelengths wide, which makes simulation of the antenna on the full craft very compute intensive. To keep the antenna evaluations fast, an infinite ground plane approximation was used in all runs. This was found to provide sufficient accuracy to achieve several good designs. Designs were then analyzed on a finite ground plane of the same shape and size as the top of the ST5 body to determine their effectiveness at meeting requirements in a realistic environment. The Numerical Electromagnetics Code, Version 4 (NEC4) (Burke and Poggio, 1981) was used to evaluate all antenna designs.

For the non-branching EA, a population of 50 individuals was used, 50% of which is kept from generation to generation. The mutation rate was 1%, with the Gaussian mutation standard deviation of 10% of the value range. The non-branching EA was halted after 100 generations had been completed, the EA's best score was stagnant for 40 generations, or EA's average score was stagnant for 10 generations. For the branching EA, a population of 200 individuals were created through either mutation or recombination, with an equal probability. For both algorithms, each antenna simulation took a few seconds of wall-clock time to run and an entire run took approximately 6-10 hours.

5.   Evolved Antenna Results

The two best evolved antennas, one from each of the EAs described above, were fabricated and tested. The antenna named ST5-3-10 was produced by the EA that allowed branching, and the antenna named ST5-4W-03 was produced by the other EA. Photographs of the prototyped antennas are shown in Figure 18-5. Due to space limitations, only performance data from antenna ST5-3-10 is presented below.

Since the goal of our work was to produce requirements-compliant antennas for ST5, no attempt was made to compare the algorithms, either to each other, nor to other search techniques. Thus statistical sampling across multiple runs was not performed.

Evolved antenna ST5-3-10 is 100% compliant with the mission antenna performance requirements. This was confirmed by testing the prototype antenna in an anechoic test chamber at NASA Goddard Space Flight Center. The data measured in the test chamber is shown in the plots below.

The genotype of antenna ST5-3-10 is shown in Figure 18-6. The complexity of this large antenna-constructing program, as compared to the antenna arm design having one branch, suggests that it is not a minimal description of the design. For example, instead of using the minimal number of rotations to specify relative angles between wires (two) there are sequences of up to a dozen rotation commands.

The 7.2 GHz max/min gain patterns for both evolved antenna ST5-3-10 and the QFH are shown in Figure 18-7. The 8.47 GHz max/min gain patterns for both antennas are shown in Figure 18-8. On the plots for antenna ST5-3-10, a box denoting the acceptable performance according to the requirements is shown. Note that the minimum gain falls off steeply below 20°. This is acceptable as those elevations were not required due to the orientation of the spacecraft with respect to Earth. As noted above, the QFH antenna was optimized at the 8.47 GHz frequency to achieve high gain in the vicinity of $75° - 90°$.

6.   Results Analysis

Antenna ST5-3-10 is a requirements-compliant antenna that was built and tested on an antenna test range. While it is slightly difficult to manufacture

(a)

(b)

Figure 18-5.   Photographs of prototype evolved antennas: (a) ST5-3-10; (b) ST5-4W-03

without the aid of automated wire-forming and soldering machines, it has a number of benefits as compared to the conventionally-designed antenna.

First, there are potential power savings. Antenna ST5-3-10 achieves high gain (2-4dB) across a wider range of elevation angles. This allows a broader range of angles over which maximum data throughput can be achieved and would result in less power being required from the solar array and batteries.

Second, unlike the QFH antenna, the evolved antenna does not require a matching network nor phasing circuit, removing two steps in design and fabrication of the antenna. A trivial transmission line may be used for the match on the flight antenna, but simulation results suggest that one is not required if small changes to the feedpoint are made.

Third, the evolved antenna has more uniform coverage in that it has a uniform pattern with small ripples in the elevations of greatest interest ($40° - 80°$). This allows for reliable performance as elevation angle relative to the ground changes.

Fourth, the evolved antenna had a shorter design cycle. It was estimated that antenna ST5-3-10 took 3 person-months to design and fabricate the first prototype as compared to 5 person-months for the quadrifilar helical antenna.

From an algorithmic perspective, both evolutionary algorithms produced antennas that were satisfactory to the mission planners. The branching antenna, evolved using a GP-style representation, slightly outperformed the non-branching antenna in terms of field pattern and VSWR. A likely reason as to why the GP-style representation performed better is that it is more flexible and allows for the evolution of new topologies.

7.   Conclusion

We have evolved and built two X-band antennas for potential use on NASA's upcoming ST5 mission to study the magnetosphere. ST5 antenna requirements, our evolutionary algorithms, and the resulting antennas and performance plots were presented.

Evolved antenna ST5-3-10 was shown to be compliant with respect to the ST5 antenna performance requirements. It has an unusual organic-looking structure, one that expert antenna designers would likely not produce.

If flight qualification testing is successful, antenna ST5-3-10 would represent the first evolved hardware in space, and the first evolved antenna to be deployed. As the mission's primary goal is to test and validate new technologies for future NASA missions, flying an evolved antenna would fulfill this goal.

Acknowledgments

The work described in this paper was supported by Mission and Science Measurement Technology, NASA Headquarters, under its Computing, Information, and Communications Technology Program. The work was performed

```
rotate-z(1.984442) 1 [rotate-x(2.251165) 1 [rotate-x(0.062240) 1
[rotate-x(0.083665) 1 [rotate-y(-2.449035) 1 [ rotate-z(-0.894357)
1 [rotate-y(-2.057702) 1 [rotate-y(0.661755) 1 [rotate-x(0.740703)
1 [rotate-y(2.057436) 1 [ forward(0.013292,0.000283) 2
[rotate-z(-1.796822) 1 [ rotate-x(-1.651348) 1 [rotate-y(-2.940880) 1
[rotate-x(0.095209) 1 [rotate-z(1.248723) 1 [forward(0.003815,0.000363)
1 [ forward(0.008289,0.000355) 1 [forward(0.008413,0.000369) 1 [
rotate-x(-0.006494) 1 [rotate-x(-0.592854) 1 [rotate-z(-2.085023) 1
[rotate-z(1.735374) 1 [rotate-x(-2.045125) 1 [ rotate-z(0.203076) 1
[rotate-z(1.750799) 1 [rotate-z(-2.038688) 1 [rotate-z(1.725007) 1
[rotate-y(1.478109) 1 [rotate-x(2.477117) 1 [rotate-x(-2.441858) 1
[forward(0.015082,0.000223) ] ] ] ] ] ] ] ] ] ] ] ] ] ] ] ] ] ] ]
rotate-y(2.335438) 1 [ rotate-y(-1.042201) 1 [rotate-y(-1.761594) 1
[rotate-x(2.518405) 1 [rotate-z(-0.739608) 1 [rotate-x(0.426553) 1 [
rotate-z(-0.291483) 1 [rotate-x(2.152738) 1 [ forward(0.013190,0.000414)
] ] ] ] ] ] ] ] ] ] ] ] ] ] ] ] ]
```

Figure 18-6.   Genotype for evolved antenna ST5-3-10.

at the Computational Sciences Division, NASA Ames Research Center, Linden Innovation Research, and NASA Goddard Space Flight Center. The support of Ken Perko of Microwave Systems Branch at NASA Goddard and Bruce Blevins of the Physical Science Laboratory at New Mexico State University is gratefully acknowledged.

References

Space technology 5 mission. http://nmp.jpl.nasa.gov/st5/.

Adewuya, A. (1996). New methods in genetic search with real-valued chromosomes. Master's thesis, Mech. Engr. Dept., MIT.

Altshuler, E. E. (20002). Electrically small self-resonant wire antennas optimized using a genetic algorithm. *IEEE Trans. Antennas Propagat*, 50:297–300.

Altshuler, E. E. and Linden, D. S. (1997a). Design of a loaded monopole having hemispherical coverage using a genetic algorithm. *IEEE Trans. Antennas & Propagation*, 45(1):1–4.

Altshuler, E. E. and Linden, D.S. (1997b). Wire antenna designs using a genetic algorithm. *IEEE Antenna & Propagation Society Magazine*, 39:33–43.

Burke, G. J. and Poggio, A. J. (1981). Numerical electromagnetics code (nec)-method of moments. Technical Report UCID18834, Lawrence Livermore Lab.

Haupt, R. L. (1995). An introduction to genetic algorithms for electromagnetics. *IEEE Antennas & Propagation Mag.*, 37:7–15.

Haupt, R. L. (1996). Genetic algorithm design of antenna arrays. In *IEEE Aerospace Applications Conf.*, volume 1, pages 103–109.

Hornby, Gregory S. and Pollack, Jordan B. (2002). Creating high-level components with a generative representation for body-brain evolution. *Artificial Life*, 8(3):223–246.

Linden, D. S. (1997). *Automated Design and Optimization of Wire Antennas using Genetic Algorithms*. PhD thesis, MIT.

Linden, D. S. (2000). Wire antennas optimized in the presence of satellite structures using genetic algorithms. In *IEEE Aerospace Conf.*

Linden, D. S. and Altshuler, E. E. (1996). Automating wire antenna design using genetic algorithms. *Microwave Journal*, 39(3):74–86.

Linden, D. S. and MacMillan, R.T. (2000). Increasing genetic algorithm efficiency for wire antenna design using clustering. *ACES Special Journal on Genetic Algorithms*.

Lohn, J. D., Kraus, W. F., and Linden, D. S. (2002). Evolutionary optimization of a quadrifilar helical antenna. In *IEEE Antenna & Propagation Society Mtg.*, volume 3, pages 814–817.

Michielssen, E., Sajer, J.-M., Ranjithan, S., and Mittra, R. (1993). Design of lightweight, broadband microwave absorbers using genetic algorithms. *IEEE Trans. Microwave Theory & Techniques*, 41(6):1024–1031.

Rahmat-Samii, Y. and Michielssen, E., editors (1999). *Electromagnetic Optimization by Genetic Algorithms*. Wiley.

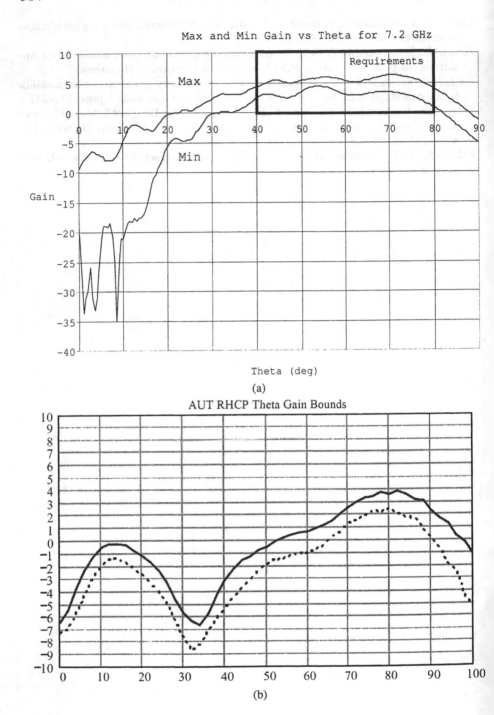

Figure 18-7. Maximum and minimum gain at 7.2 GHz for antennas (a) ST5-3-10; (b) QFH.

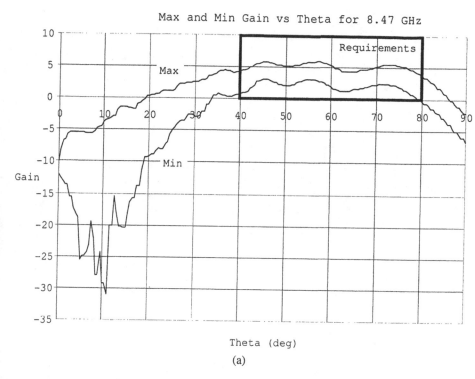

(a)

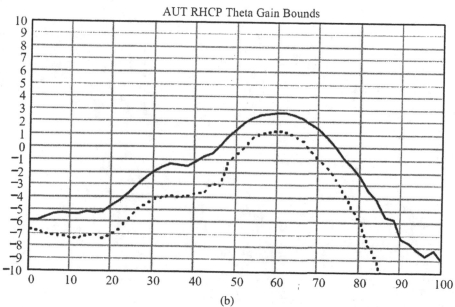

(b)

Figure 18-8.   Maximum and minimum gain at 8.47 GHz for antennas (a) ST5-3-10; (b) QFH.

Index